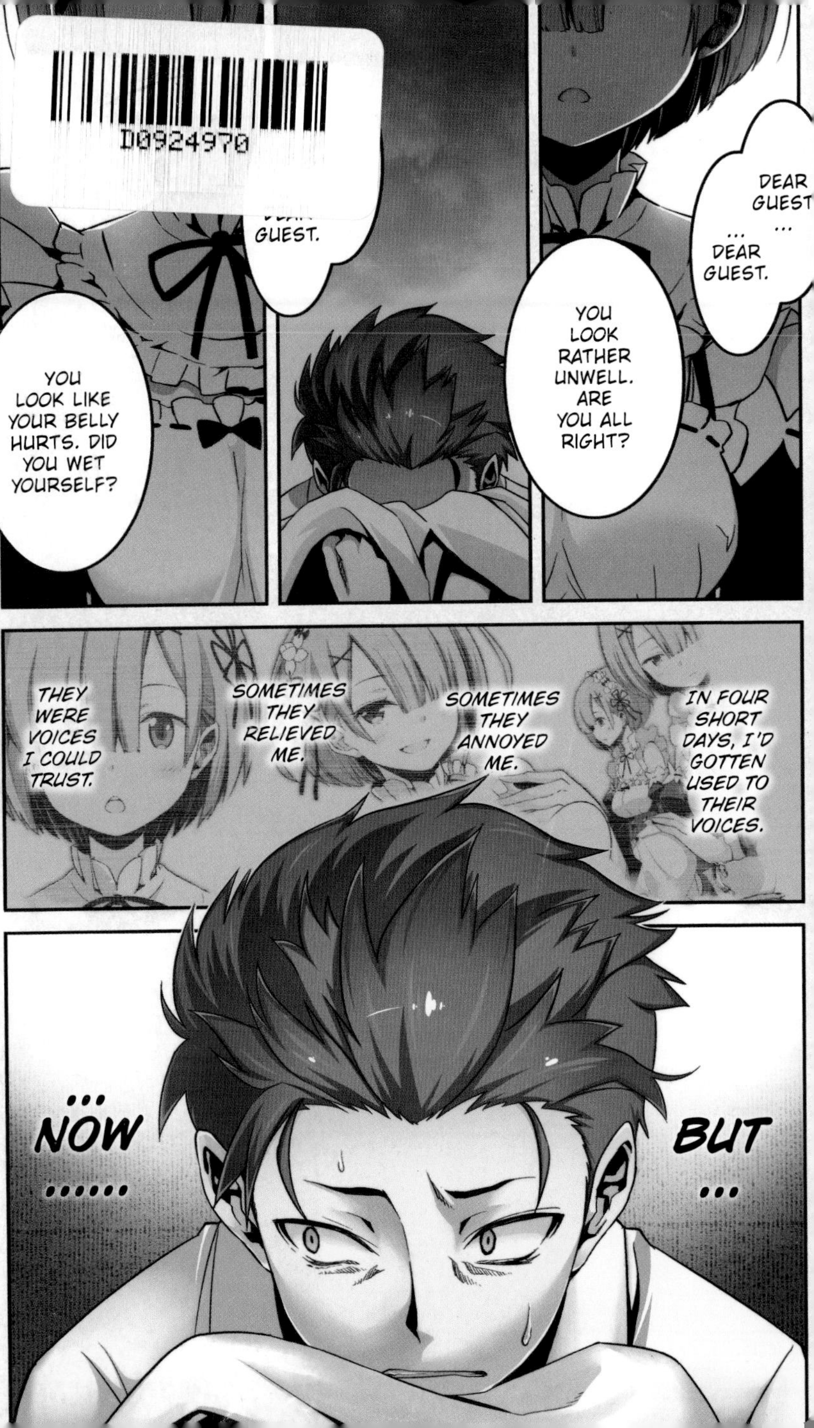
DEAR GUEST ...
... DEAR GUEST.
YOU LOOK RATHER UNWELL. ARE YOU ALL RIGHT?
GUEST.
YOU LOOK LIKE YOUR BELLY HURTS. DID YOU WET YOURSELF?
IN FOUR SHORT DAYS, I'D GOTTEN USED TO THEIR VOICES.
SOMETIMES THEY ANNOYED ME.
SOMETIMES THEY RELIEVED ME.
THEY WERE VOICES I COULD TRUST.
BUT ...
... NOW ......

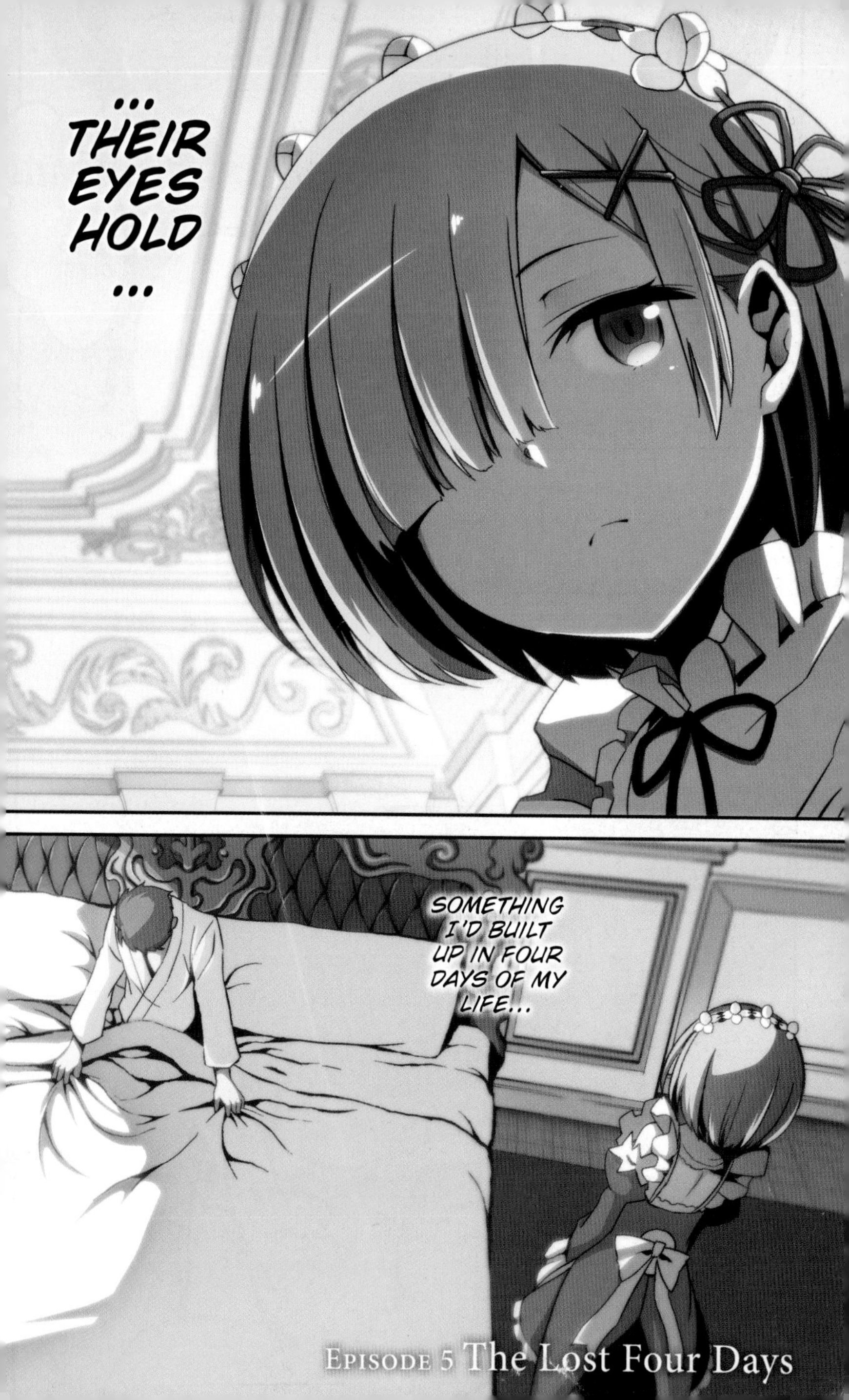
... THEIR EYES HOLD ...
SOMETHING I'D BUILT UP IN FOUR DAYS OF MY LIFE...

# Episode 5 The Lost Four Days

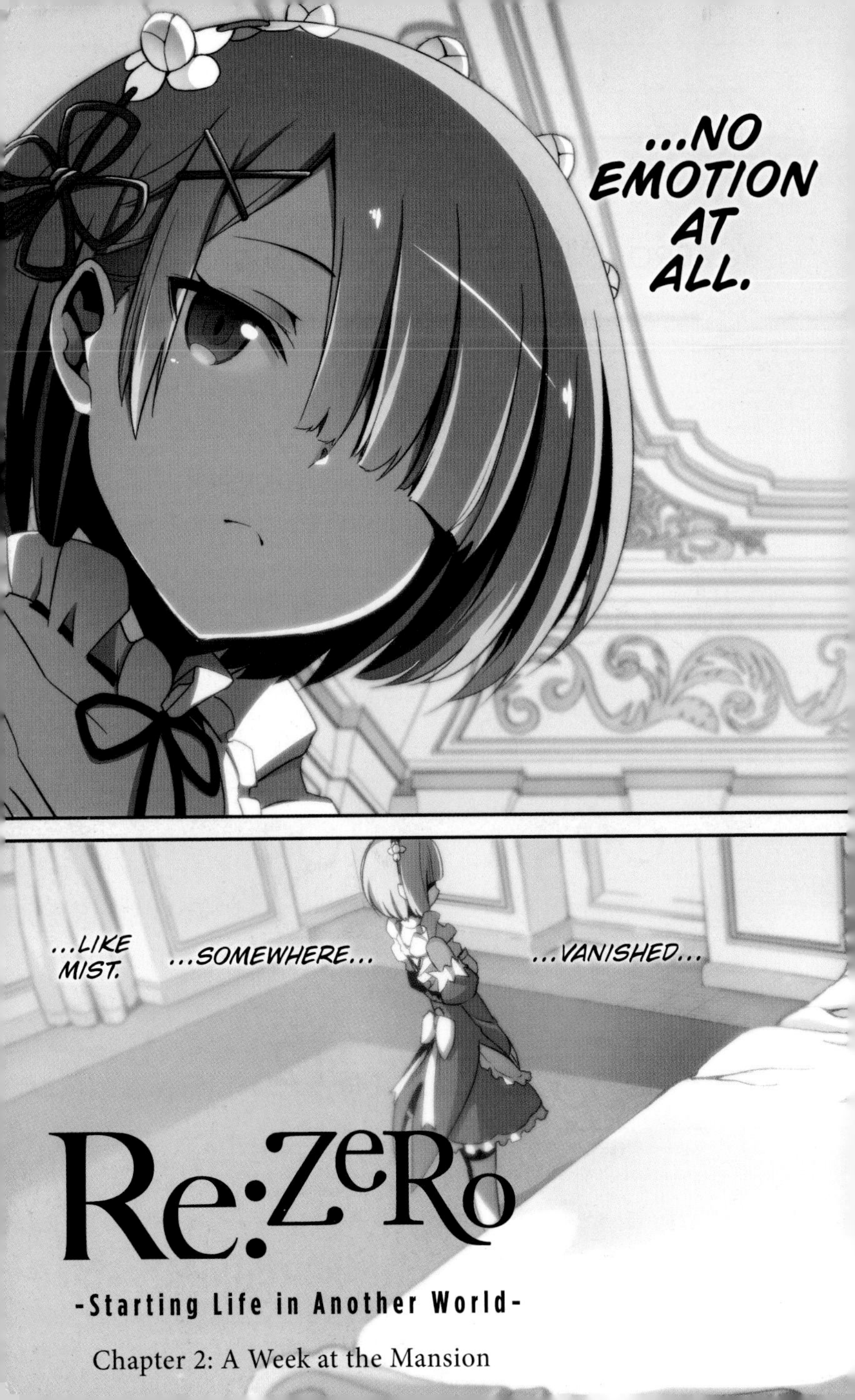
...NO EMOTION AT ALL.
...VANISHED...
...SOMEWHERE...
...LIKE MIST.

# Re:ZeRo

-Starting Life in Another World-

## Chapter 2: A Week at the Mansion

# Re:ZERO -Starting Life in Another World-

### Chapter 2: A Week at the Mansion

The only ability Subaru Natsuki gets when he's summoned to another world is time travel via his own death. But to save her, he'll die as many times as it takes.

## Contents

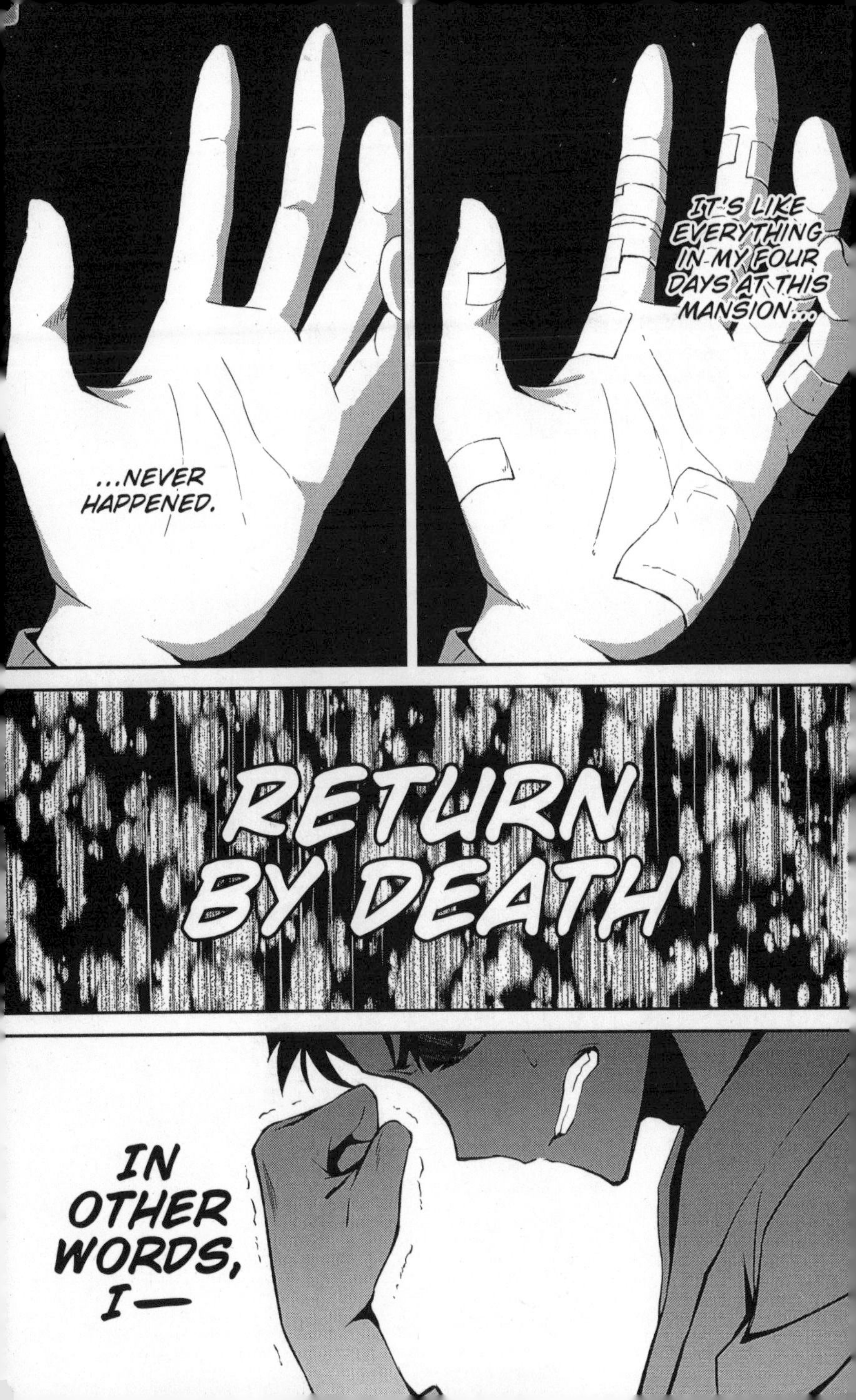
IT'S LIKE EVERYTHING IN MY FOUR DAYS AT THIS MANSION...
...NEVER HAPPENED.
RETURN BY DEATH
IN OTHER WORDS, I—

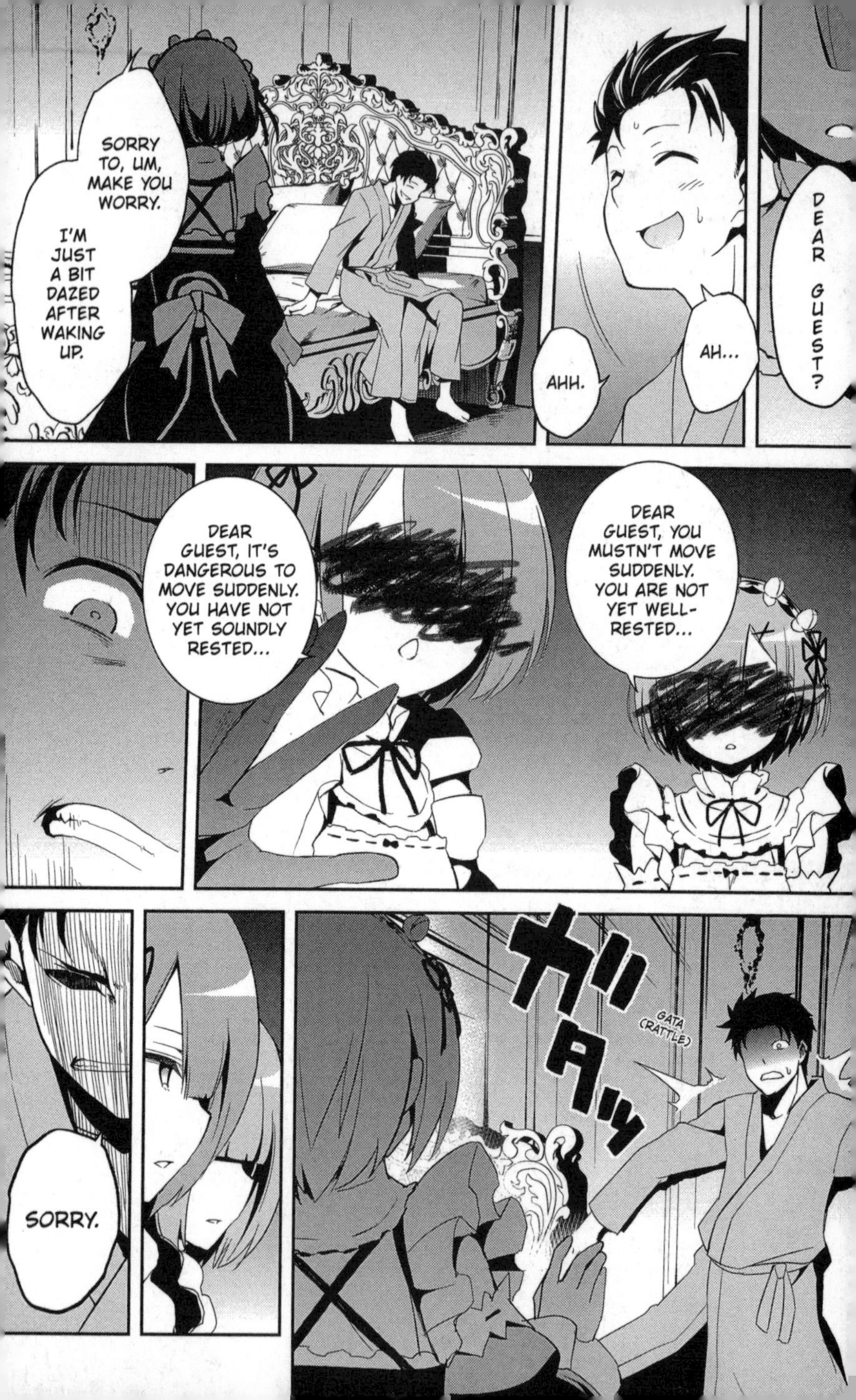
DEAR GUEST?
AH...
AHH.
SORRY TO, UM, MAKE YOU WORRY.
I'M JUST A BIT DAZED AFTER WAKING UP.
DEAR GUEST, YOU MUSTN'T MOVE SUDDENLY. YOU ARE NOT YET WELL-RESTED...
DEAR GUEST, IT'S DANGEROUS TO MOVE SUDDENLY. YOU HAVE NOT YET SOUNDLY RESTED...
ガタッ
GATA (RATTLE)
SORRY.

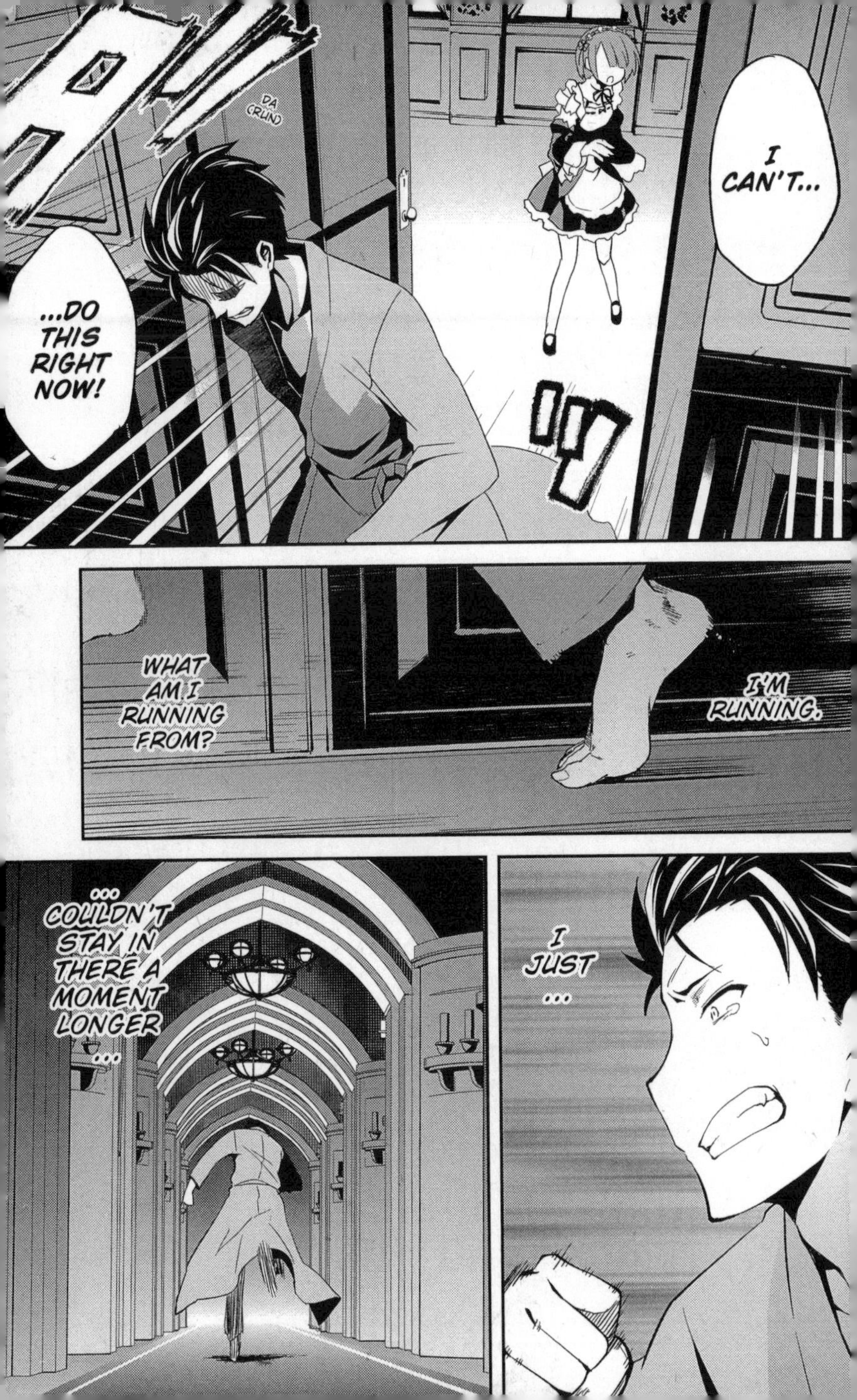
I CAN'T...
DA (RUN)
...DO THIS RIGHT NOW!
I'M RUNNING.
WHAT AM I RUNNING FROM?
I JUST ...
...COULDN'T STAY IN THERE A MOMENT LONGER ...

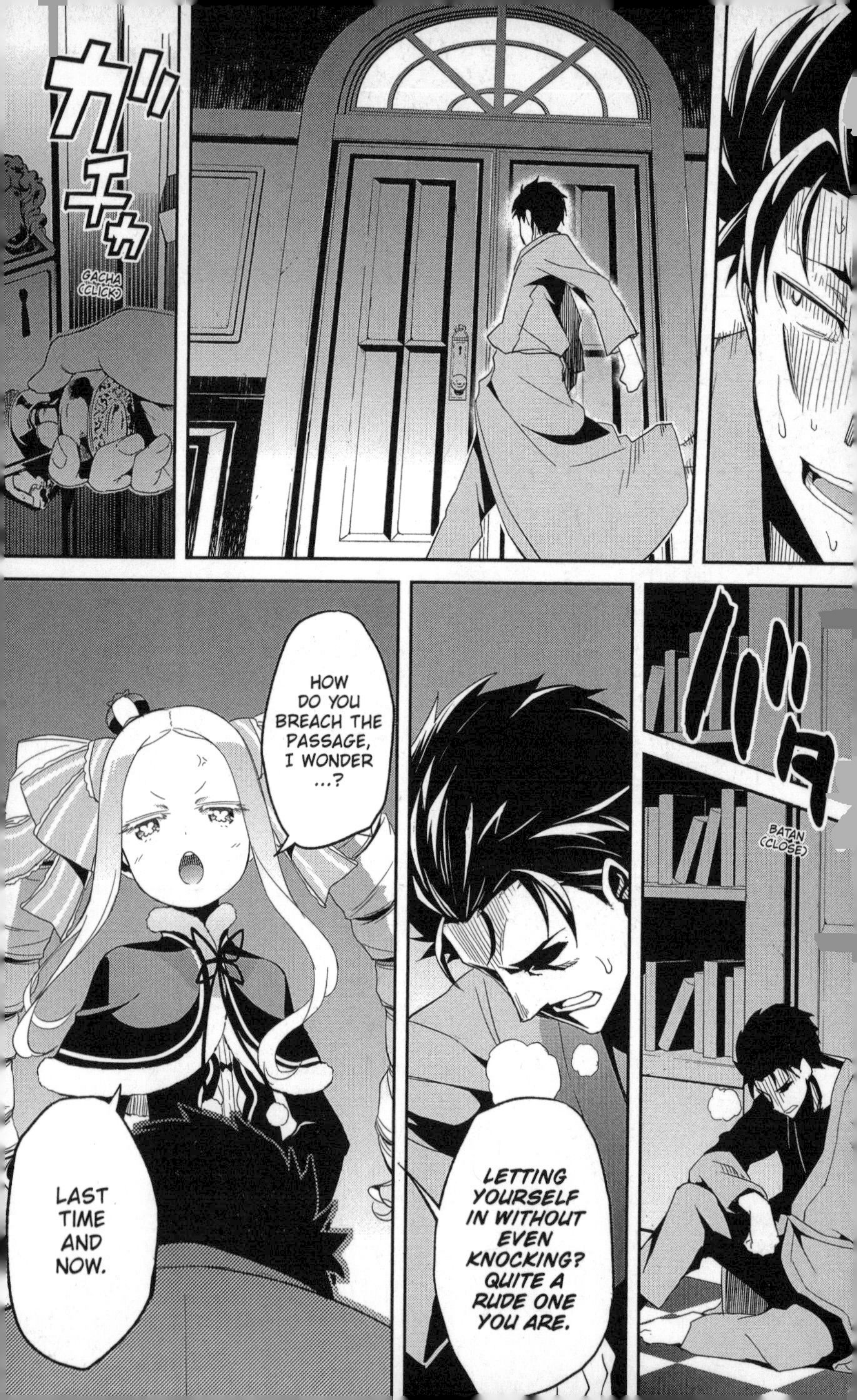
ガチャ
GACHA (CLICK)
BATAN (CLOSE)
LETTING YOURSELF IN WITHOUT EVEN KNOCKING? QUITE A RUDE ONE YOU ARE.
HOW DO YOU BREACH THE PASSAGE, I WONDER ...?
LAST TIME AND NOW.

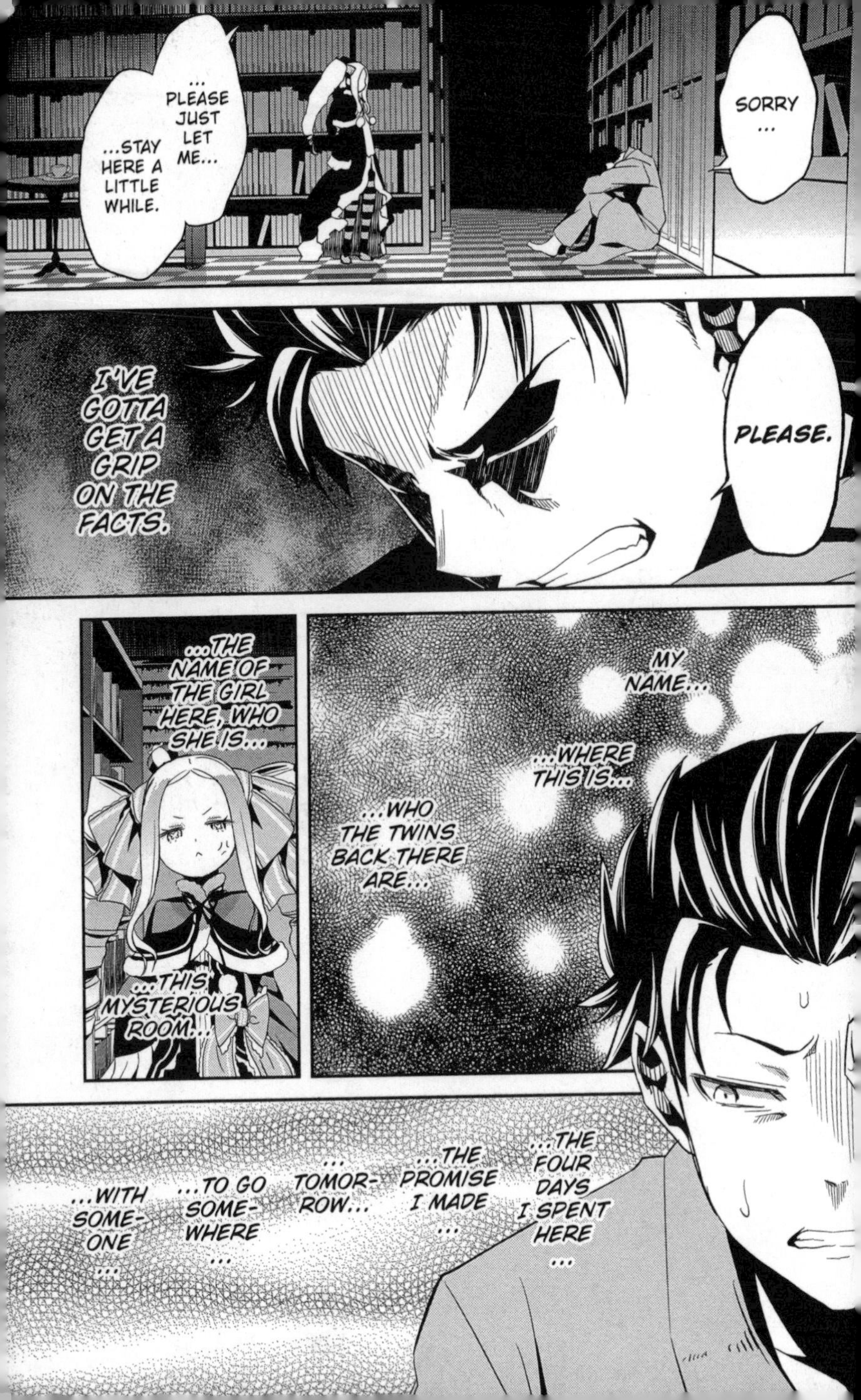
SORRY...
...PLEASE JUST LET ME...
...STAY HERE A LITTLE WHILE.
PLEASE.
I'VE GOTTA GET A GRIP ON THE FACTS.
MY NAME...
...WHERE THIS IS...
...WHO THE TWINS BACK THERE ARE...
...THE NAME OF THE GIRL HERE, WHO SHE IS...
...THIS MYSTERIOUS ROOM...
...THE FOUR DAYS I SPENT HERE...
...THE PROMISE I MADE...
...TOMORROW...
...TO GO SOMEWHERE...
...WITH SOMEONE...

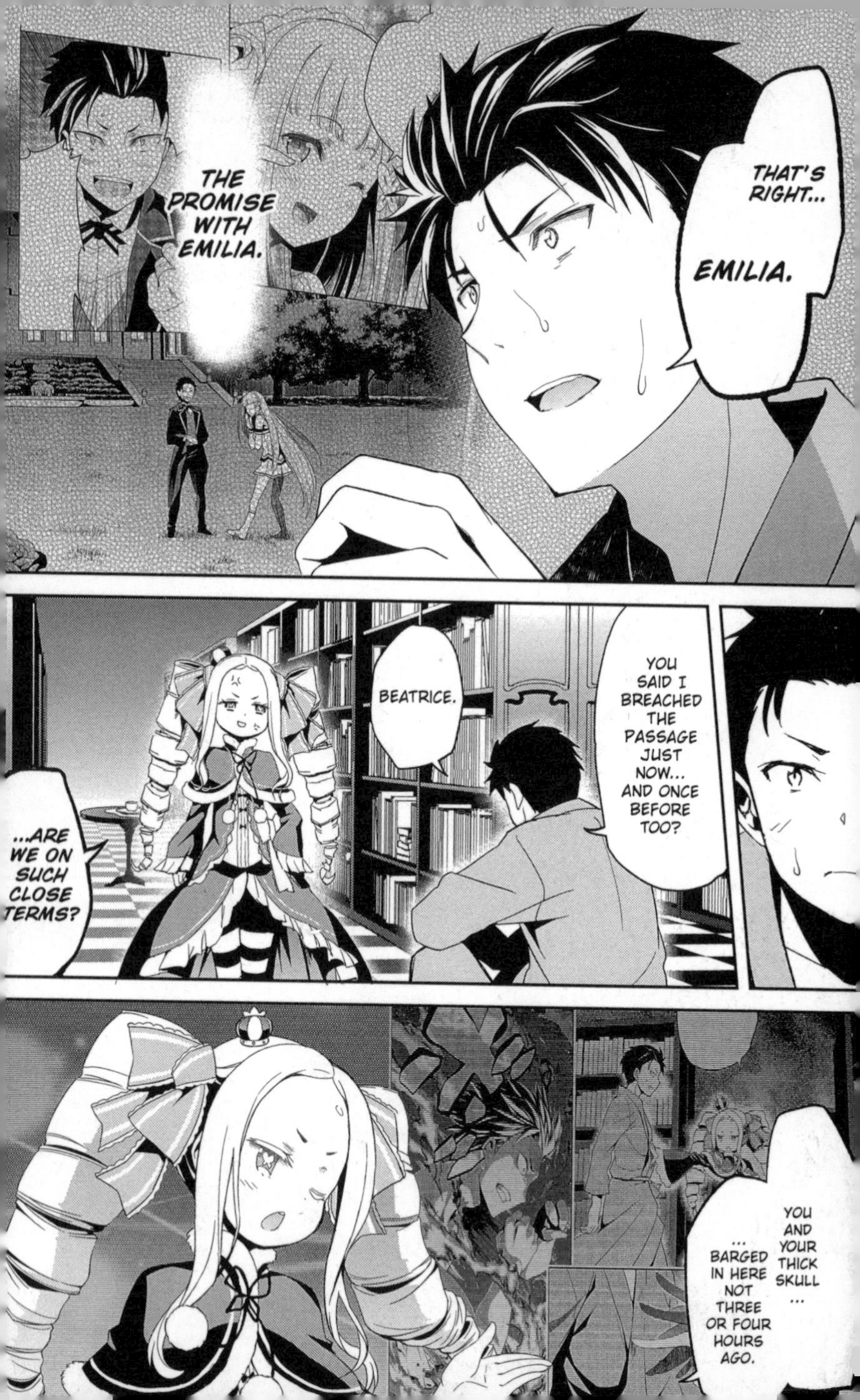
THAT'S RIGHT...
EMILIA.
THE PROMISE WITH EMILIA.
YOU SAID I BREACHED THE PASSAGE JUST NOW... AND ONCE BEFORE TOO?
BEATRICE.
...ARE WE ON SUCH CLOSE TERMS?
YOU AND YOUR THICK SKULL...
...BARGED IN HERE NOT THREE OR FOUR HOURS AGO.

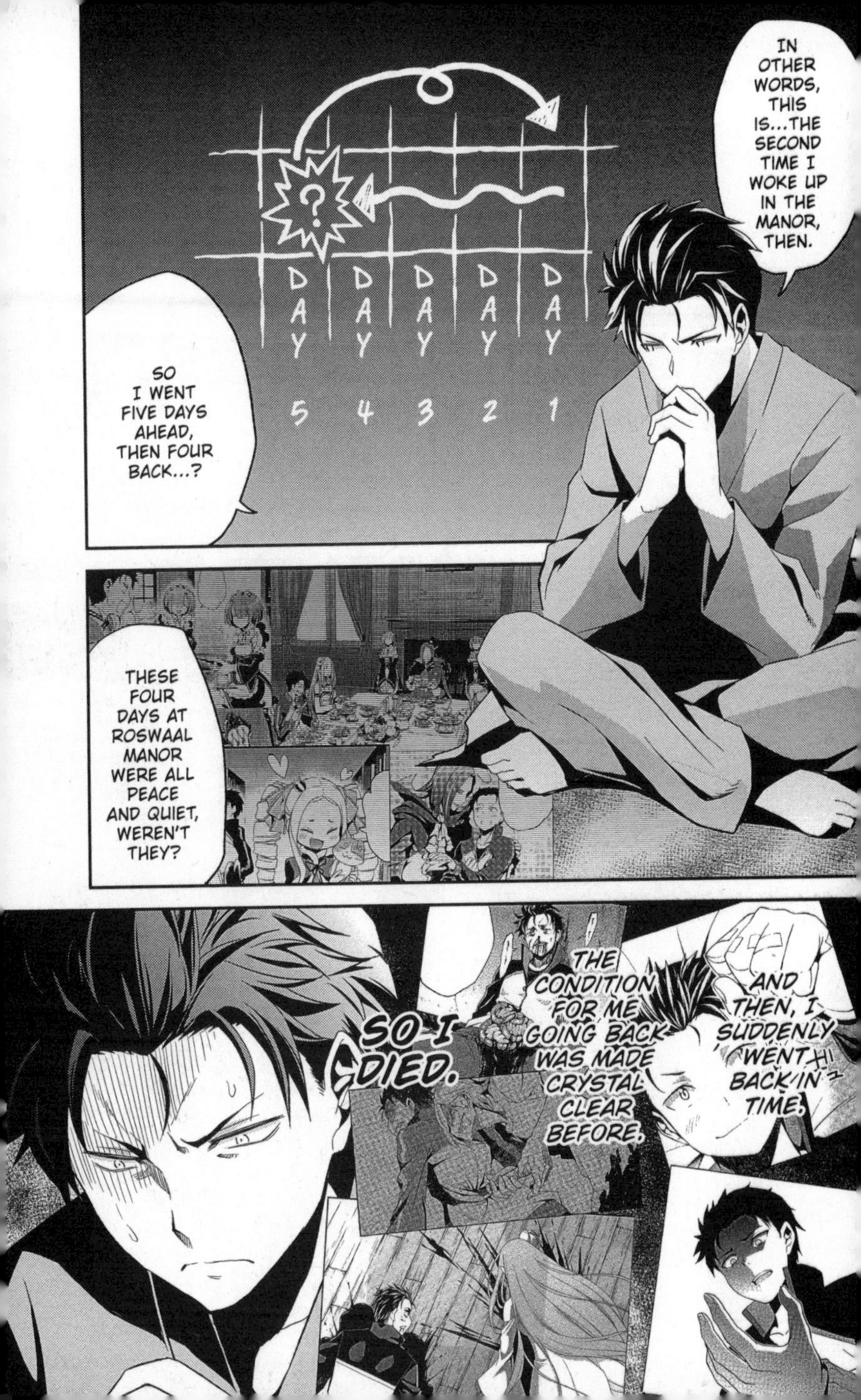

IN OTHER WORDS, THIS IS...THE SECOND TIME I WOKE UP IN THE MANOR, THEN.
?
DAY 5
DAY 4
DAY 3
DAY 2
DAY 1
SO I WENT FIVE DAYS AHEAD, THEN FOUR BACK...?
THESE FOUR DAYS AT ROSWAAL MANOR WERE ALL PEACE AND QUIET, WEREN'T THEY?
AND THEN, I SUDDENLY WENT BACK IN TIME.
THE CONDITION FOR ME GOING BACK WAS MADE CRYSTAL CLEAR BEFORE.
SO I DIED.

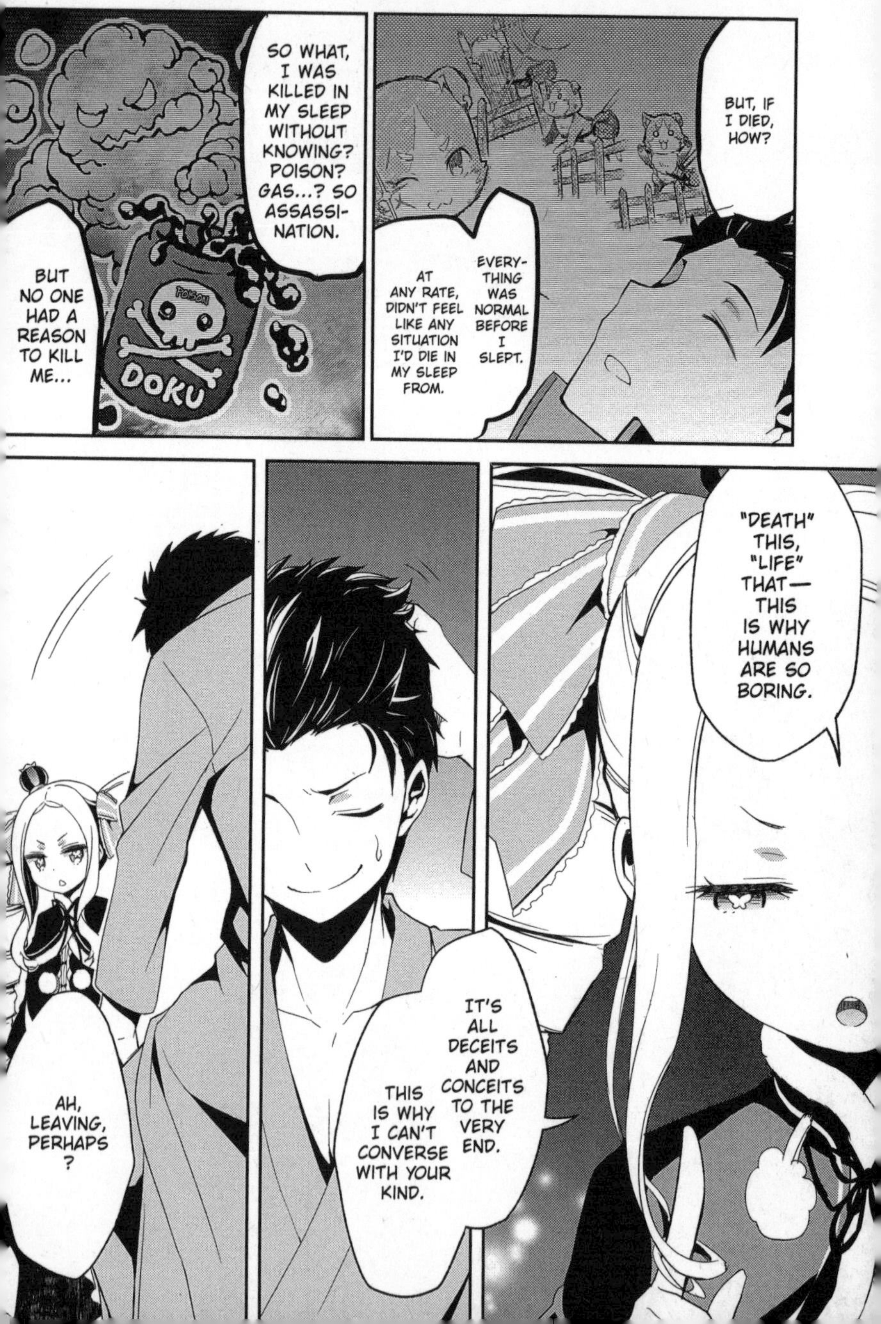
BUT, IF I DIED, HOW?
EVERYTHING WAS NORMAL BEFORE I SLEPT.
AT ANY RATE, DIDN'T FEEL LIKE ANY SITUATION I'D DIE IN MY SLEEP FROM.
SO WHAT, I WAS KILLED IN MY SLEEP WITHOUT KNOWING? POISON? GAS...? SO ASSASSINATION.
POISON
DOKU
BUT NO ONE HAD A REASON TO KILL ME...
"DEATH" THIS, "LIFE" THAT—THIS IS WHY HUMANS ARE SO BORING.
IT'S ALL DECEITS AND CONCEITS TO THE VERY END.
THIS IS WHY I CAN'T CONVERSE WITH YOUR KIND.
AH, LEAVING, PERHAPS?

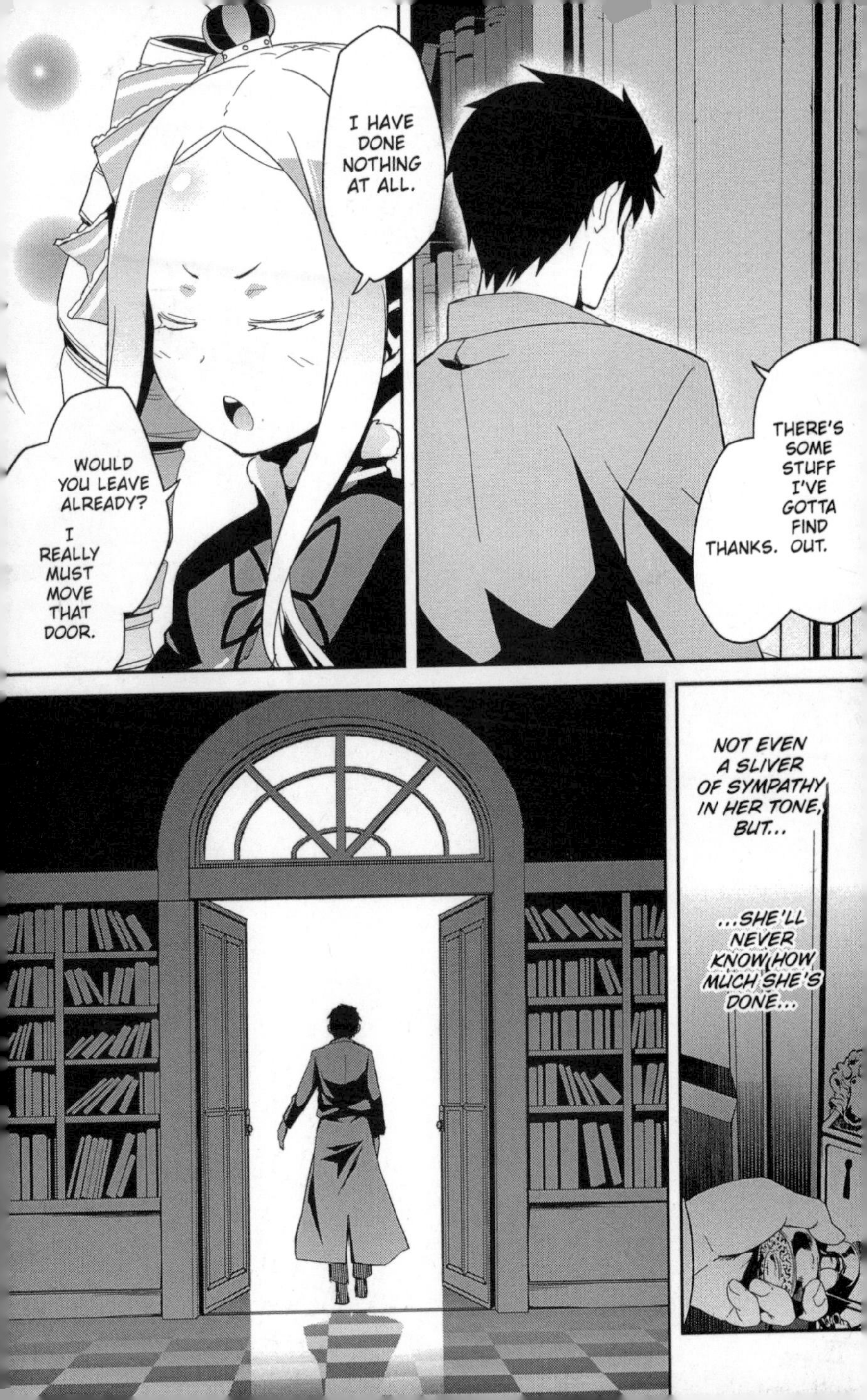
THERE'S SOME STUFF I'VE GOTTA FIND OUT.
THANKS.
I HAVE DONE NOTHING AT ALL.
WOULD YOU LEAVE ALREADY?
I REALLY MUST MOVE THAT DOOR.
NOT EVEN A SLIVER OF SYMPATHY IN HER TONE, BUT...
...SHE'LL NEVER KNOW HOW MUCH SHE'S DONE...

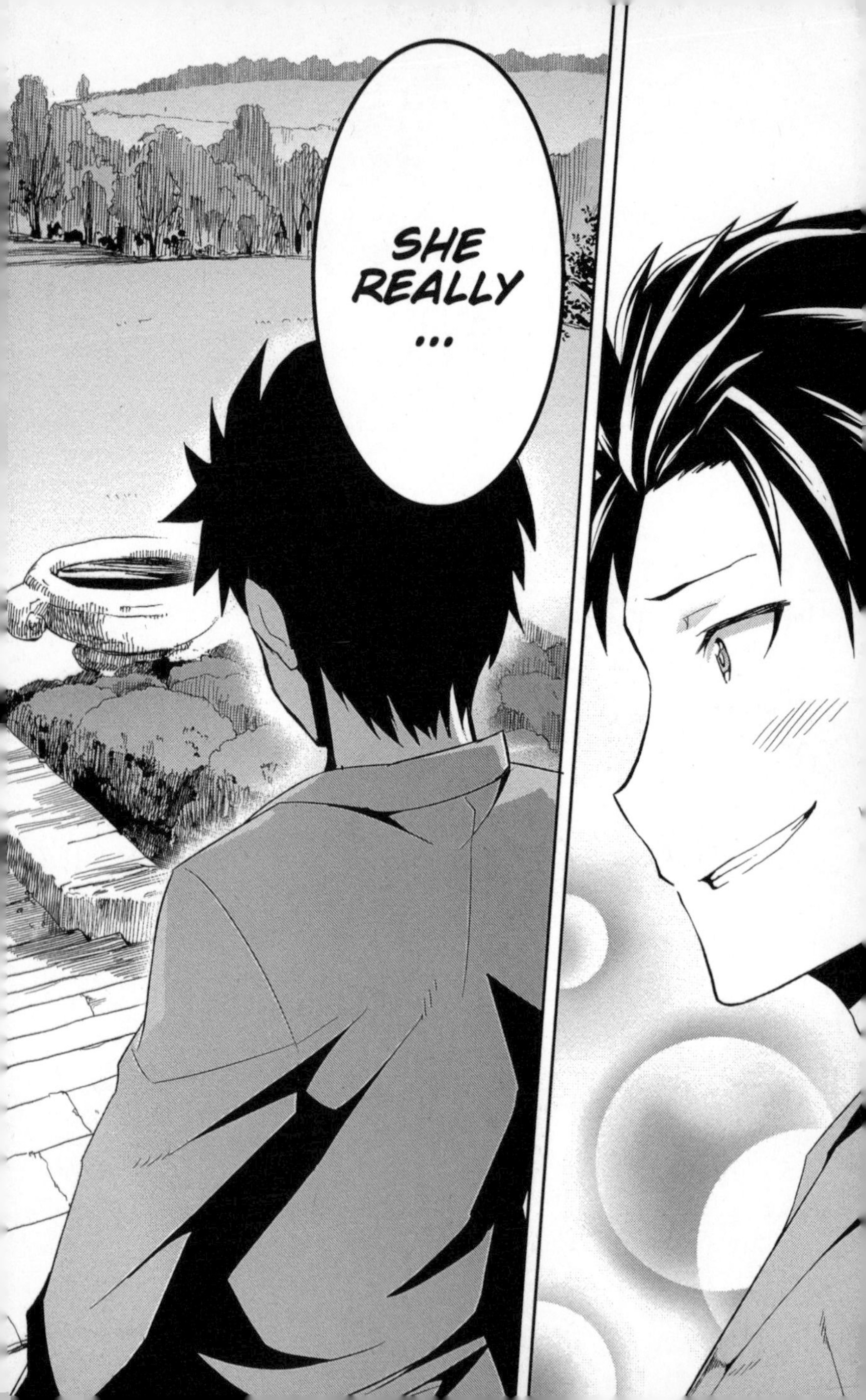
SHE REALLY ...

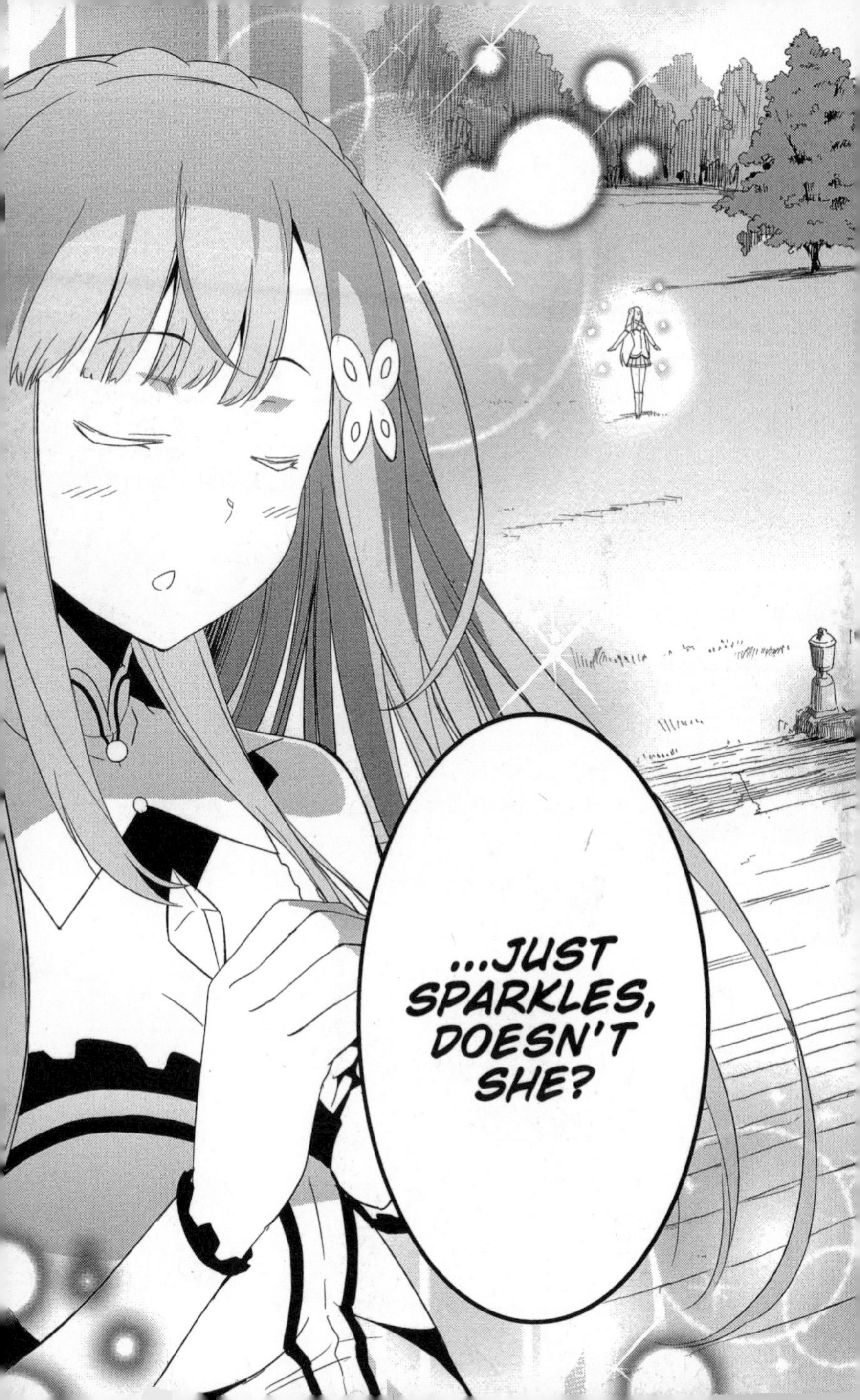
...JUST SPARKLES, DOESN'T SHE?

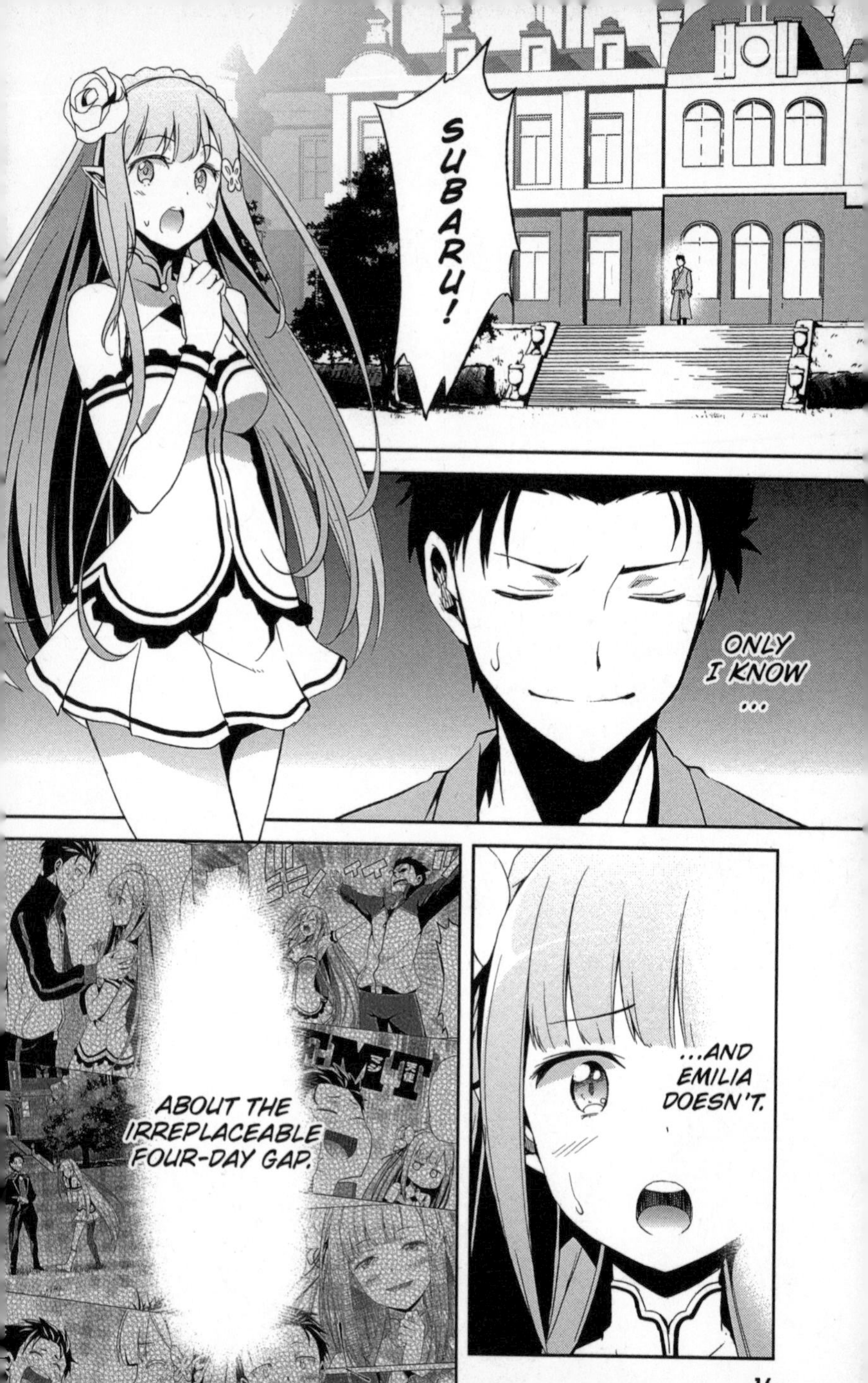
SUBARU!
ONLY I KNOW ...
...AND EMILIA DOESN'T.
ABOUT THE IRREPLACEABLE FOUR-DAY GAP.

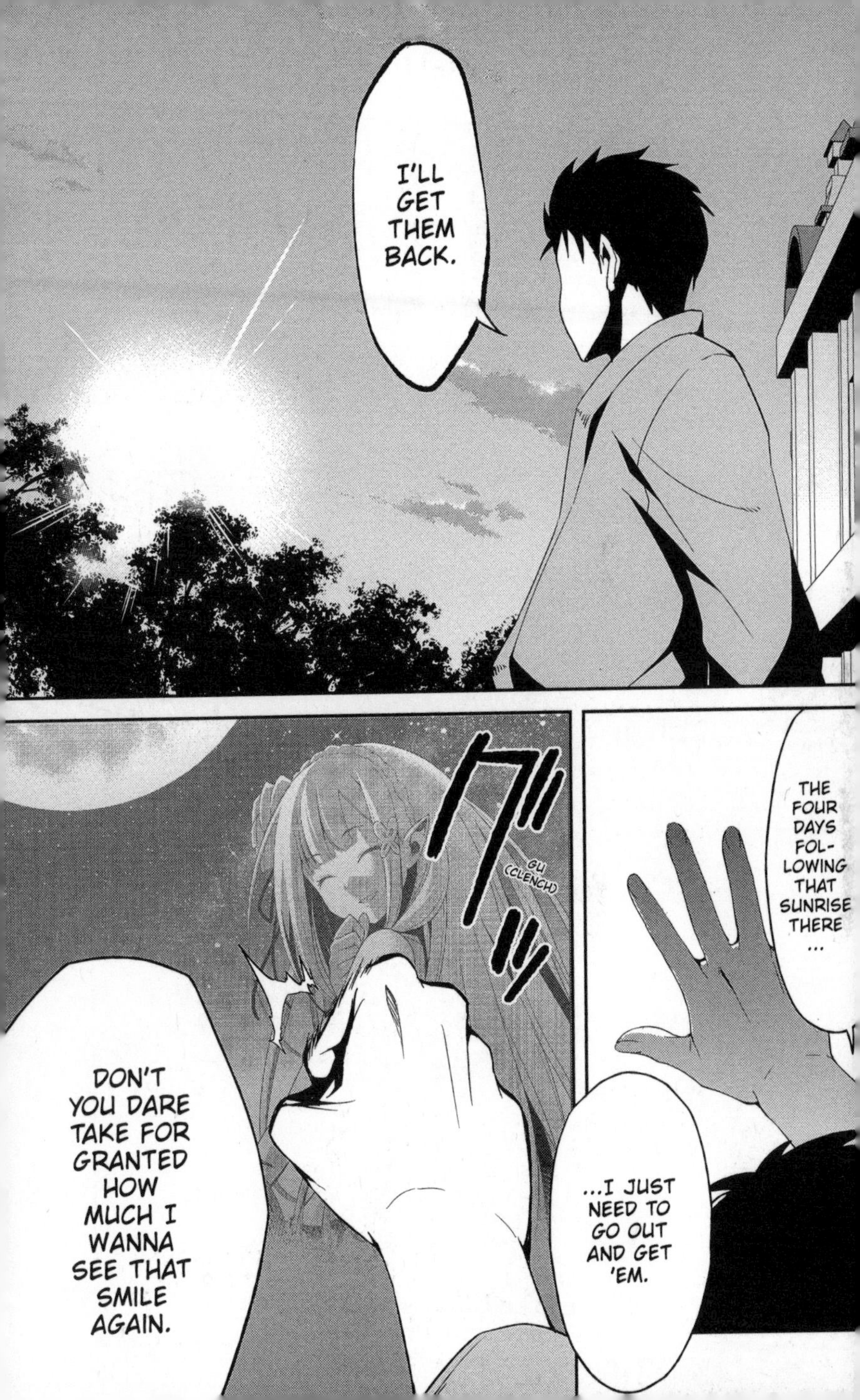
I'LL GET THEM BACK.
THE FOUR DAYS FOL-LOWING THAT SUNRISE THERE ...
...I JUST NEED TO GO OUT AND GET 'EM.
GU (CLENCH)
DON'T YOU DARE TAKE FOR GRANTED HOW MUCH I WANNA SEE THAT SMILE AGAIN.

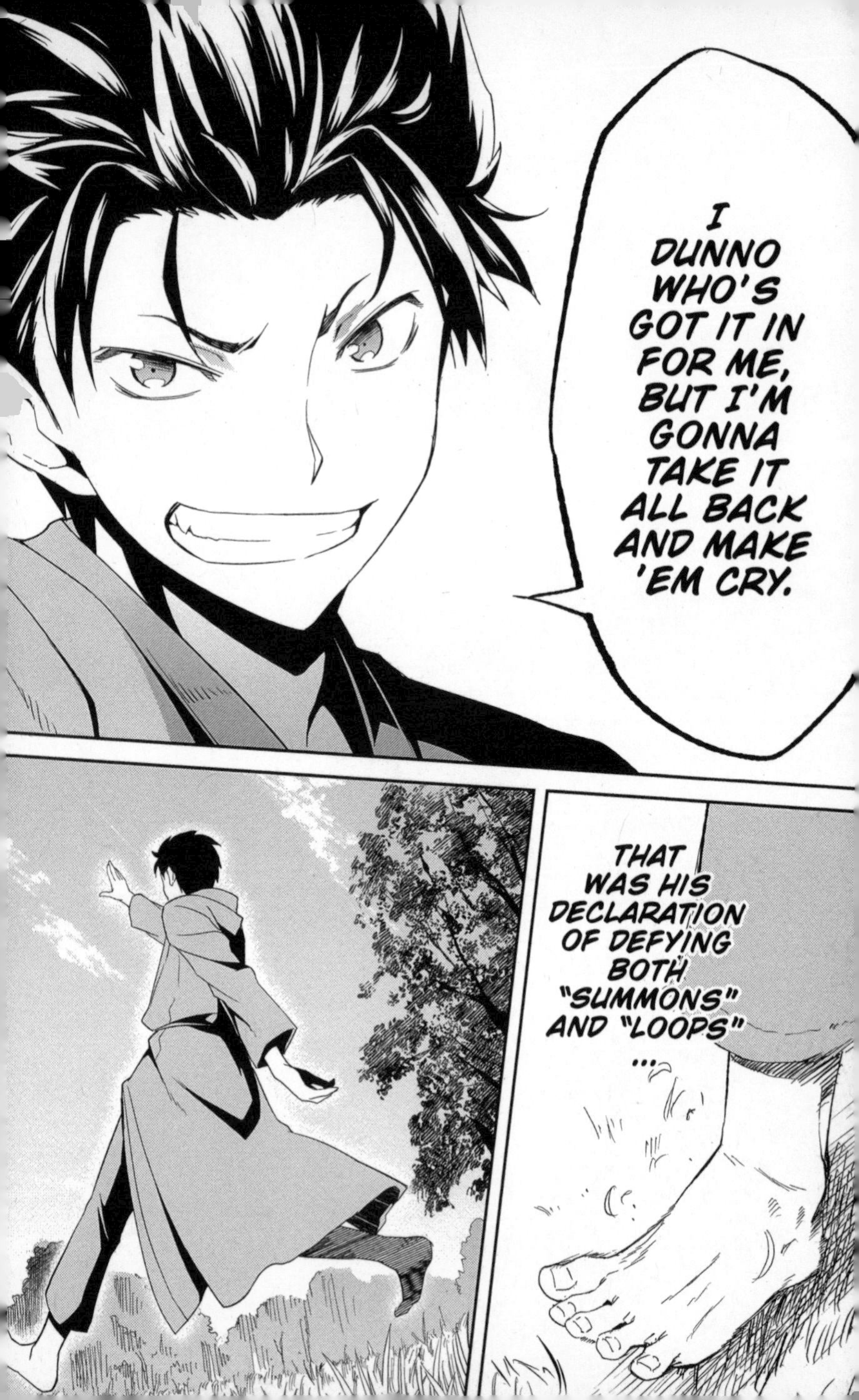
I DUNNO WHO'S GOT IT IN FOR ME, BUT I'M GONNA TAKE IT ALL BACK AND MAKE 'EM CRY.
THAT WAS HIS DECLARATION OF DEFYING BOTH "SUMMONS" AND "LOOPS"...

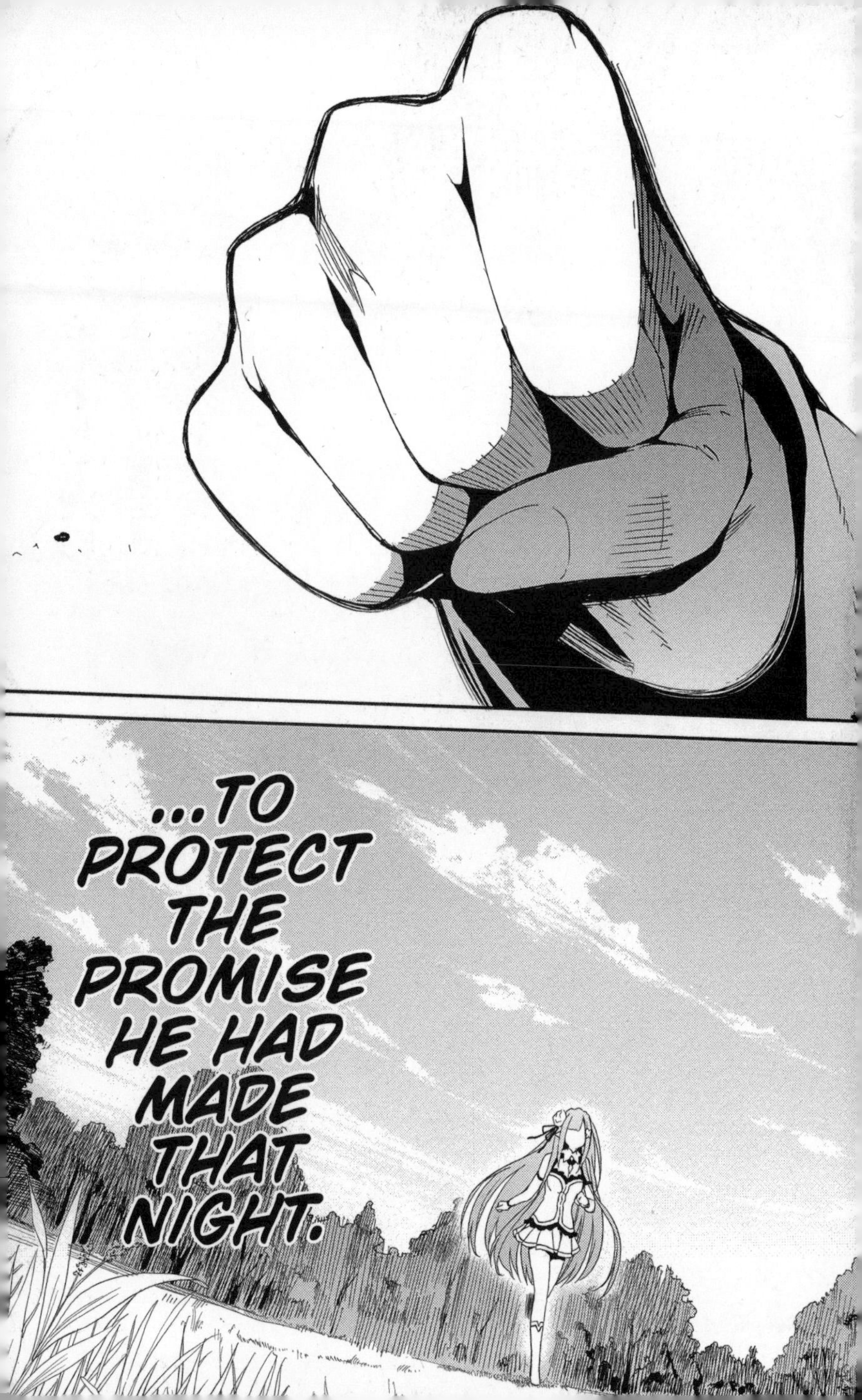
...TO PROTECT THE PROMISE HE HAD MADE THAT NIGHT.

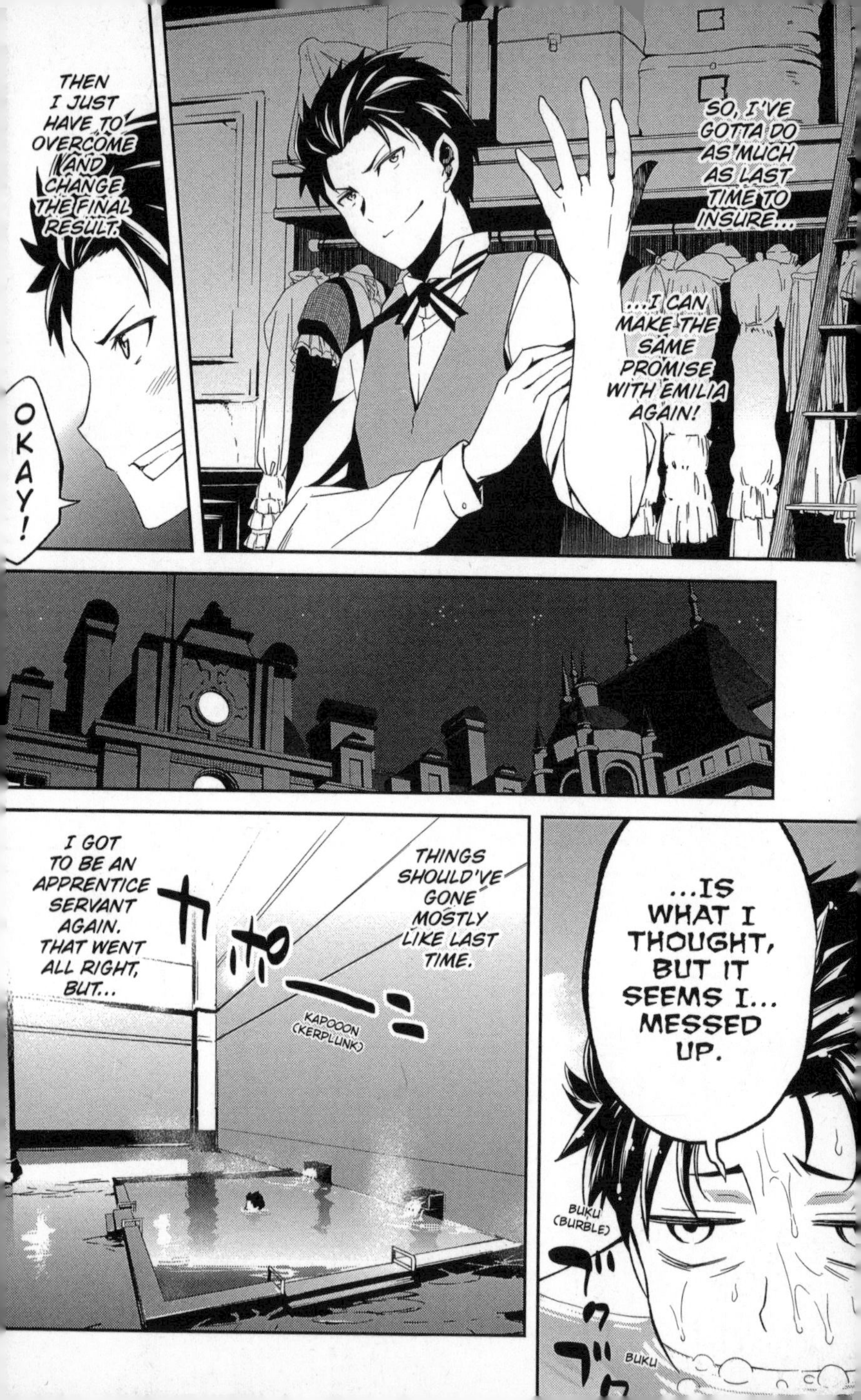
THEN I JUST HAVE TO OVERCOME AND CHANGE THE FINAL RESULT.
OKAY!
SO, I'VE GOTTA DO AS MUCH AS LAST TIME TO INSURE...
...I CAN MAKE THE SAME PROMISE WITH EMILIA AGAIN!
I GOT TO BE AN APPRENTICE SERVANT AGAIN. THAT WENT ALL RIGHT, BUT...
THINGS SHOULD'VE GONE MOSTLY LIKE LAST TIME.
KAPOOON (KERPLUNK)
...IS WHAT I THOUGHT, BUT IT SEEMS I... MESSED UP.
BUKU (BURBLE)
BUKU

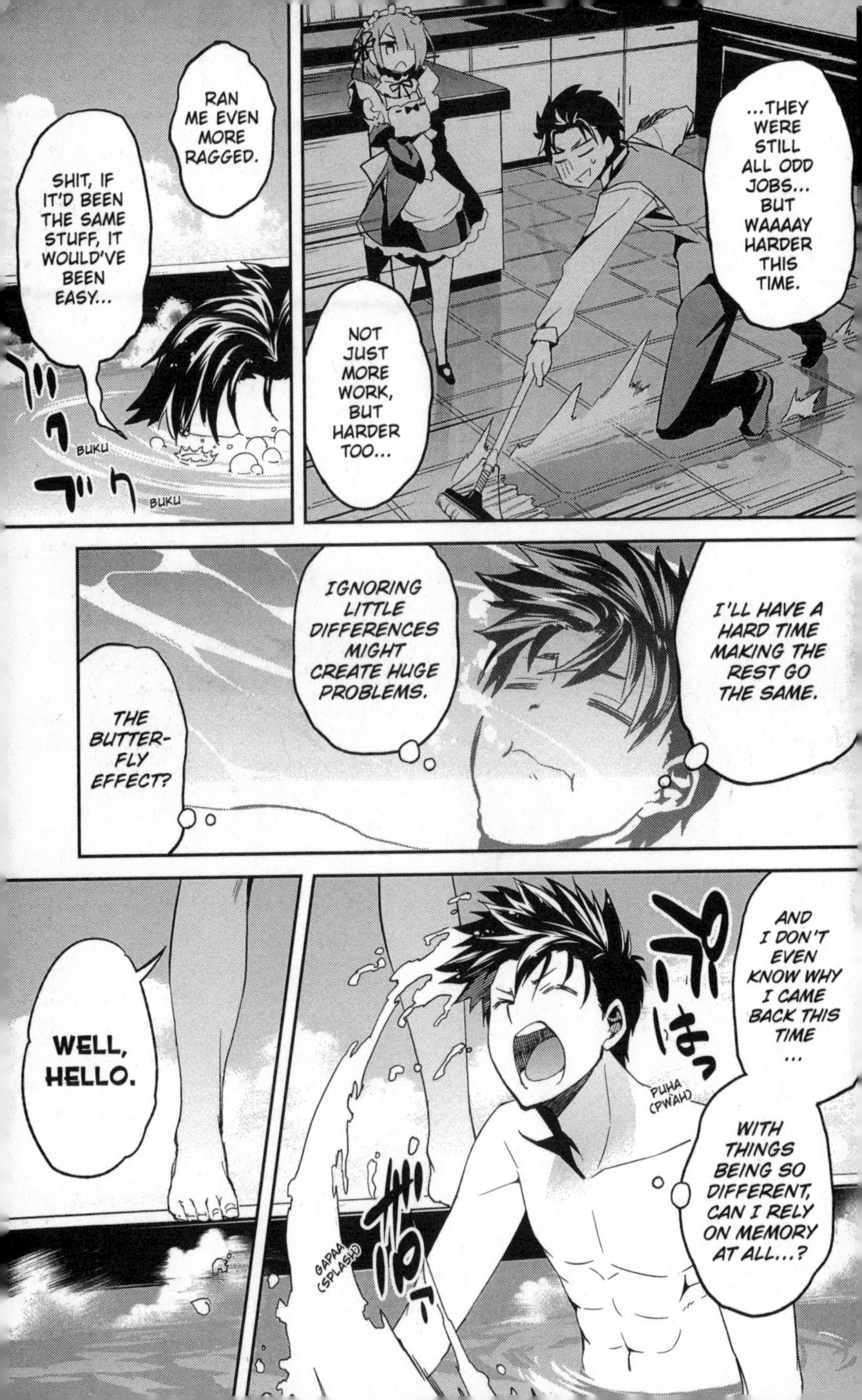
...THEY WERE STILL ALL ODD JOBS... BUT WAAAAY HARDER THIS TIME.
NOT JUST MORE WORK, BUT HARDER TOO...
RAN ME EVEN MORE RAGGED.
SHIT, IF IT'D BEEN THE SAME STUFF, IT WOULD'VE BEEN EASY...
BUKU
BUKU
I'LL HAVE A HARD TIME MAKING THE REST GO THE SAME.
IGNORING LITTLE DIFFERENCES MIGHT CREATE HUGE PROBLEMS.
THE BUTTER-FLY EFFECT?
AND I DON'T EVEN KNOW WHY I CAME BACK THIS TIME ...
PUHA (PWAH)
WITH THINGS BEING SO DIFFERENT, CAN I RELY ON MEMORY AT ALL...?
GAPAA (SPLASH)
WELL, HELLO.

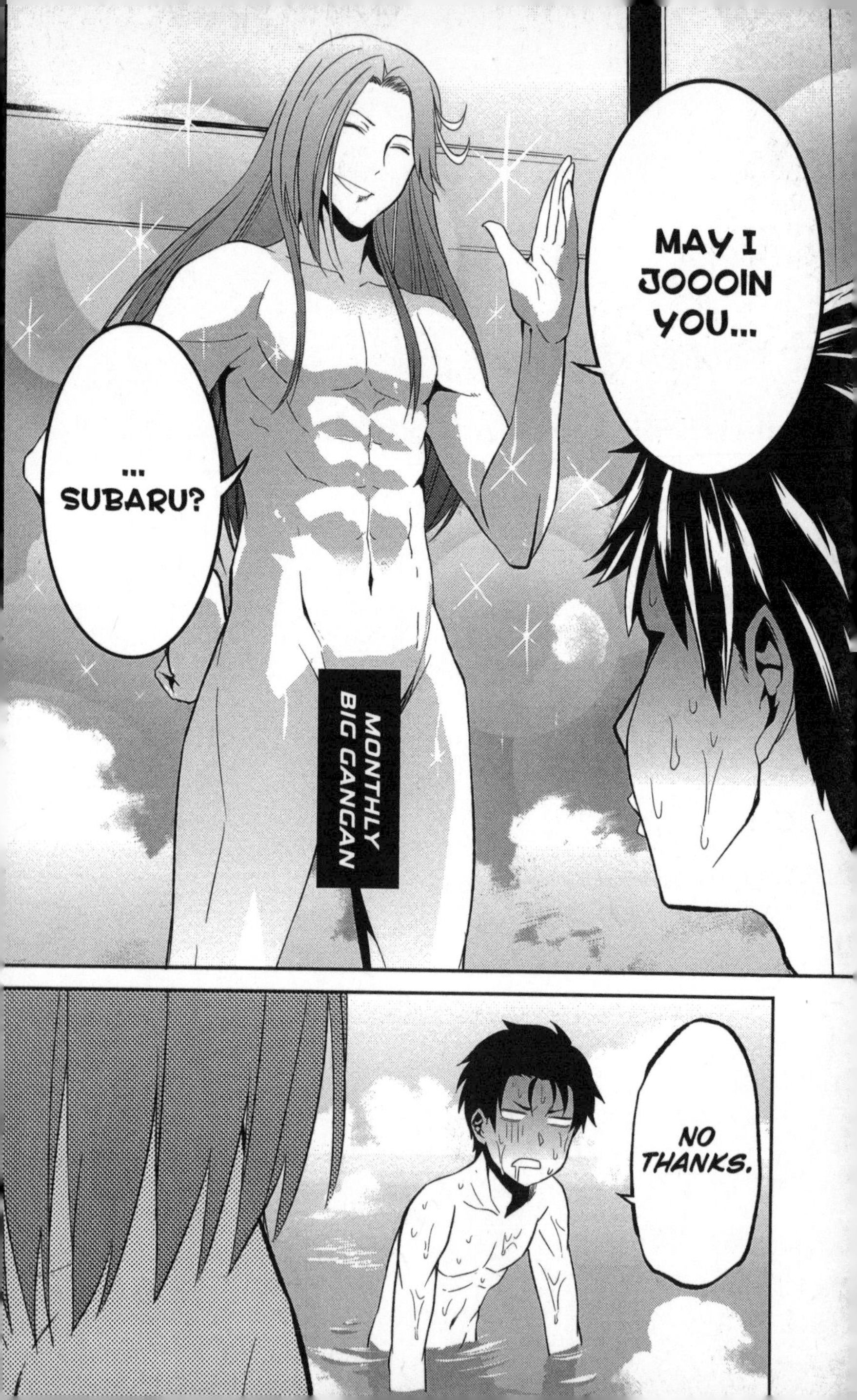
MAY I JOOOIN YOU...
... SUBARU?
MONTHLY BIG GANGAN
NO THANKS.

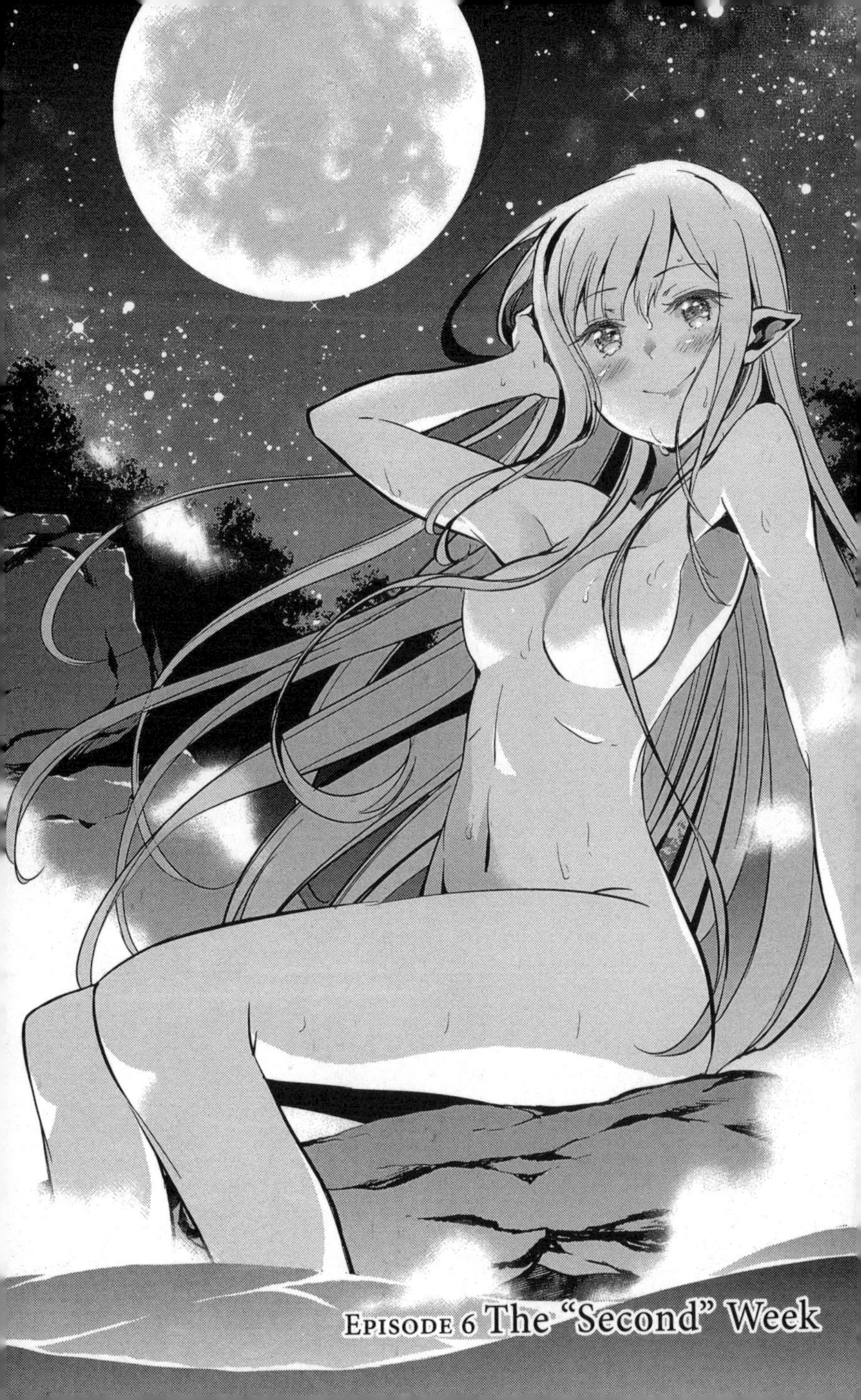

# Episode 6 The “Second” Week

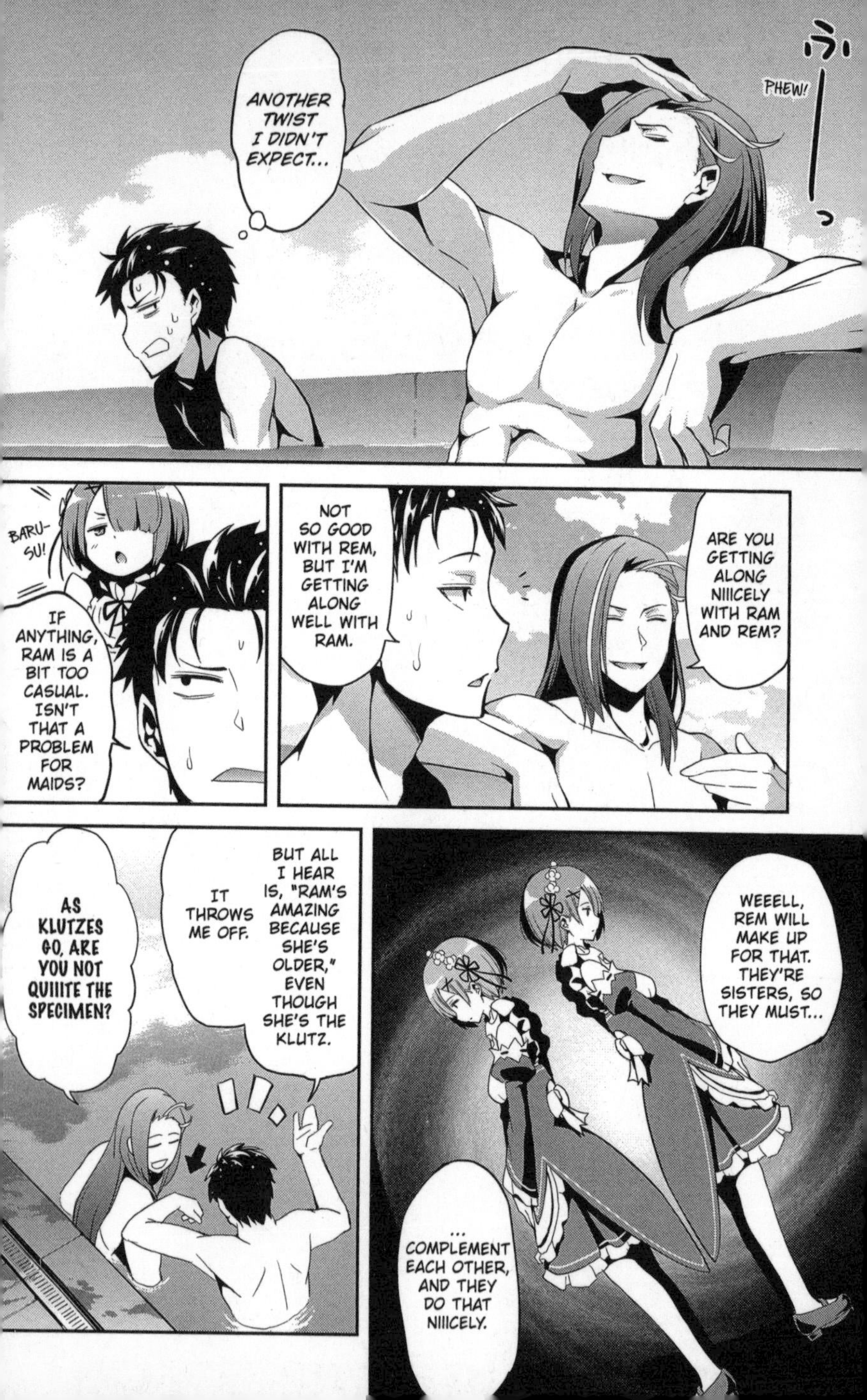
ふー
PHEW!
ANOTHER TWIST I DIDN'T EXPECT...
ARE YOU GETTING ALONG NIIICELY WITH RAM AND REM?
NOT SO GOOD WITH REM, BUT I'M GETTING ALONG WELL WITH RAM.
BARU-SU!
IF ANYTHING, RAM IS A BIT TOO CASUAL. ISN'T THAT A PROBLEM FOR MAIDS?
WEEELL, REM WILL MAKE UP FOR THAT. THEY'RE SISTERS, SO THEY MUST...
...COMPLEMENT EACH OTHER, AND THEY DO THAT NIIICELY.
BUT ALL I HEAR IS, "RAM'S AMAZING BECAUSE SHE'S OLDER," EVEN THOUGH SHE'S THE KLUTZ.
IT THROWS ME OFF.
AS KLUTZES GO, ARE YOU NOT QUIIITE THE SPECIMEN?

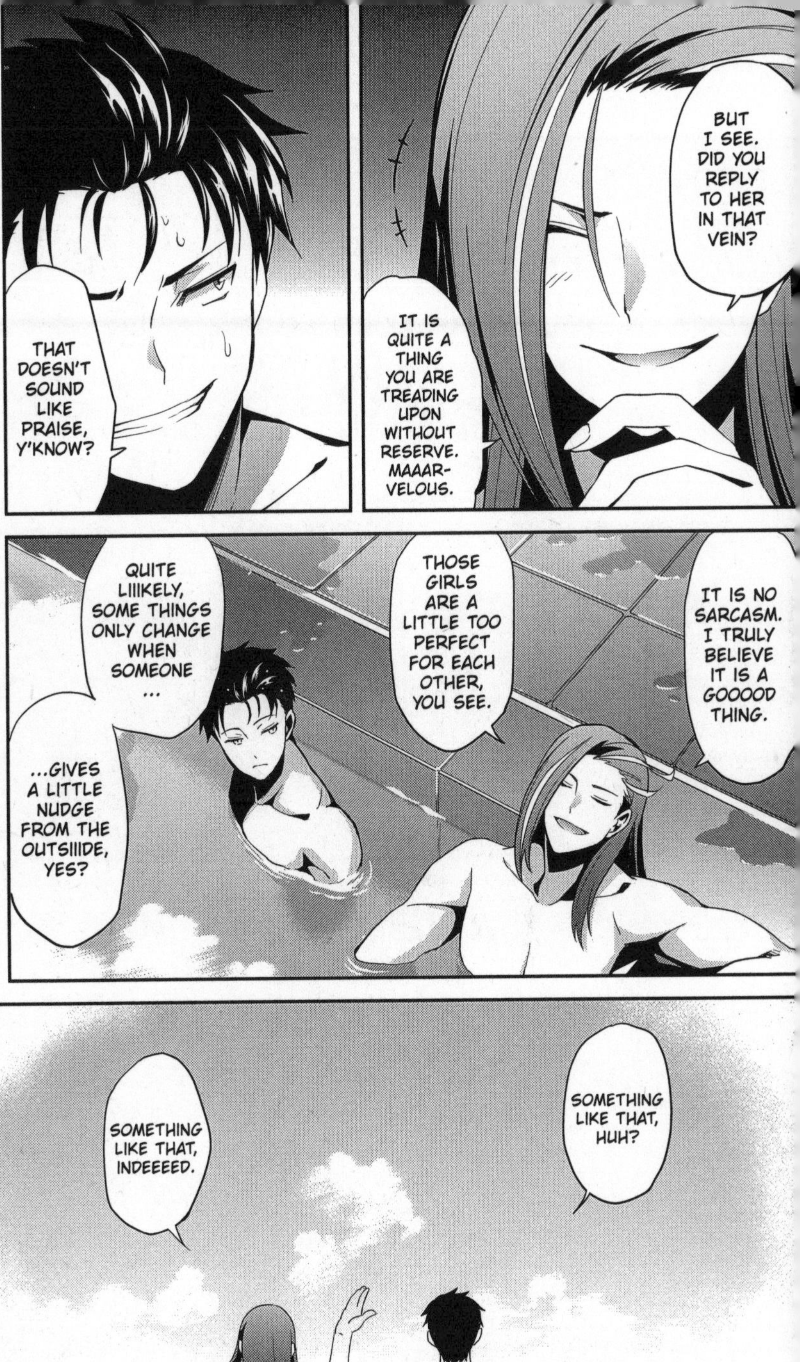
BUT I SEE. DID YOU REPLY TO HER IN THAT VEIN?
IT IS QUITE A THING YOU ARE TREADING UPON WITHOUT RESERVE. MAAAR-VELOUS.
THAT DOESN'T SOUND LIKE PRAISE, Y'KNOW?
IT IS NO SARCASM. I TRULY BELIEVE IT IS A GOOOOD THING.
THOSE GIRLS ARE A LITTLE TOO PERFECT FOR EACH OTHER, YOU SEE.
QUITE LIIIKELY, SOME THINGS ONLY CHANGE WHEN SOMEONE ...
...GIVES A LITTLE NUDGE FROM THE OUTSIIIDE, YES?
SOMETHING LIKE THAT, HUH?
SOMETHING LIKE THAT, INDEEEED.

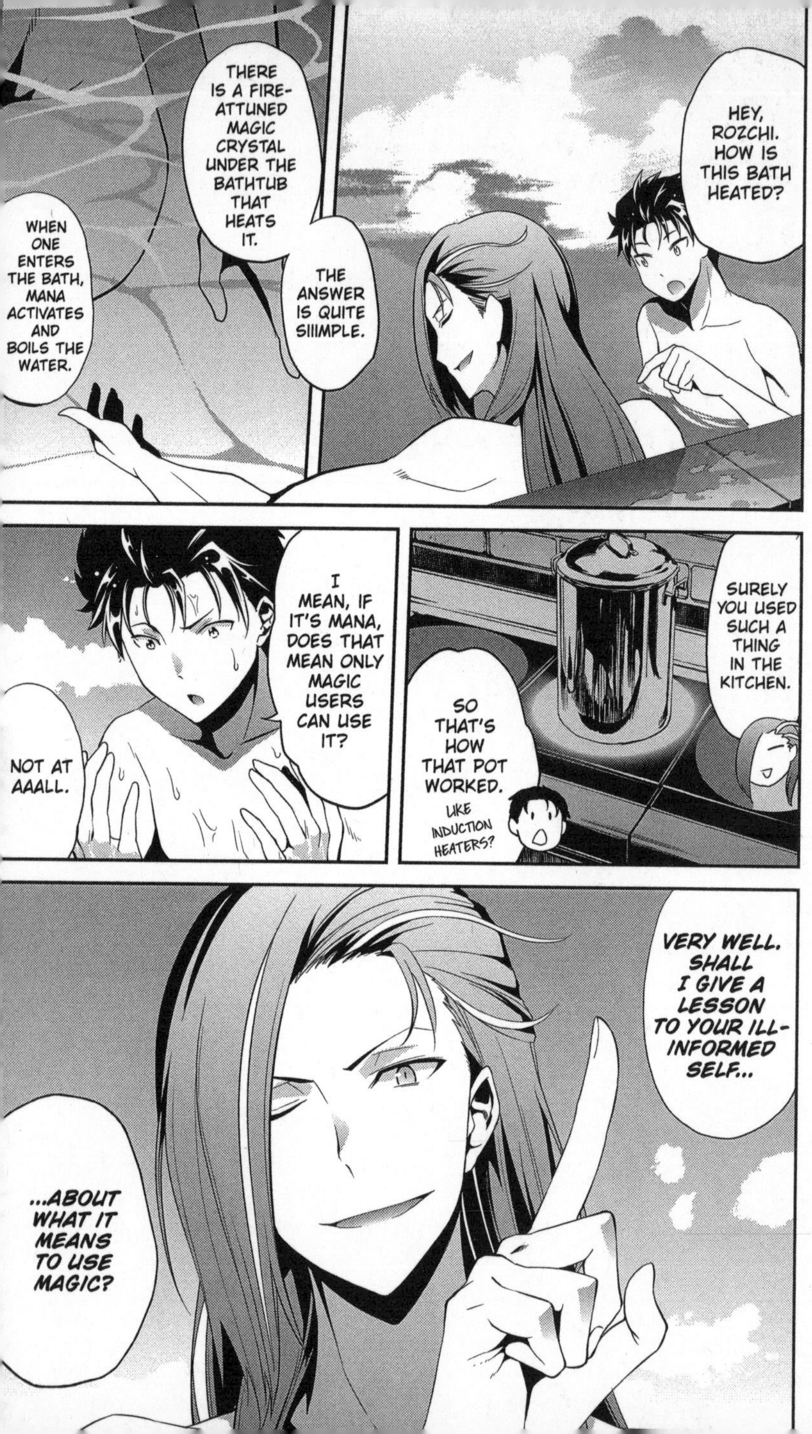
HEY, ROZCHI. HOW IS THIS BATH HEATED?
THE ANSWER IS QUITE SIIIMPLE.
THERE IS A FIRE-ATTUNED MAGIC CRYSTAL UNDER THE BATHTUB THAT HEATS IT.
WHEN ONE ENTERS THE BATH, MANA ACTIVATES AND BOILS THE WATER.
SURELY YOU USED SUCH A THING IN THE KITCHEN.
SO THAT'S HOW THAT POT WORKED.
LIKE INDUCTION HEATERS?
I MEAN, IF IT'S MANA, DOES THAT MEAN ONLY MAGIC USERS CAN USE IT?
NOT AT AAALL.
VERY WELL. SHALL I GIVE A LESSON TO YOUR ILL-INFORMED SELF...
...ABOUT WHAT IT MEANS TO USE MAGIC?

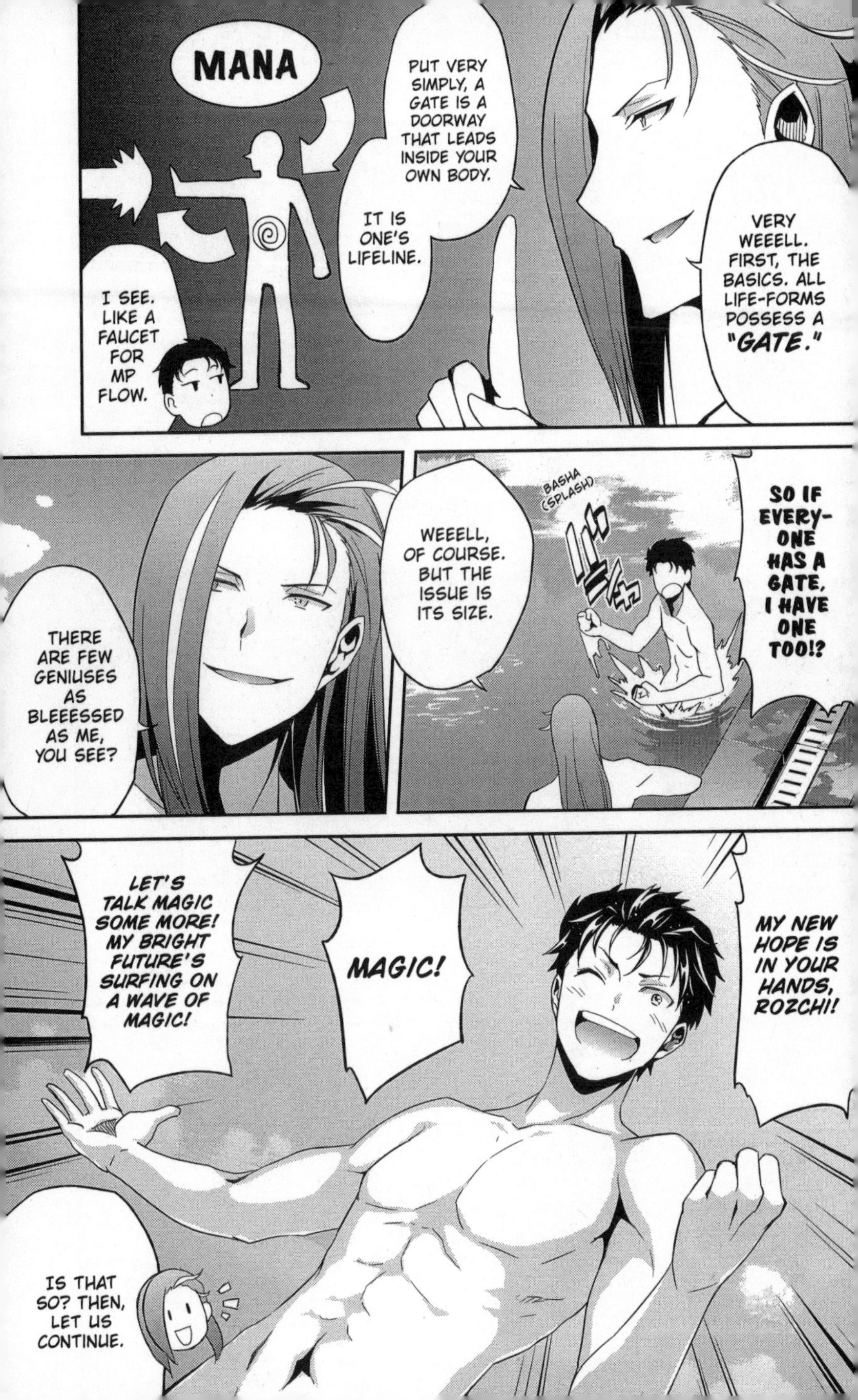
VERY WEEELL. FIRST, THE BASICS. ALL LIFE-FORMS POSSESS A "GATE."
PUT VERY SIMPLY, A GATE IS A DOORWAY THAT LEADS INSIDE YOUR OWN BODY.
IT IS ONE'S LIFELINE.
MANA
I SEE. LIKE A FAUCET FOR MP FLOW.
BASHA (SPLASH)
SO IF EVERYONE HAS A GATE, I HAVE ONE TOO!?
WEEELL, OF COURSE. BUT THE ISSUE IS ITS SIZE.
THERE ARE FEW GENIUSES AS BLEEESSED AS ME, YOU SEE?
MY NEW HOPE IS IN YOUR HANDS, ROZCHI!
MAGIC!
LET'S TALK MAGIC SOME MORE! MY BRIGHT FUTURE'S SURFING ON A WAVE OF MAGIC!
IS THAT SO? THEN, LET US CONTINUE.

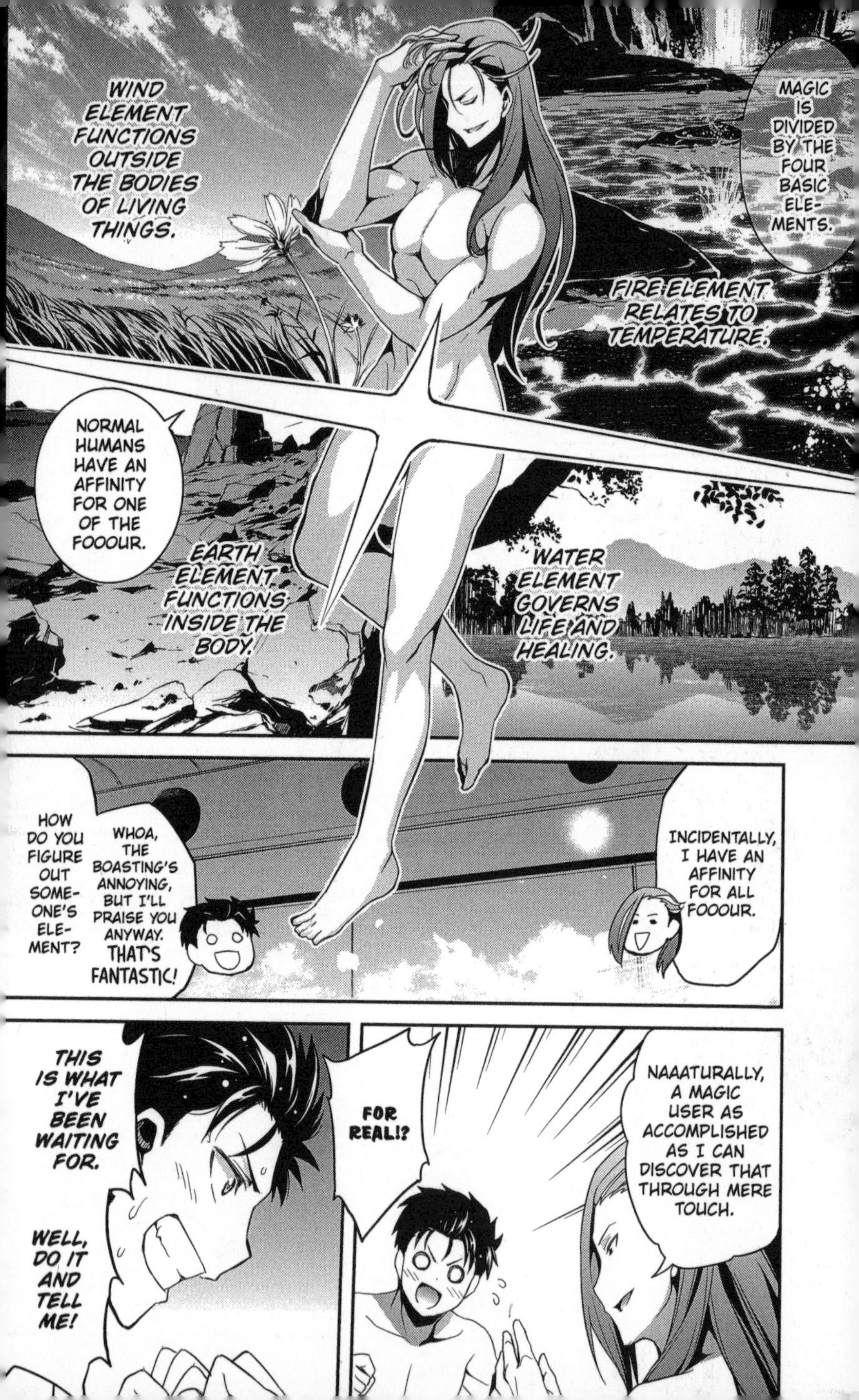

MAGIC IS DIVIDED BY THE FOUR BASIC ELEMENTS.
FIRE ELEMENT RELATES TO TEMPERATURE.
WIND ELEMENT FUNCTIONS OUTSIDE THE BODIES OF LIVING THINGS.
WATER ELEMENT GOVERNS LIFE AND HEALING.
EARTH ELEMENT FUNCTIONS INSIDE THE BODY.
NORMAL HUMANS HAVE AN AFFINITY FOR ONE OF THE FOOOUR.
INCIDENTALLY, I HAVE AN AFFINITY FOR ALL FOOOUR.
WHOA, THE BOASTING'S ANNOYING, BUT I'LL PRAISE YOU ANYWAY.
THAT'S FANTASTIC!
HOW DO YOU FIGURE OUT SOME-ONE'S ELE-MENT?
NAAATURALLY, A MAGIC USER AS ACCOMPLISHED AS I CAN DISCOVER THAT THROUGH MERE TOUCH.
FOR REAL!?
THIS IS WHAT I'VE BEEN WAITING FOR.
WELL, DO IT AND TELL ME!

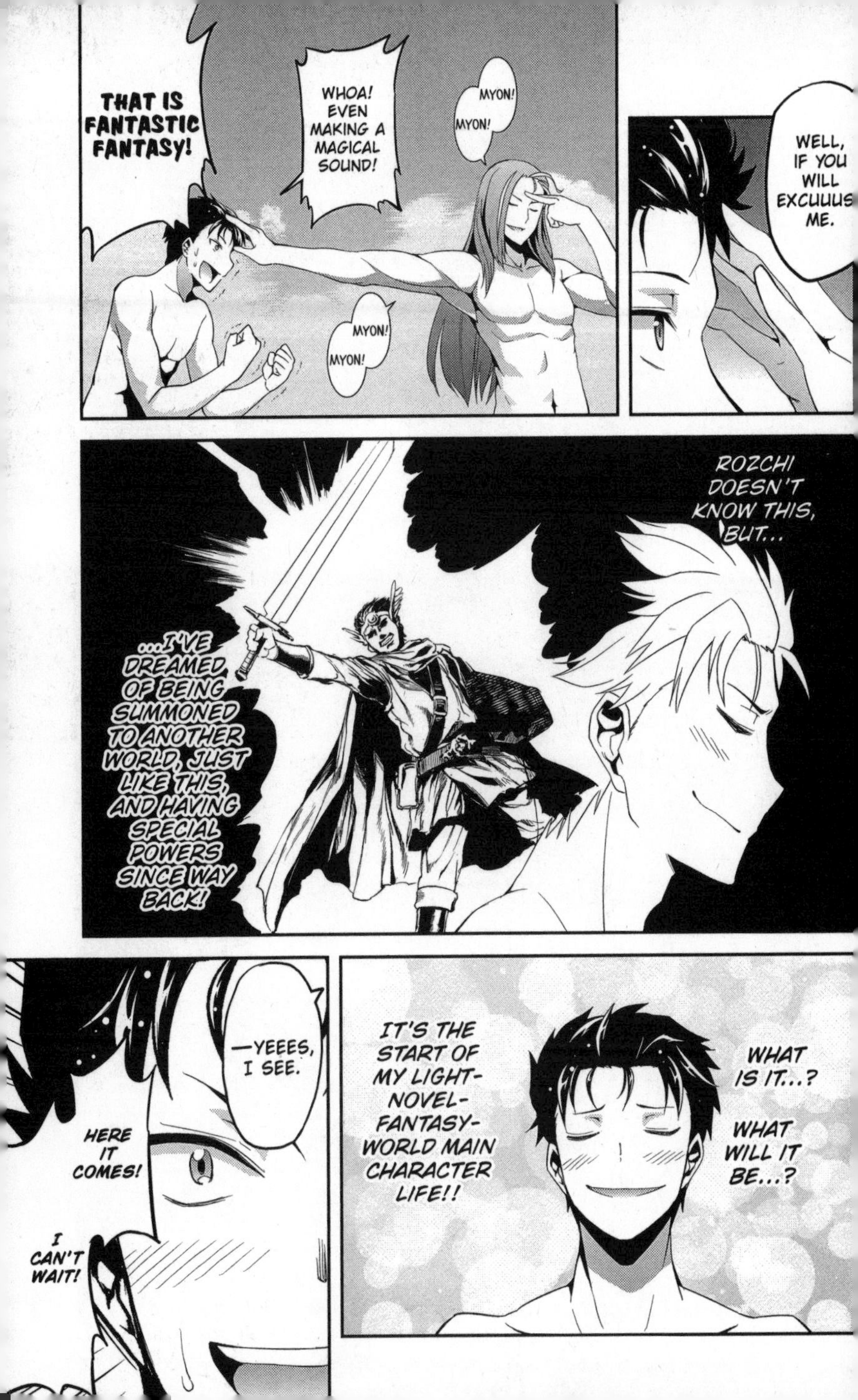
WELL, IF YOU WILL EXCUUUS ME.
MYON! MYON!
WHOA! EVEN MAKING A MAGICAL SOUND!
THAT IS FANTASTIC FANTASY!
MYON! MYON!
ROZCHI DOESN'T KNOW THIS, BUT...
...I'VE DREAMED OF BEING SUMMONED TO ANOTHER WORLD, JUST LIKE THIS, AND HAVING SPECIAL POWERS SINCE WAY BACK!
WHAT IS IT...?
WHAT WILL IT BE...?
IT'S THE START OF MY LIGHT-NOVEL-FANTASY-WORLD MAIN CHARACTER LIFE!!
—YEEES, I SEE.
HERE IT COMES!
I CAN'T WAIT!

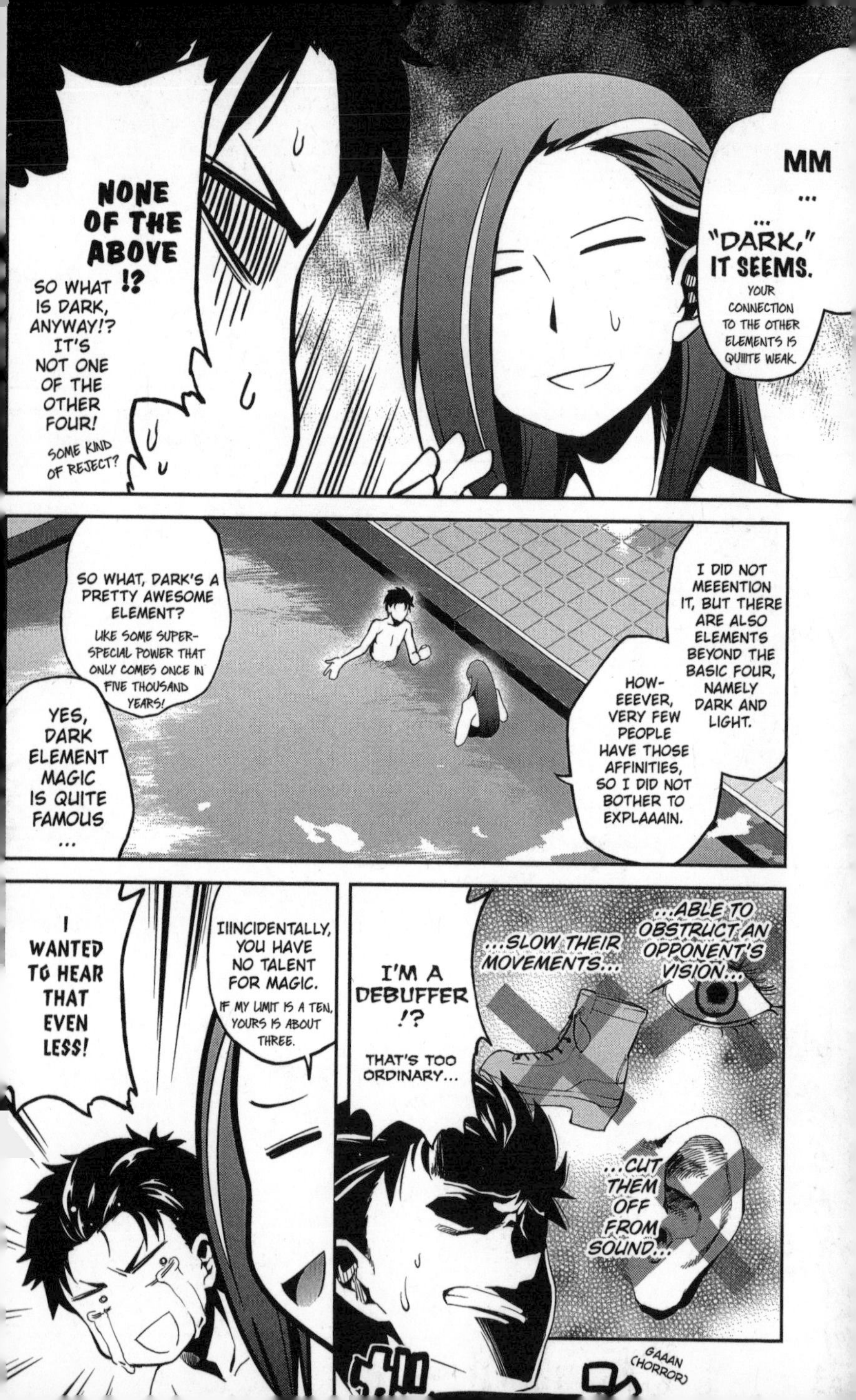
MM... ... "DARK," IT SEEMS.
YOUR CONNECTION TO THE OTHER ELEMENTS IS QUIIITE WEAK.
NONE OF THE ABOVE !?
SO WHAT IS DARK, ANYWAY!? IT'S NOT ONE OF THE OTHER FOUR!
SOME KIND OF REJECT?
I DID NOT MEEENTION IT, BUT THERE ARE ALSO ELEMENTS BEYOND THE BASIC FOUR, NAMELY DARK AND LIGHT.
HOW-EEEVER, VERY FEW PEOPLE HAVE THOSE AFFINITIES, SO I DID NOT BOTHER TO EXPLAAAIN.
SO WHAT, DARK'S A PRETTY AWESOME ELEMENT?
LIKE SOME SUPER-SPECIAL POWER THAT ONLY COMES ONCE IN FIVE THOUSAND YEARS!
YES, DARK ELEMENT MAGIC IS QUITE FAMOUS...
...ABLE TO OBSTRUCT AN OPPONENT'S VISION...
...SLOW THEIR MOVEMENTS...
I'M A DEBUFFER !?
THAT'S TOO ORDINARY...
...CUT THEM OFF FROM SOUND...
GAAAN (HORROR)
IIINCIDENTALLY, YOU HAVE NO TALENT FOR MAGIC.
IF MY LIMIT IS A TEN, YOURS IS ABOUT THREE.
I WANTED TO HEAR THAT EVEN LESS!

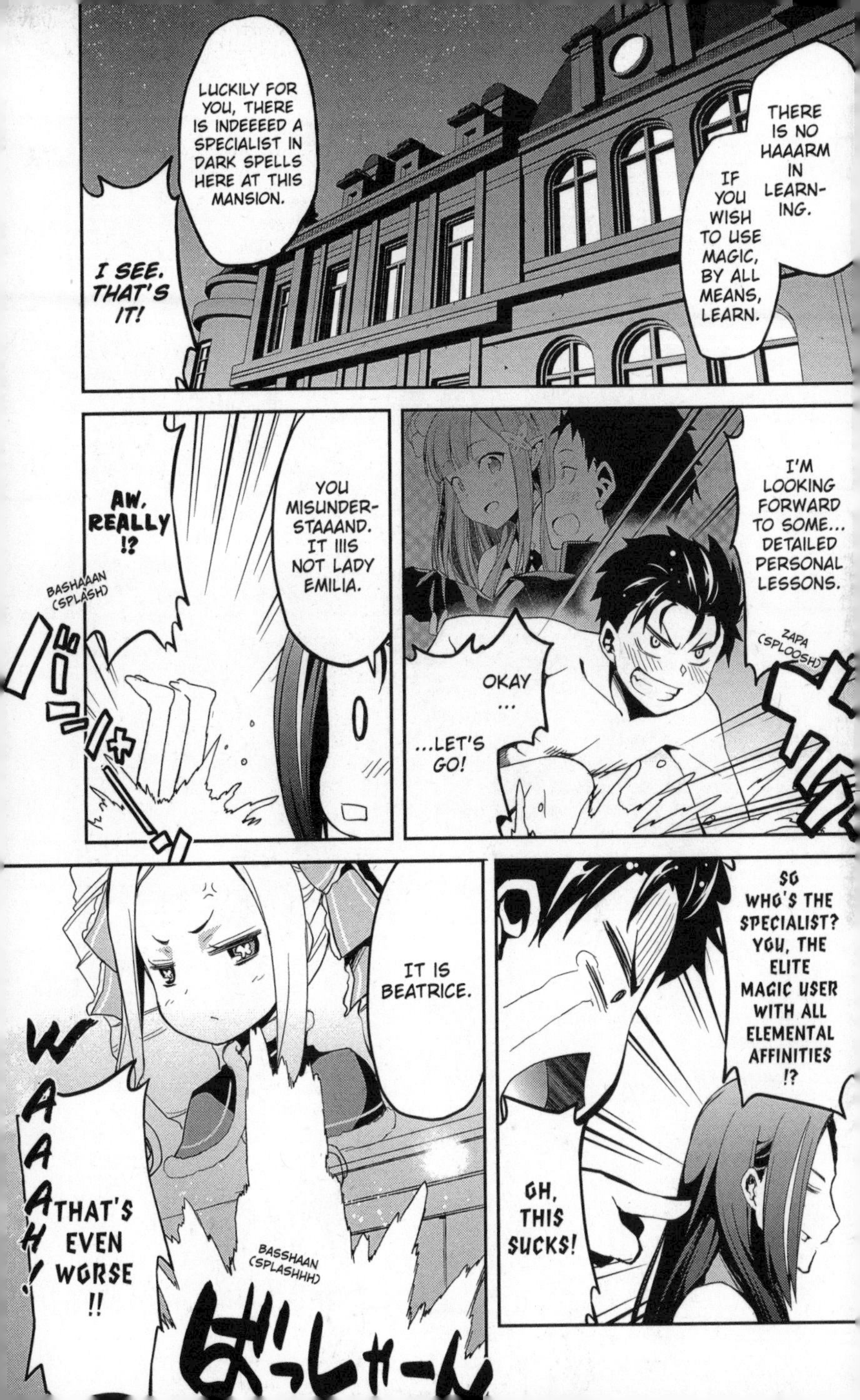
THERE IS NO HAAARM IN LEARNING.
IF YOU WISH TO USE MAGIC, BY ALL MEANS, LEARN.
LUCKILY FOR YOU, THERE IS INDEEEED A SPECIALIST IN DARK SPELLS HERE AT THIS MANSION.
I SEE. THAT'S IT!
I'M LOOKING FORWARD TO SOME... DETAILED PERSONAL LESSONS.
ZAPA (SPLOOSH)
OKAY ...
...LET'S GO!
YOU MISUNDERSTAAAND. IT IIIS NOT LADY EMILIA.
AW, REALLY!?
BASHAAAN (SPLASH)
SO WHO'S THE SPECIALIST? YOU, THE ELITE MAGIC USER WITH ALL ELEMENTAL AFFINITIES!?
OH, THIS SUCKS!
IT IS BEATRICE.
WAAAAH!
THAT'S EVEN WORSE!!
BASSHAAN (SPLASHHH)
ばっしゃーん

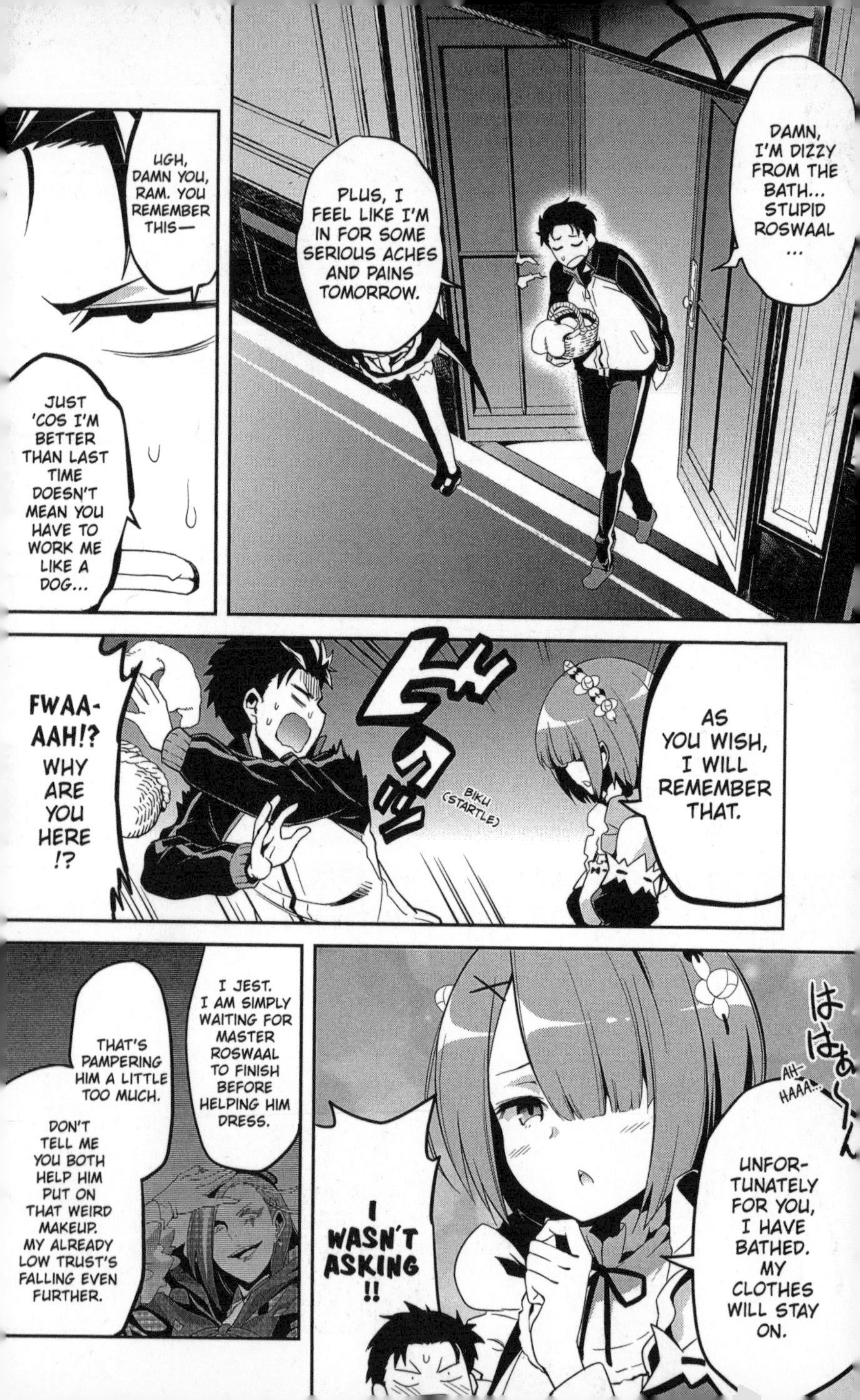
DAMN, I'M DIZZY FROM THE BATH... STUPID ROSWAAL...
PLUS, I FEEL LIKE I'M IN FOR SOME SERIOUS ACHES AND PAINS TOMORROW.
UGH, DAMN YOU, RAM. YOU REMEMBER THIS—
JUST 'COS I'M BETTER THAN LAST TIME DOESN'T MEAN YOU HAVE TO WORK ME LIKE A DOG...
AS YOU WISH, I WILL REMEMBER THAT.
BIKU (STARTLE)
FWAA-AAH!? WHY ARE YOU HERE!?
AH-HAAA...
UNFORTUNATELY FOR YOU, I HAVE BATHED. MY CLOTHES WILL STAY ON.
I WASN'T ASKING!!
I JEST. I AM SIMPLY WAITING FOR MASTER ROSWAAL TO FINISH BEFORE HELPING HIM DRESS.
THAT'S PAMPERING HIM A LITTLE TOO MUCH.
DON'T TELL ME YOU BOTH HELP HIM PUT ON THAT WEIRD MAKEUP. MY ALREADY LOW TRUST'S FALLING EVEN FURTHER.

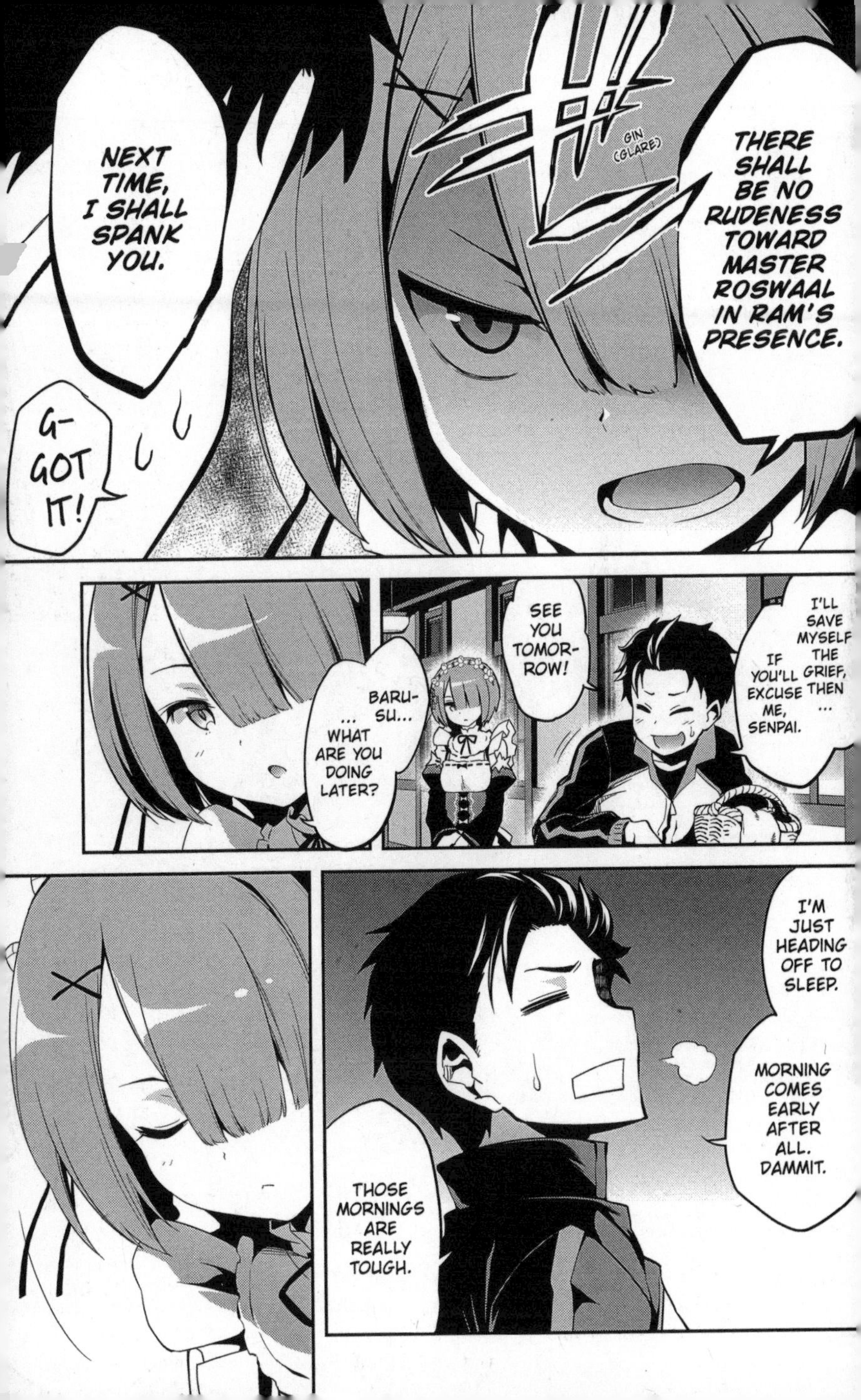
THERE SHALL BE NO RUDENESS TOWARD MASTER ROSWAAL IN RAM'S PRESENCE.
GIN (GLARE)
NEXT TIME, I SHALL SPANK YOU.
G-GOT IT!
I'LL SAVE MYSELF THE GRIEF, THEN...
IF YOU'LL EXCUSE ME, SENPAI.
SEE YOU TOMORROW!
BARU-SU... ...WHAT ARE YOU DOING LATER?
I'M JUST HEADING OFF TO SLEEP.
MORNING COMES EARLY AFTER ALL. DAMMIT.
THOSE MORNINGS ARE REALLY TOUGH.

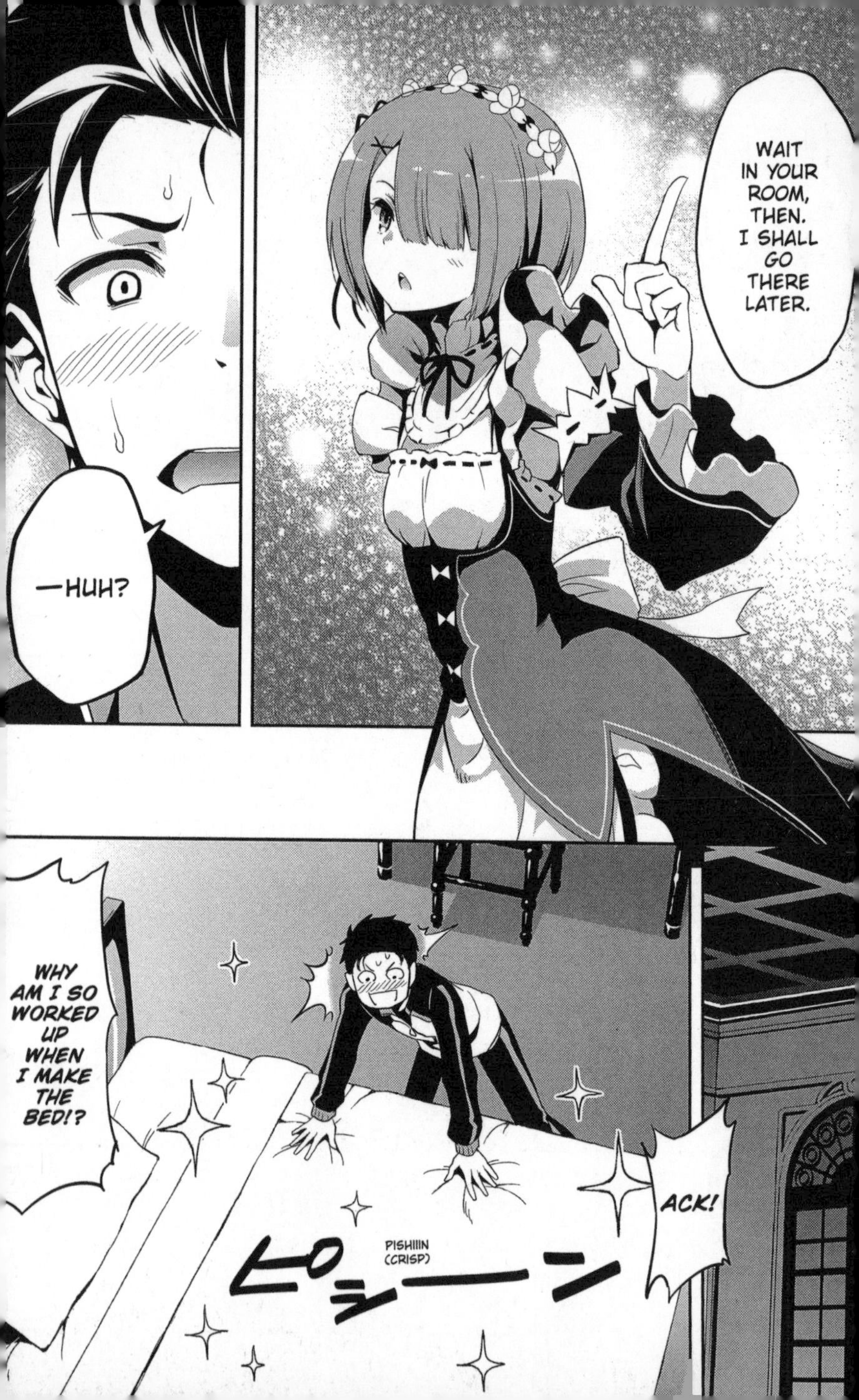
WAIT IN YOUR ROOM, THEN. I SHALL GO THERE LATER.
—HUH?
ACK!
WHY AM I SO WORKED UP WHEN I MAKE THE BED!?
PISHIIIN (CRISP)

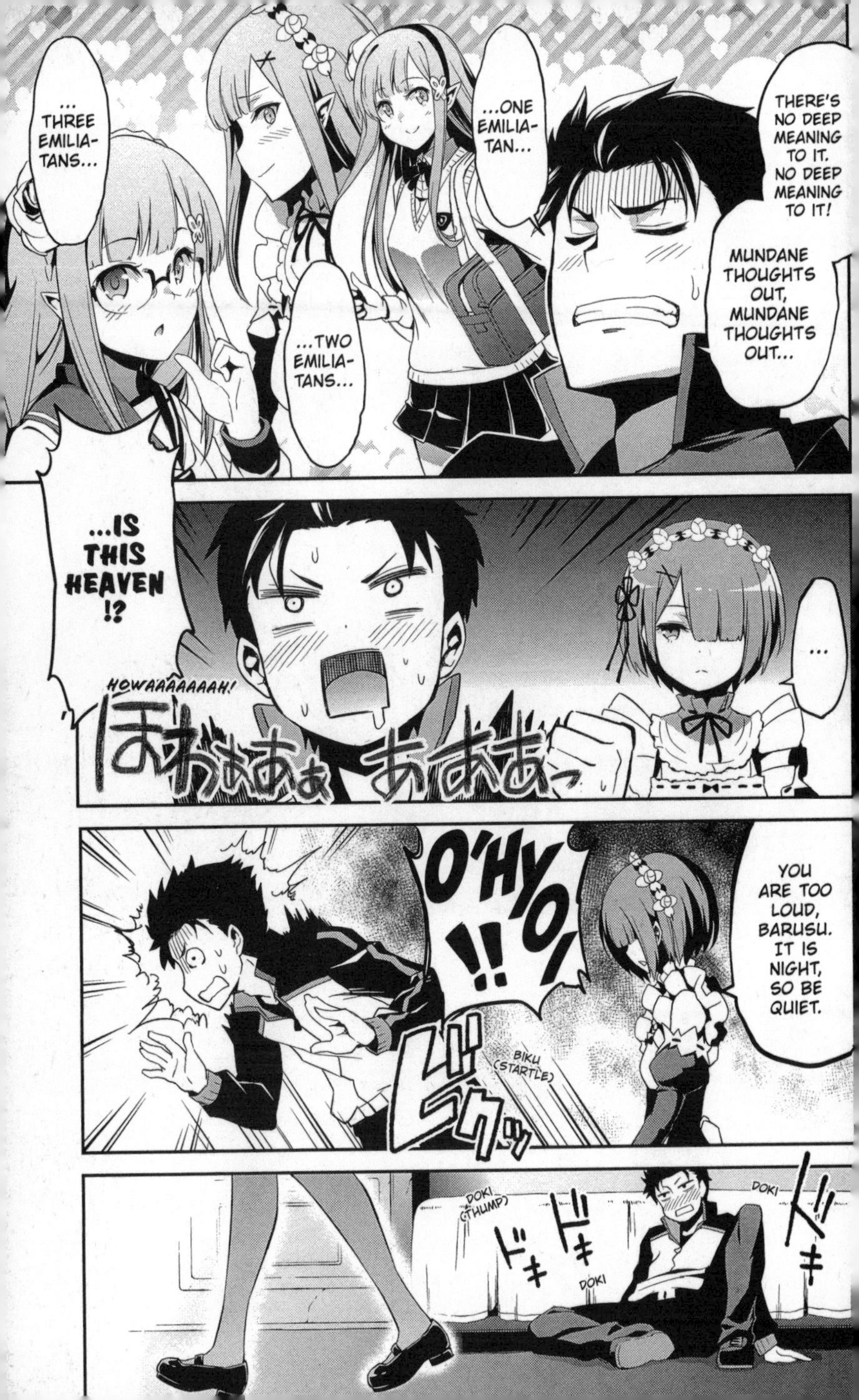
THERE'S NO DEEP MEANING TO IT. NO DEEP MEANING TO IT!
MUNDANE THOUGHTS OUT, MUNDANE THOUGHTS OUT...
...ONE EMILIA-TAN...
...TWO EMILIA-TANS...
...THREE EMILIA-TANS...
...
...IS THIS HEAVEN!?
HOWAAAAAAAH!
YOU ARE TOO LOUD, BARUSU. IT IS NIGHT, SO BE QUIET.
O'HYO!!
BIKU (STARTLE)
ドキ
DOKI
ドキ
DOKI
ドキ
DOKI (THUMP)

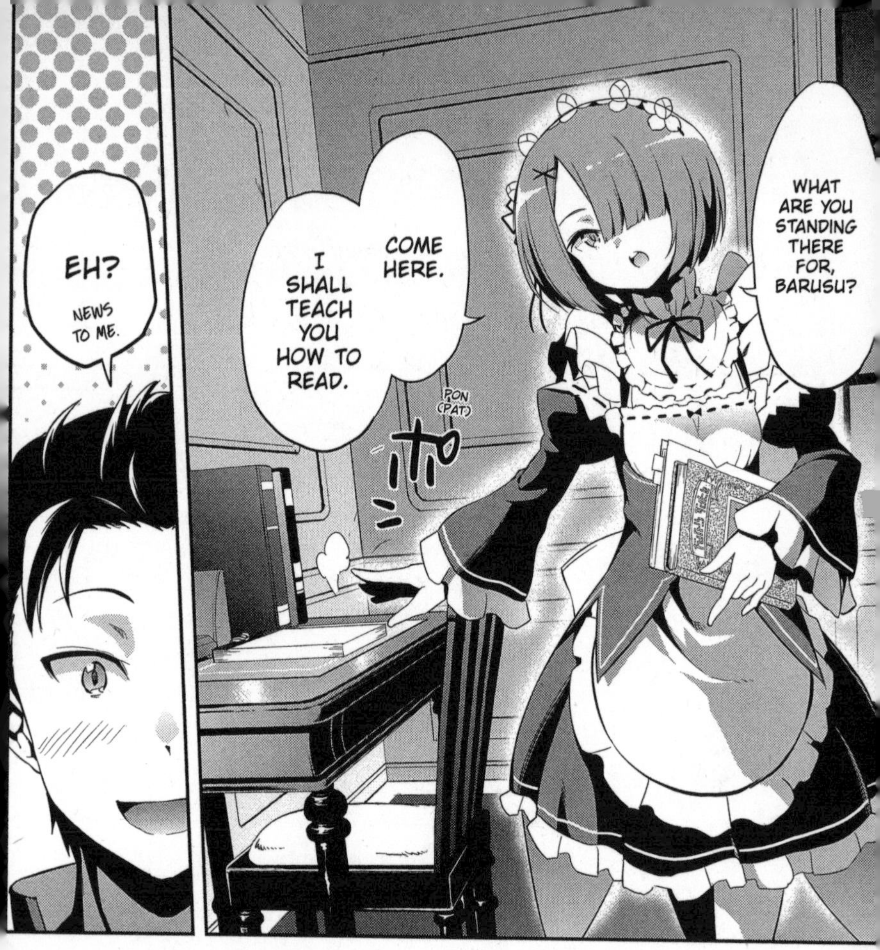
WHAT ARE YOU STANDING THERE FOR, BARUSU?
COME HERE.
I SHALL TEACH YOU HOW TO READ.
PON (PAT)
EH?
NEWS TO ME.

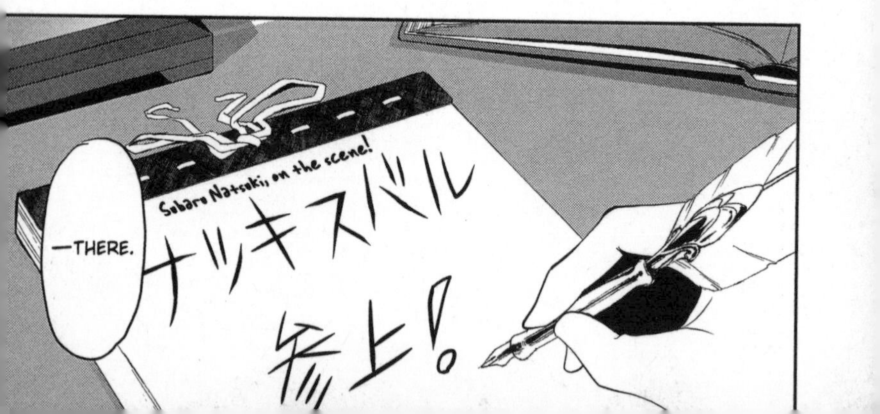
Subaru Natsuki, on the scene!
ナツキスバル
—THERE.

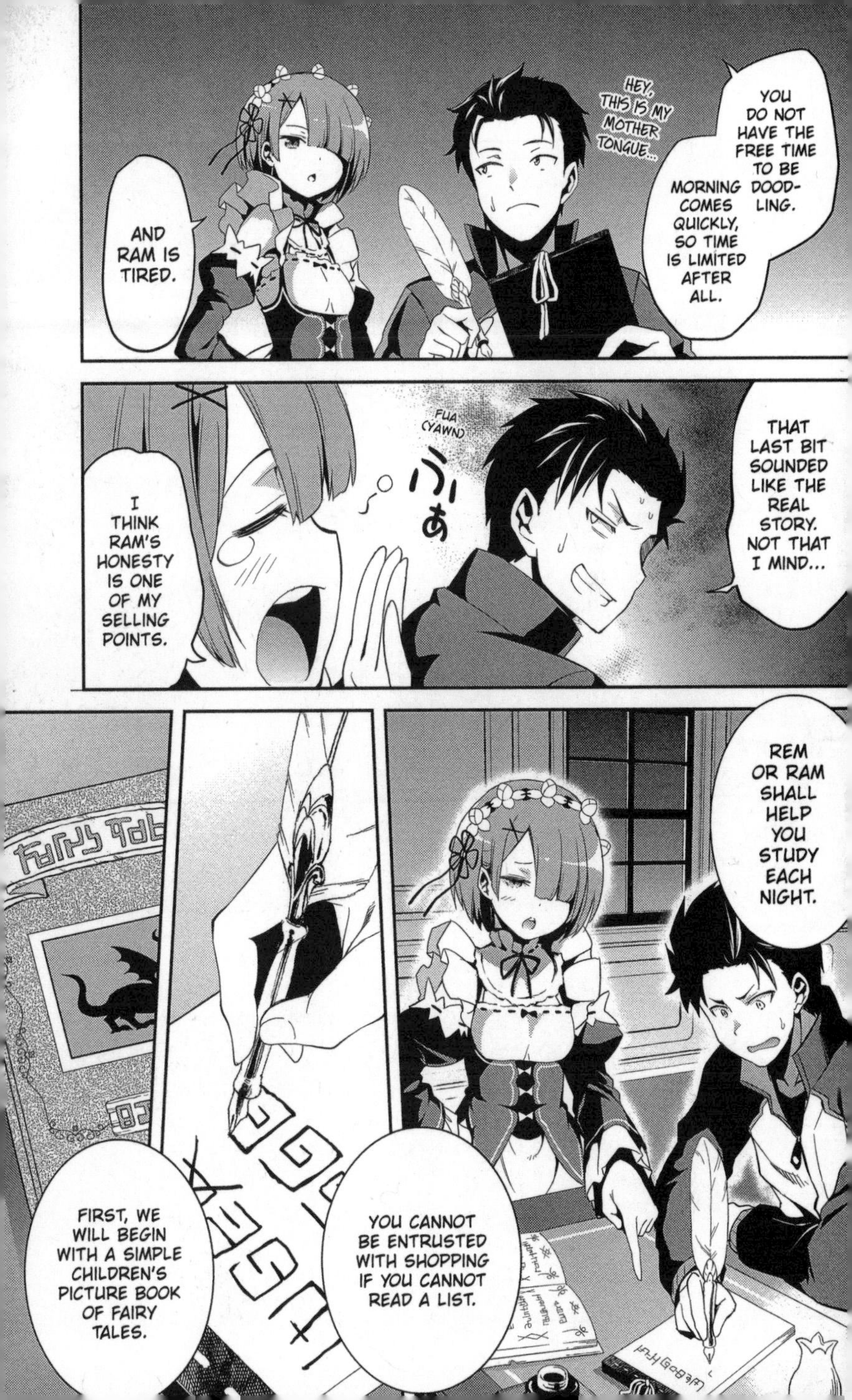
YOU DO NOT HAVE THE FREE TIME TO BE DOODLING.
HEY, THIS IS MY MOTHER TONGUE...
MORNING COMES QUICKLY, SO TIME IS LIMITED AFTER ALL.
AND RAM IS TIRED.
THAT LAST BIT SOUNDED LIKE THE REAL STORY. NOT THAT I MIND...
FUA (YAWN)
ふぁ
I THINK RAM'S HONESTY IS ONE OF MY SELLING POINTS.
REM OR RAM SHALL HELP YOU STUDY EACH NIGHT.
YOU CANNOT BE ENTRUSTED WITH SHOPPING IF YOU CANNOT READ A LIST.
FIRST, WE WILL BEGIN WITH A SIMPLE CHILDREN'S PICTURE BOOK OF FAIRY TALES.

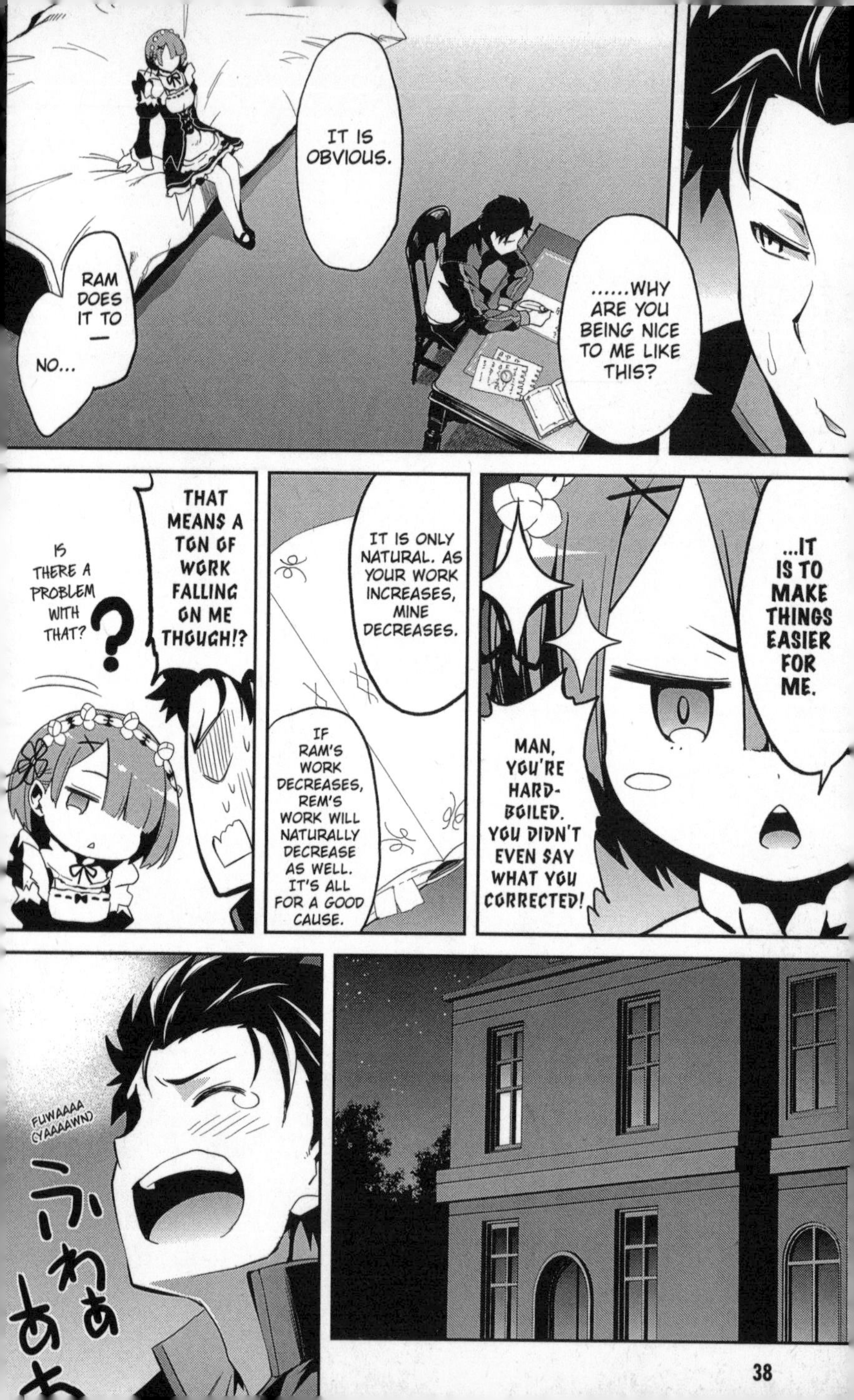
......WHY ARE YOU BEING NICE TO ME LIKE THIS?
IT IS OBVIOUS.
RAM DOES IT TO— NO...
...IT IS TO MAKE THINGS EASIER FOR ME.
MAN, YOU'RE HARD-BOILED. YOU DIDN'T EVEN SAY WHAT YOU CORRECTED!
IT IS ONLY NATURAL. AS YOUR WORK INCREASES, MINE DECREASES.
IF RAM'S WORK DECREASES, REM'S WORK WILL NATURALLY DECREASE AS WELL. IT'S ALL FOR A GOOD CAUSE.
THAT MEANS A TON OF WORK FALLING ON ME THOUGH!?
IS THERE A PROBLEM WITH THAT?
FUWAAAA (YAAAAWN)

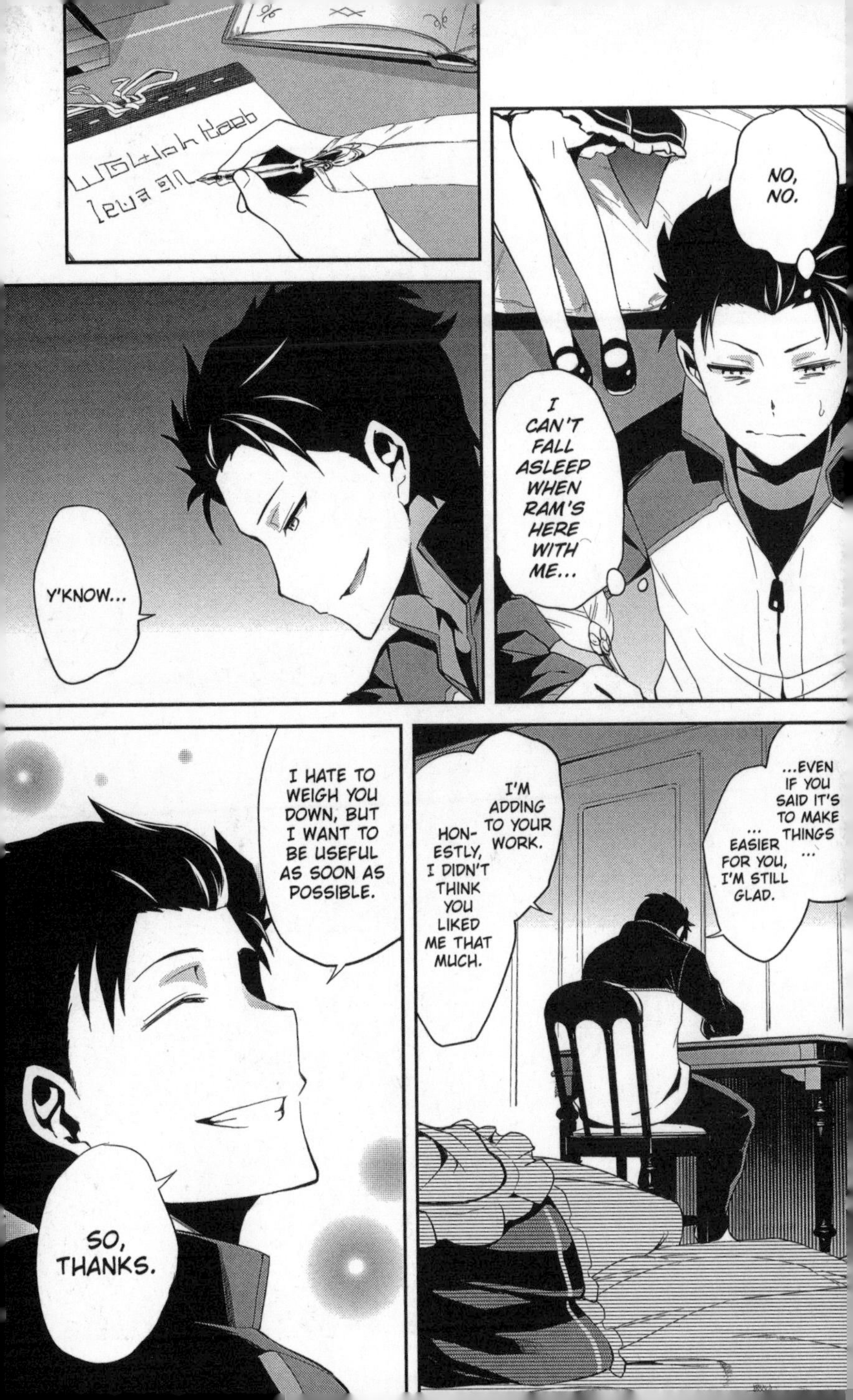

NO, NO.
I CAN'T FALL ASLEEP WHEN RAM'S HERE WITH ME...
Y'KNOW...
...EVEN IF YOU SAID IT'S TO MAKE THINGS...
...EASIER FOR YOU, I'M STILL GLAD.
I'M ADDING TO YOUR WORK.
HON-ESTLY, I DIDN'T THINK YOU LIKED ME THAT MUCH.
I HATE TO WEIGH YOU DOWN, BUT I WANT TO BE USEFUL AS SOON AS POSSIBLE.
SO, THANKS.

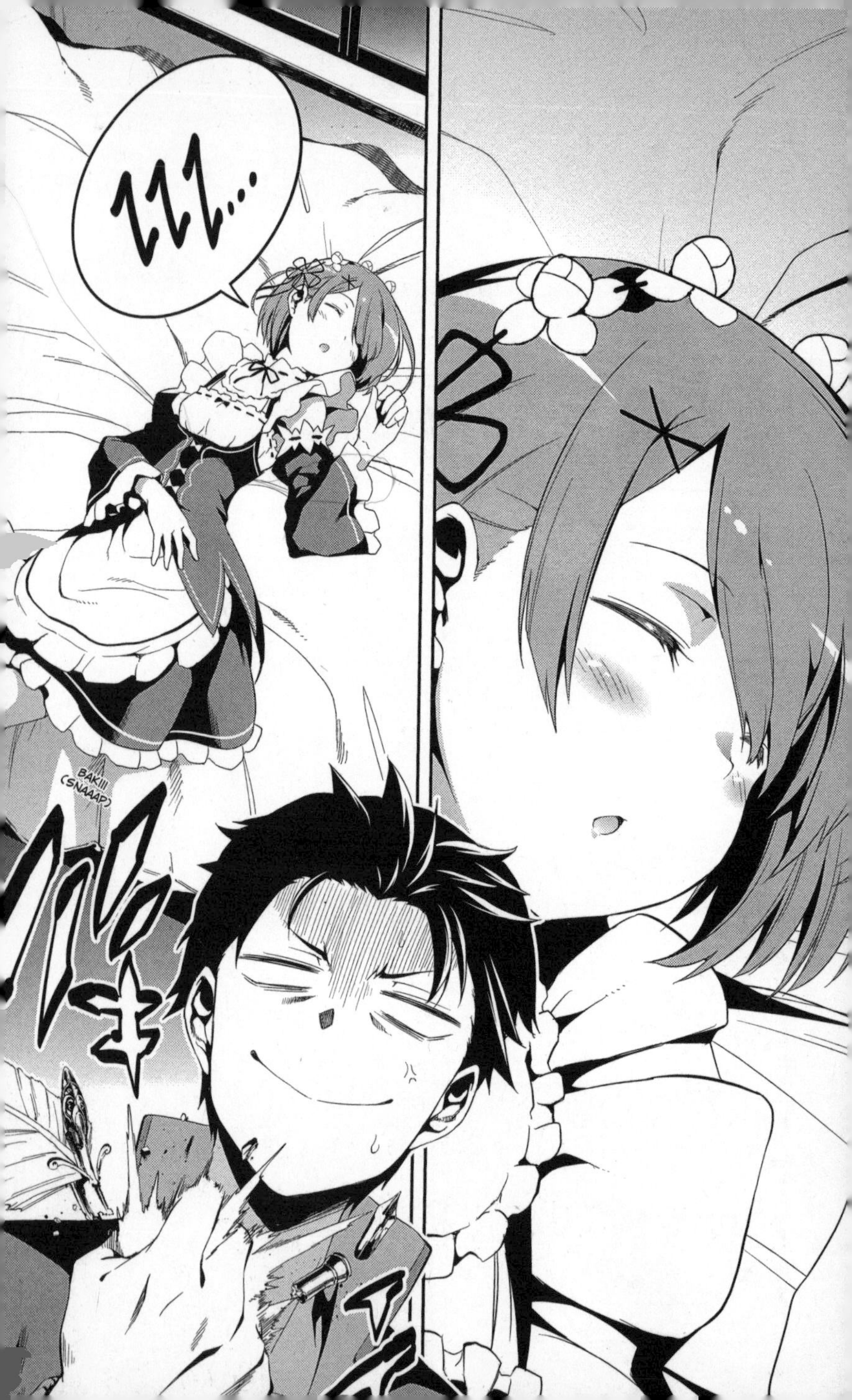
ZZZ...
BAKIII
(SNAAAP)

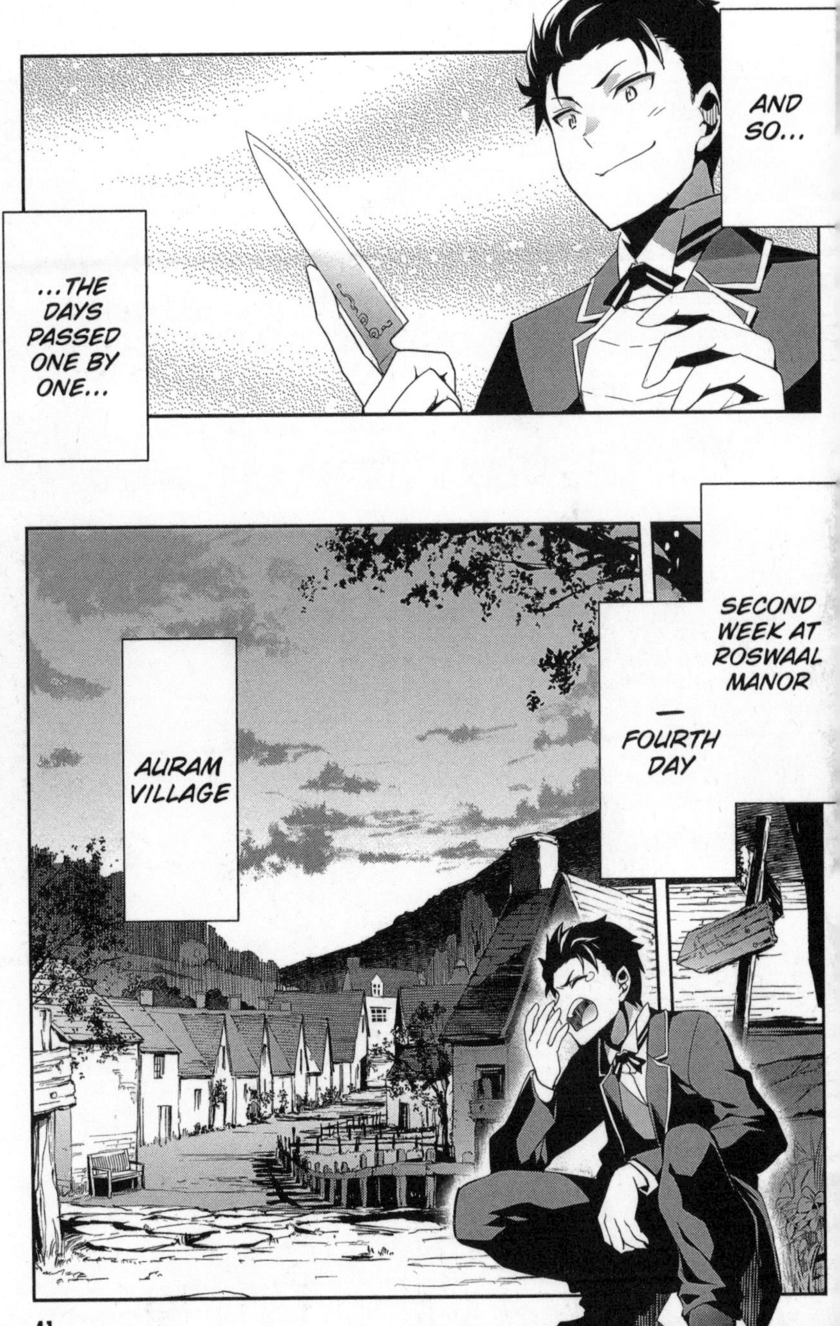
AND SO...
...THE DAYS PASSED ONE BY ONE...
SECOND WEEK AT ROSWAAL MANOR
—
FOURTH DAY
AURAM VILLAGE

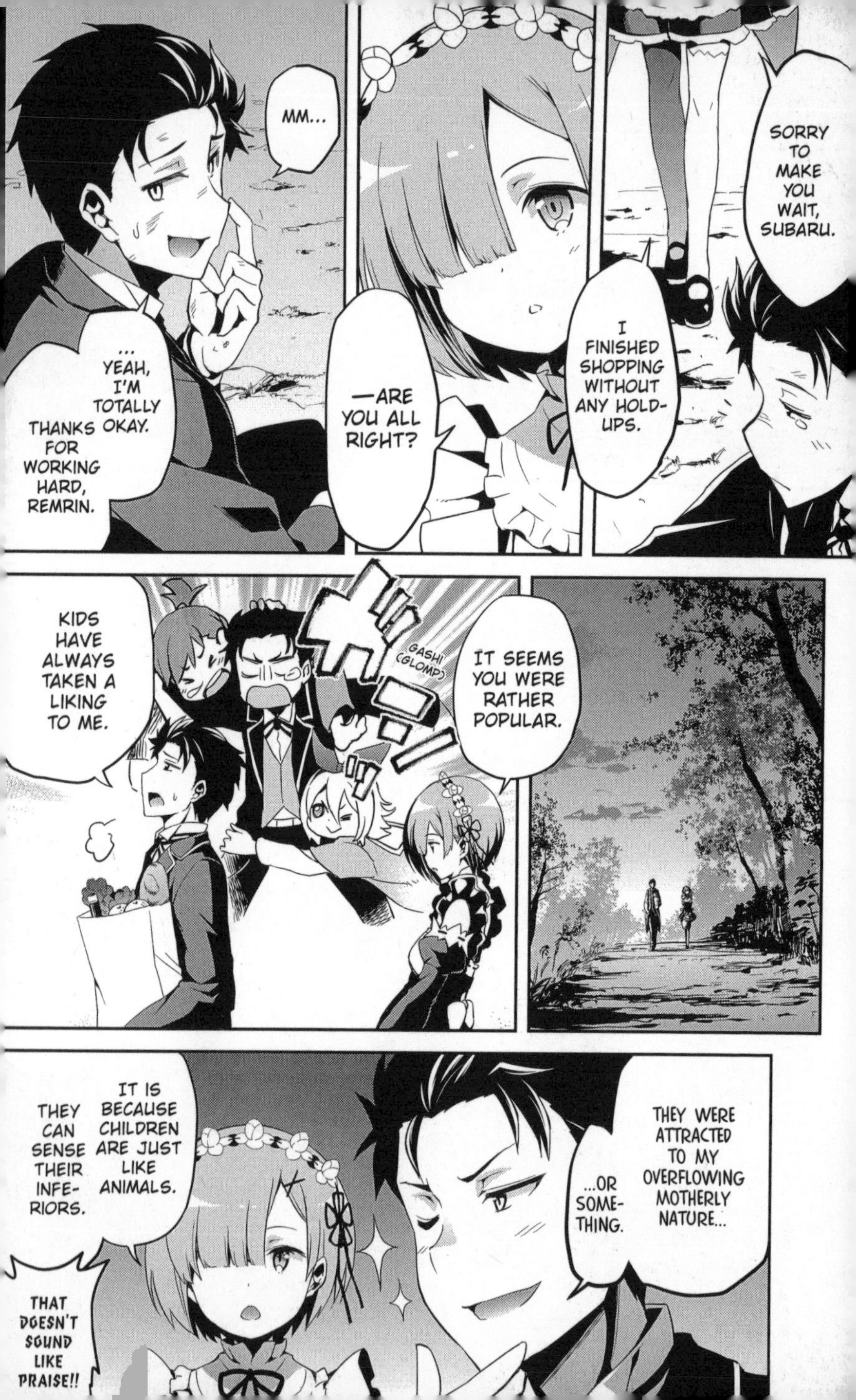
SORRY TO MAKE YOU WAIT, SUBARU.
I FINISHED SHOPPING WITHOUT ANY HOLD-UPS.
—ARE YOU ALL RIGHT?
MM...
...YEAH, I'M TOTALLY OKAY.
THANKS FOR WORKING HARD, REMRIN.
IT SEEMS YOU WERE RATHER POPULAR.
GASHI (GLOMP)
KIDS HAVE ALWAYS TAKEN A LIKING TO ME.
THEY WERE ATTRACTED TO MY OVERFLOWING MOTHERLY NATURE...
...OR SOME-THING.
IT IS BECAUSE CHILDREN ARE JUST LIKE ANIMALS.
THEY CAN SENSE THEIR INFE-RIORS.
THAT DOESN'T SOUND LIKE PRAISE!!

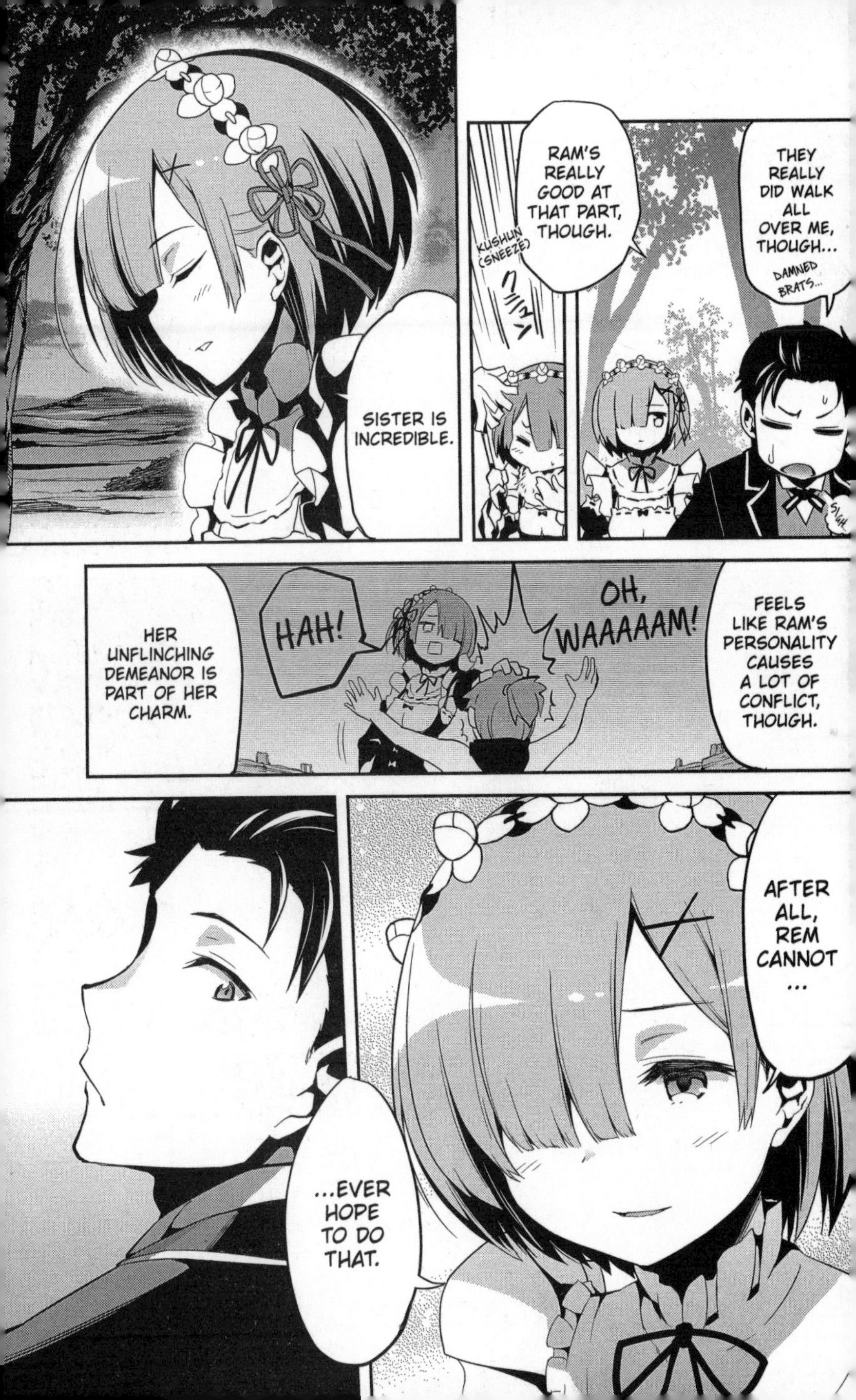
THEY REALLY DID WALK ALL OVER ME, THOUGH...
DAMNED BRATS...
SIGH
RAM'S REALLY GOOD AT THAT PART, THOUGH.
KUSHUN (SNEEZE)
SISTER IS INCREDIBLE.
FEELS LIKE RAM'S PERSONALITY CAUSES A LOT OF CONFLICT, THOUGH.
OH, WAAAAAM!
HAH!
HER UNFLINCHING DEMEANOR IS PART OF HER CHARM.
AFTER ALL, REM CANNOT ...
...EVER HOPE TO DO THAT.

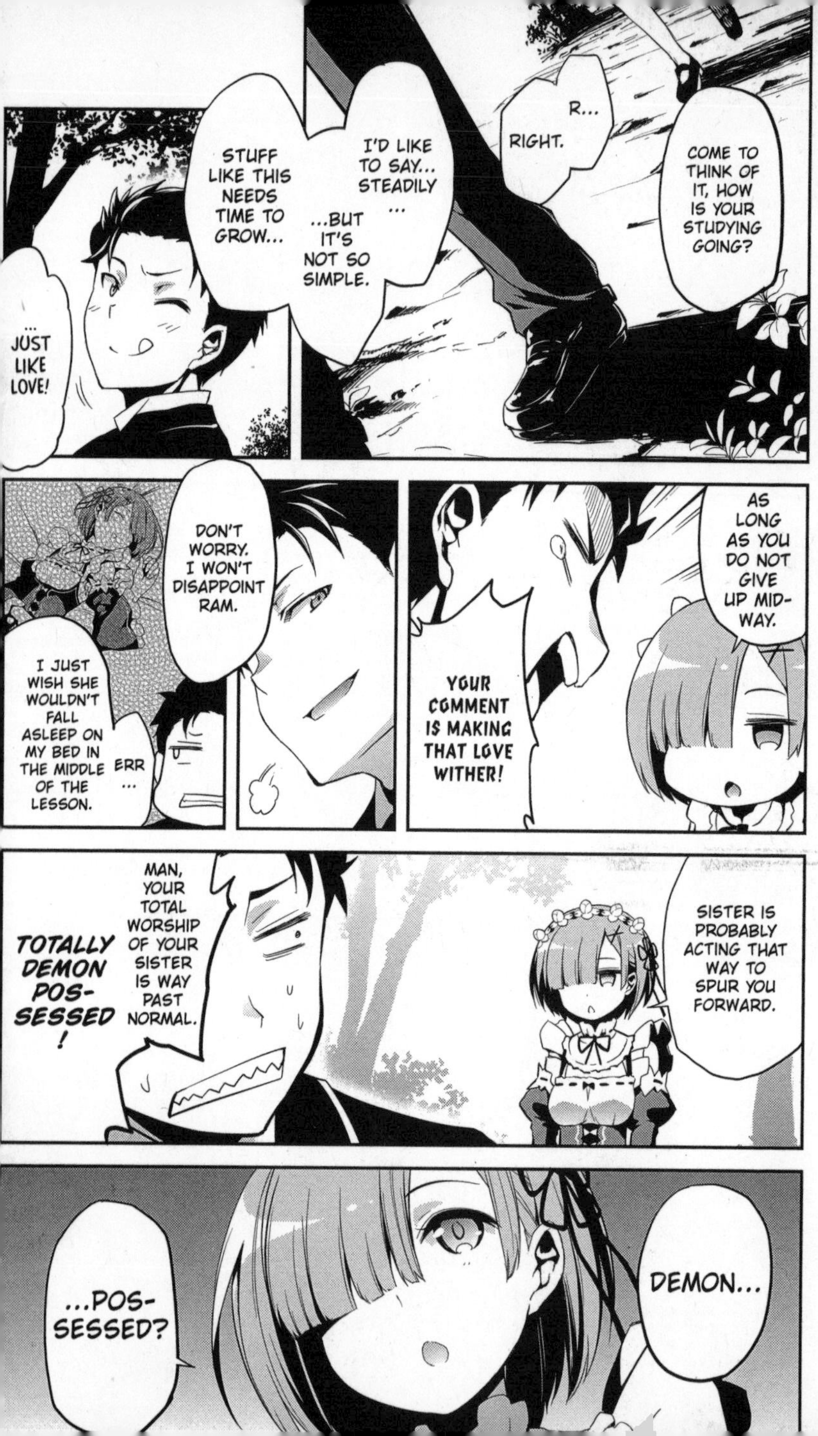
COME TO THINK OF IT, HOW IS YOUR STUDYING GOING?
R... RIGHT.
I'D LIKE TO SAY... STEADILY ...
...BUT IT'S NOT SO SIMPLE.
STUFF LIKE THIS NEEDS TIME TO GROW...
...JUST LIKE LOVE!
AS LONG AS YOU DO NOT GIVE UP MID-WAY.
YOUR COMMENT IS MAKING THAT LOVE WITHER!
DON'T WORRY. I WON'T DISAPPOINT RAM.
I JUST WISH SHE WOULDN'T FALL ASLEEP ON MY BED IN THE MIDDLE OF THE LESSON.
ERR ...
SISTER IS PROBABLY ACTING THAT WAY TO SPUR YOU FORWARD.
MAN, YOUR TOTAL WORSHIP OF YOUR SISTER IS WAY PAST NORMAL.
TOTALLY DEMON POS-SESSED!
DEMON...
...POS-SESSED?

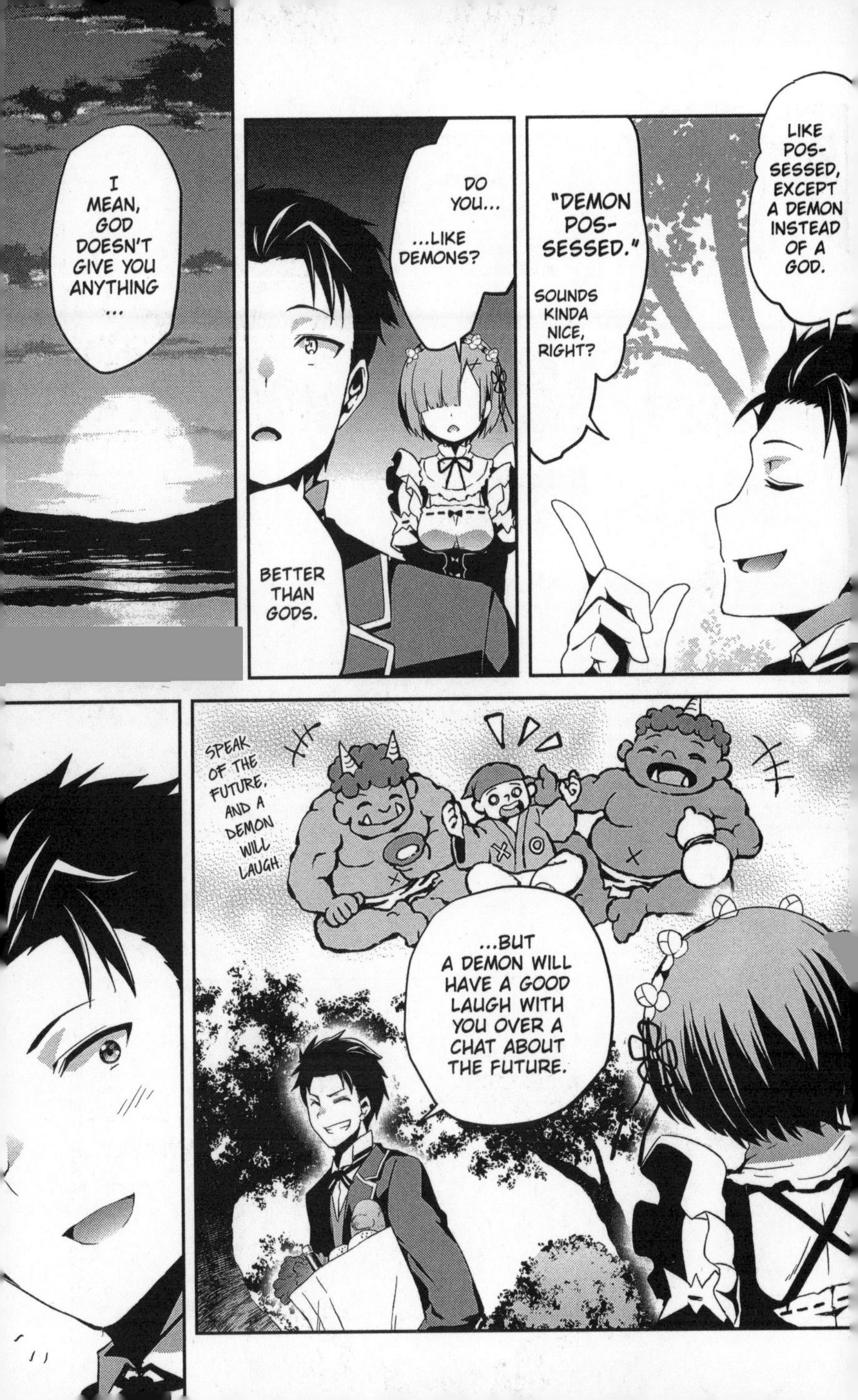
LIKE POSSESSED, EXCEPT A DEMON INSTEAD OF A GOD.
"DEMON POSSESSED."
SOUNDS KINDA NICE, RIGHT?
DO YOU... ...LIKE DEMONS?
BETTER THAN GODS.
I MEAN, GOD DOESN'T GIVE YOU ANYTHING...
...BUT A DEMON WILL HAVE A GOOD LAUGH WITH YOU OVER A CHAT ABOUT THE FUTURE.
SPEAK OF THE FUTURE, AND A DEMON WILL LAUGH.

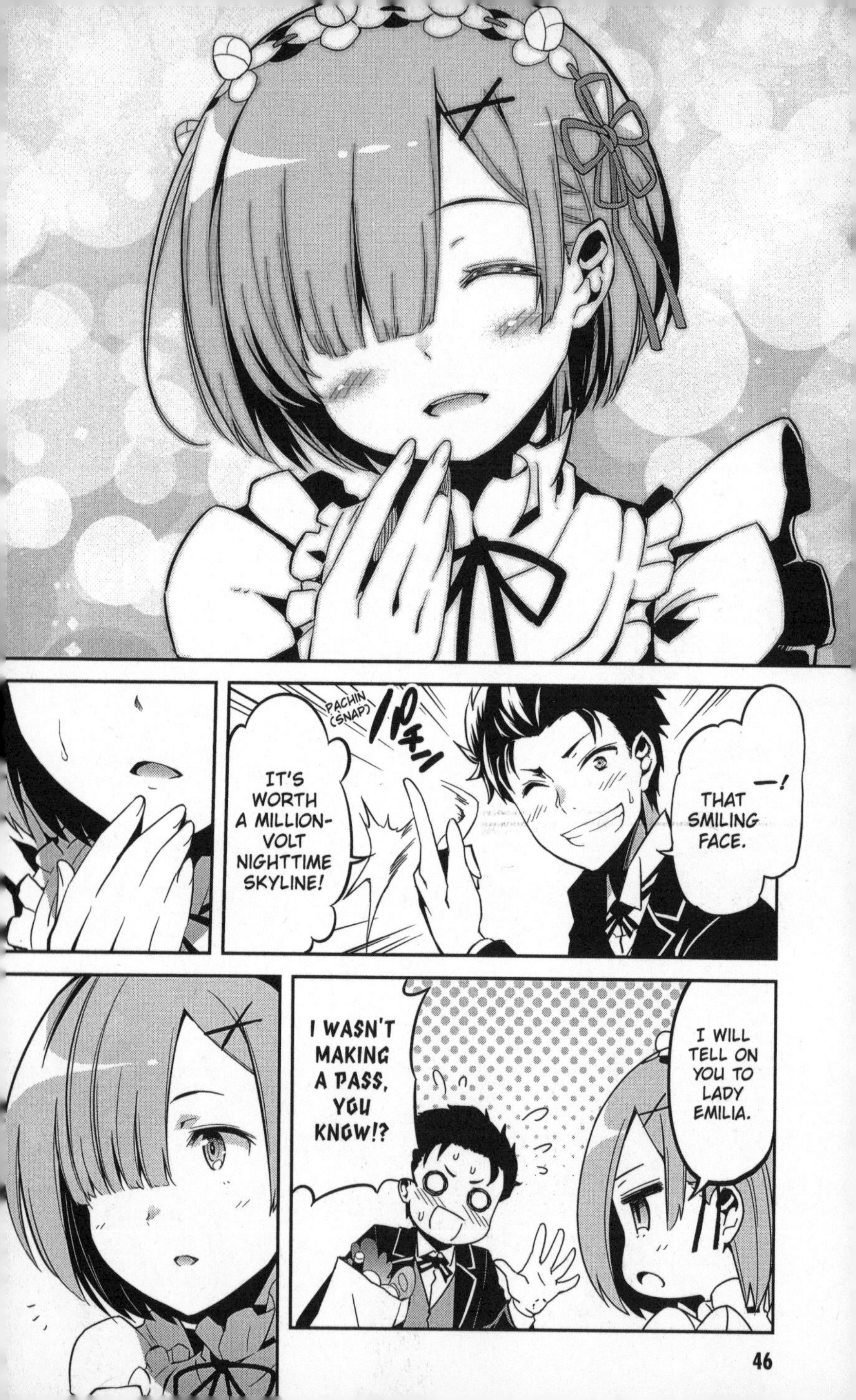
—!
THAT SMILING FACE.
PACHIN (SNAP)
IT'S WORTH A MILLION-VOLT NIGHTTIME SKYLINE!
I WILL TELL ON YOU TO LADY EMILIA.
I WASN'T MAKING A PASS, YOU KNOW!?

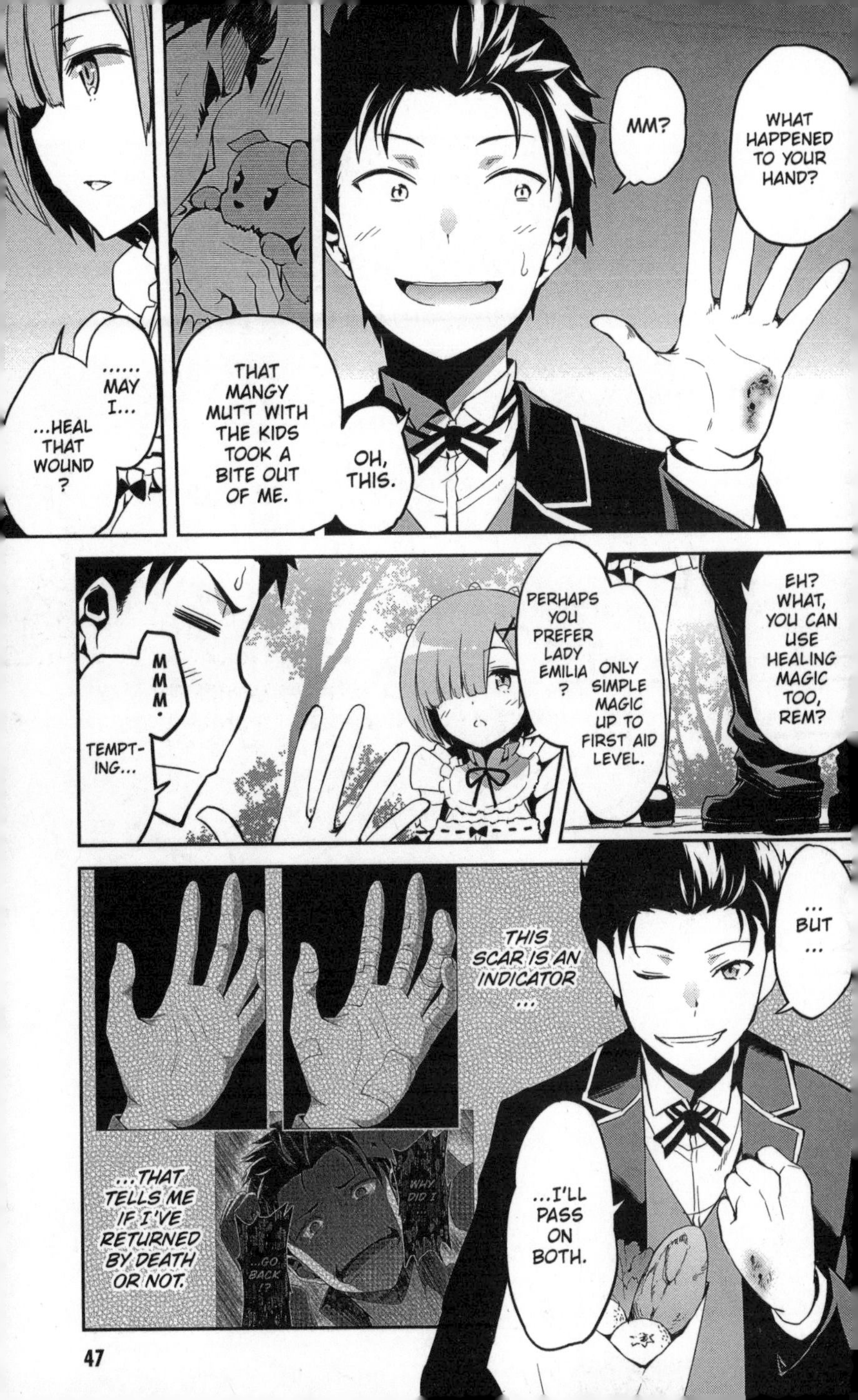
WHAT HAPPENED TO YOUR HAND?
MM?
OH, THIS.
THAT MANGY MUTT WITH THE KIDS TOOK A BITE OUT OF ME.
......MAY I... ...HEAL THAT WOUND?
EH? WHAT, YOU CAN USE HEALING MAGIC TOO, REM?
ONLY SIMPLE MAGIC UP TO FIRST AID LEVEL.
PERHAPS YOU PREFER LADY EMILIA?
MMM.
TEMPTING...
...BUT...
THIS SCAR IS AN INDICATOR...
...THAT TELLS ME IF I'VE RETURNED BY DEATH OR NOT.
WHY DID I ...GO BACK!?
...I'LL PASS ON BOTH.

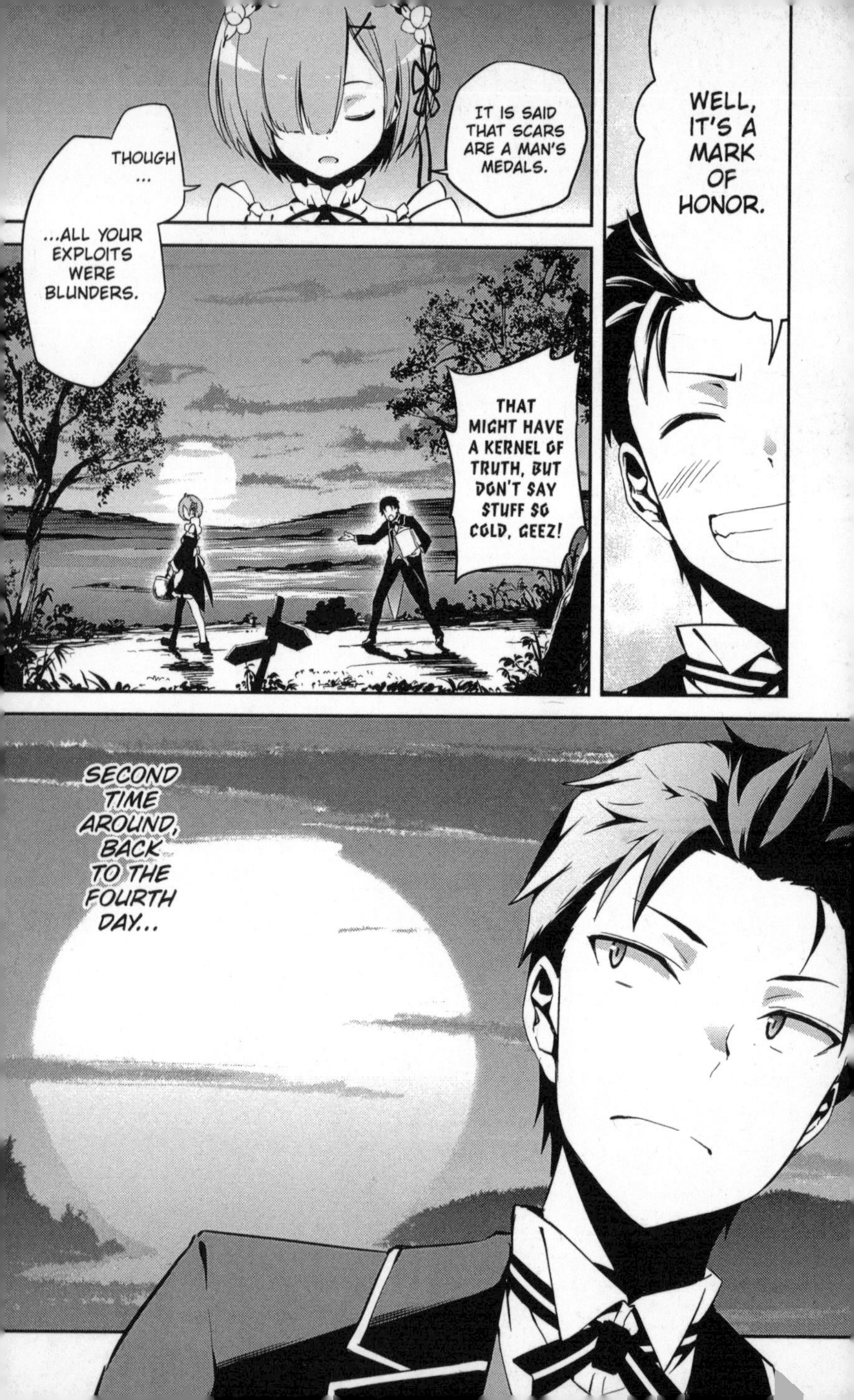
WELL, IT'S A MARK OF HONOR.
IT IS SAID THAT SCARS ARE A MAN'S MEDALS.
THOUGH ...
...ALL YOUR EXPLOITS WERE BLUNDERS.
THAT MIGHT HAVE A KERNEL OF TRUTH, BUT DON'T SAY STUFF SO COLD, GEEZ!
SECOND TIME AROUND, BACK TO THE FOURTH DAY...

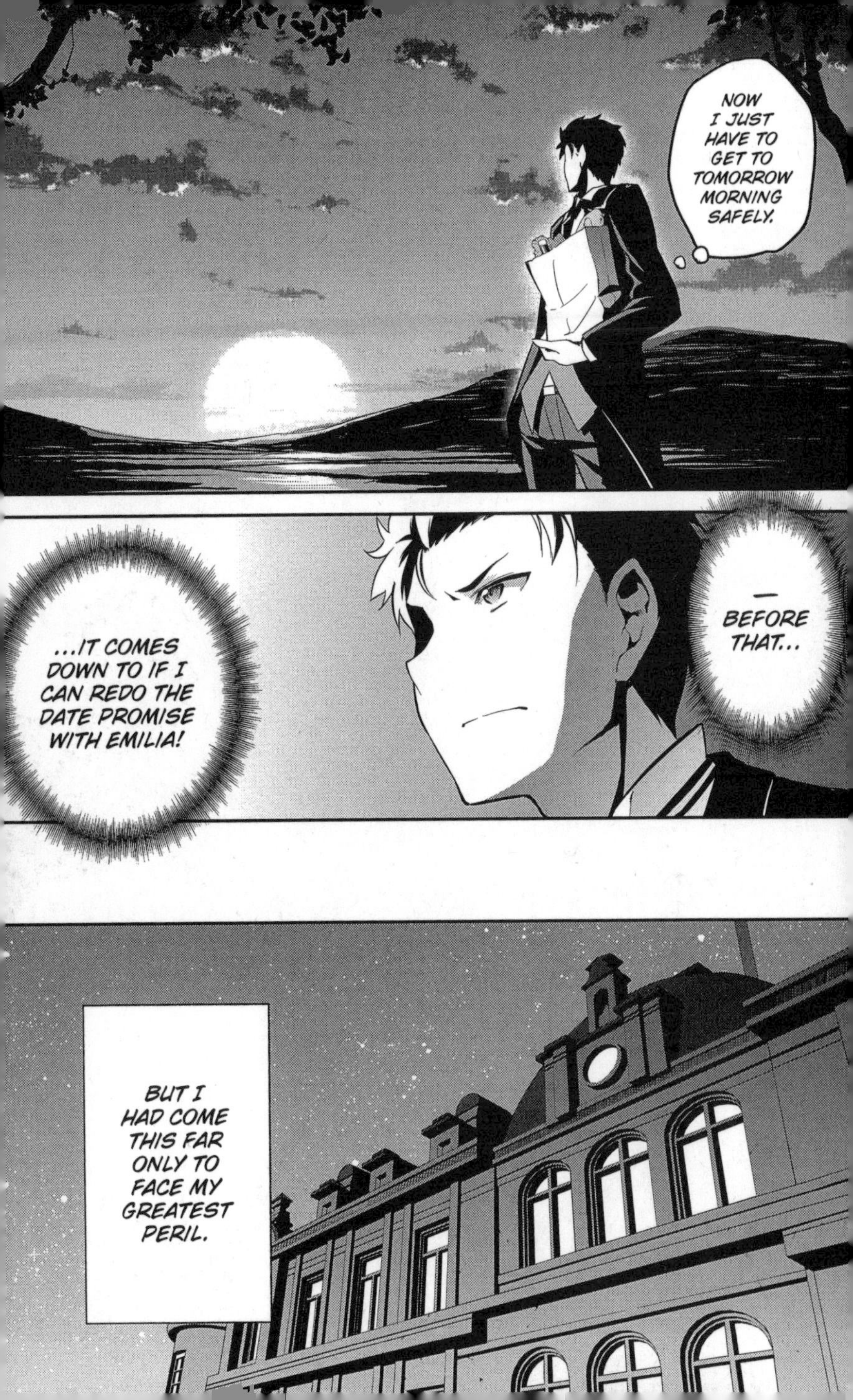
NOW I JUST HAVE TO GET TO TOMORROW MORNING SAFELY.
—BEFORE THAT...
...IT COMES DOWN TO IF I CAN REDO THE DATE PROMISE WITH EMILIA!
BUT I HAD COME THIS FAR ONLY TO FACE MY GREATEST PERIL.

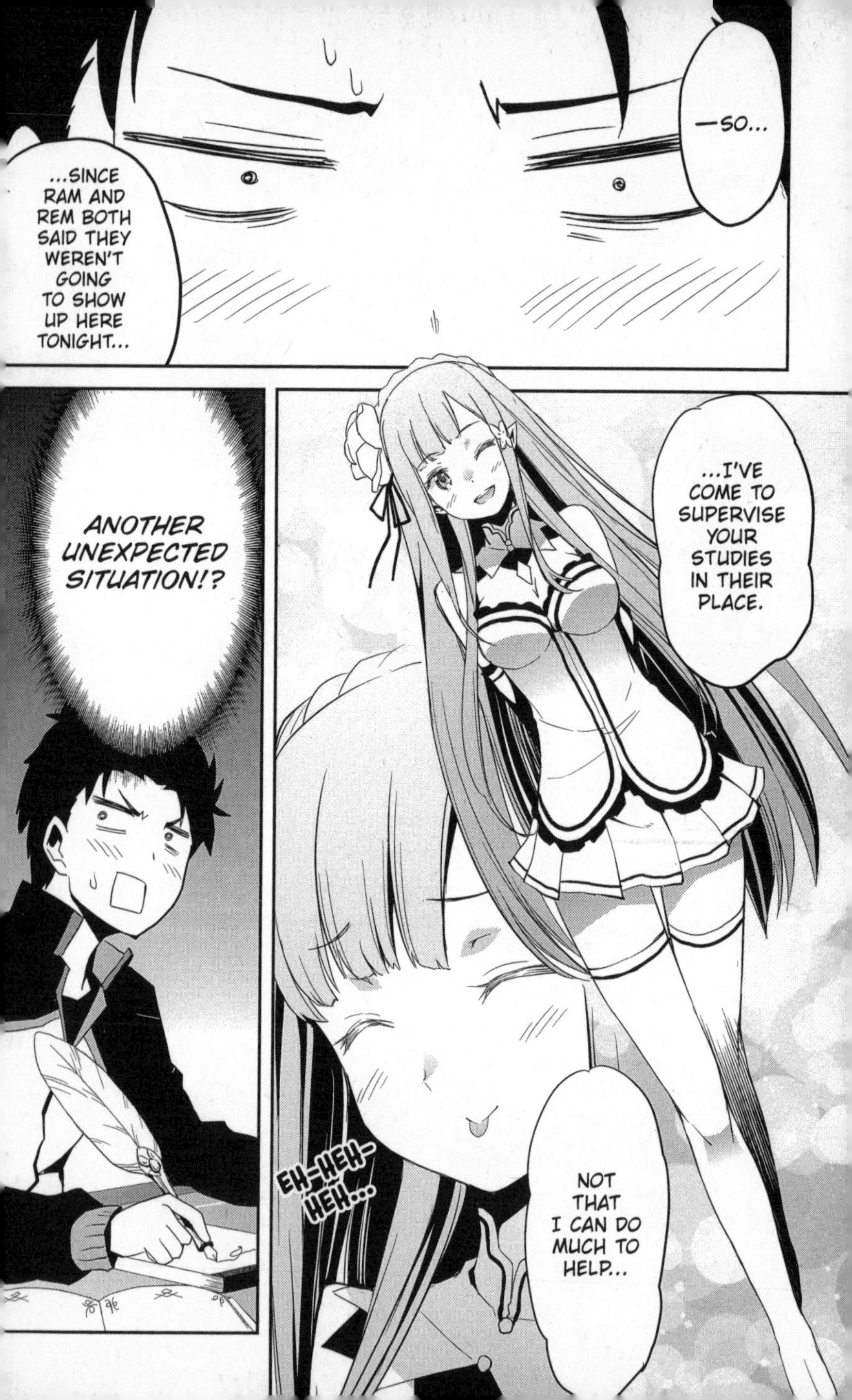
—SO...
...SINCE RAM AND REM BOTH SAID THEY WEREN'T GOING TO SHOW UP HERE TONIGHT...
...I'VE COME TO SUPERVISE YOUR STUDIES IN THEIR PLACE.
NOT THAT I CAN DO MUCH TO HELP...
EH-HEH-HEH...
ANOTHER UNEXPECTED SITUATION!?

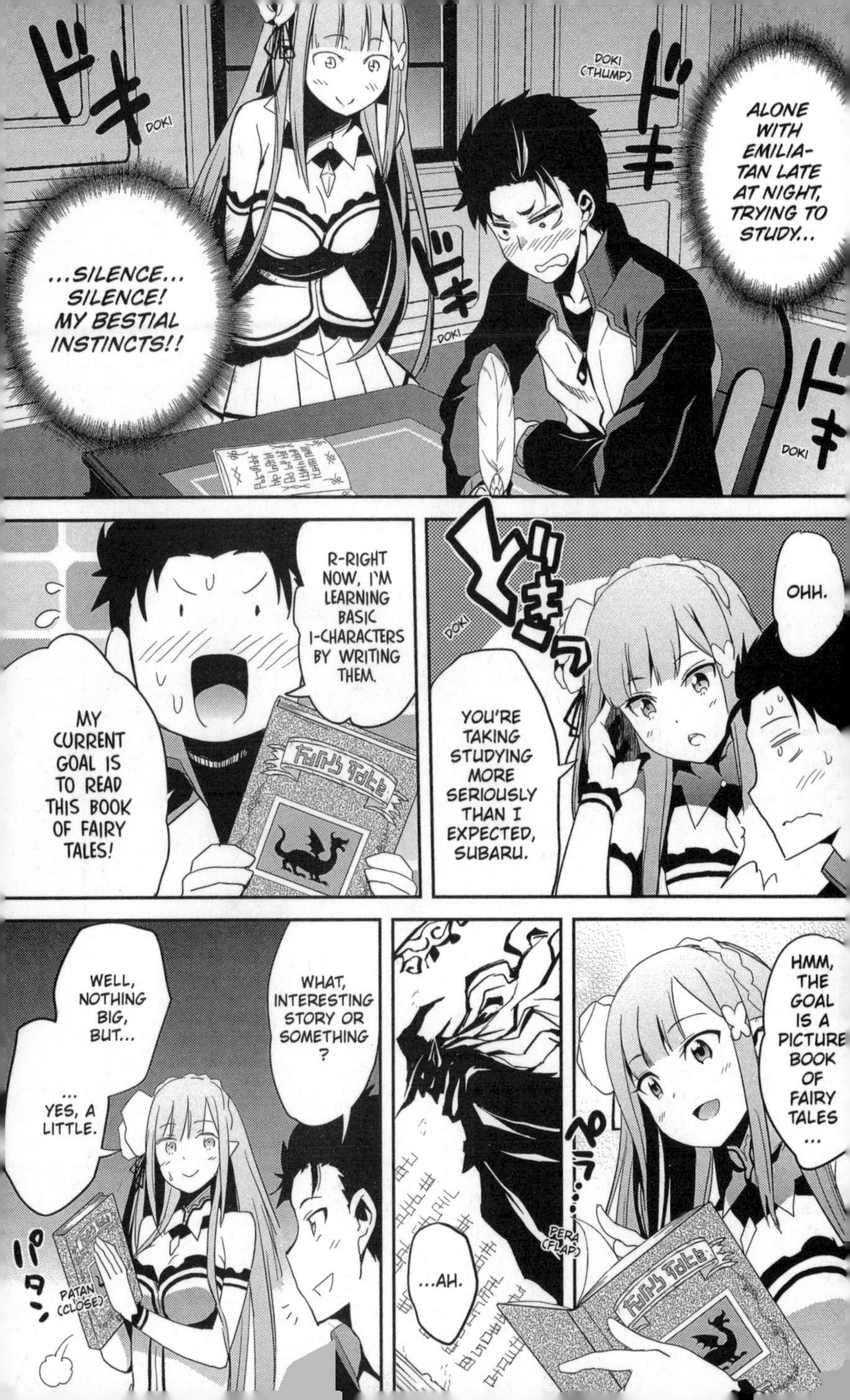
ドキ
DOKI (THUMP)
ALONE WITH EMILIA-TAN LATE AT NIGHT, TRYING TO STUDY...
ドキ
DOKI
ドキ
DOKI
ドキ
DOKI
...SILENCE... SILENCE! MY BESTIAL INSTINCTS!!
OHH.
どきっ
DOKI
YOU'RE TAKING STUDYING MORE SERIOUSLY THAN I EXPECTED, SUBARU.
R-RIGHT NOW, I'M LEARNING BASIC I-CHARACTERS BY WRITING THEM.
MY CURRENT GOAL IS TO READ THIS BOOK OF FAIRY TALES!
HMM, THE GOAL IS A PICTURE BOOK OF FAIRY TALES...
ペラ…
PERA (FLAP)
...AH.
WHAT, INTERESTING STORY OR SOMETHING?
WELL, NOTHING BIG, BUT...
... YES, A LITTLE.
パタン
PATAN (CLOSE)

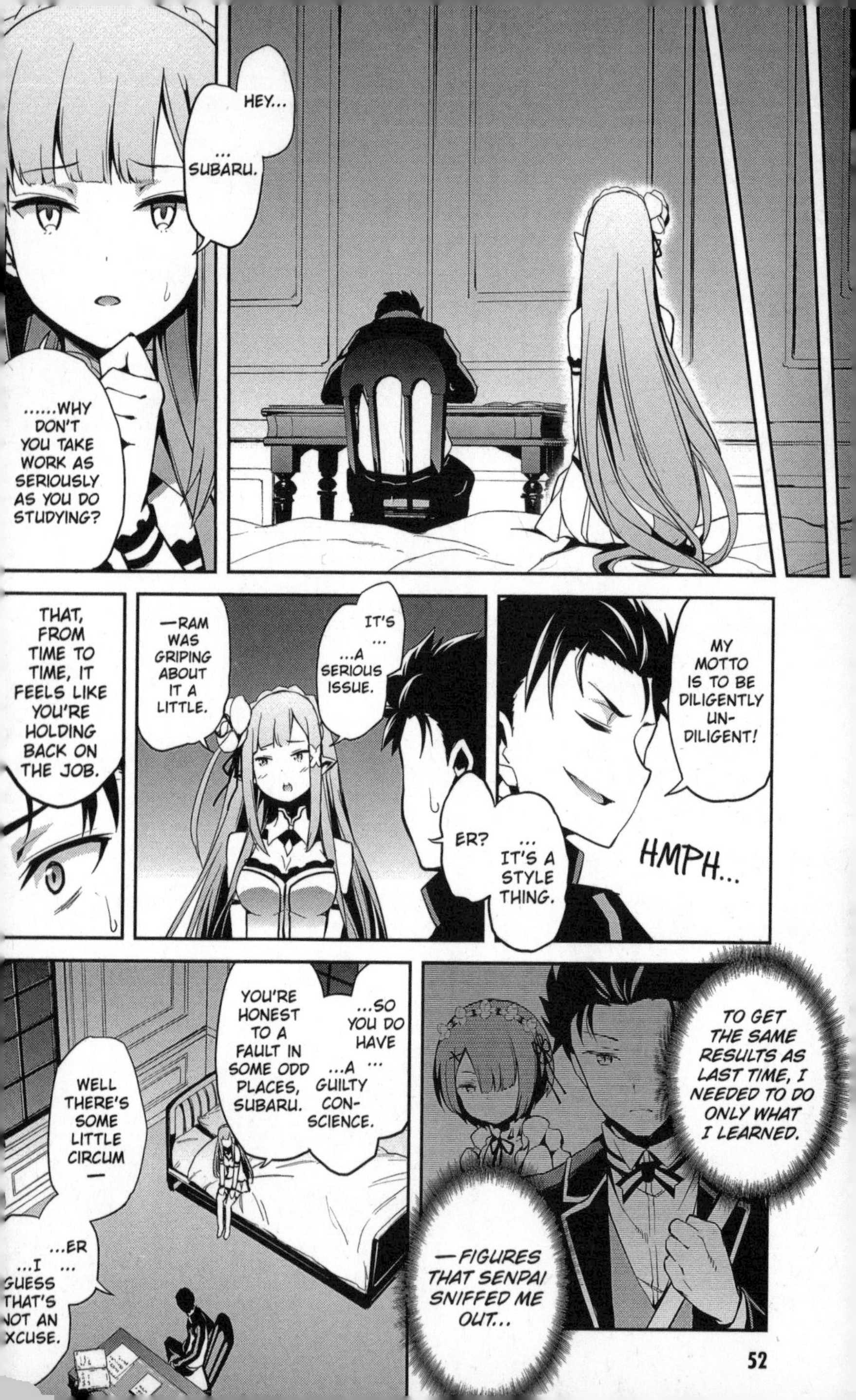
HEY...
...SUBARU.
......WHY DON'T YOU TAKE WORK AS SERIOUSLY AS YOU DO STUDYING?
MY MOTTO IS TO BE DILIGENTLY UN-DILIGENT!
HMPH...
ER? ...IT'S A STYLE THING.
IT'S... ...A SERIOUS ISSUE.
—RAM WAS GRIPING ABOUT IT A LITTLE.
THAT, FROM TIME TO TIME, IT FEELS LIKE YOU'RE HOLDING BACK ON THE JOB.
TO GET THE SAME RESULTS AS LAST TIME, I NEEDED TO DO ONLY WHAT I LEARNED.
—FIGURES THAT SENPAI SNIFFED ME OUT...
...SO YOU DO HAVE... ...A GUILTY CON-SCIENCE.
YOU'RE HONEST TO A FAULT IN SOME ODD PLACES, SUBARU.
WELL THERE'S SOME LITTLE CIRCUM—
...ER ...I ... GUESS THAT'S NOT AN XCUSE.

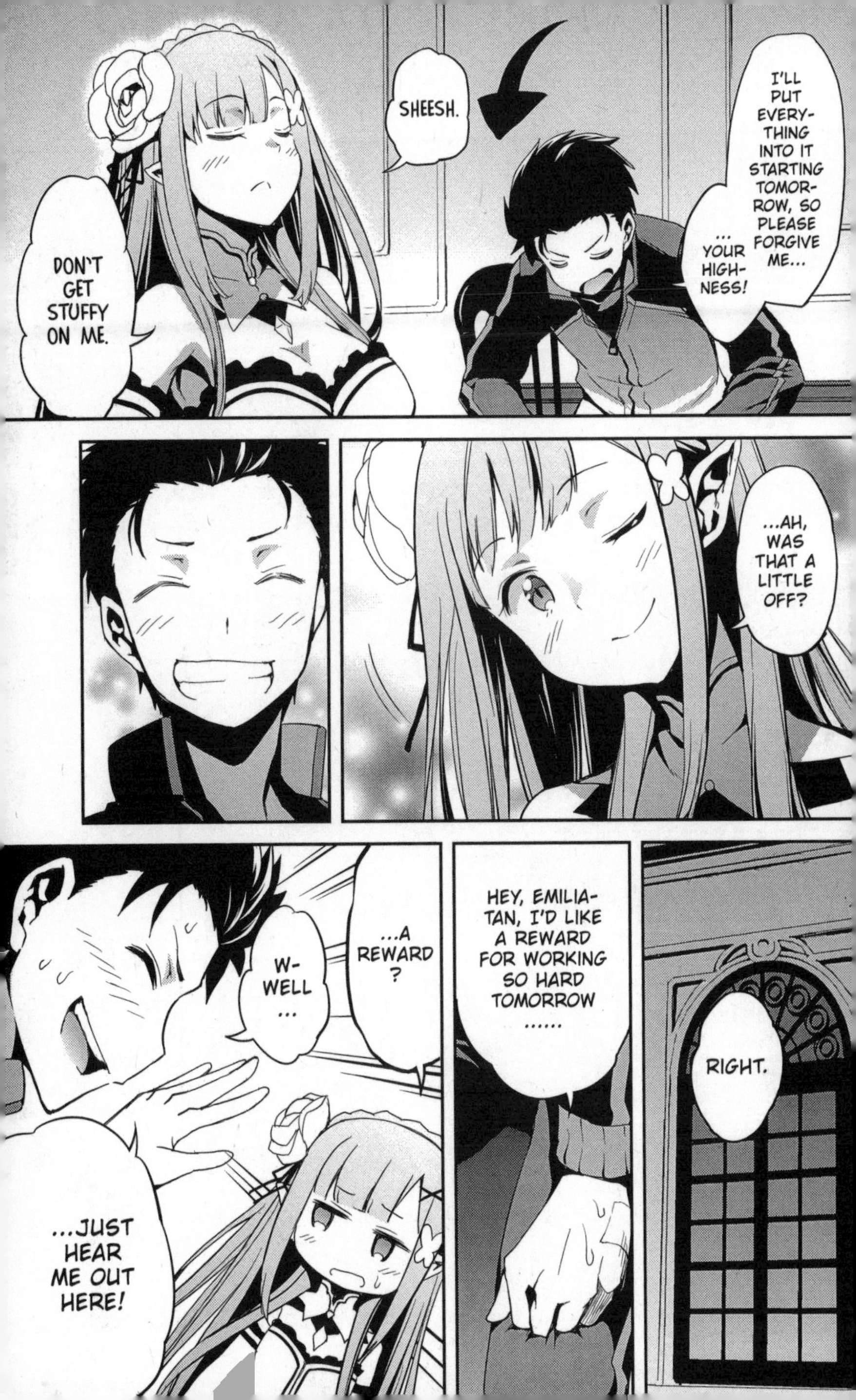
I'LL PUT EVERYTHING INTO IT STARTING TOMORROW, SO PLEASE FORGIVE ME...
...YOUR HIGHNESS!
SHEESH.
DON'T GET STUFFY ON ME.
...AH, WAS THAT A LITTLE OFF?
RIGHT.
HEY, EMILIA-TAN, I'D LIKE A REWARD FOR WORKING SO HARD TOMORROW ......
...A REWARD?
W-WELL...
...JUST HEAR ME OUT HERE!

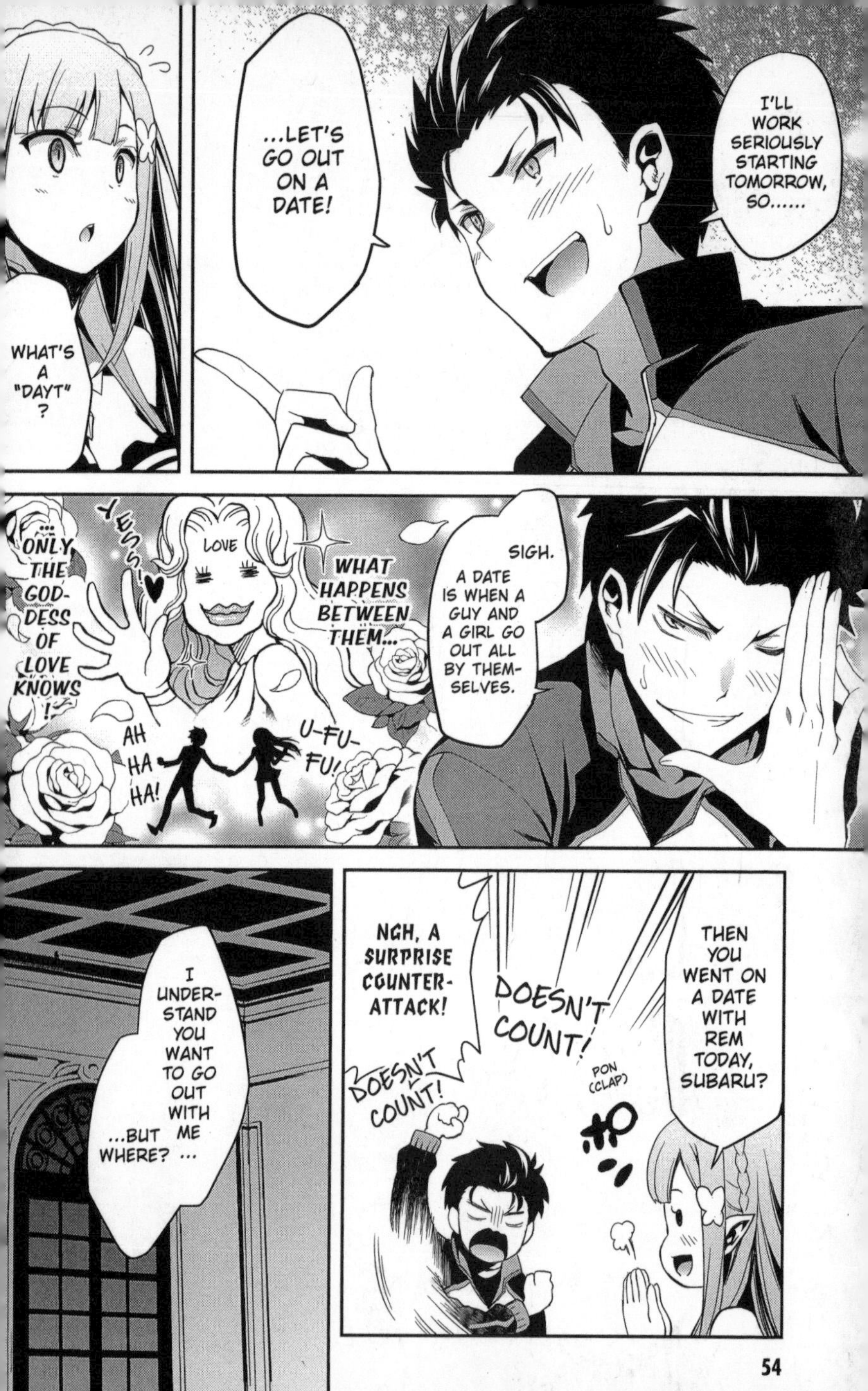
I'LL WORK SERIOUSLY STARTING TOMORROW, SO......
...LET'S GO OUT ON A DATE!
WHAT'S A "DAYT" ?
SIGH.
A DATE IS WHEN A GUY AND A GIRL GO OUT ALL BY THEMSELVES.
WHAT HAPPENS BETWEEN THEM...
LOVE
YESS!
...ONLY THE GODDESS OF LOVE KNOWS!
U-FU-FU!
AH HA HA!
THEN YOU WENT ON A DATE WITH REM TODAY, SUBARU?
PON (CLAP)
DOESN'T COUNT!
DOESN'T COUNT!
NGH, A SURPRISE COUNTER-ATTACK!
I UNDERSTAND YOU WANT TO GO OUT WITH ME...
...BUT WHERE?

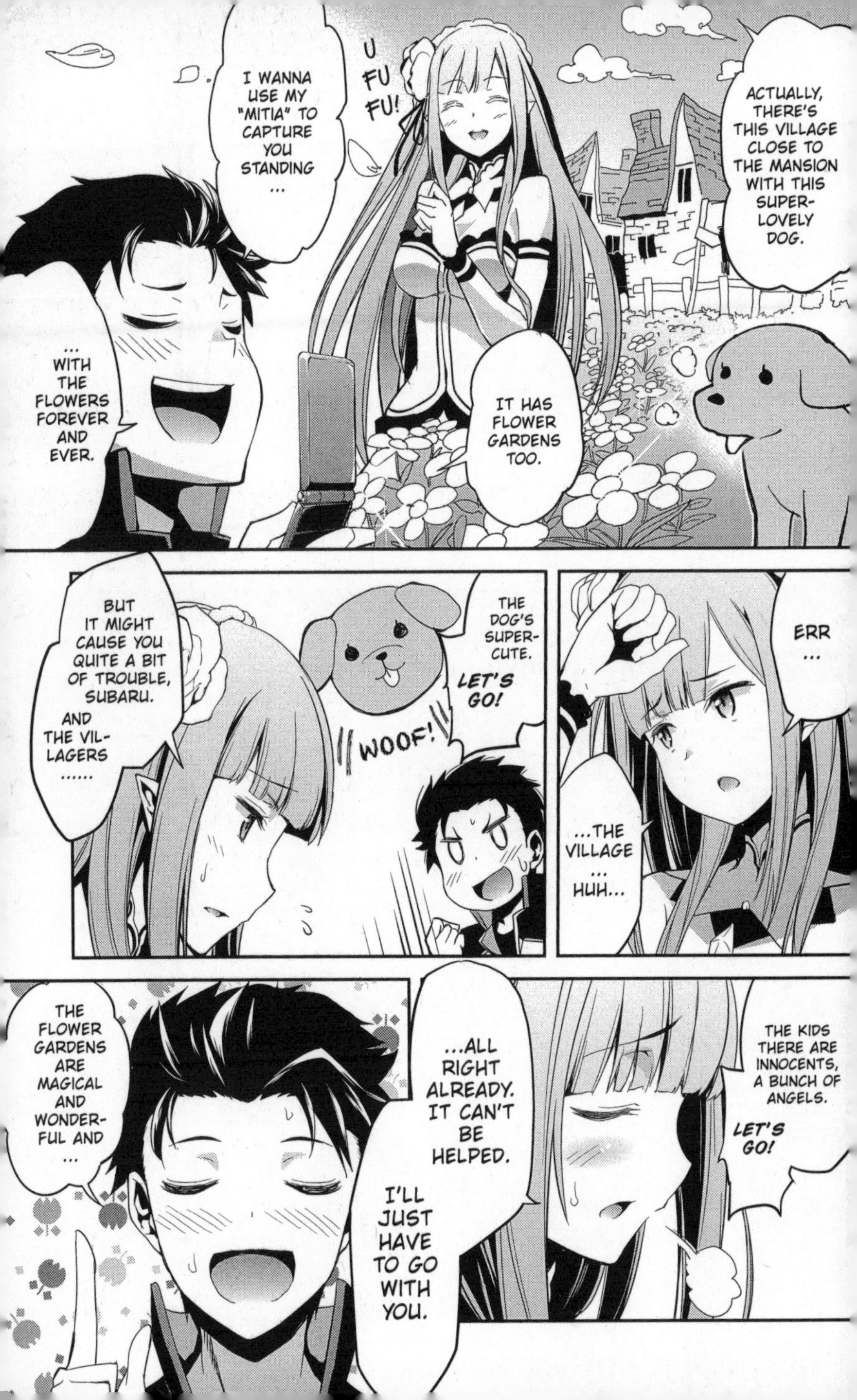
ACTUALLY, THERE'S THIS VILLAGE CLOSE TO THE MANSION WITH THIS SUPER-LOVELY DOG.
IT HAS FLOWER GARDENS TOO.
U FU FU!
I WANNA USE MY "MITIA" TO CAPTURE YOU STANDING ...
... WITH THE FLOWERS FOREVER AND EVER.
ERR ...
...THE VILLAGE ... HUH...
THE DOG'S SUPER-CUTE.
LET'S GO!
WOOF!
BUT IT MIGHT CAUSE YOU QUITE A BIT OF TROUBLE, SUBARU.
AND THE VIL-LAGERS ......
THE KIDS THERE ARE INNOCENTS, A BUNCH OF ANGELS.
LET'S GO!
...ALL RIGHT ALREADY. IT CAN'T BE HELPED.
I'LL JUST HAVE TO GO WITH YOU.
THE FLOWER GARDENS ARE MAGICAL AND WONDER-FUL AND ...

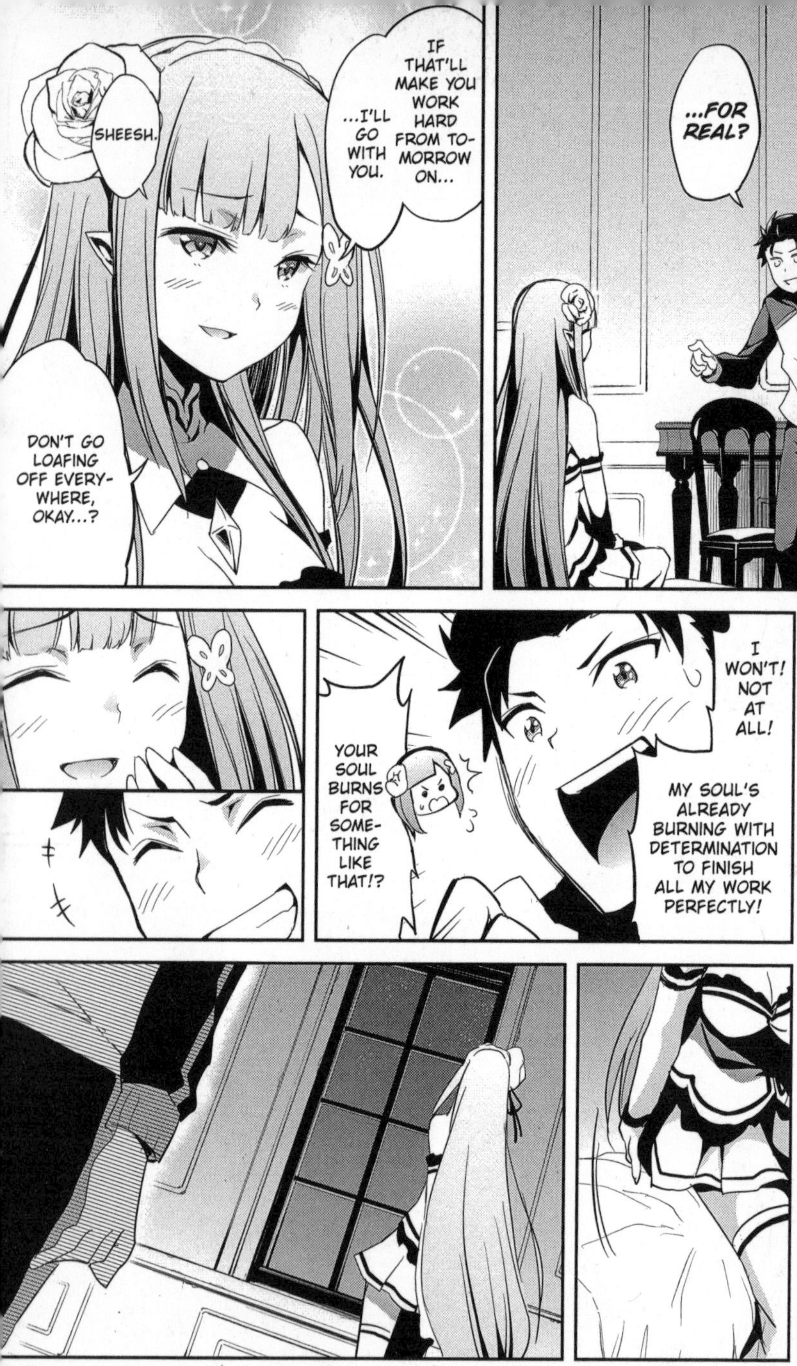
...FOR REAL?
IF THAT'LL MAKE YOU WORK HARD FROM TO-MORROW ON...
...I'LL GO WITH YOU.
SHEESH.
DON'T GO LOAFING OFF EVERY-WHERE, OKAY...?
I WON'T! NOT AT ALL!
MY SOUL'S ALREADY BURNING WITH DETERMINATION TO FINISH ALL MY WORK PERFECTLY!
YOUR SOUL BURNS FOR SOME-THING LIKE THAT!?

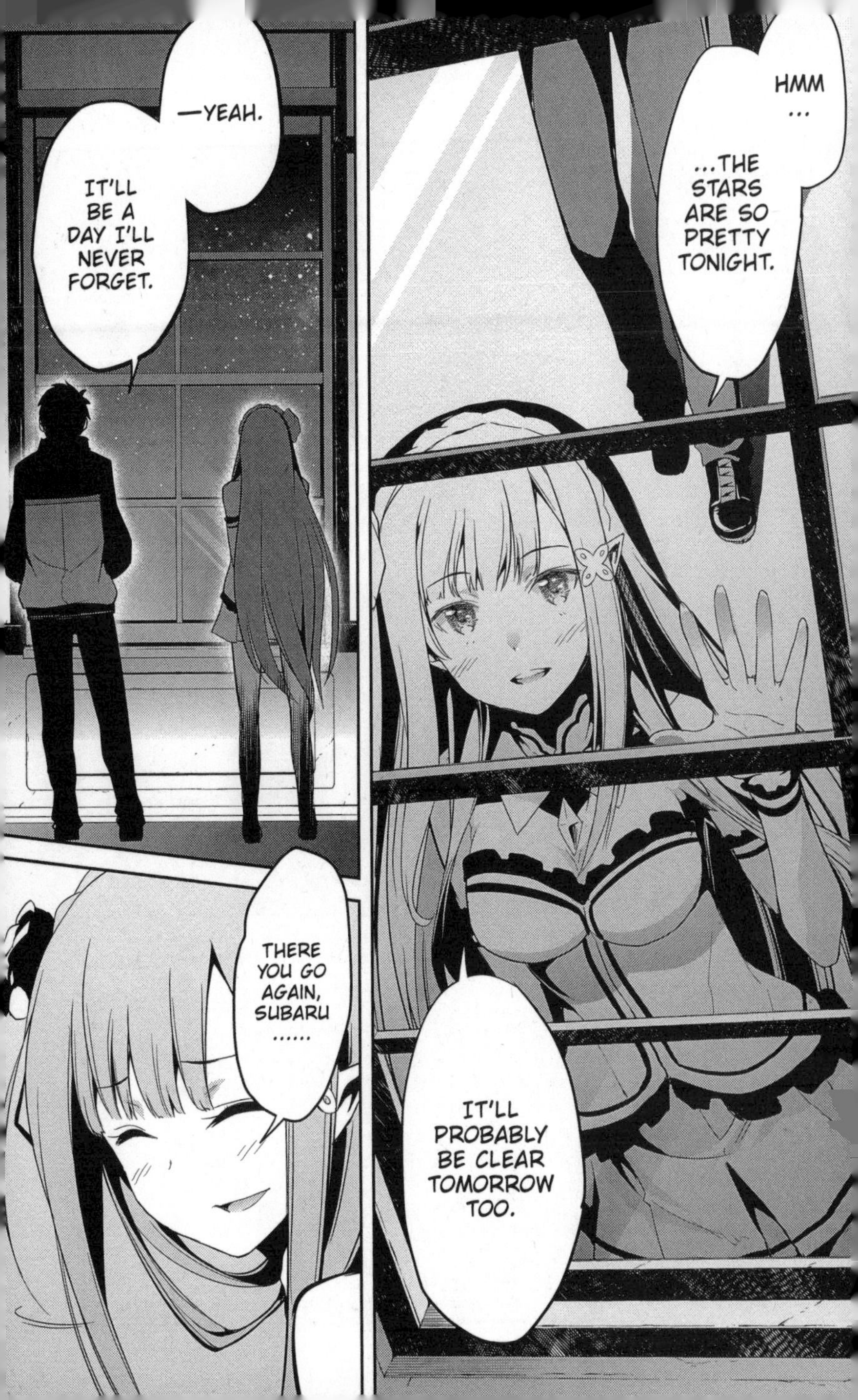
HMM …
...THE STARS ARE SO PRETTY TONIGHT.
IT'LL PROBABLY BE CLEAR TOMORROW TOO.
—YEAH.
IT'LL BE A DAY I'LL NEVER FORGET.
THERE YOU GO AGAIN, SUBARU ......

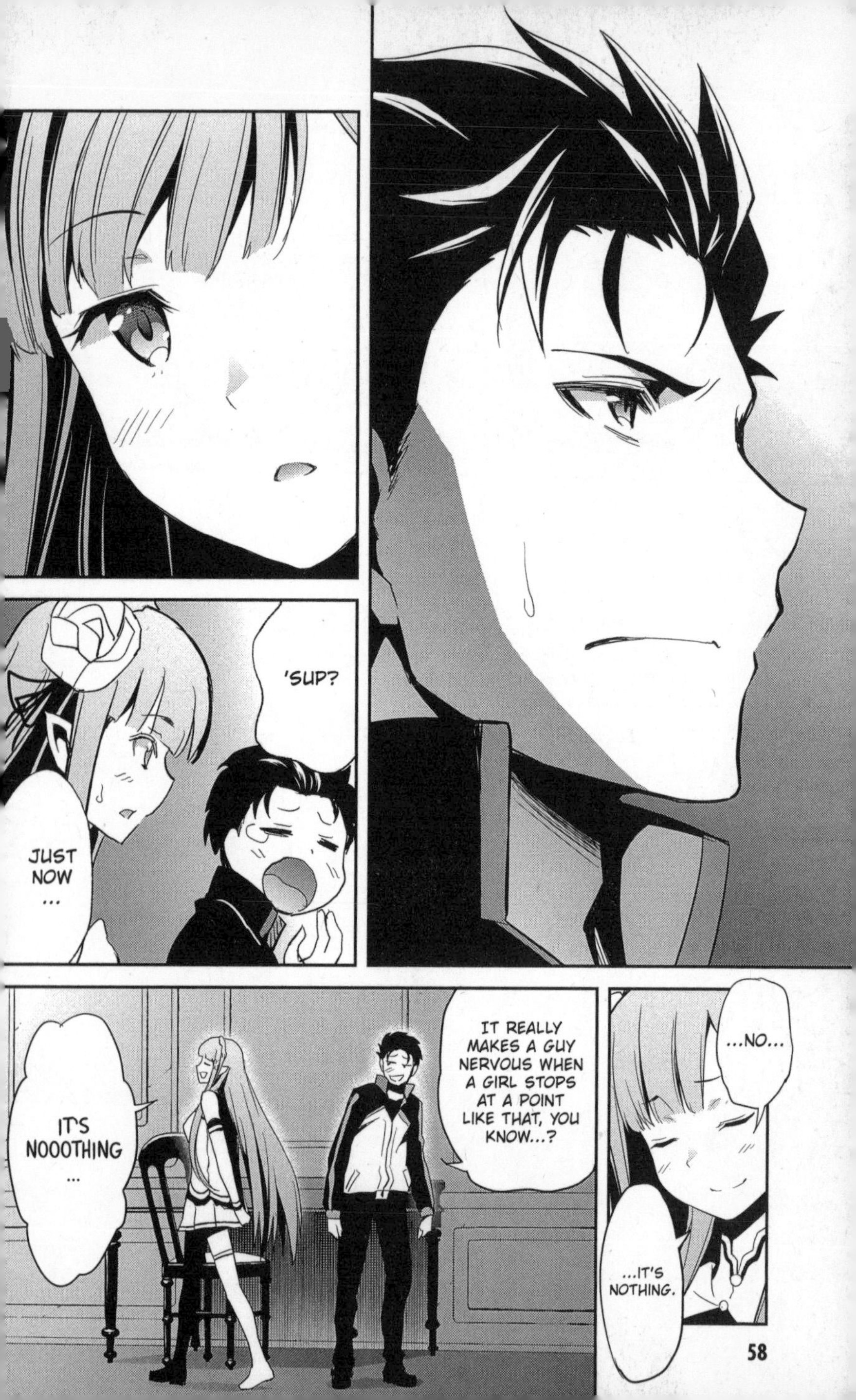
'SUP?
JUST NOW ...
...NO...
...IT'S NOTHING.
IT REALLY MAKES A GUY NERVOUS WHEN A GIRL STOPS AT A POINT LIKE THAT, YOU KNOW...?
IT'S NOOOTHING ...

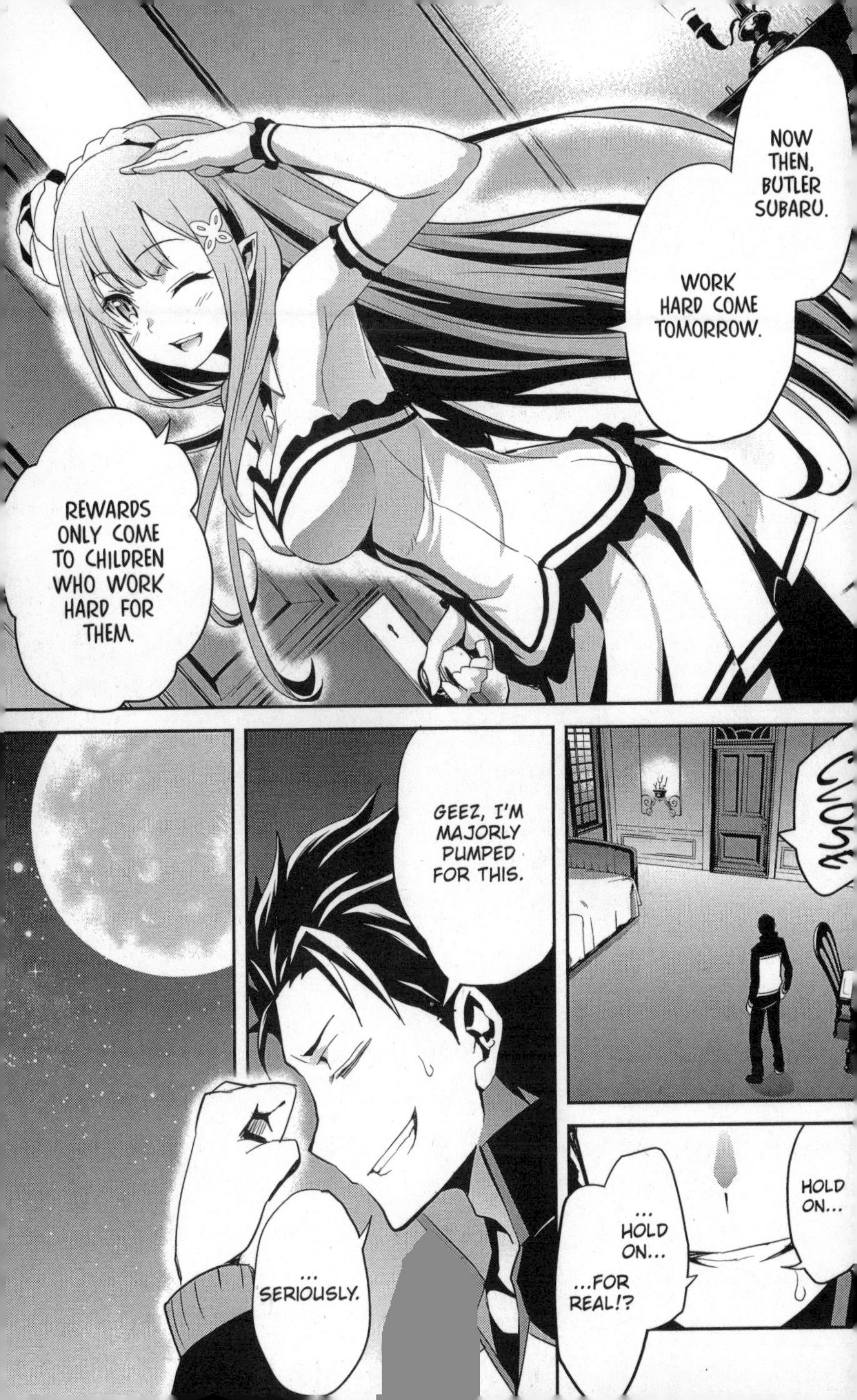
NOW THEN, BUTLER SUBARU.
WORK HARD COME TOMORROW.
REWARDS ONLY COME TO CHILDREN WHO WORK HARD FOR THEM.
HOLD ON...
... HOLD ON...
...FOR REAL!?
GEEZ, I'M MAJORLY PUMPED FOR THIS.
... SERIOUSLY.

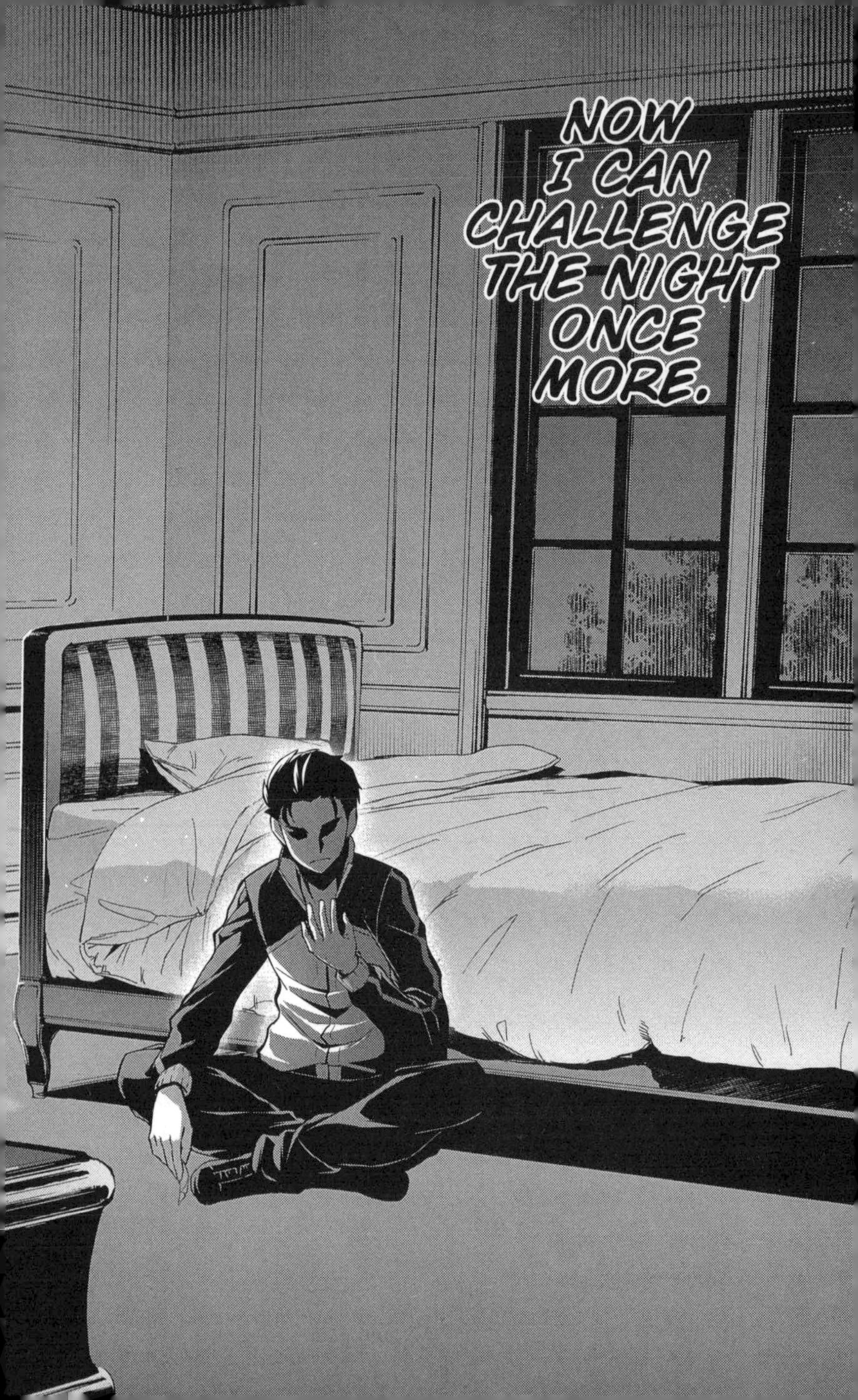
NOW I CAN CHALLENGE THE NIGHT ONCE MORE.

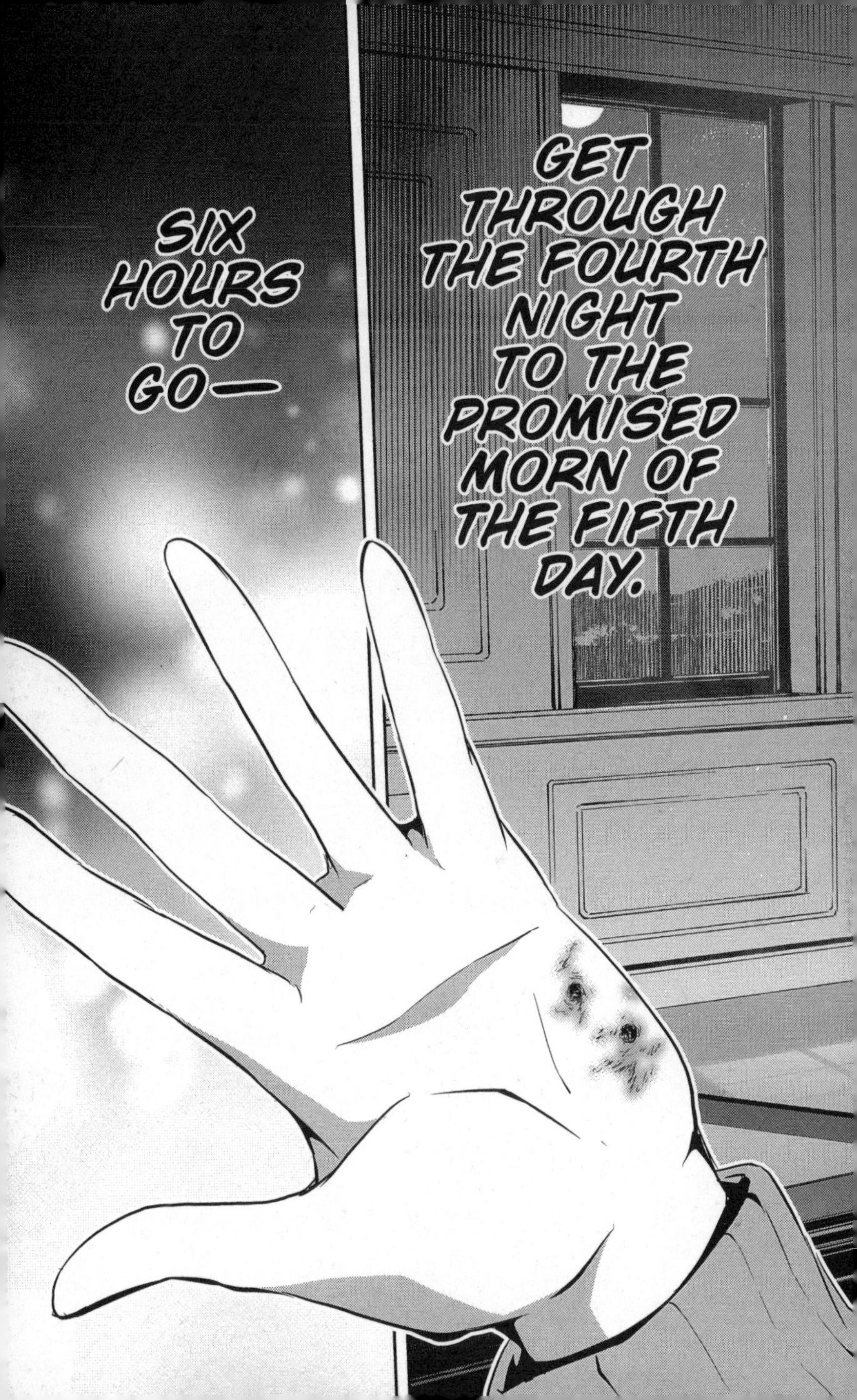
GET THROUGH THE FOURTH NIGHT TO THE PROMISED MORN OF THE FIFTH DAY.
SIX HOURS TO GO—

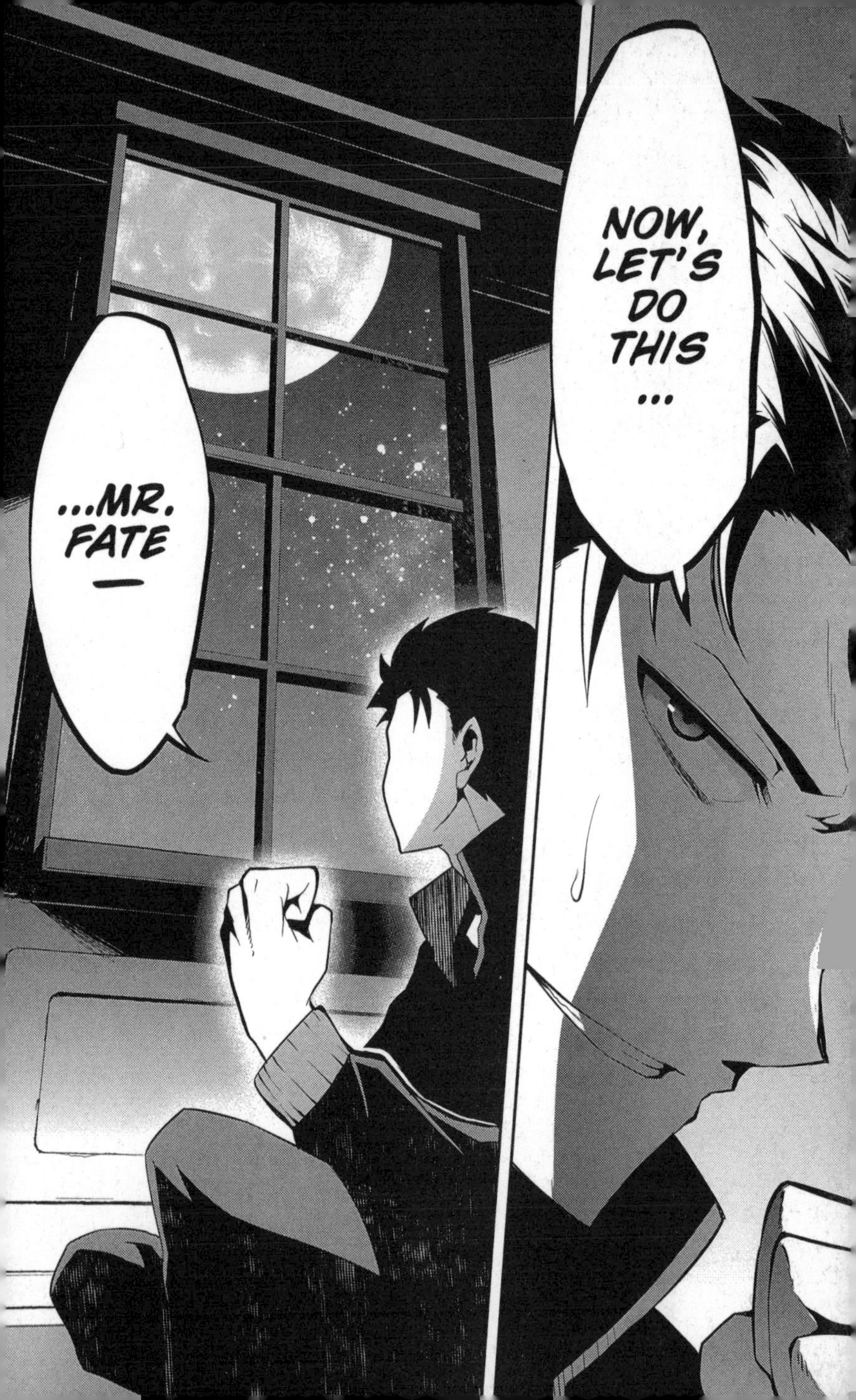
NOW, LET'S DO THIS ...
...MR. FATE —

The bath. What dreams are made of. And yet!

It's just men!!

No, it was indeed a fun encounter in a certain sense. Do enjoy the bath short story that Nagatsuki-sensei wrote.

# Re:ZeRo

-Starting Life in Another World-

## Episode 7 The Sound of Chains

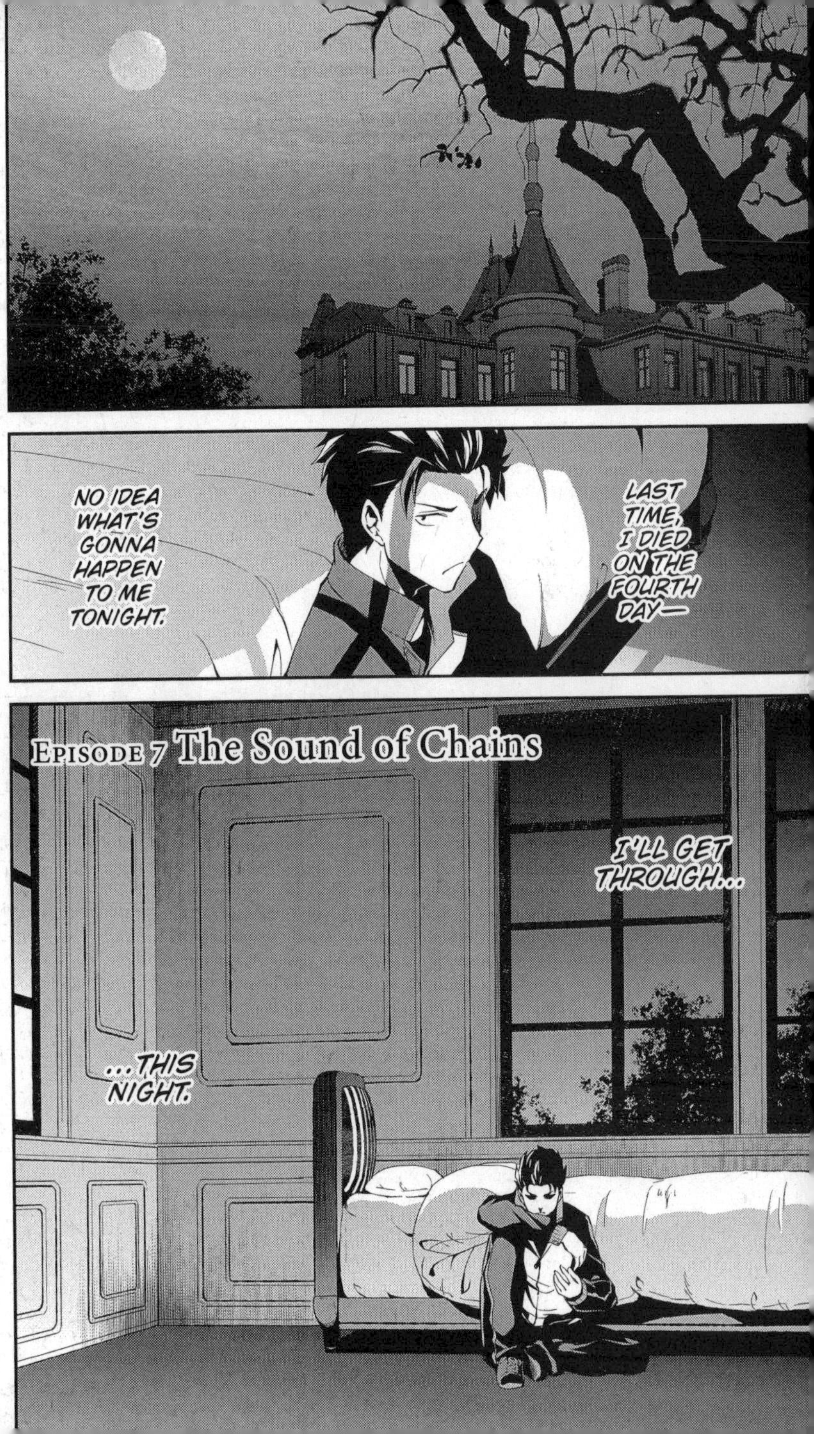
LAST TIME, I DIED ON THE FOURTH DAY—
NO IDEA WHAT'S GONNA HAPPEN TO ME TONIGHT.
I'LL GET THROUGH...
...THIS NIGHT.

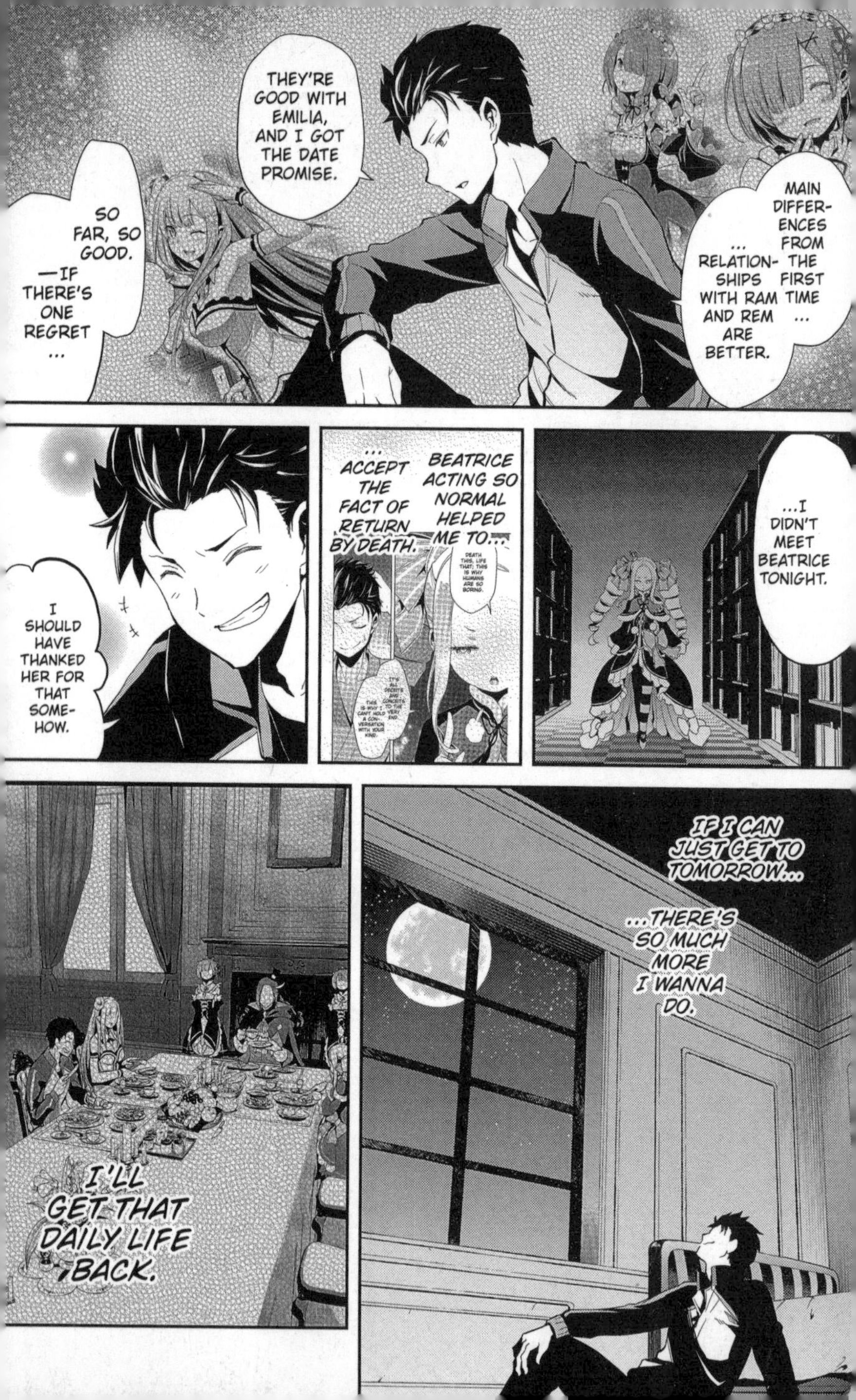
MAIN DIFFERENCES FROM THE FIRST TIME ...
... RELATIONSHIPS WITH RAM AND REM ARE BETTER.
THEY'RE GOOD WITH EMILIA, AND I GOT THE DATE PROMISE.
SO FAR, SO GOOD. —IF THERE'S ONE REGRET ...
...I DIDN'T MEET BEATRICE TONIGHT.
BEATRICE ACTING SO NORMAL HELPED ME TO...
... ACCEPT THE FACT OF RETURN BY DEATH.
DEATH THIS, LIFE THAT; THIS IS WHY HUMANS ARE SO BORING.
IT'S ALL DECEITS AND CONCEITS TO THE VERY END.
THIS IS WHY I CAN'T HOLD A CONVERSATION WITH YOUR KIND.
I SHOULD HAVE THANKED HER FOR THAT SOMEHOW.
IF I CAN JUST GET TO TOMORROW...
...THERE'S SO MUCH MORE I WANNA DO.
I'LL GET THAT DAILY LIFE BACK.

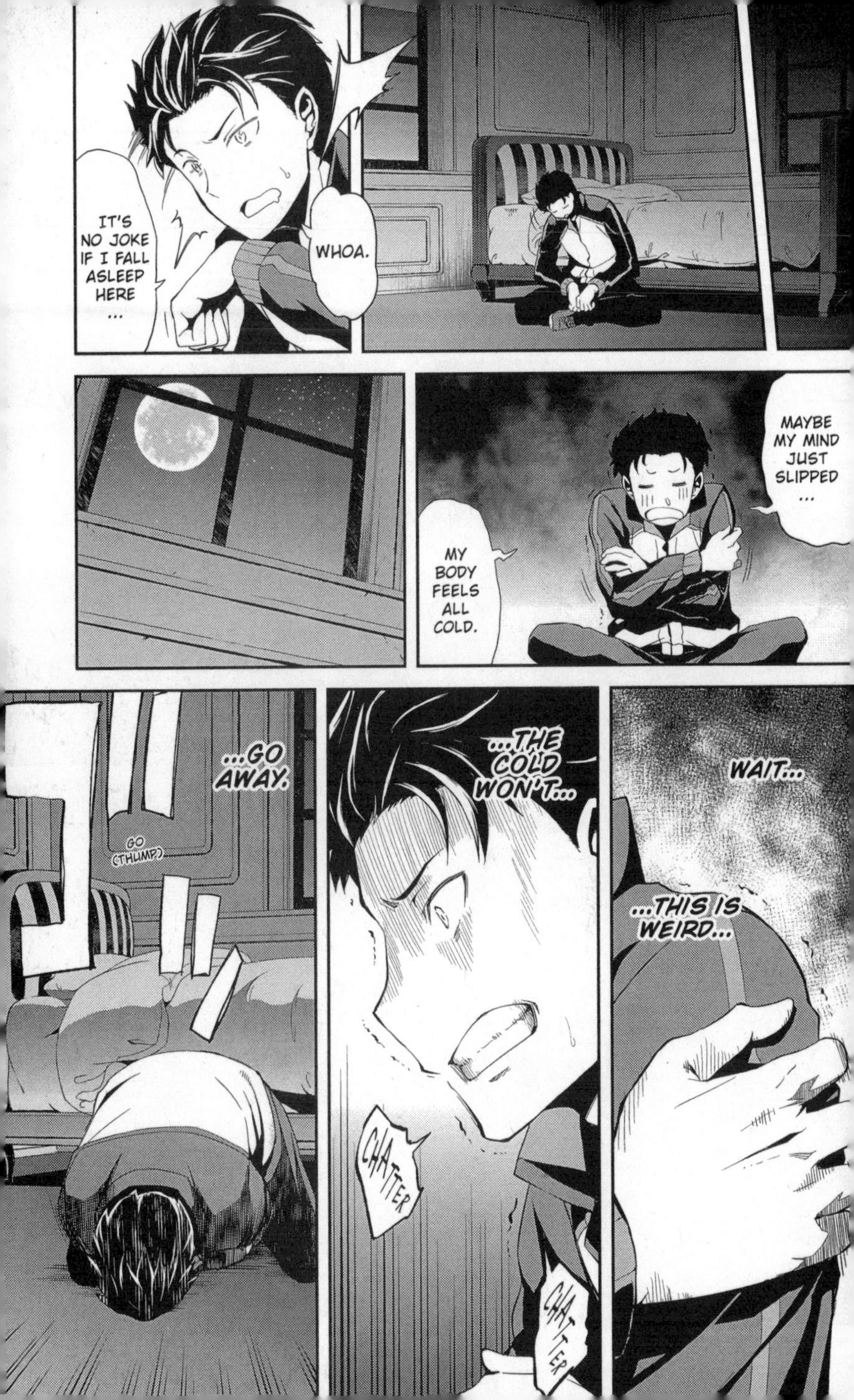
WHOA.
IT'S NO JOKE IF I FALL ASLEEP HERE...
MAYBE MY MIND JUST SLIPPED...
MY BODY FEELS ALL COLD.
WAIT...
...THIS IS WEIRD...
...THE COLD WON'T...
CHATTER
CHATTER
...GO AWAY.
GO (THUMP)

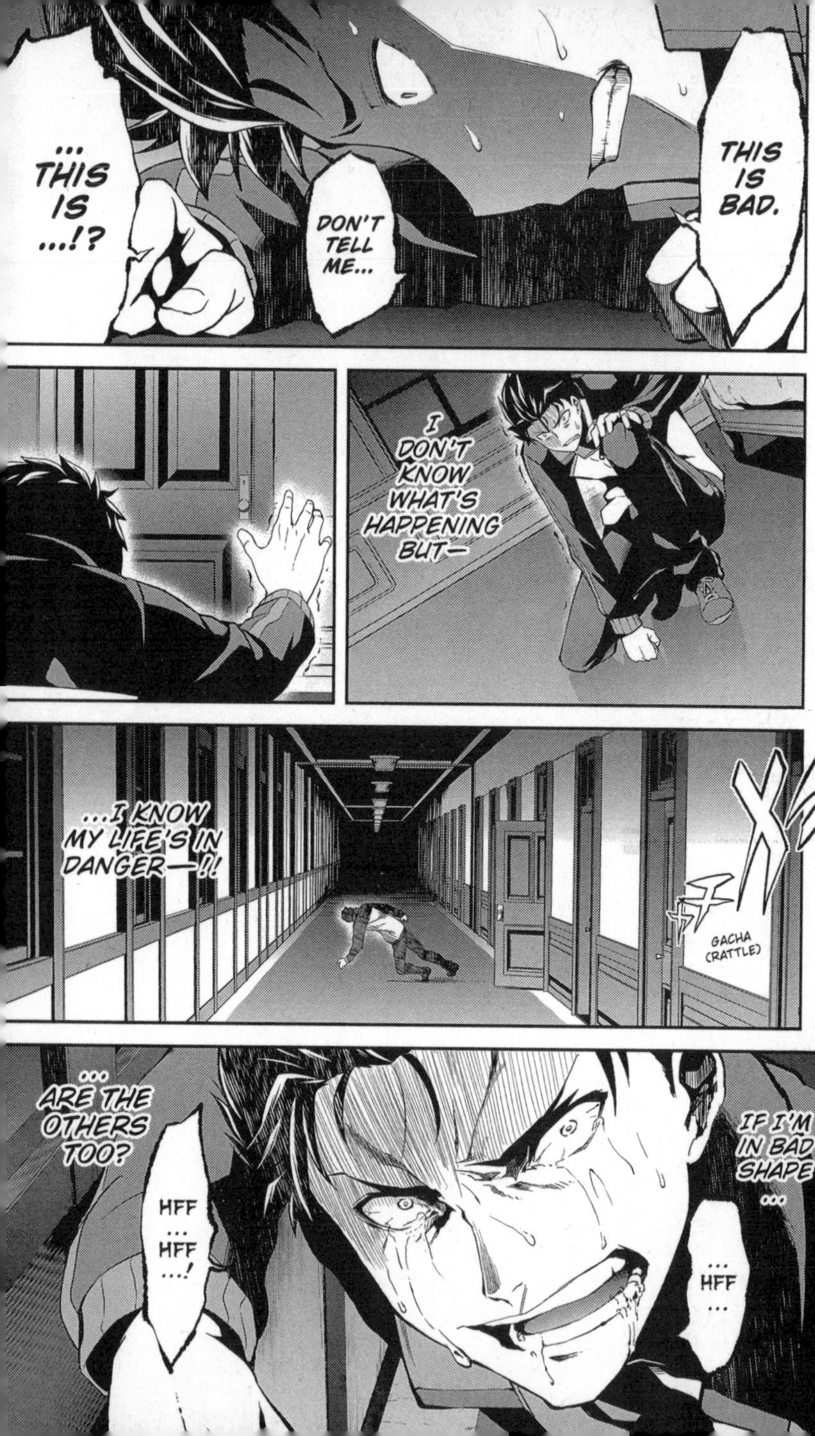
THIS IS BAD.
DON'T TELL ME...
...THIS IS ...!?
I DON'T KNOW WHAT'S HAPPENING BUT—
GACHA (RATTLE)
...I KNOW MY LIFE'S IN DANGER—!!
IF I'M IN BAD SHAPE...
...HFF...
...ARE THE OTHERS TOO?
HFF ... HFF ...!

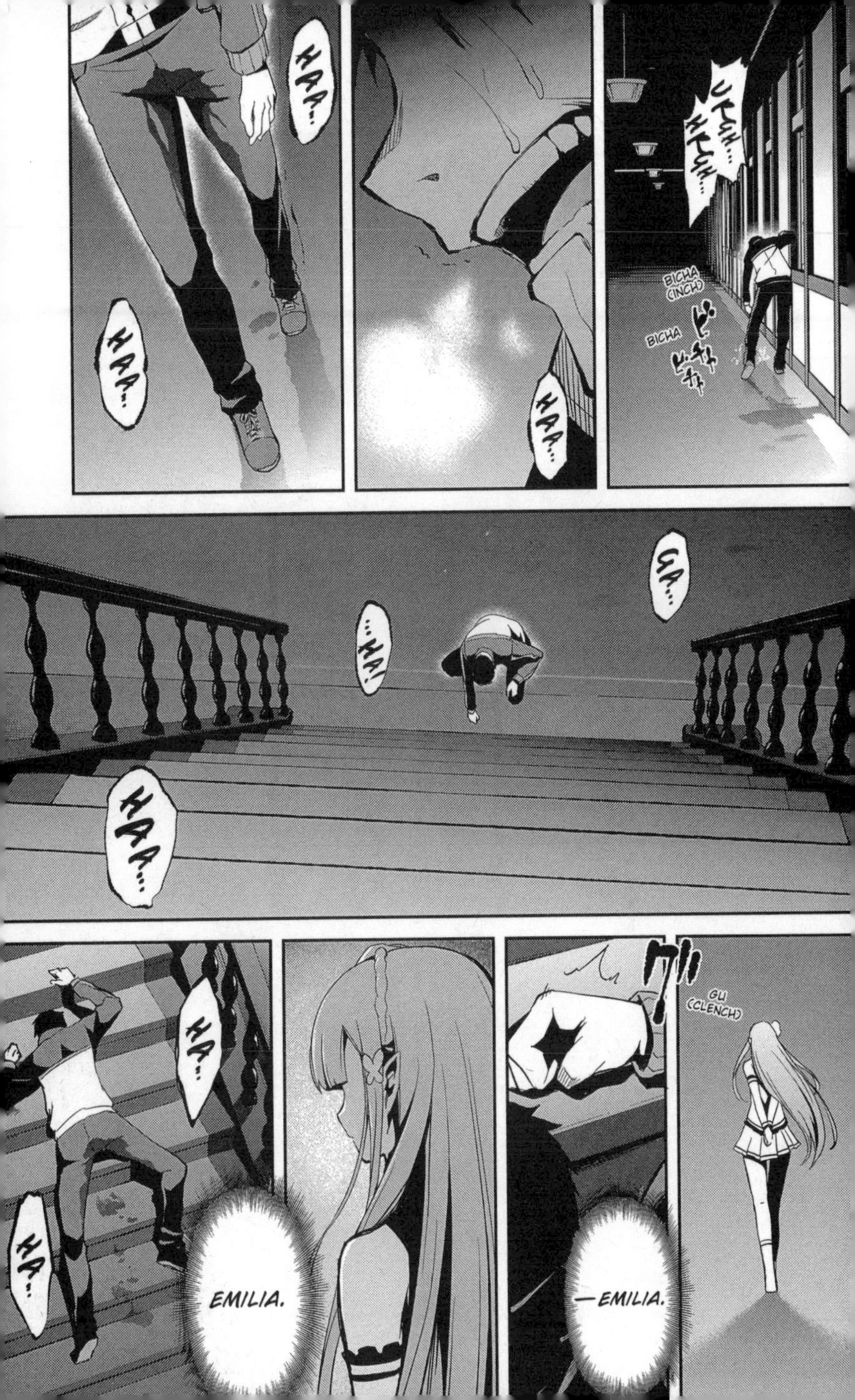
UKGH... HKGH...
BICHA (INCH)
BICHA
HAA...
HAA...
HAA...
GA...
...HA!
HAA...
GU (CLENCH)
—EMILIA.
EMILIA.
HA...
HA...

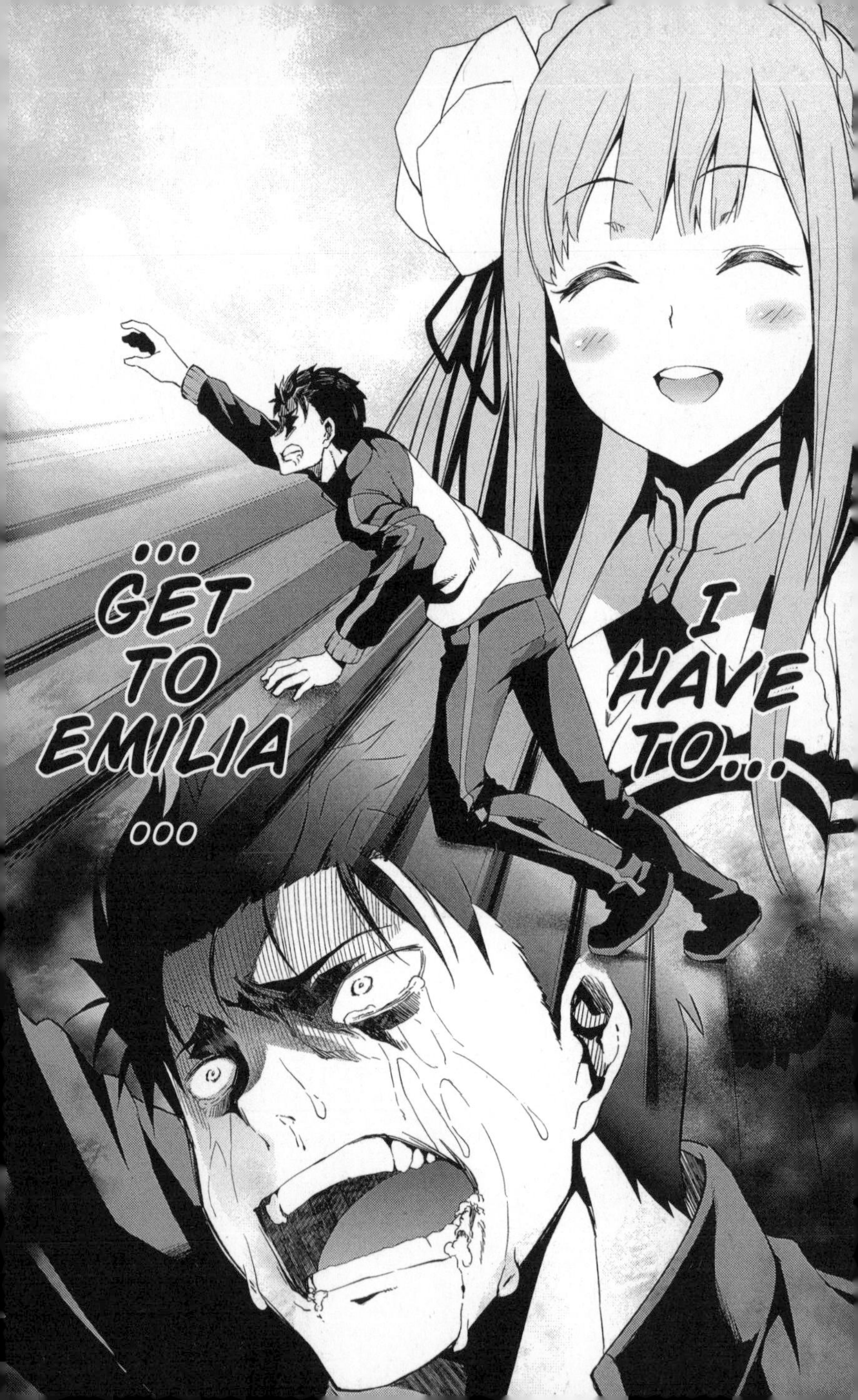
I HAVE TO...
...GET TO EMILIA...

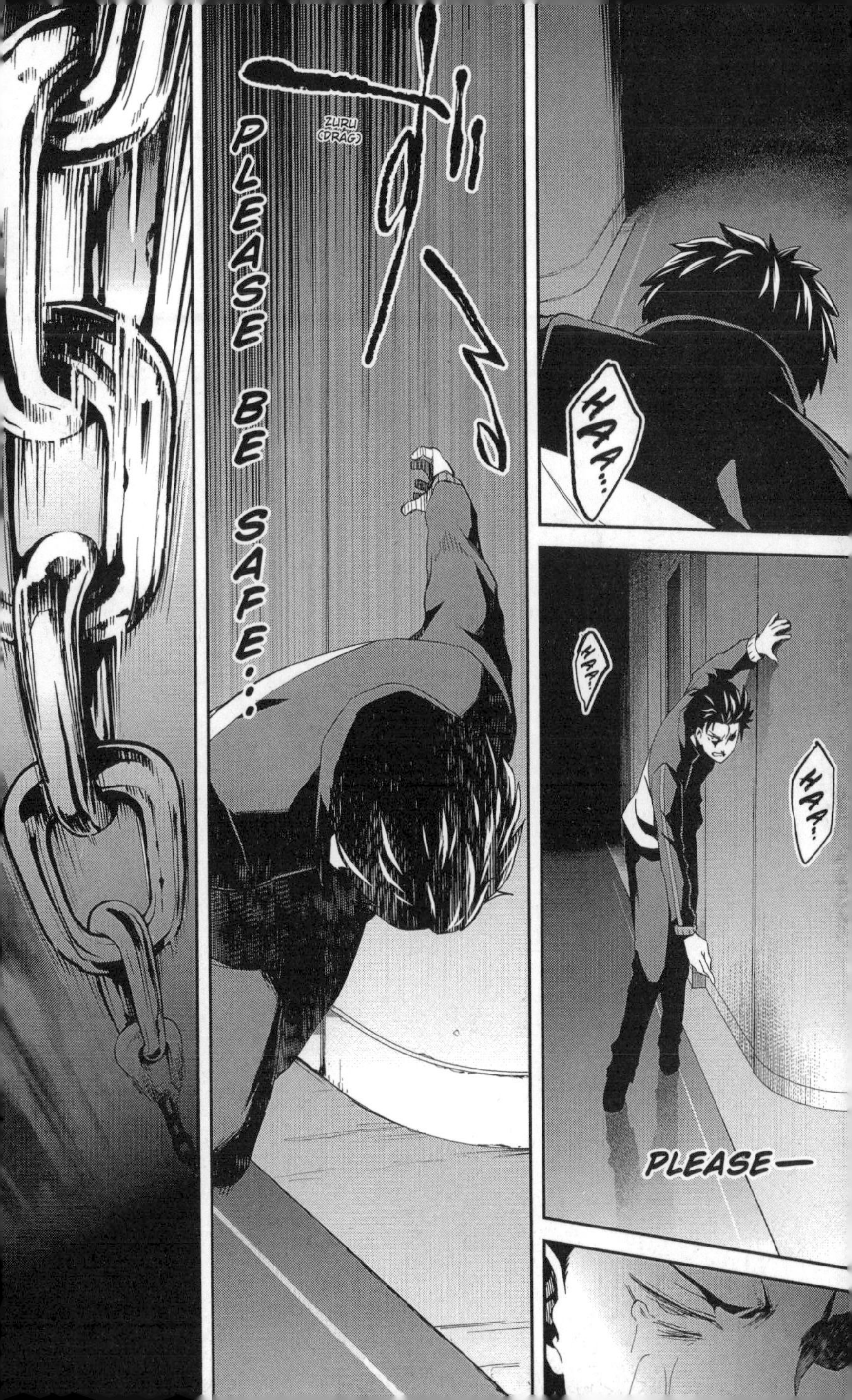
HAA...
HAA...
HAA...
PLEASE—
ZURU (DRAG)
PLEASE BE SAFE...

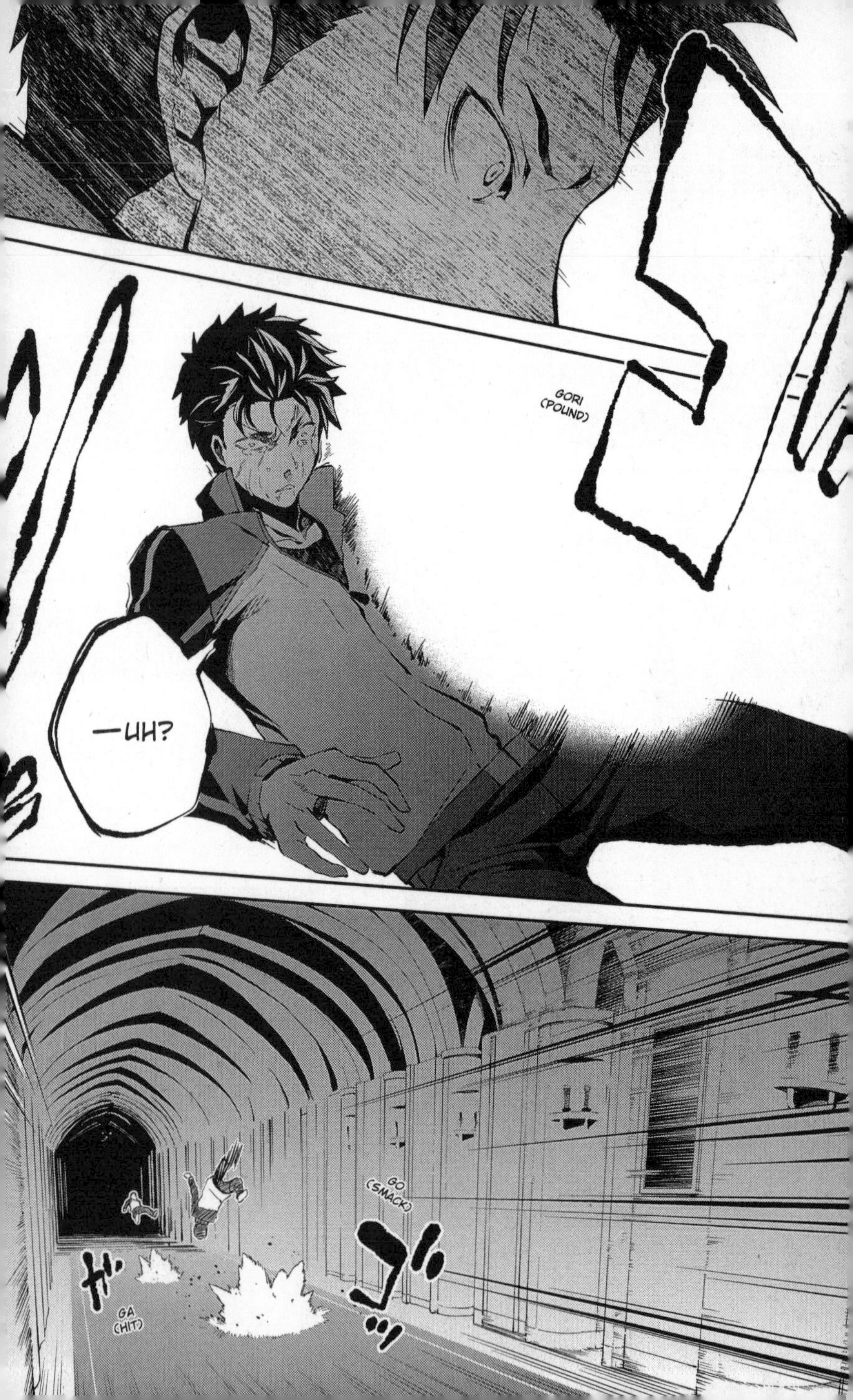
GORI
(POUND)
—UH?
GO
(SMACK)
GA
(HIT)

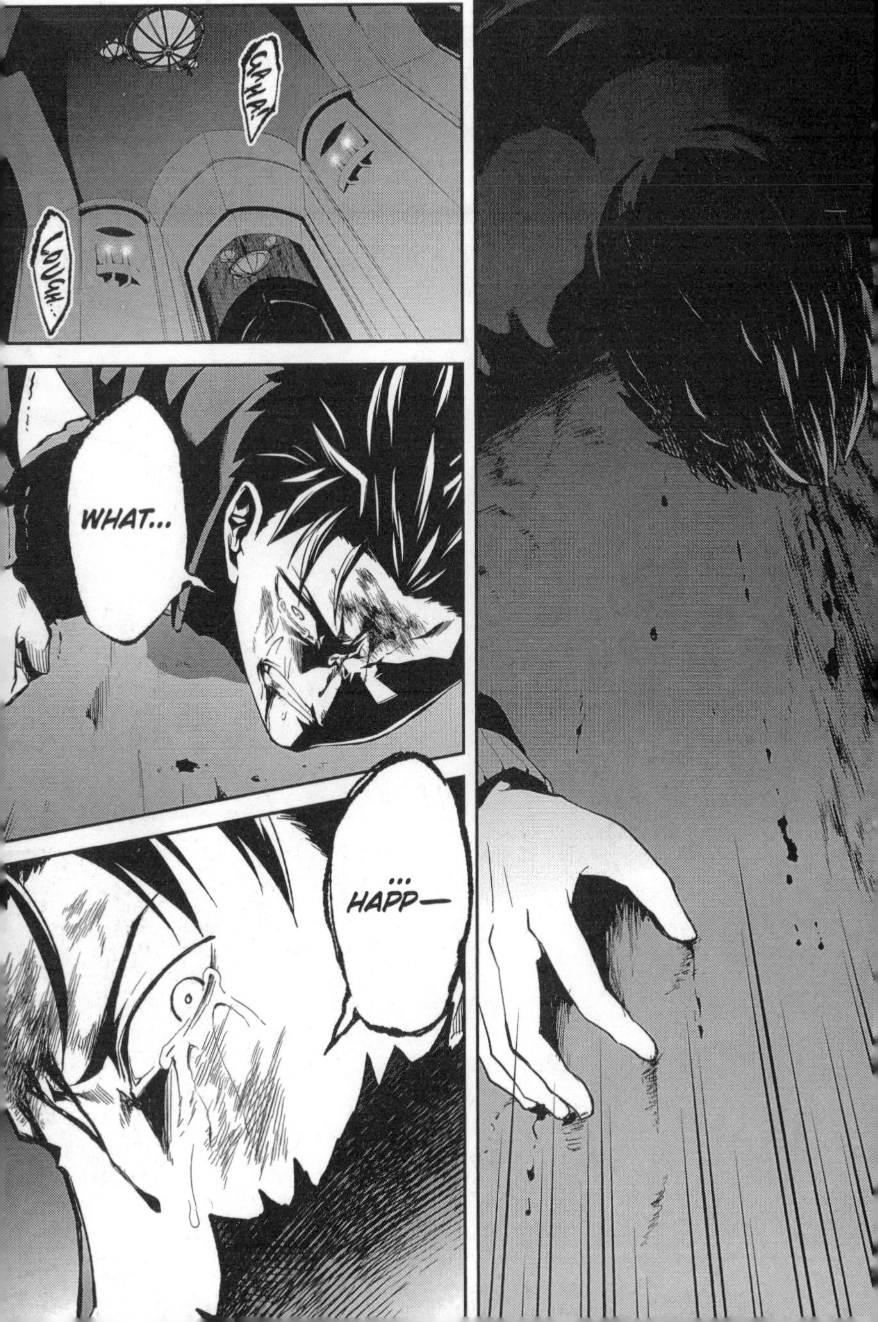
GAHA!
COUGH...
WHAT...
...HAPP—

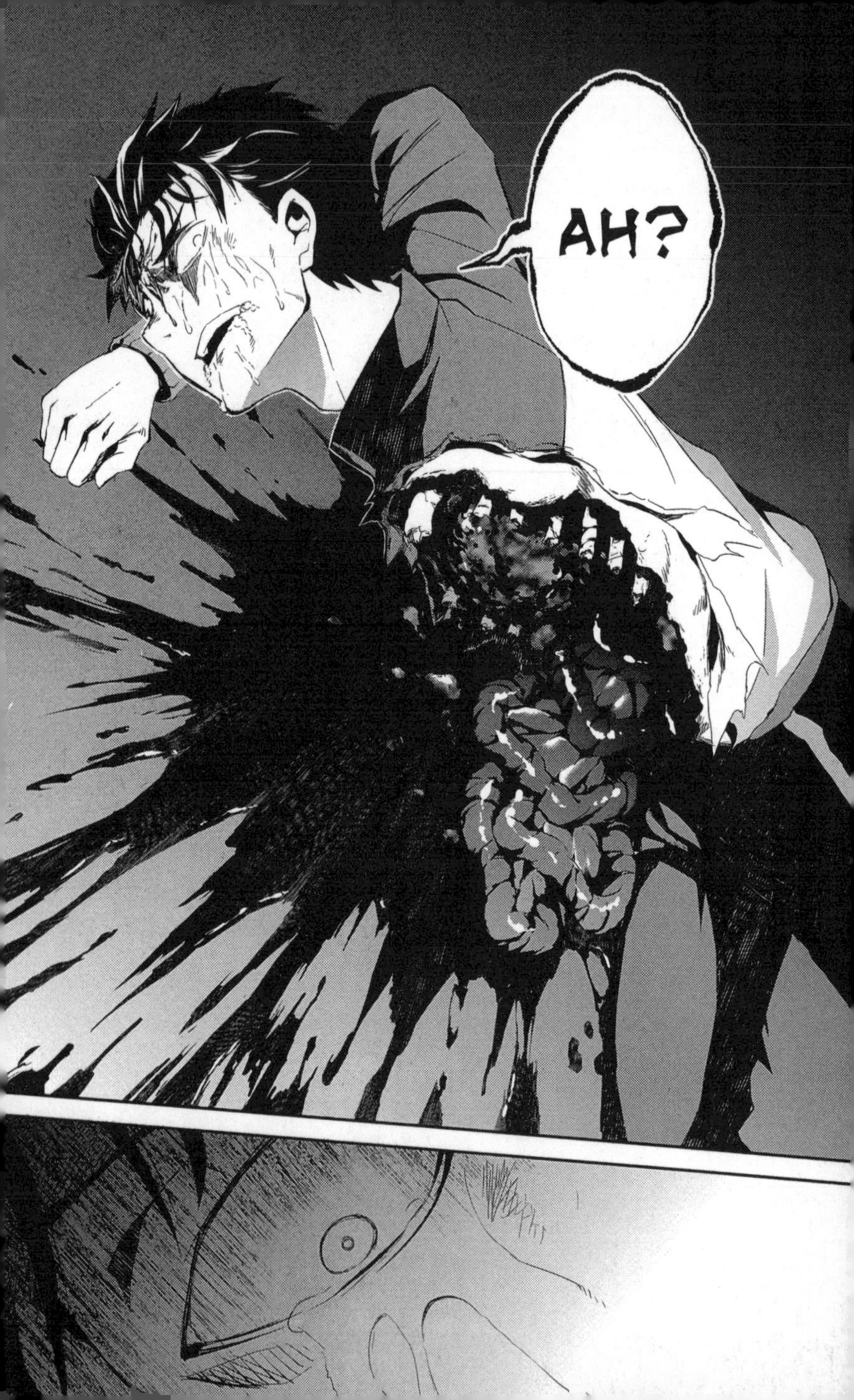
AH?

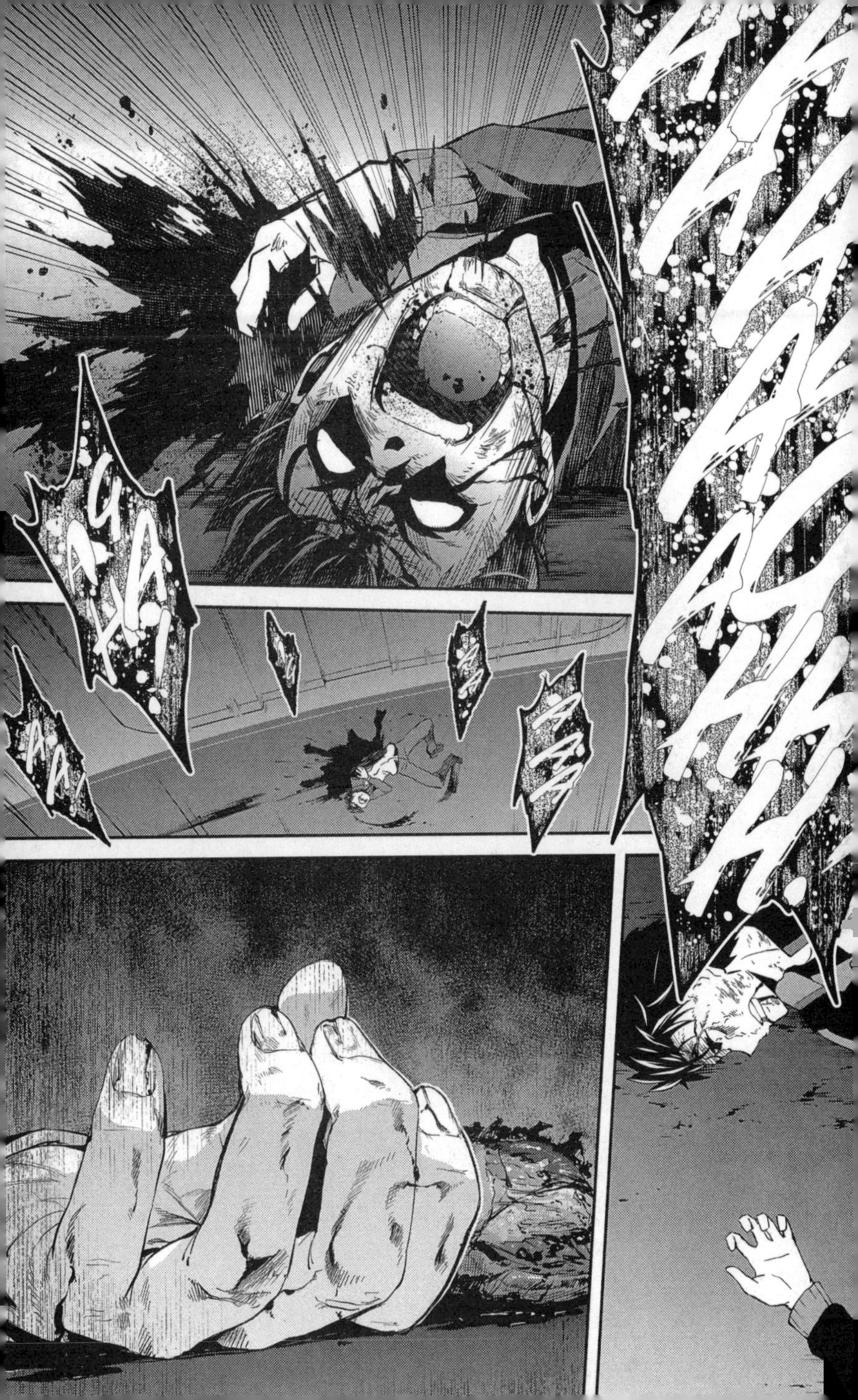
AAAA
AA!

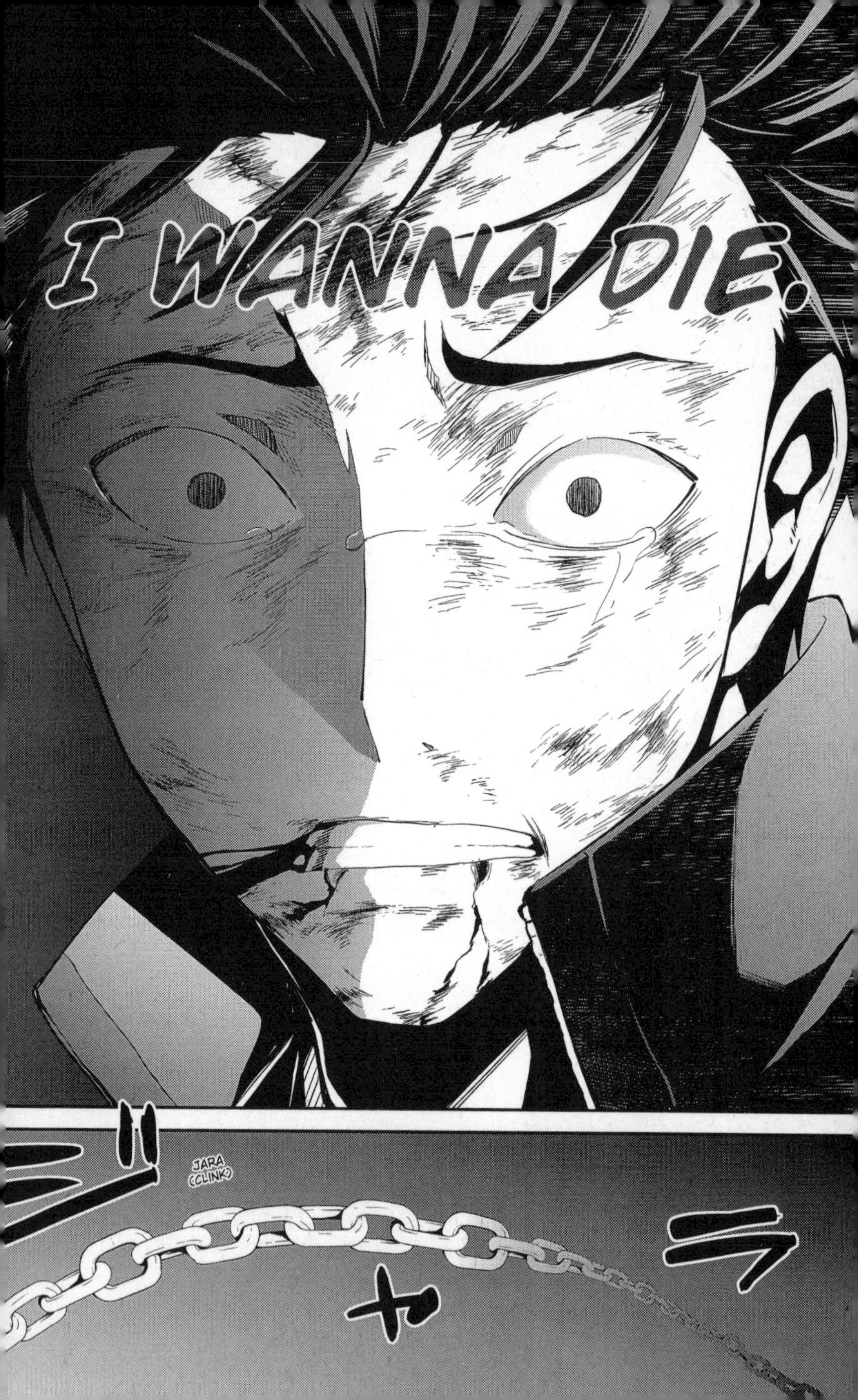
I WANNA DIE.
ジャラ
JARA (CLINK)

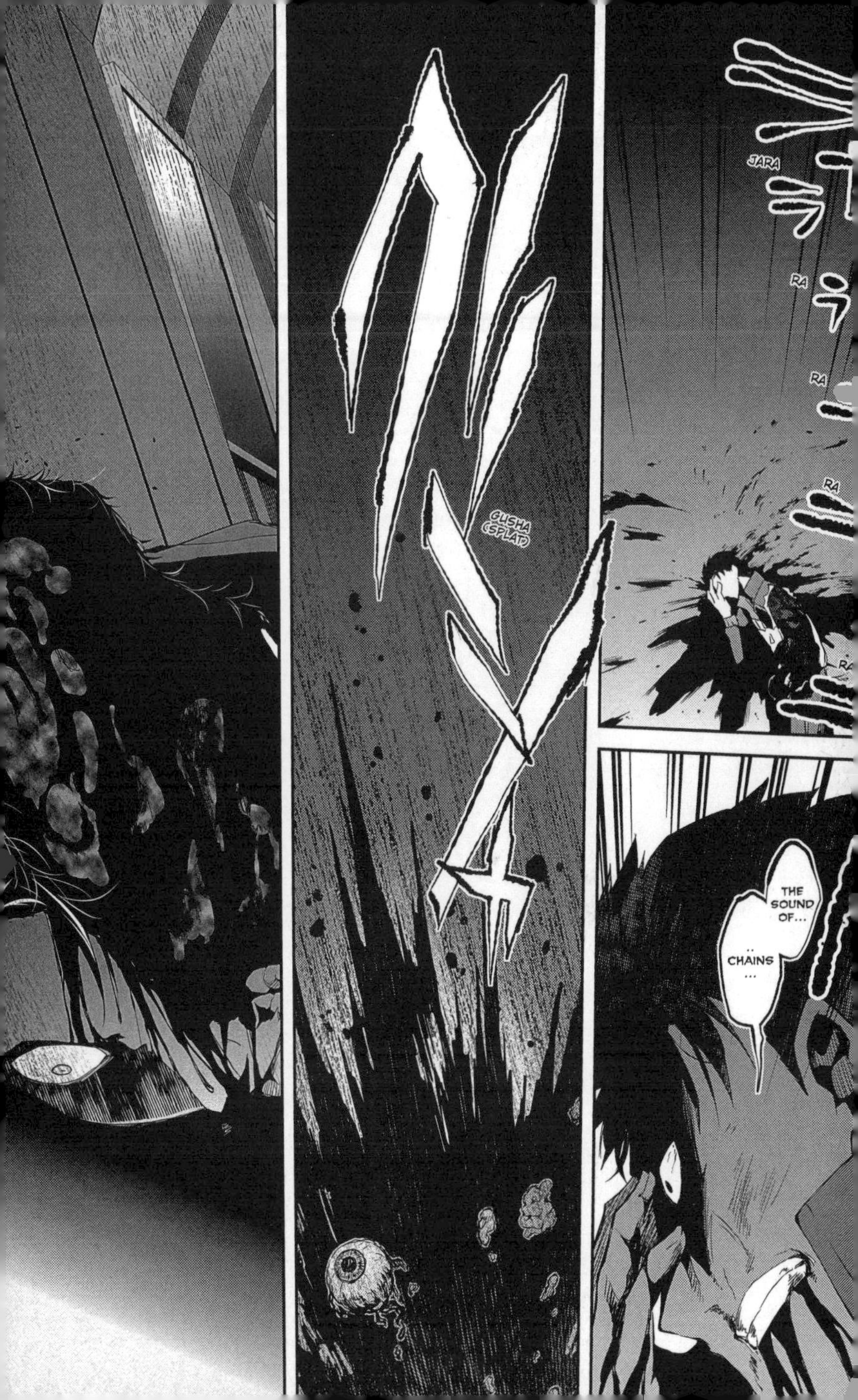
JARA
RA
RA
RA
RA
THE SOUND OF...
.. CHAINS ...
GUSHA (SPLAT)

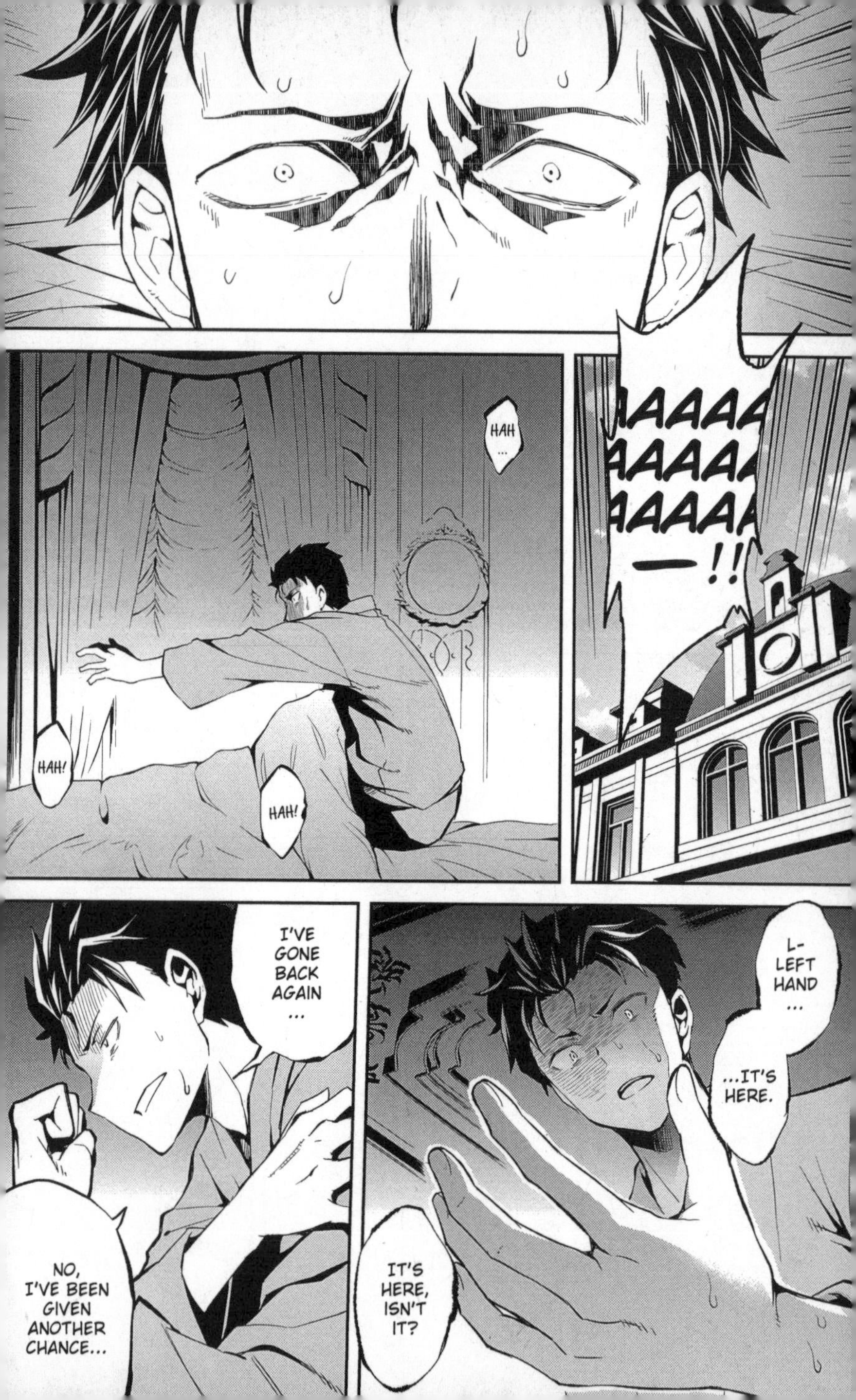
AAAAAAAAAAAAAAA—!!
HAH...
HAH!
HAH!
L-LEFT HAND...
...IT'S HERE.
IT'S HERE, ISN'T IT?
I'VE GONE BACK AGAIN...
NO, I'VE BEEN GIVEN ANOTHER CHANCE...

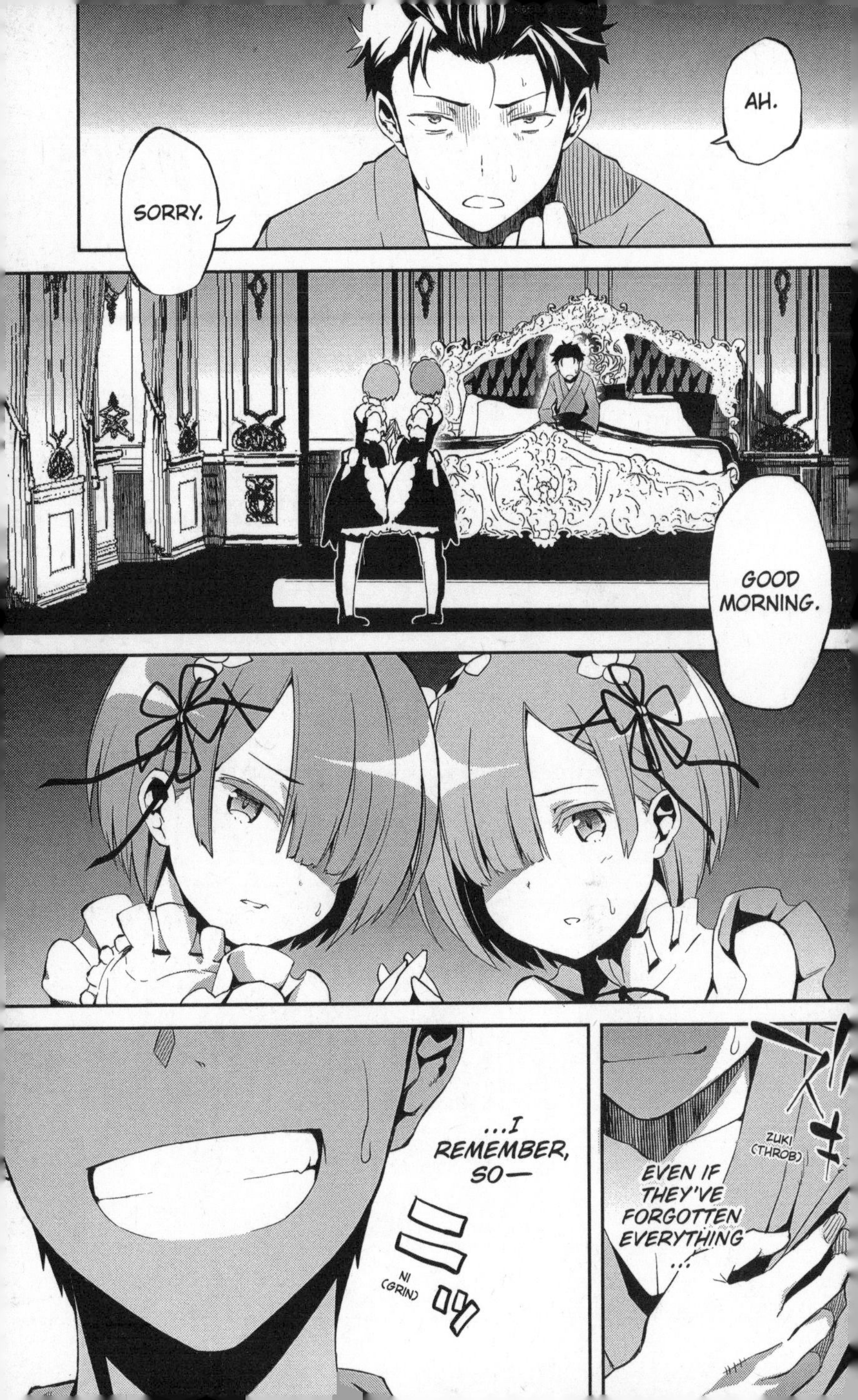
AH.
SORRY.
GOOD MORNING.
ZUKI (THROB)
EVEN IF THEY'VE FORGOTTEN EVERYTHING...
...I REMEMBER, SO—
NI (GRIN)

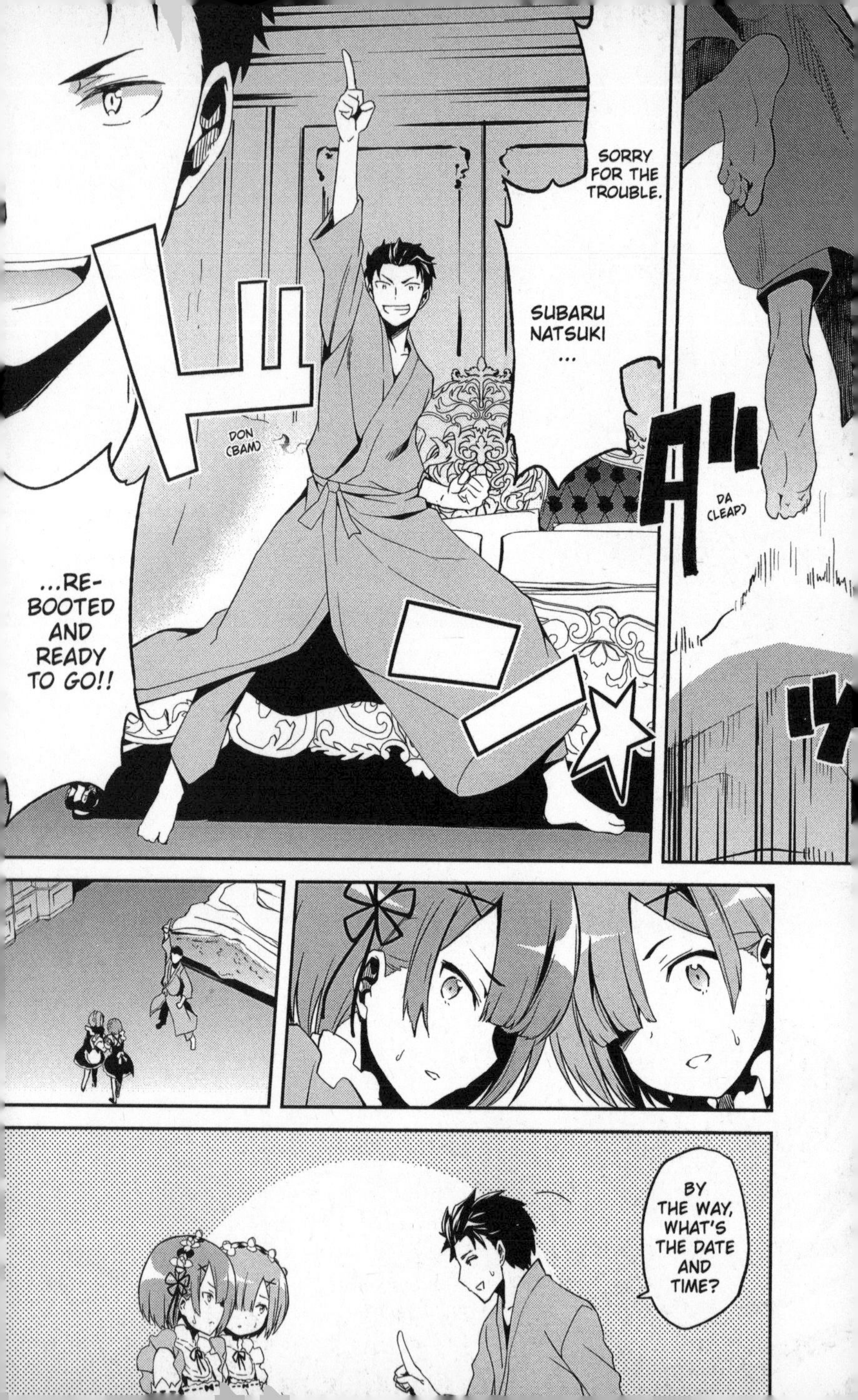
DA (LEAP)
SORRY FOR THE TROUBLE.
SUBARU NATSUKI ...
DON (BAM)
...RE-BOOTED AND READY TO GO!!
BY THE WAY, WHAT'S THE DATE AND TIME?

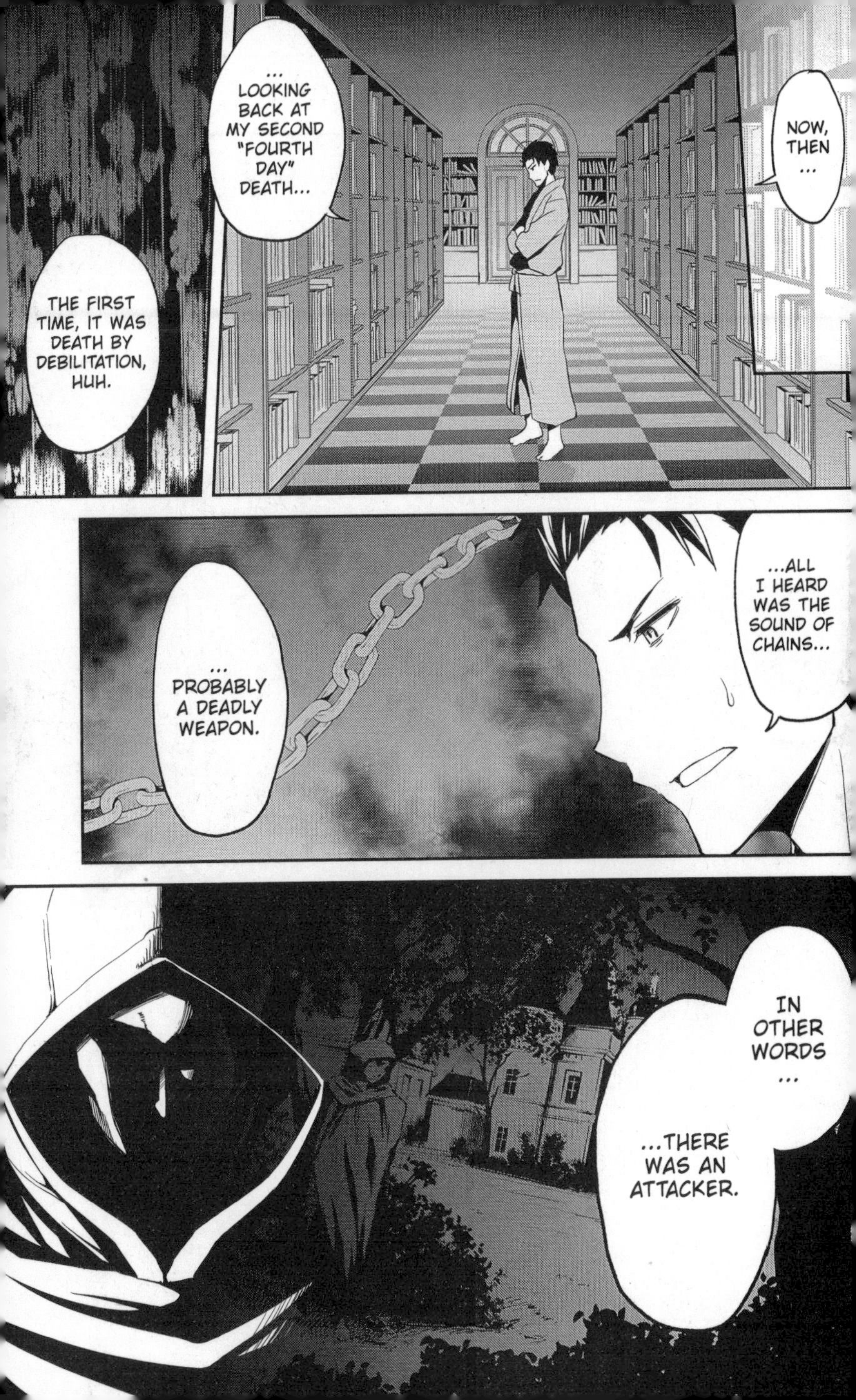
NOW, THEN ...
... LOOKING BACK AT MY SECOND "FOURTH DAY" DEATH...
THE FIRST TIME, IT WAS DEATH BY DEBILITATION, HUH.
...ALL I HEARD WAS THE SOUND OF CHAINS...
... PROBABLY A DEADLY WEAPON.
IN OTHER WORDS ...
...THERE WAS AN ATTACKER.

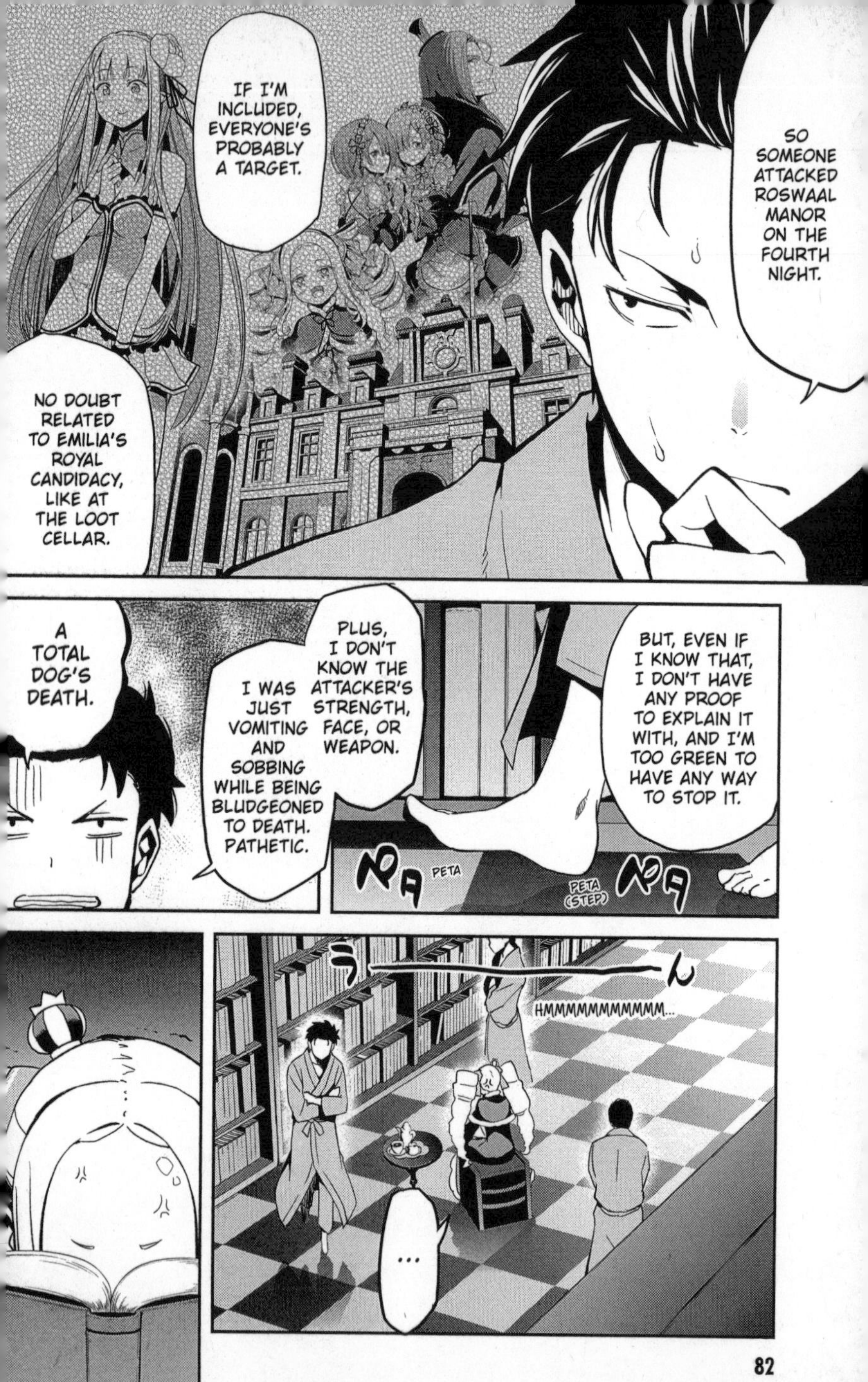
SO SOMEONE ATTACKED ROSWAAL MANOR ON THE FOURTH NIGHT.
IF I'M INCLUDED, EVERYONE'S PROBABLY A TARGET.
NO DOUBT RELATED TO EMILIA'S ROYAL CANDIDACY, LIKE AT THE LOOT CELLAR.
BUT, EVEN IF I KNOW THAT, I DON'T HAVE ANY PROOF TO EXPLAIN IT WITH, AND I'M TOO GREEN TO HAVE ANY WAY TO STOP IT.
ペタ
PETA (STEP)
ペタ
PETA
PLUS, I DON'T KNOW THE ATTACKER'S STRENGTH, FACE, OR WEAPON.
I WAS JUST VOMITING AND SOBBING WHILE BEING BLUDGEONED TO DEATH. PATHETIC.
A TOTAL DOG'S DEATH.
う————ん
HMMMMMMMMMMM...
...

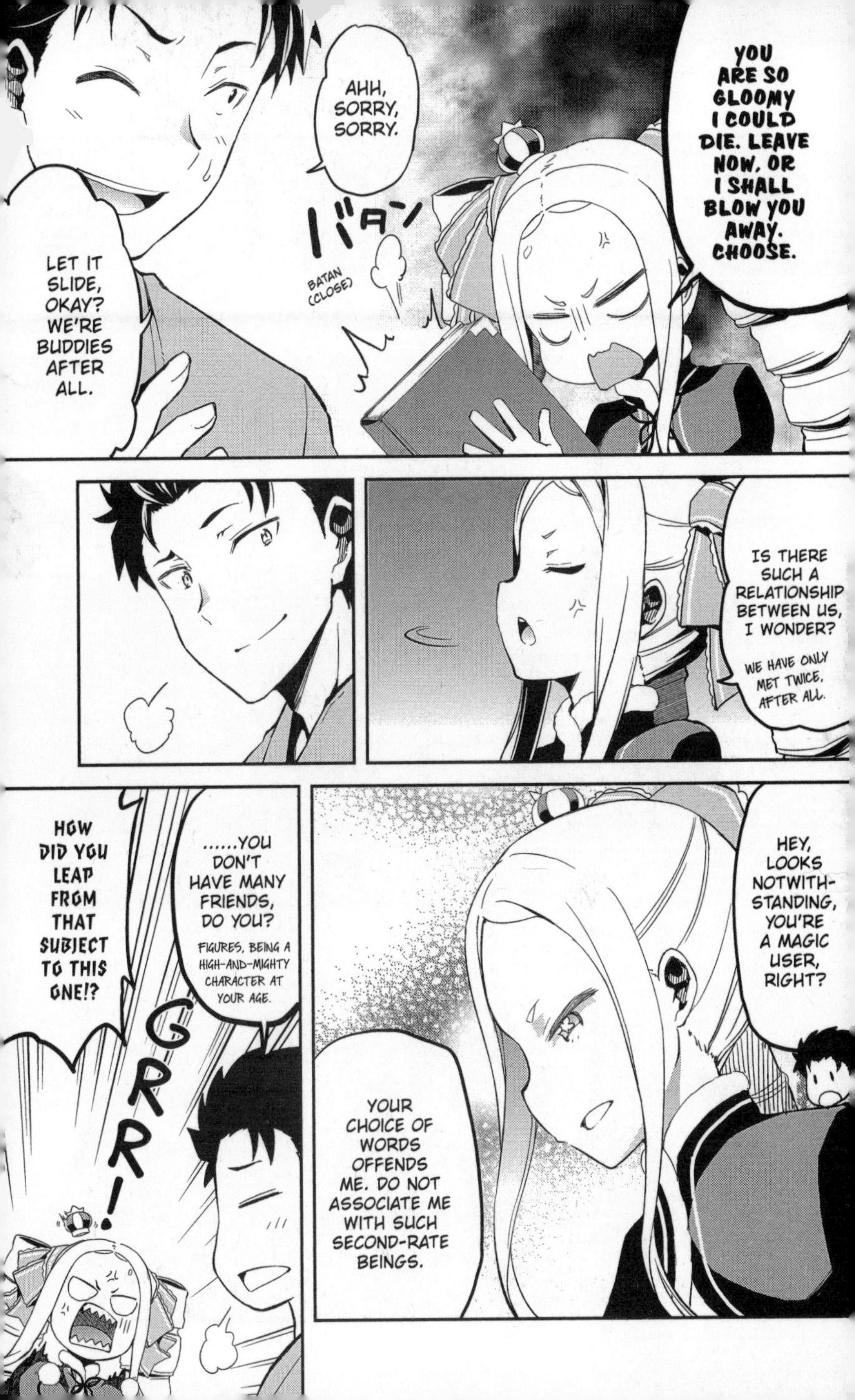
YOU ARE SO GLOOMY I COULD DIE. LEAVE NOW, OR I SHALL BLOW YOU AWAY. CHOOSE.
AHH, SORRY, SORRY.
バタン
BATAN (CLOSE)
LET IT SLIDE, OKAY? WE'RE BUDDIES AFTER ALL.
IS THERE SUCH A RELATIONSHIP BETWEEN US, I WONDER?
WE HAVE ONLY MET TWICE, AFTER ALL.
HEY, LOOKS NOTWITH-STANDING, YOU'RE A MAGIC USER, RIGHT?
YOUR CHOICE OF WORDS OFFENDS ME. DO NOT ASSOCIATE ME WITH SUCH SECOND-RATE BEINGS.
......YOU DON'T HAVE MANY FRIENDS, DO YOU?
FIGURES, BEING A HIGH-AND-MIGHTY CHARACTER AT YOUR AGE.
HOW DID YOU LEAP FROM THAT SUBJECT TO THIS ONE!?
GRRR!

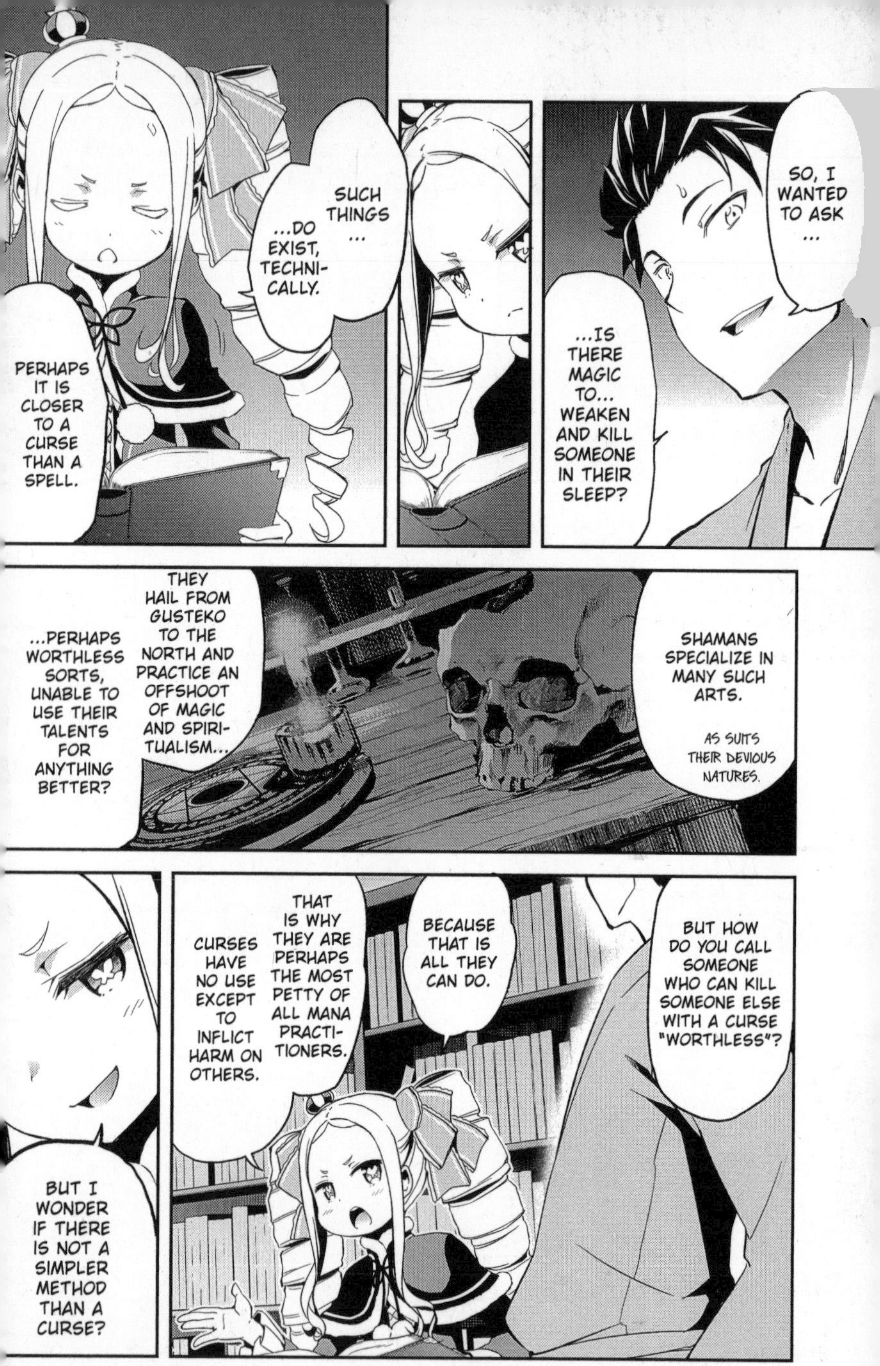
SO, I WANTED TO ASK ...
...IS THERE MAGIC TO... WEAKEN AND KILL SOMEONE IN THEIR SLEEP?
SUCH THINGS ...
...DO EXIST, TECHNICALLY.
PERHAPS IT IS CLOSER TO A CURSE THAN A SPELL.
SHAMANS SPECIALIZE IN MANY SUCH ARTS.
AS SUITS THEIR DEVIOUS NATURES.
THEY HAIL FROM GUSTEKO TO THE NORTH AND PRACTICE AN OFFSHOOT OF MAGIC AND SPIRITUALISM...
...PERHAPS WORTHLESS SORTS, UNABLE TO USE THEIR TALENTS FOR ANYTHING BETTER?
BUT HOW DO YOU CALL SOMEONE WHO CAN KILL SOMEONE ELSE WITH A CURSE "WORTHLESS"?
BECAUSE THAT IS ALL THEY CAN DO.
THAT IS WHY THEY ARE PERHAPS THE MOST PETTY OF ALL MANA PRACTITIONERS.
CURSES HAVE NO USE EXCEPT TO INFLICT HARM ON OTHERS.
BUT I WONDER IF THERE IS NOT A SIMPLER METHOD THAN A CURSE?

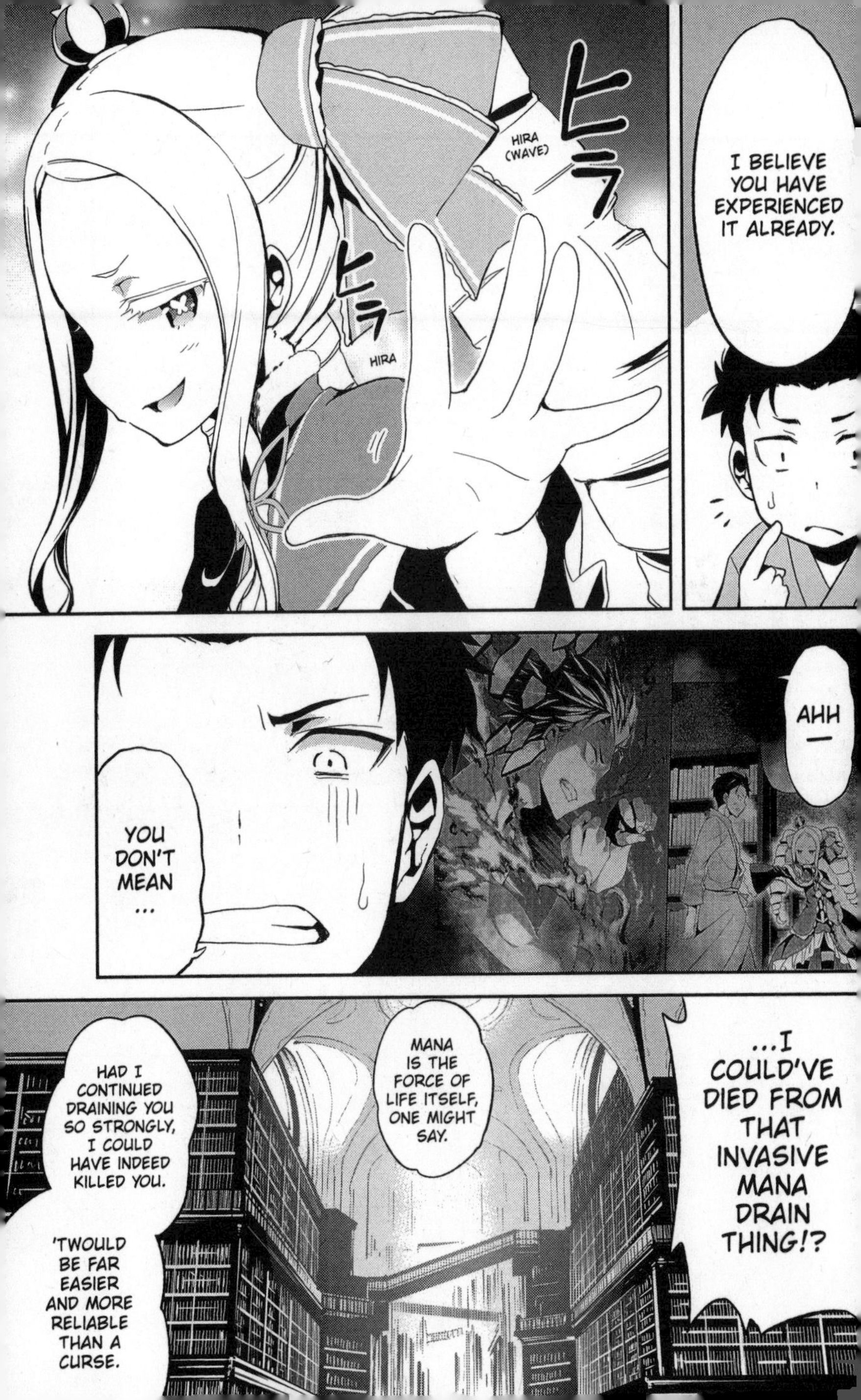
I BELIEVE YOU HAVE EXPERIENCED IT ALREADY.
ヒラ
HIRA (WAVE)
ヒラ
HIRA
AHH—
YOU DON'T MEAN...
...I COULD'VE DIED FROM THAT INVASIVE MANA DRAIN THING!?
MANA IS THE FORCE OF LIFE ITSELF, ONE MIGHT SAY.
HAD I CONTINUED DRAINING YOU SO STRONGLY, I COULD HAVE INDEED KILLED YOU.
'TWOULD BE FAR EASIER AND MORE RELIABLE THAN A CURSE.

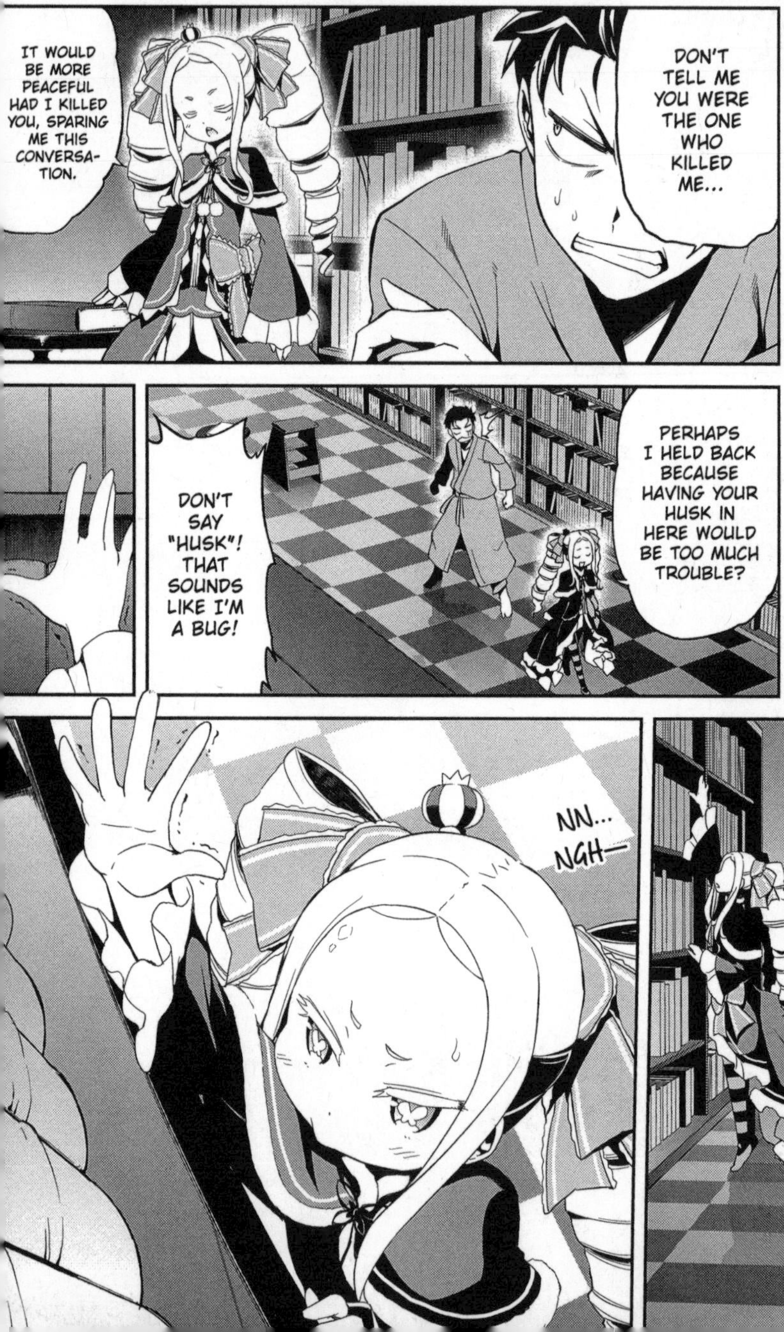
DON'T TELL ME YOU WERE THE ONE WHO KILLED ME...
IT WOULD BE MORE PEACEFUL HAD I KILLED YOU, SPARING ME THIS CONVERSA-TION.
PERHAPS I HELD BACK BECAUSE HAVING YOUR HUSK IN HERE WOULD BE TOO MUCH TROUBLE?
DON'T SAY "HUSK"! THAT SOUNDS LIKE I'M A BUG!
NN... NGH—

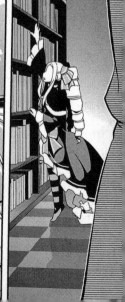

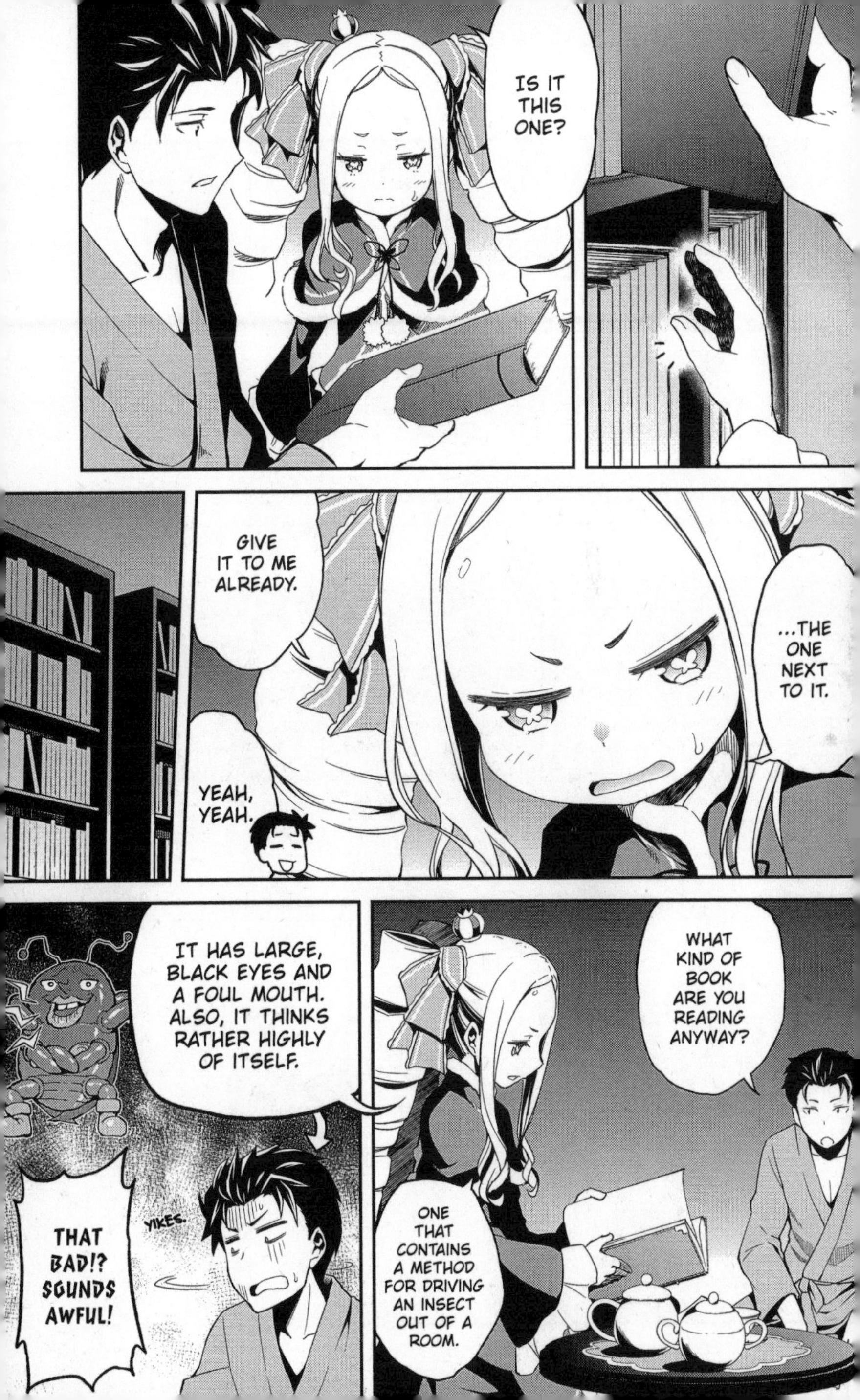
IS IT THIS ONE?
...THE ONE NEXT TO IT.
GIVE IT TO ME ALREADY.
YEAH, YEAH.
WHAT KIND OF BOOK ARE YOU READING ANYWAY?
ONE THAT CONTAINS A METHOD FOR DRIVING AN INSECT OUT OF A ROOM.
IT HAS LARGE, BLACK EYES AND A FOUL MOUTH. ALSO, IT THINKS RATHER HIGHLY OF ITSELF.
YIKES.
THAT BAD!? SOUNDS AWFUL!

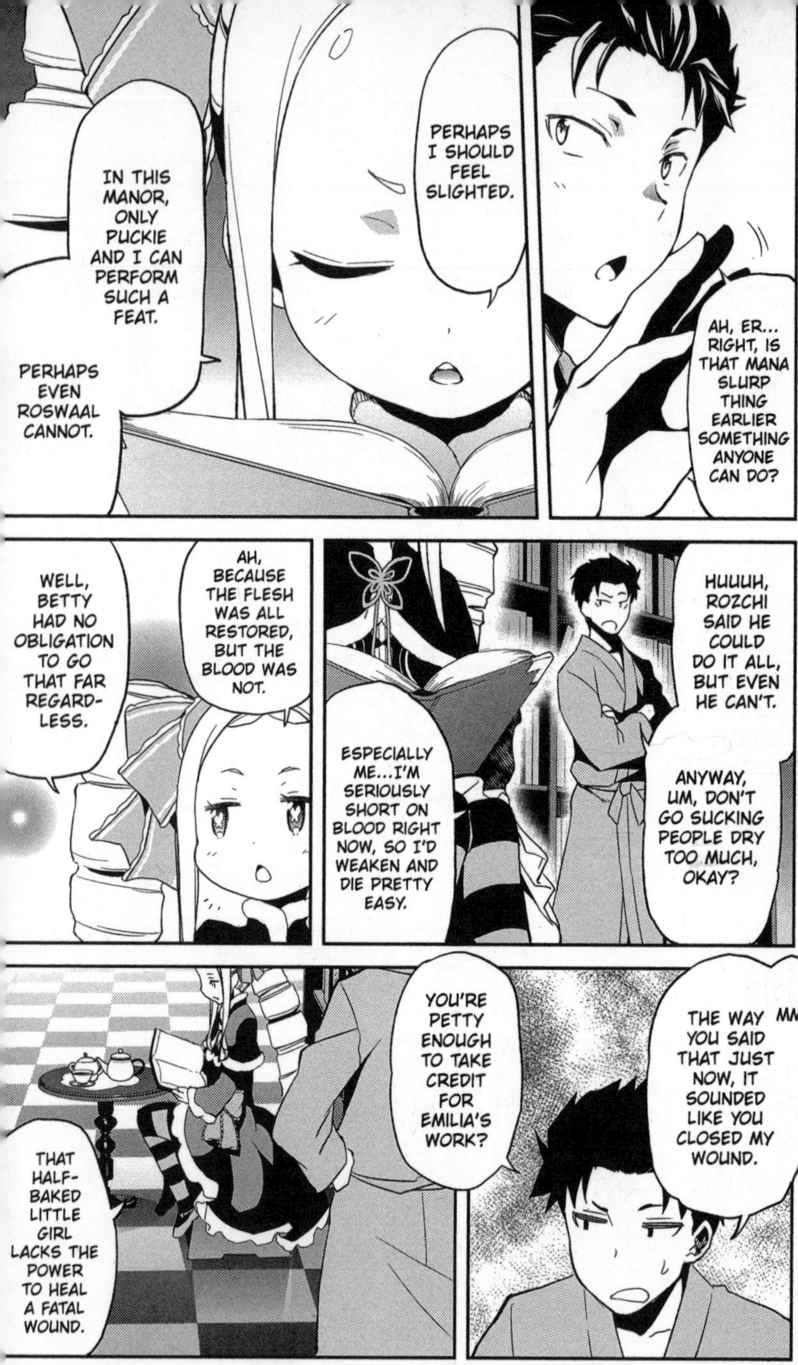
AH, ER... RIGHT, IS THAT MANA SLURP THING EARLIER SOMETHING ANYONE CAN DO?
PERHAPS I SHOULD FEEL SLIGHTED.
IN THIS MANOR, ONLY PUCKIE AND I CAN PERFORM SUCH A FEAT.
PERHAPS EVEN ROSWAAL CANNOT.
HUUUH, ROZCHI SAID HE COULD DO IT ALL, BUT EVEN HE CAN'T.
ANYWAY, UM, DON'T GO SUCKING PEOPLE DRY TOO MUCH, OKAY?
ESPECIALLY ME...I'M SERIOUSLY SHORT ON BLOOD RIGHT NOW, SO I'D WEAKEN AND DIE PRETTY EASY.
AH, BECAUSE THE FLESH WAS ALL RESTORED, BUT THE BLOOD WAS NOT.
WELL, BETTY HAD NO OBLIGATION TO GO THAT FAR REGARDLESS.
MM?
THE WAY YOU SAID THAT JUST NOW, IT SOUNDED LIKE YOU CLOSED MY WOUND.
YOU'RE PETTY ENOUGH TO TAKE CREDIT FOR EMILIA'S WORK?
THAT HALF-BAKED LITTLE GIRL LACKS THE POWER TO HEAL A FATAL WOUND.

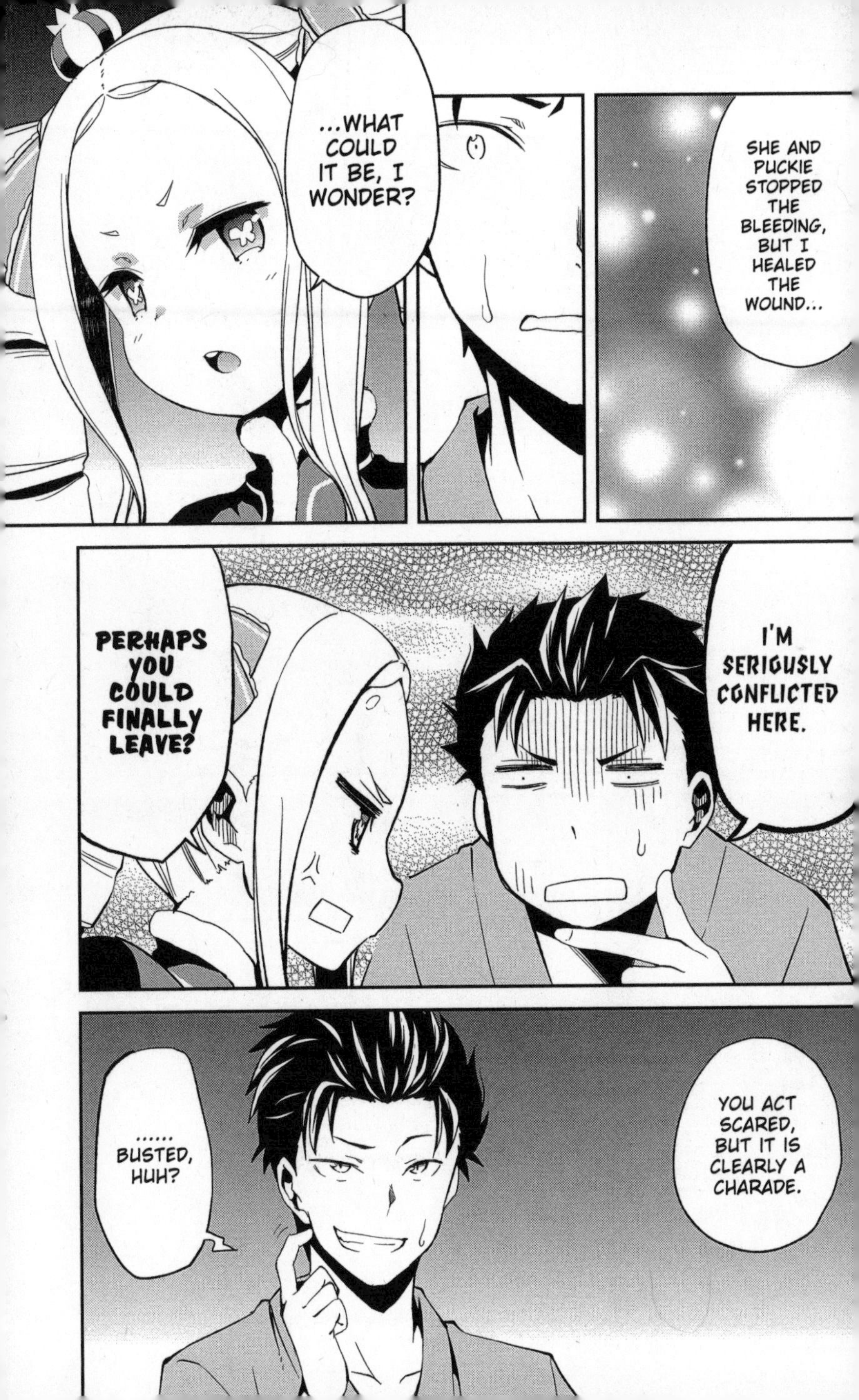
SHE AND PUCKIE STOPPED THE BLEEDING, BUT I HEALED THE WOUND...
...WHAT COULD IT BE, I WONDER?
I'M SERIOUSLY CONFLICTED HERE.
PERHAPS YOU COULD FINALLY LEAVE?
YOU ACT SCARED, BUT IT IS CLEARLY A CHARADE.
...... BUSTED, HUH?

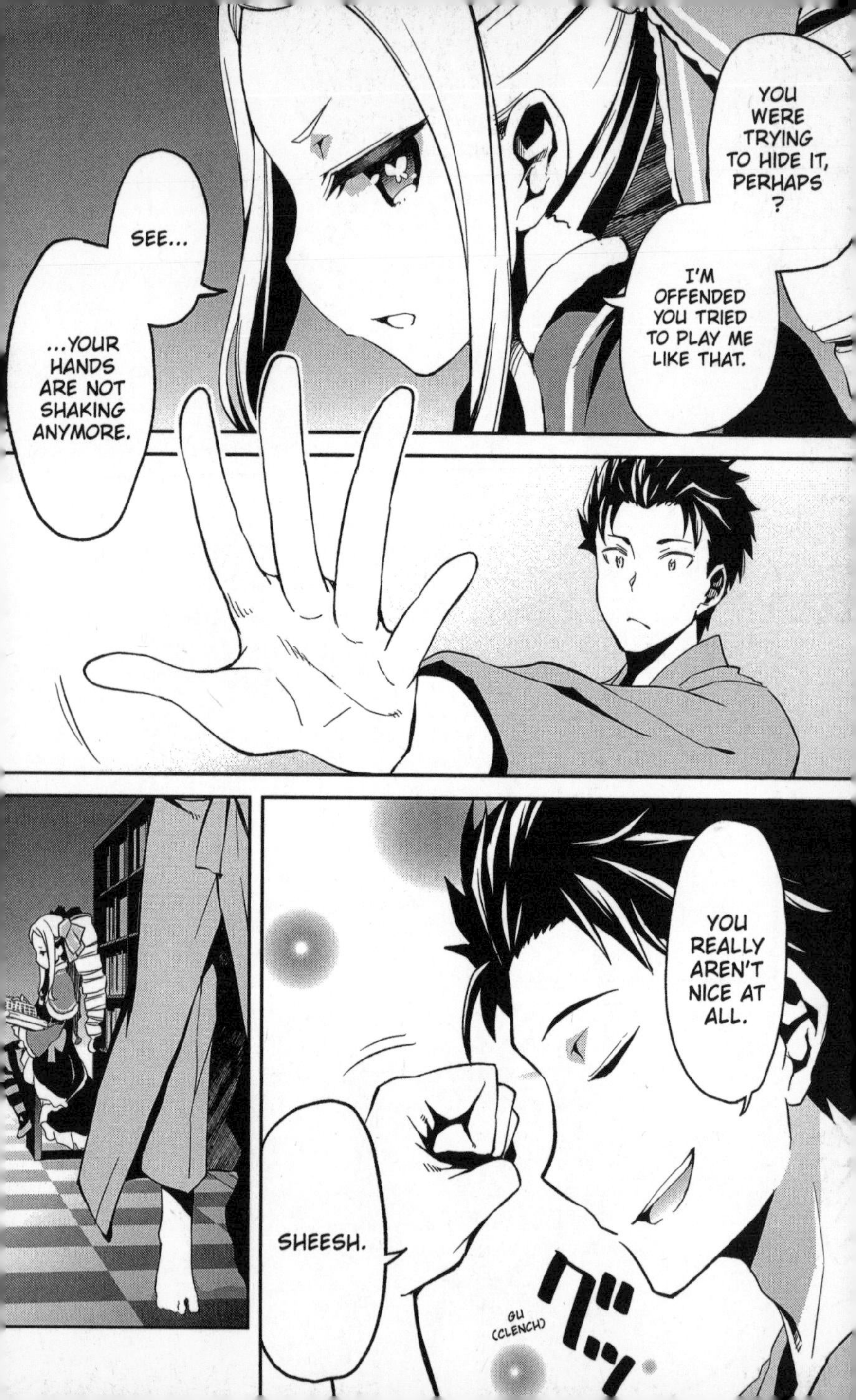
YOU WERE TRYING TO HIDE IT, PERHAPS?
I'M OFFENDED YOU TRIED TO PLAY ME LIKE THAT.
SEE...
...YOUR HANDS ARE NOT SHAKING ANYMORE.
YOU REALLY AREN'T NICE AT ALL.
SHEESH.
GU (CLENCH)

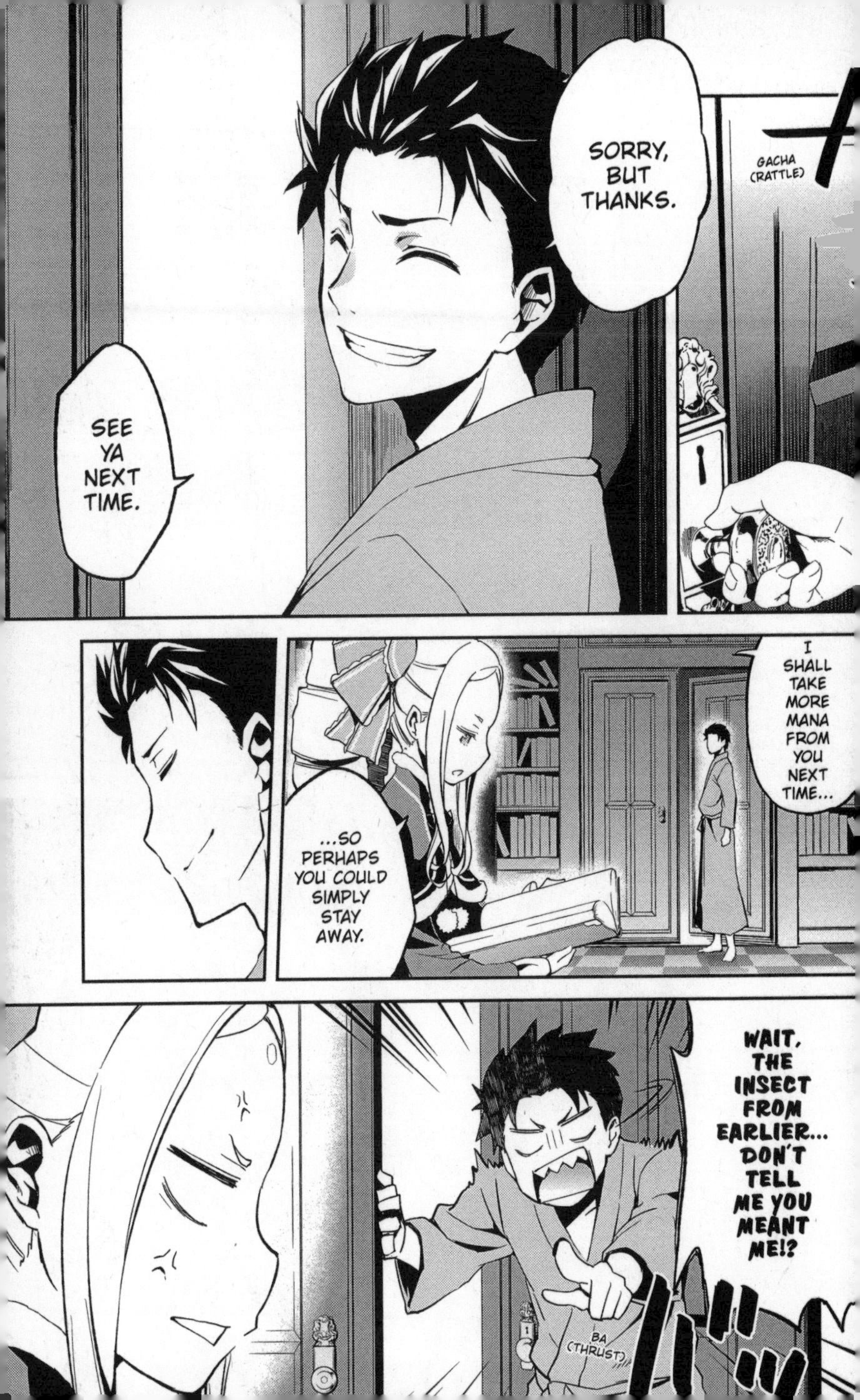
GACHA (RATTLE)
SORRY, BUT THANKS.
SEE YA NEXT TIME.
I SHALL TAKE MORE MANA FROM YOU NEXT TIME...
...SO PERHAPS YOU COULD SIMPLY STAY AWAY.
WAIT, THE INSECT FROM EARLIER... DON'T TELL ME YOU MEANT ME!?
BA (THRUST)

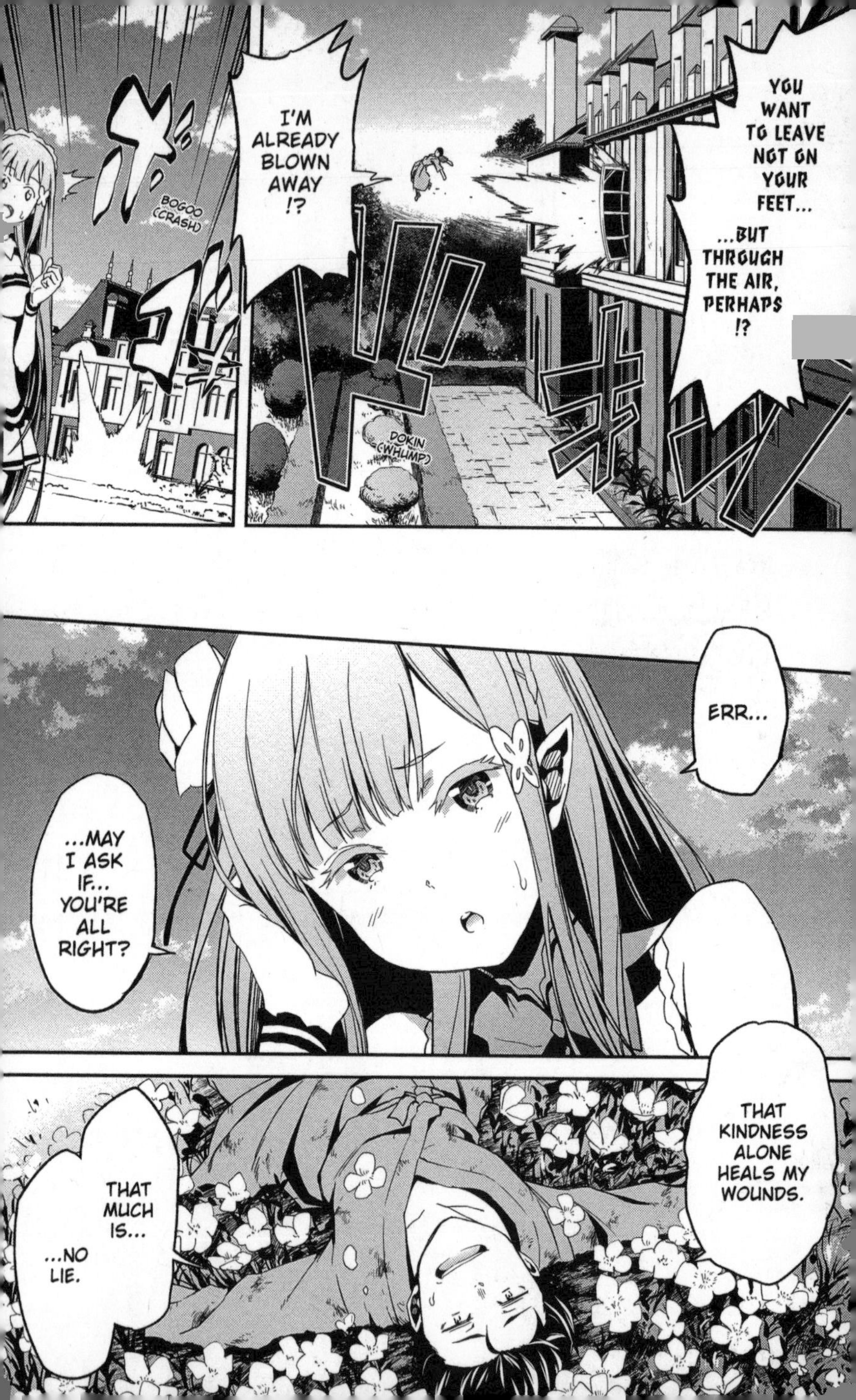
YOU WANT TO LEAVE NOT ON YOUR FEET...
...BUT THROUGH THE AIR, PERHAPS !?
I'M ALREADY BLOWN AWAY !?
DOKIN (WHUMP)
BOGOO (CRASH)
ERR...
...MAY I ASK IF... YOU'RE ALL RIGHT?
THAT KINDNESS ALONE HEALS MY WOUNDS.
THAT MUCH IS...
...NO LIE.

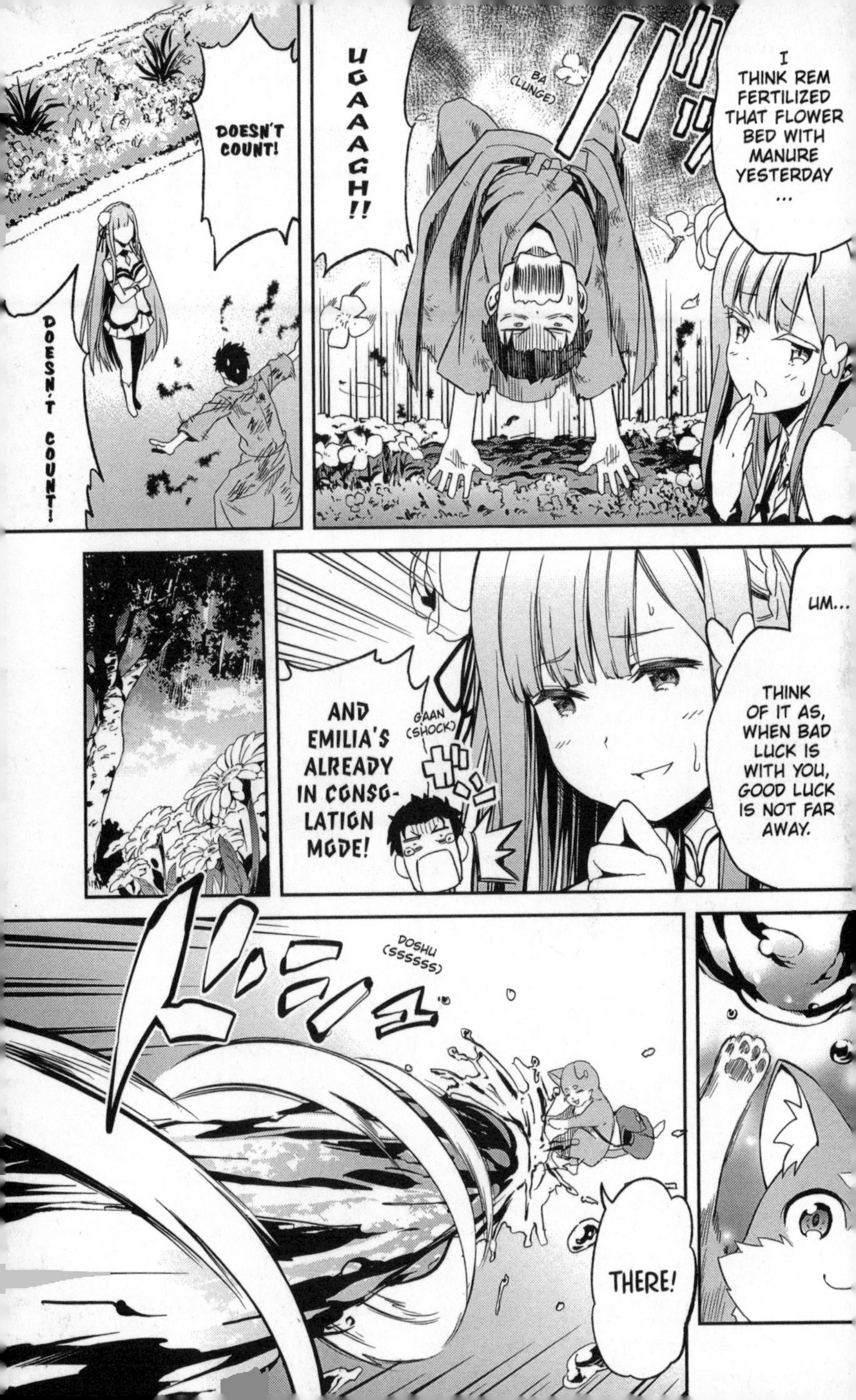
I THINK REM FERTILIZED THAT FLOWER BED WITH MANURE YESTERDAY...
BA (LUNGE)
UGAAAAGH!!
DOESN'T COUNT!
DOESN'T COUNT!
UM...
THINK OF IT AS, WHEN BAD LUCK IS WITH YOU, GOOD LUCK IS NOT FAR AWAY.
GAAN (SHOCK)
AND EMILIA'S ALREADY IN CONSO-LATION MODE!
THERE!
DOSHU (SSSSSS)

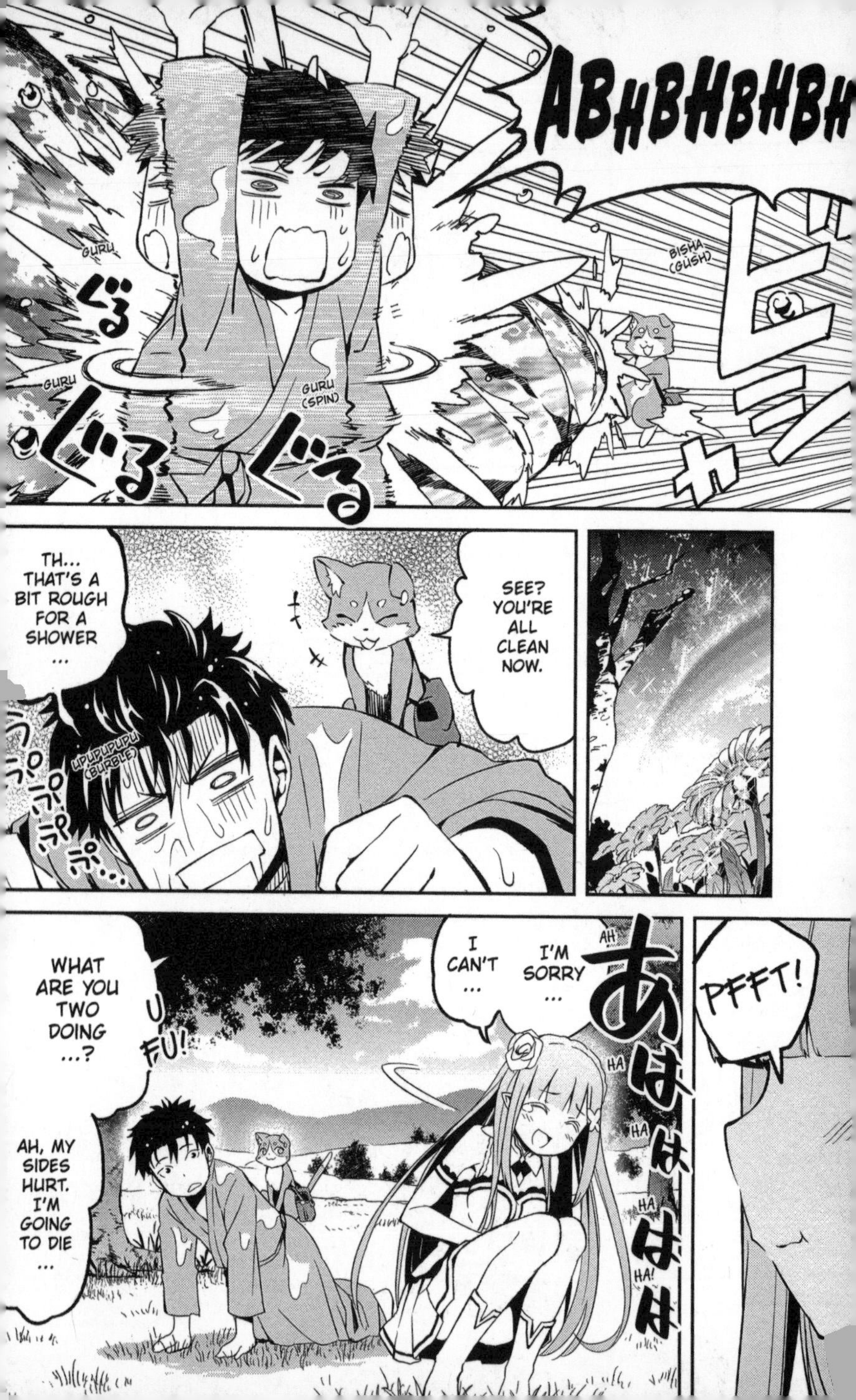
ABHBHBHBH
BISHA (GUSH)
ビシャ
GURU (SPIN)
ぐる
GURU
ぐる
GURU
ぐる
SEE? YOU'RE ALL CLEAN NOW.
TH... THAT'S A BIT ROUGH FOR A SHOWER ...
UPUPUPUPU (BURBLE)
うぷぷぷぷ...
PFFT!
AH HA HA HA!
あははは
I'M SORRY ...
I CAN'T ...
U FU!
WHAT ARE YOU TWO DOING ...?
AH, MY SIDES HURT. I'M GOING TO DIE ...

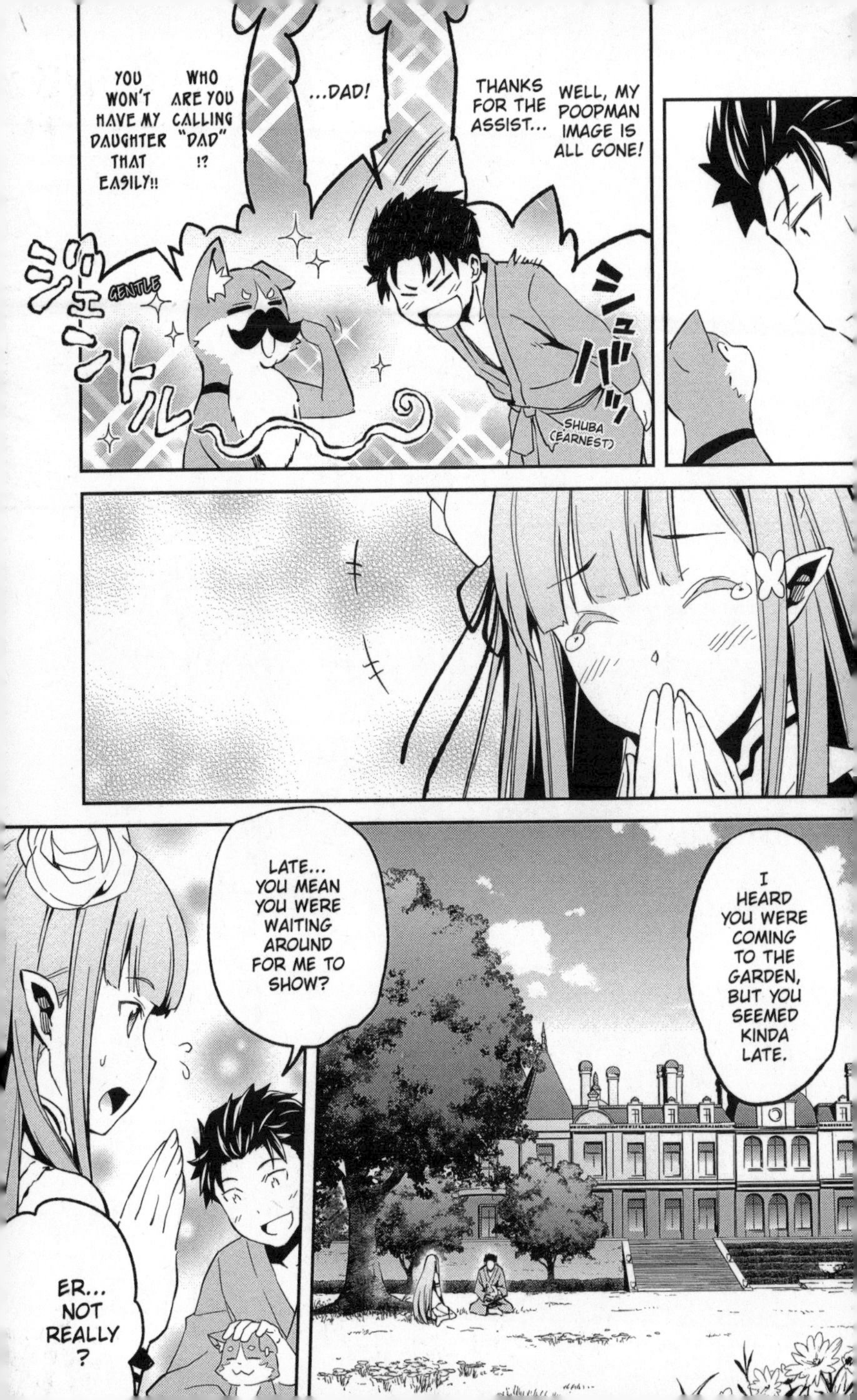
WELL, MY POOPMAN IMAGE IS ALL GONE!
THANKS FOR THE ASSIST...
SHUBA (EARNEST)
...DAD!
WHO ARE YOU CALLING "DAD" !?
YOU WON'T HAVE MY DAUGHTER THAT EASILY!!
ジェーントル
GENTLE
I HEARD YOU WERE COMING TO THE GARDEN, BUT YOU SEEMED KINDA LATE.
LATE... YOU MEAN YOU WERE WAITING AROUND FOR ME TO SHOW?
ER... NOT REALLY ?

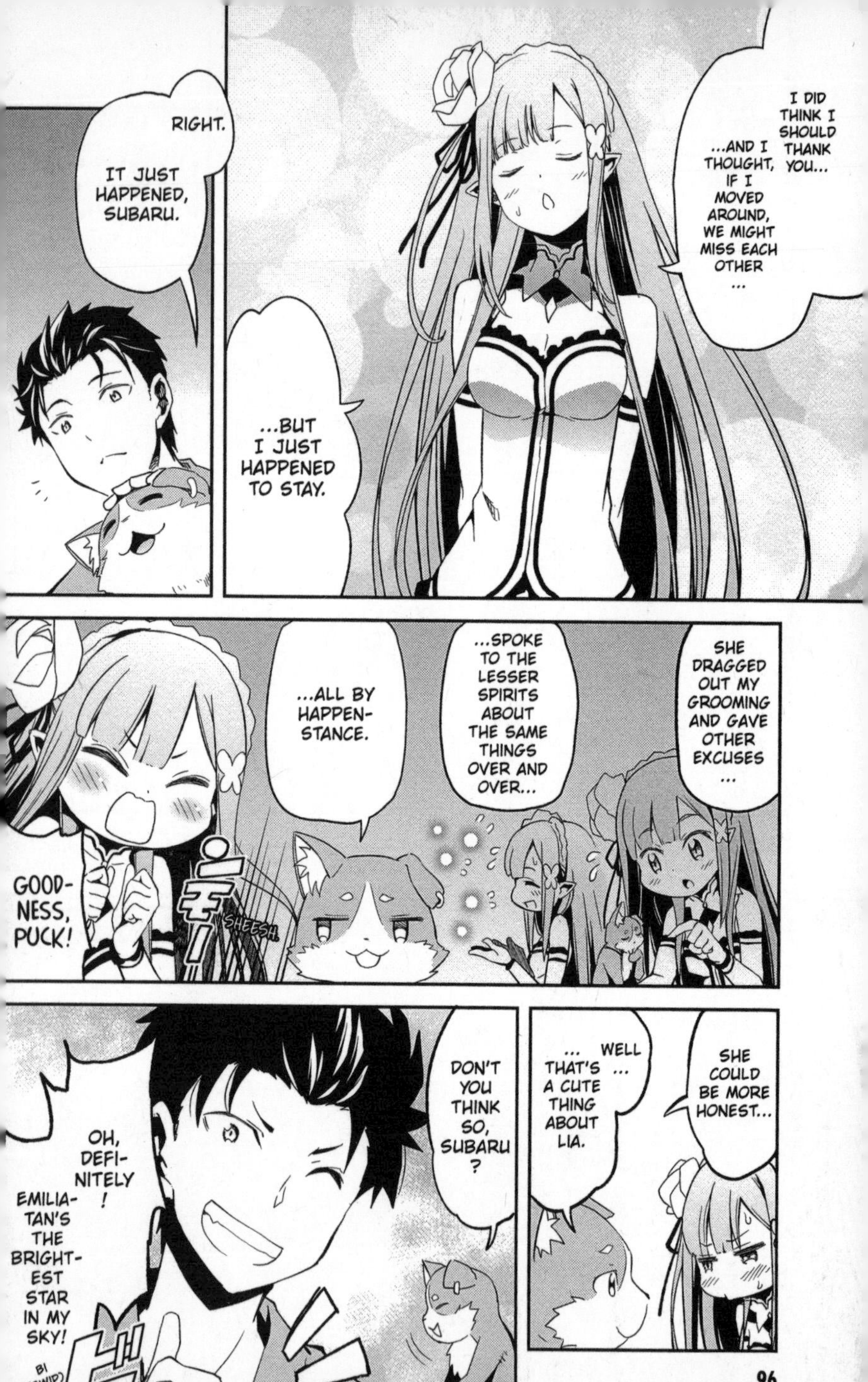
I DID THINK I SHOULD THANK YOU...
...AND I THOUGHT, IF I MOVED AROUND, WE MIGHT MISS EACH OTHER ...
...BUT I JUST HAPPENED TO STAY.
RIGHT.
IT JUST HAPPENED, SUBARU.
SHE DRAGGED OUT MY GROOMING AND GAVE OTHER EXCUSES ...
...SPOKE TO THE LESSER SPIRITS ABOUT THE SAME THINGS OVER AND OVER...
...ALL BY HAPPEN-STANCE.
SHEESH
GOOD-NESS, PUCK!
SHE COULD BE MORE HONEST...
WELL ...
... THAT'S A CUTE THING ABOUT LIA.
DON'T YOU THINK SO, SUBARU?
OH, DEFI-NITELY!
EMILIA-TAN'S THE BRIGHT-EST STAR IN MY SKY!
BI (FWIP)

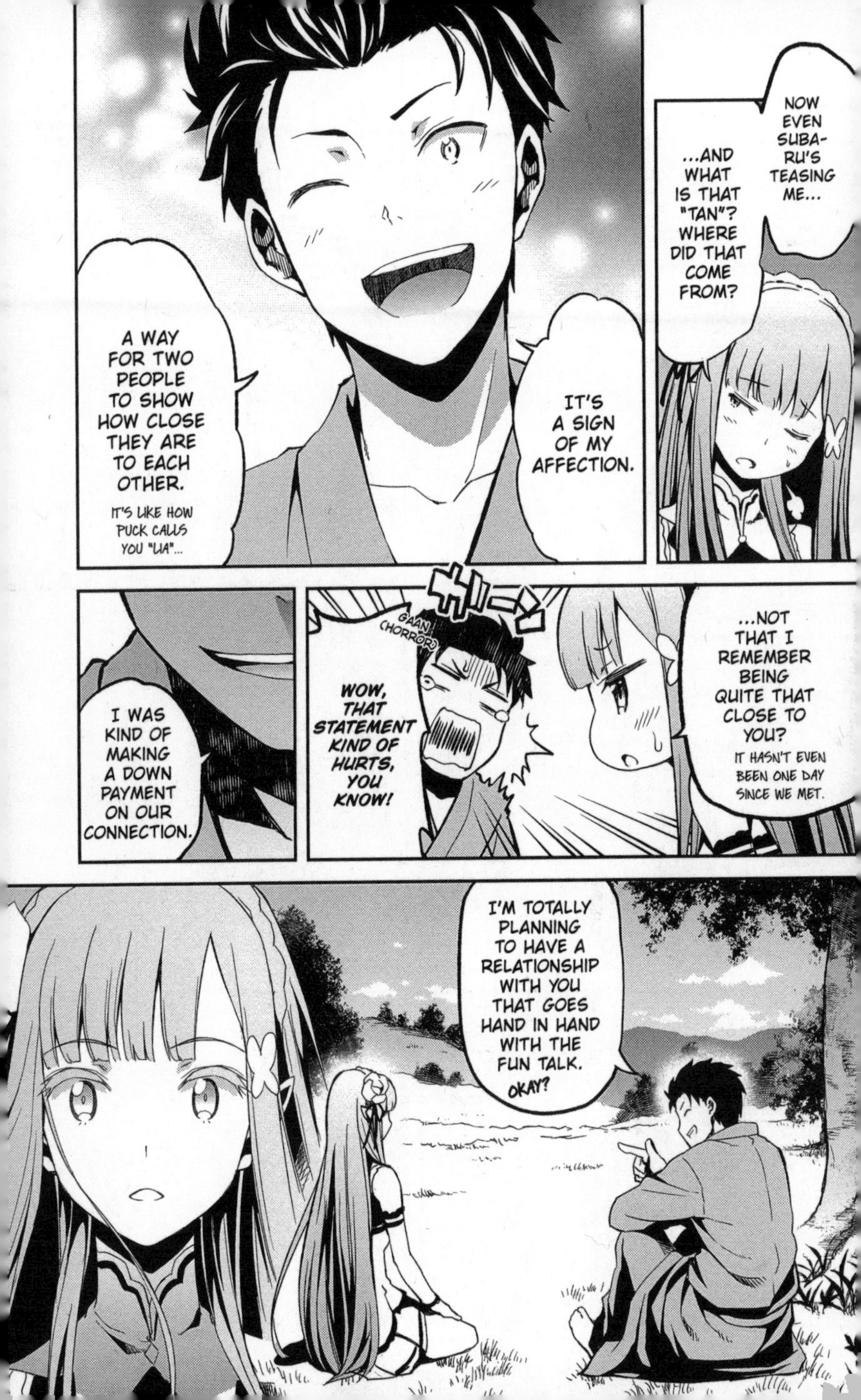
NOW EVEN SUBARU'S TEASING ME...
...AND WHAT IS THAT "TAN"? WHERE DID THAT COME FROM?
IT'S A SIGN OF MY AFFECTION.
A WAY FOR TWO PEOPLE TO SHOW HOW CLOSE THEY ARE TO EACH OTHER.
IT'S LIKE HOW PUCK CALLS YOU "LIA"...
...NOT THAT I REMEMBER BEING QUITE THAT CLOSE TO YOU?
IT HASN'T EVEN BEEN ONE DAY SINCE WE MET.
GAAN (HORROR)
WOW, THAT STATEMENT KIND OF HURTS, YOU KNOW!
I WAS KIND OF MAKING A DOWN PAYMENT ON OUR CONNECTION.
I'M TOTALLY PLANNING TO HAVE A RELATIONSHIP WITH YOU THAT GOES HAND IN HAND WITH THE FUN TALK.
OKAY?

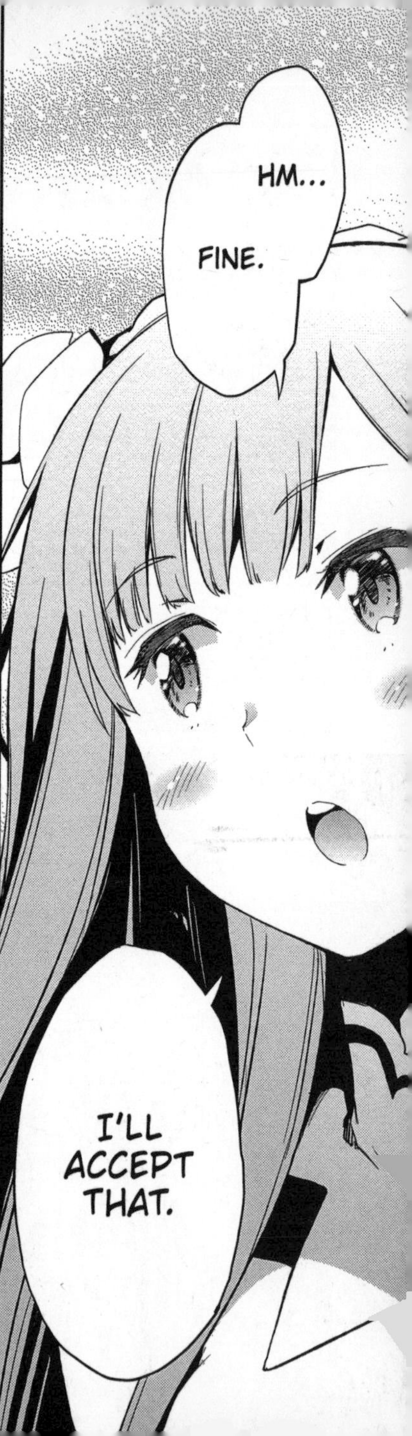
HM...
FINE.
I'LL ACCEPT THAT.

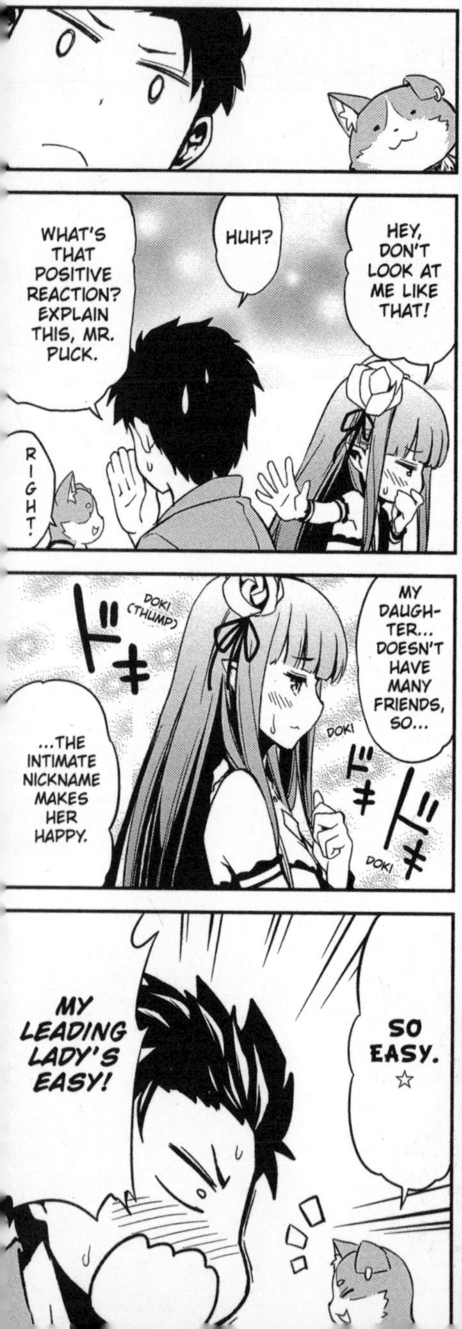
HEY, DON'T LOOK AT ME LIKE THAT!
HUH?
WHAT'S THAT POSITIVE REACTION? EXPLAIN THIS, MR. PUCK.
RIGHT!
MY DAUGHTER... DOESN'T HAVE MANY FRIENDS, SO...
ドキ DOKI (THUMP)
...THE INTIMATE NICKNAME MAKES HER HAPPY.
ドキ DOKI
ドキ DOKI
SO EASY. ☆
MY LEADING LADY'S EASY!

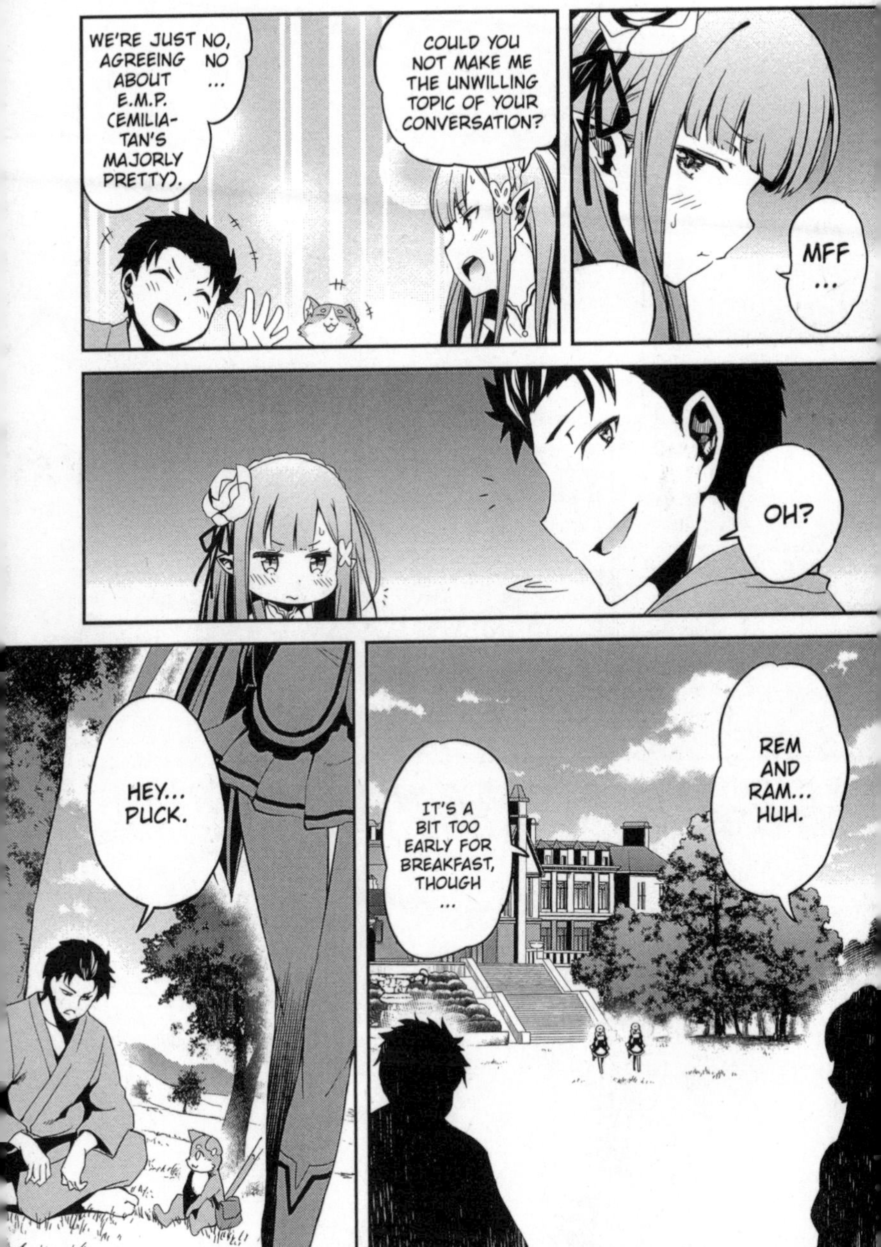
MFF...
COULD YOU NOT MAKE ME THE UNWILLING TOPIC OF YOUR CONVERSATION?
NO, NO...
WE'RE JUST AGREEING ABOUT E.M.P. (EMILIA-TAN'S MAJORLY PRETTY).
OH?
REM AND RAM... HUH.
IT'S A BIT TOO EARLY FOR BREAKFAST, THOUGH...
HEY... PUCK.

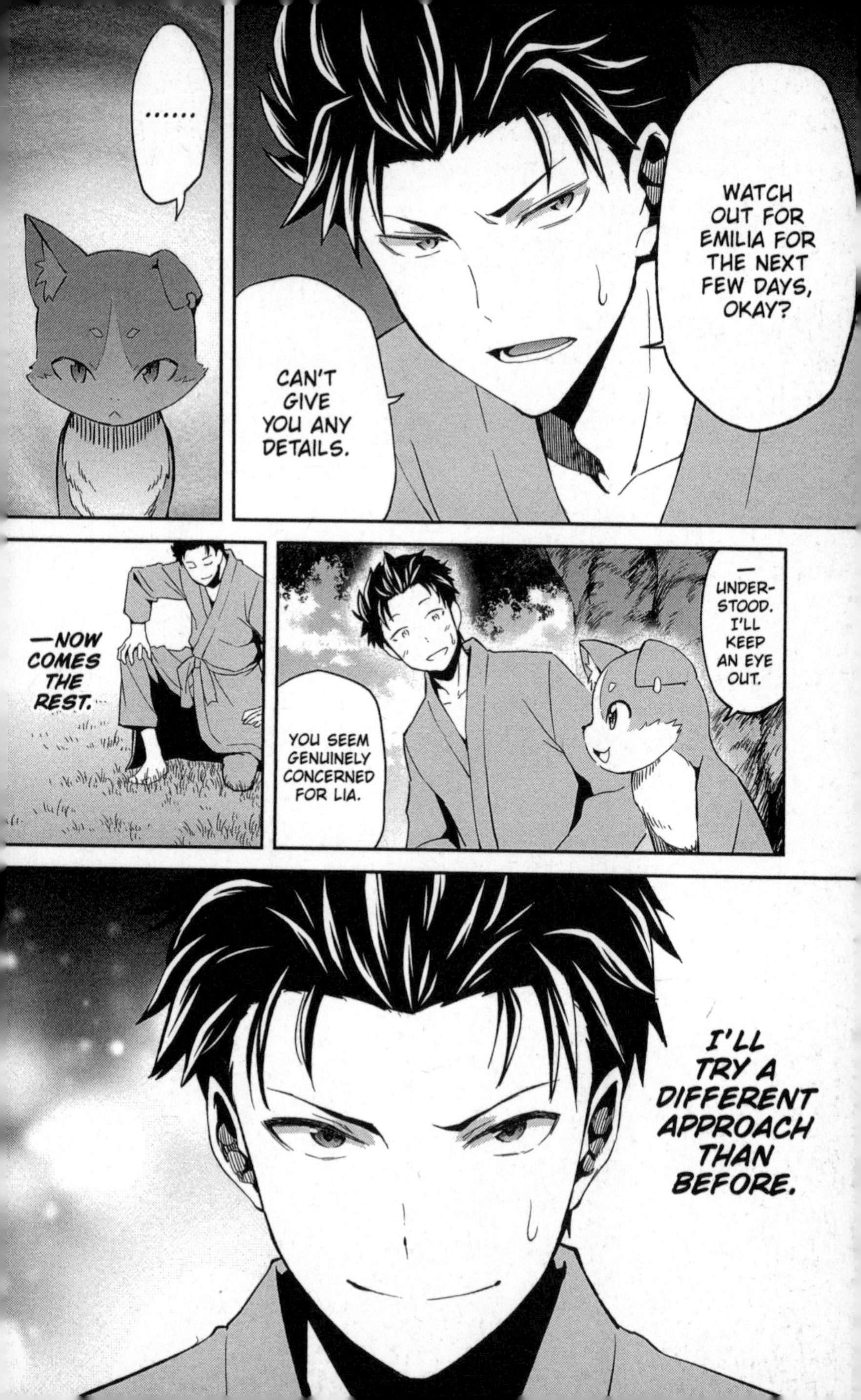
WATCH OUT FOR EMILIA FOR THE NEXT FEW DAYS, OKAY?
CAN'T GIVE YOU ANY DETAILS.
......
—UNDERSTOOD. I'LL KEEP AN EYE OUT.
YOU SEEM GENUINELY CONCERNED FOR LIA.
—NOW COMES THE REST.
I'LL TRY A DIFFERENT APPROACH THAN BEFORE.

A spectacular death his second time around. And thus, a new chapter commences.

With Subaru's struggle, the real charm of *Re:ZERO* begins.

The only ability Subaru Natsuki gets when he's summoned to another world is time travel via his own death. But to save her, he'll die as many times as it takes.

Re:ZERO -Starting Life in Another World-

A Week at the Mansion

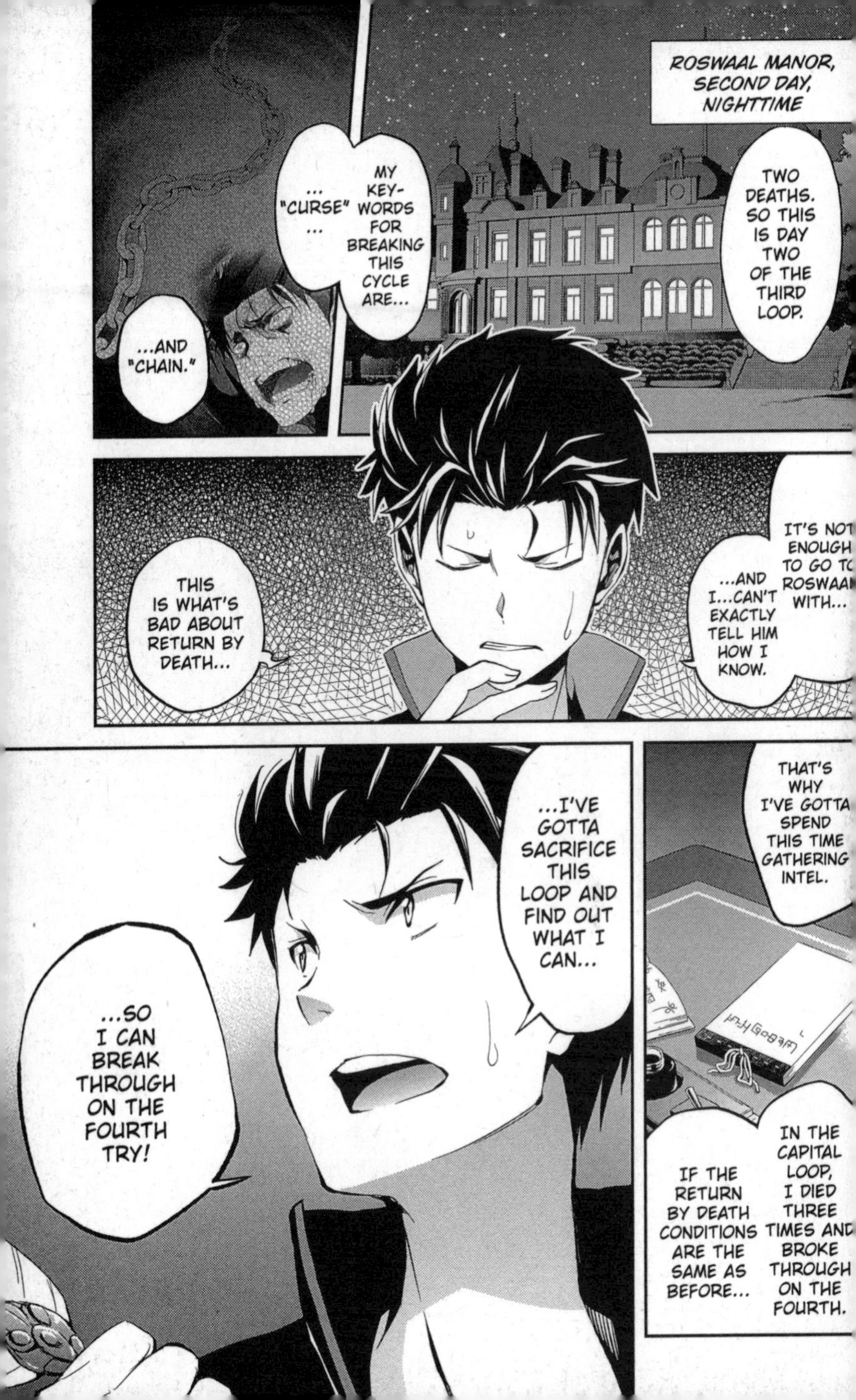
ROSWAAL MANOR, SECOND DAY, NIGHTTIME
TWO DEATHS. SO THIS IS DAY TWO OF THE THIRD LOOP.
MY KEY-WORDS FOR BREAKING THIS CYCLE ARE...
... "CURSE" ...
...AND "CHAIN."
IT'S NOT ENOUGH TO GO TO ROSWAAL WITH...
...AND I...CAN'T EXACTLY TELL HIM HOW I KNOW.
THIS IS WHAT'S BAD ABOUT RETURN BY DEATH...
THAT'S WHY I'VE GOTTA SPEND THIS TIME GATHERING INTEL.
IN THE CAPITAL LOOP, I DIED THREE TIMES AND BROKE THROUGH ON THE FOURTH.
IF THE RETURN BY DEATH CONDITIONS ARE THE SAME AS BEFORE...
...I'VE GOTTA SACRIFICE THIS LOOP AND FIND OUT WHAT I CAN...
...SO I CAN BREAK THROUGH ON THE FOURTH TRY!

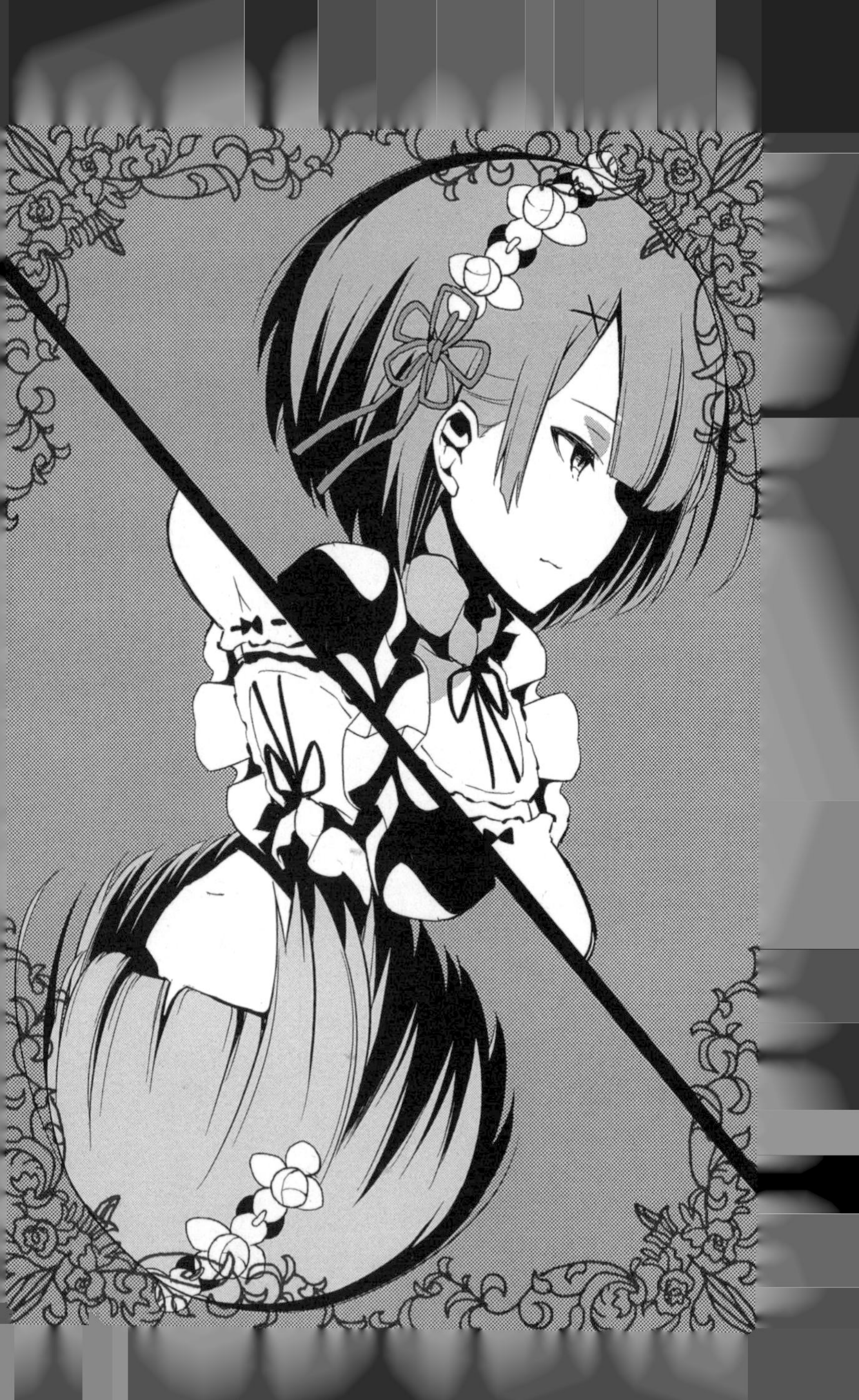

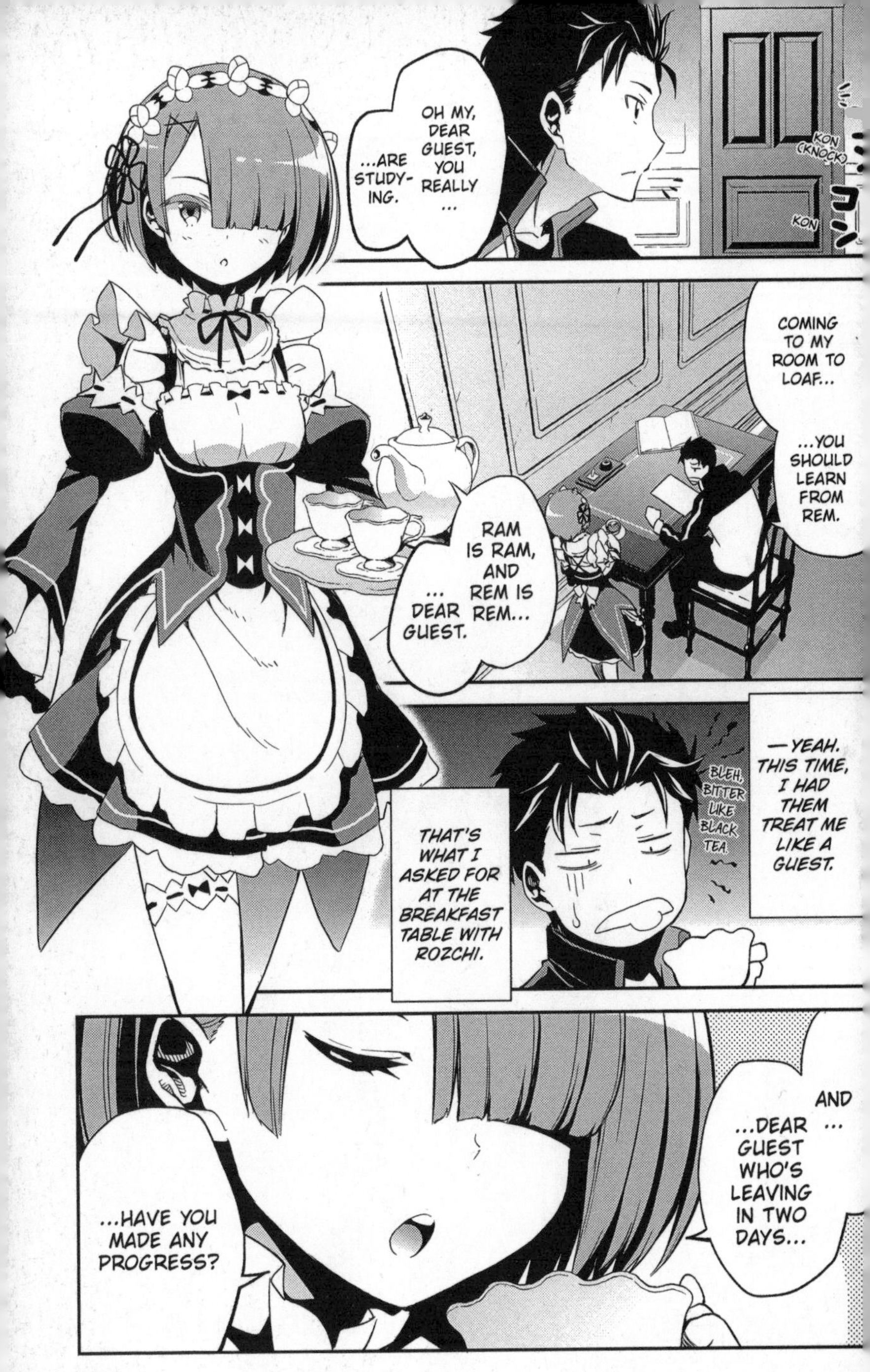
KON (KNOCK)
KON
OH MY, DEAR GUEST, YOU REALLY ...
...ARE STUDYING.
COMING TO MY ROOM TO LOAF...
...YOU SHOULD LEARN FROM REM.
RAM IS RAM, AND REM IS REM...
... DEAR GUEST.
—YEAH. THIS TIME, I HAD THEM TREAT ME LIKE A GUEST.
BLEH, BITTER LIKE BLACK TEA.
THAT'S WHAT I ASKED FOR AT THE BREAKFAST TABLE WITH ROZCHI.
AND ...
...DEAR GUEST WHO'S LEAVING IN TWO DAYS...
...HAVE YOU MADE ANY PROGRESS?

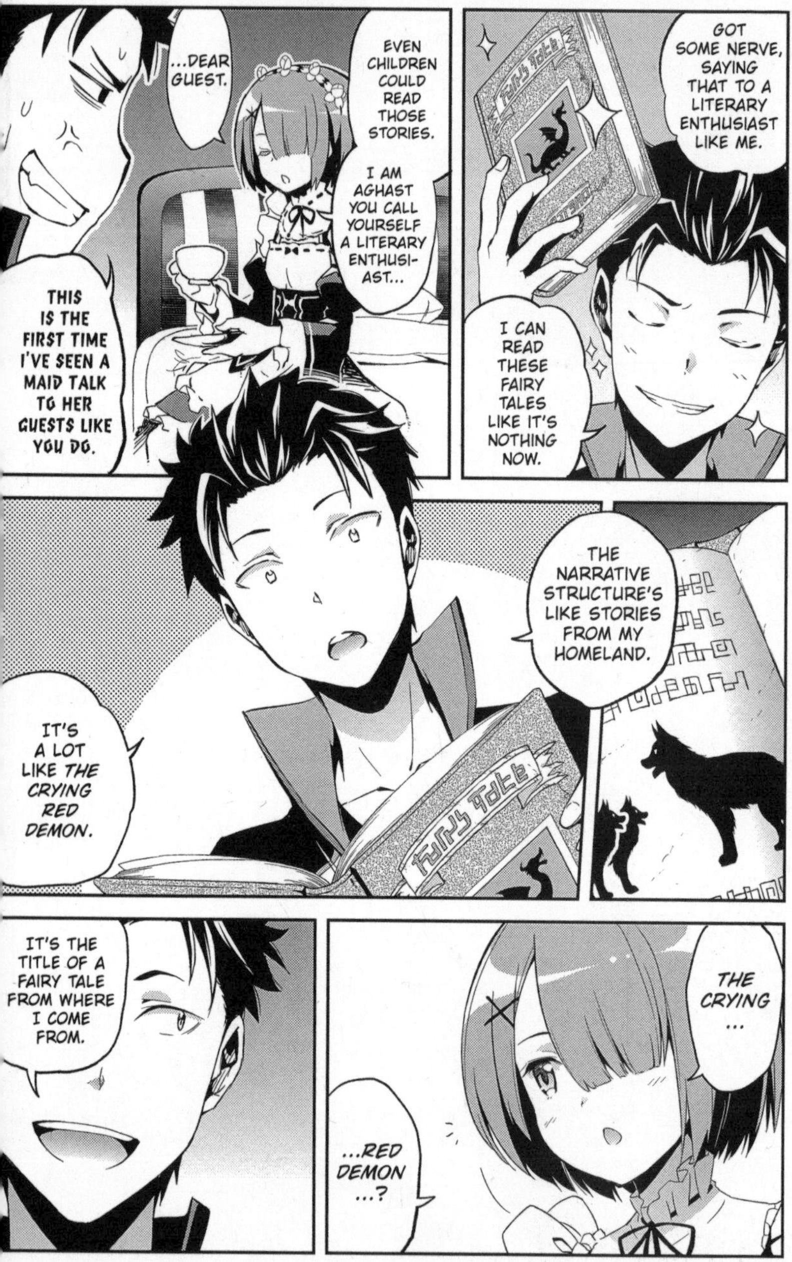
GOT SOME NERVE, SAYING THAT TO A LITERARY ENTHUSIAST LIKE ME.
I CAN READ THESE FAIRY TALES LIKE IT'S NOTHING NOW.
EVEN CHILDREN COULD READ THOSE STORIES.
...DEAR GUEST.
I AM AGHAST YOU CALL YOURSELF A LITERARY ENTHUSI-AST...
THIS IS THE FIRST TIME I'VE SEEN A MAID TALK TO HER GUESTS LIKE YOU DO.
THE NARRATIVE STRUCTURE'S LIKE STORIES FROM MY HOMELAND.
IT'S A LOT LIKE *THE CRYING RED DEMON*.
*THE CRYING* ...
*...RED DEMON ...?*
IT'S THE TITLE OF A FAIRY TALE FROM WHERE I COME FROM.

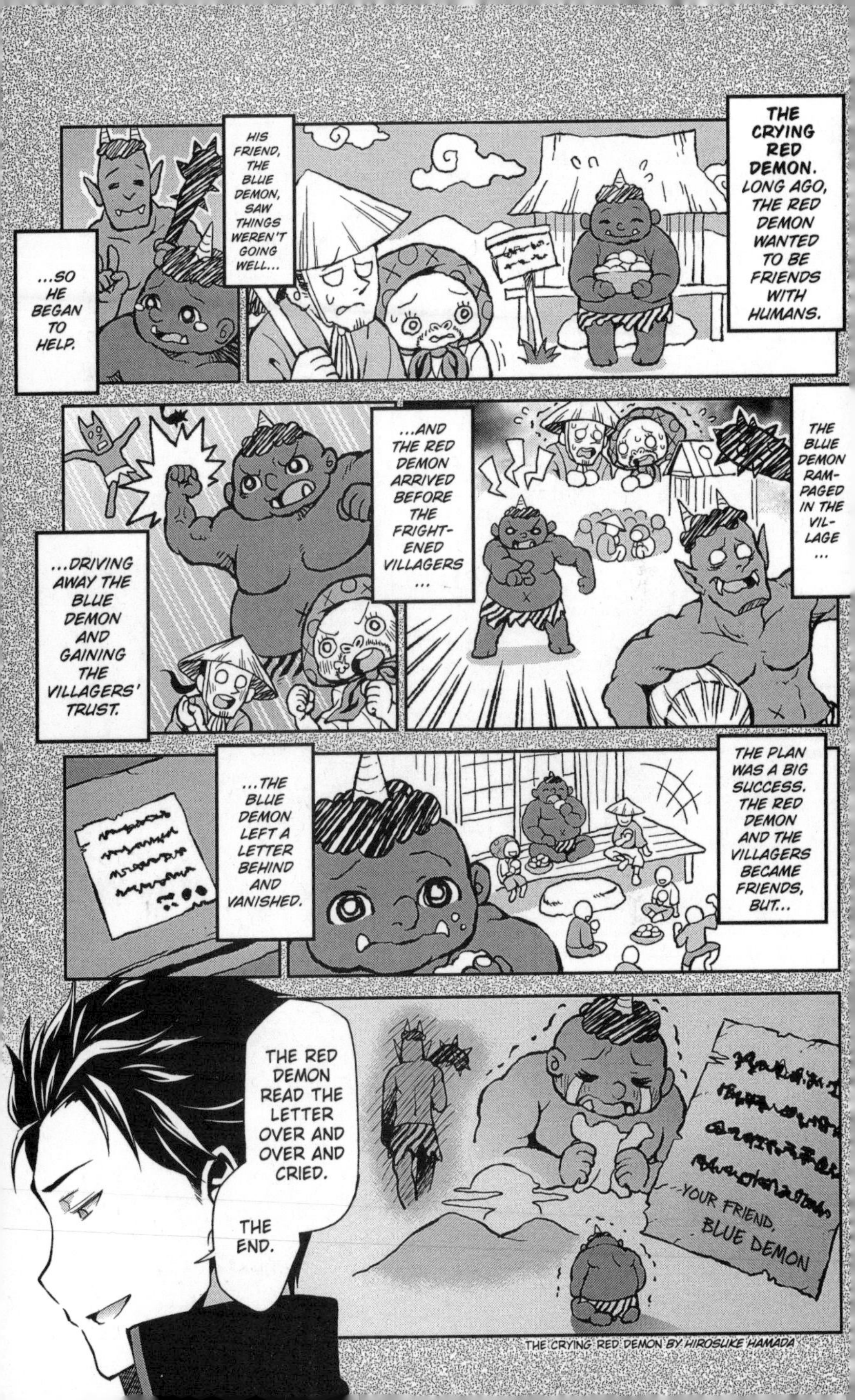
THE CRYING RED DEMON. LONG AGO, THE RED DEMON WANTED TO BE FRIENDS WITH HUMANS.
HIS FRIEND, THE BLUE DEMON, SAW THINGS WEREN'T GOING WELL...
...SO HE BEGAN TO HELP.
THE BLUE DEMON RAMPAGED IN THE VILLAGE...
...AND THE RED DEMON ARRIVED BEFORE THE FRIGHTENED VILLAGERS...
...DRIVING AWAY THE BLUE DEMON AND GAINING THE VILLAGERS' TRUST.
THE PLAN WAS A BIG SUCCESS. THE RED DEMON AND THE VILLAGERS BECAME FRIENDS, BUT...
...THE BLUE DEMON LEFT A LETTER BEHIND AND VANISHED.
YOUR FRIEND, BLUE DEMON
THE RED DEMON READ THE LETTER OVER AND OVER AND CRIED.
THE END.

THE CRYING RED DEMON BY HIROSUKE HAMADA

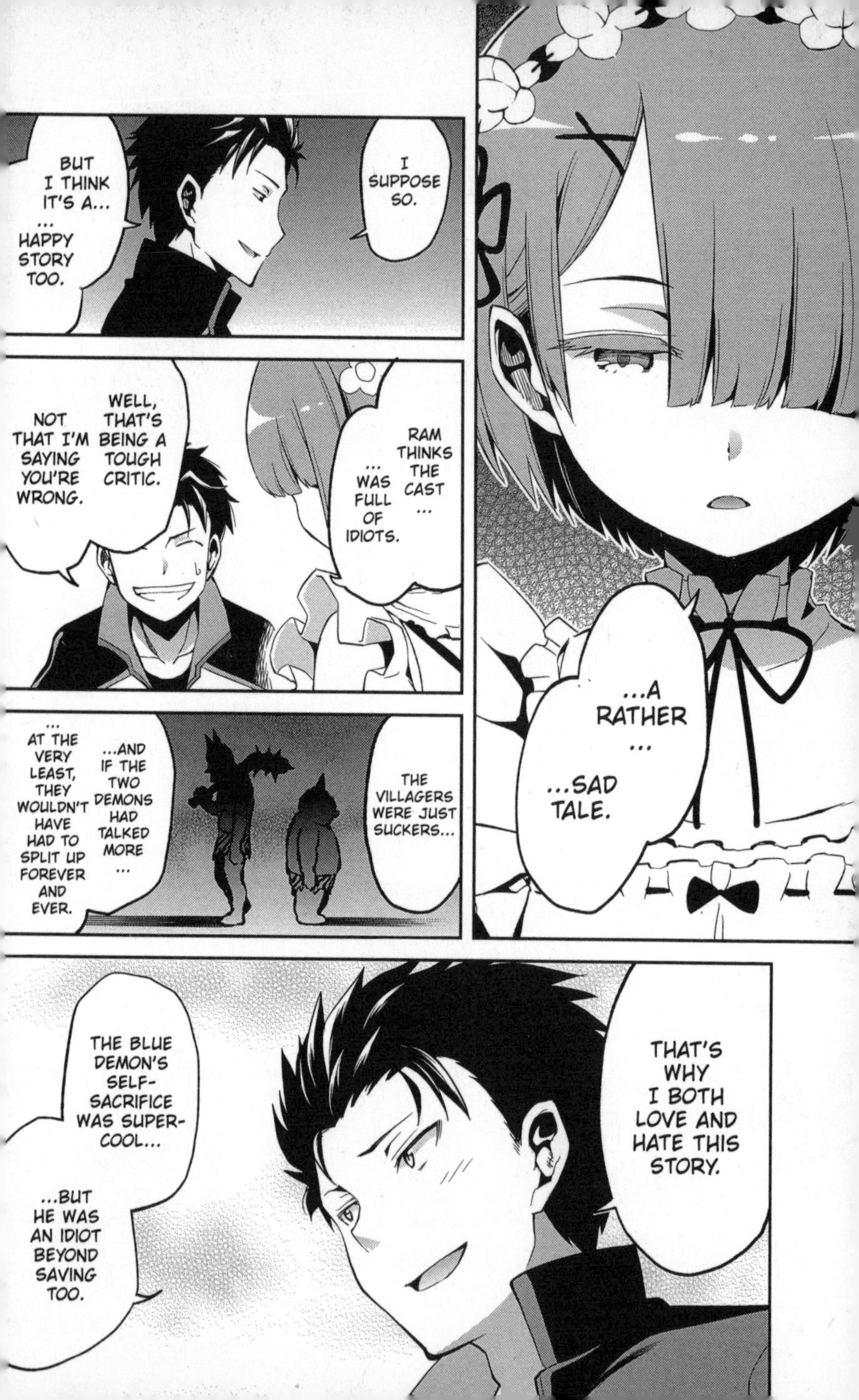
...A RATHER ... ...SAD TALE.
I SUPPOSE SO.
BUT I THINK IT'S A... ... HAPPY STORY TOO.
RAM THINKS THE CAST ...
... WAS FULL OF IDIOTS.
WELL, THAT'S BEING A TOUGH CRITIC.
NOT THAT I'M SAYING YOU'RE WRONG.
THE VILLAGERS WERE JUST SUCKERS...
...AND IF THE TWO DEMONS HAD TALKED MORE ...
... AT THE VERY LEAST, THEY WOULDN'T HAVE HAD TO SPLIT UP FOREVER AND EVER.
THAT'S WHY I BOTH LOVE AND HATE THIS STORY.
THE BLUE DEMON'S SELF-SACRIFICE WAS SUPER-COOL...
...BUT HE WAS AN IDIOT BEYOND SAVING TOO.

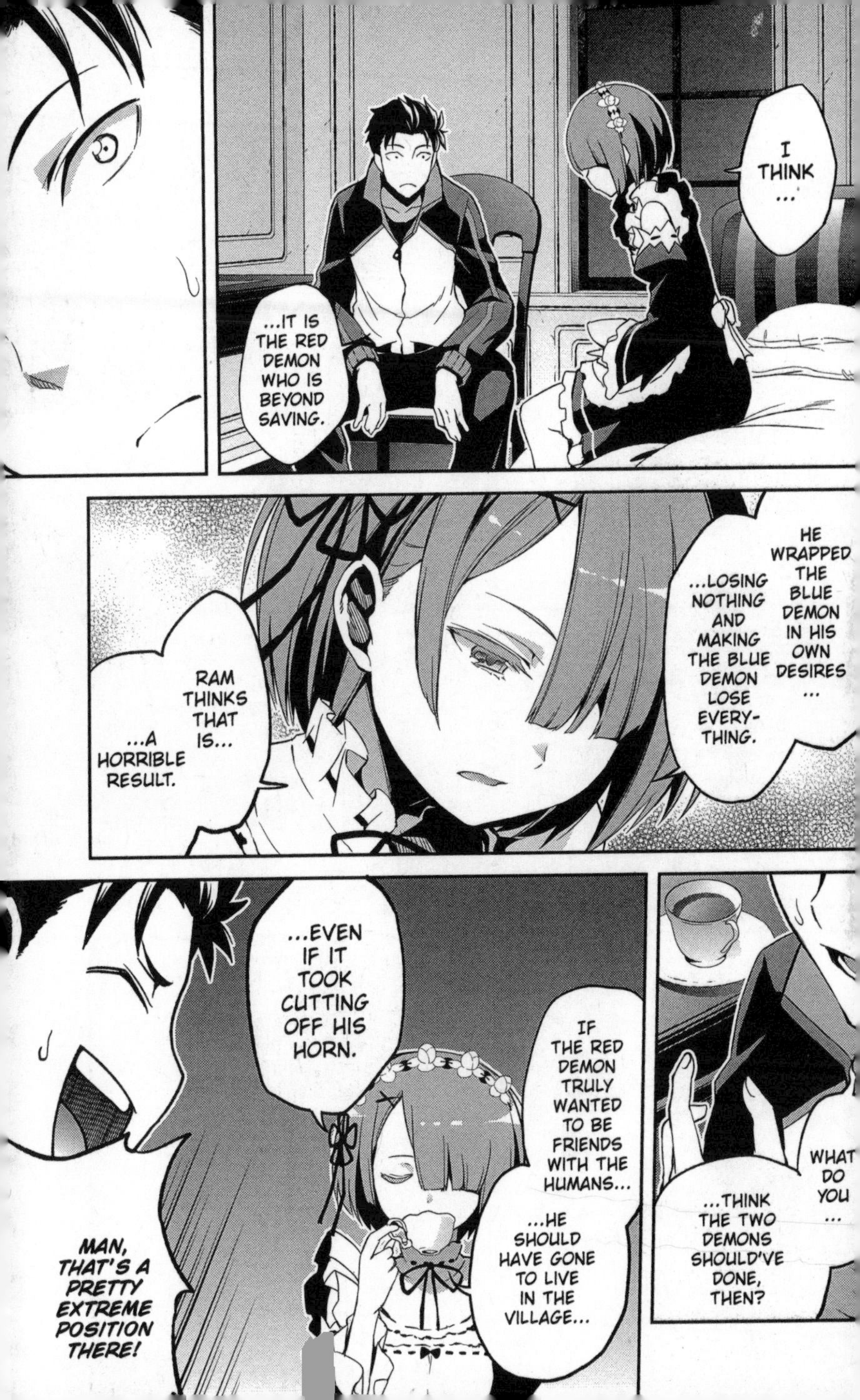
I THINK...
...IT IS THE RED DEMON WHO IS BEYOND SAVING.
HE WRAPPED THE BLUE DEMON IN HIS OWN DESIRES...
...LOSING NOTHING AND MAKING THE BLUE DEMON LOSE EVERYTHING.
RAM THINKS THAT IS...
...A HORRIBLE RESULT.
WHAT DO YOU...
...THINK THE TWO DEMONS SHOULD'VE DONE, THEN?
IF THE RED DEMON TRULY WANTED TO BE FRIENDS WITH THE HUMANS...
...HE SHOULD HAVE GONE TO LIVE IN THE VILLAGE...
...EVEN IF IT TOOK CUTTING OFF HIS HORN.
MAN, THAT'S A PRETTY EXTREME POSITION THERE!

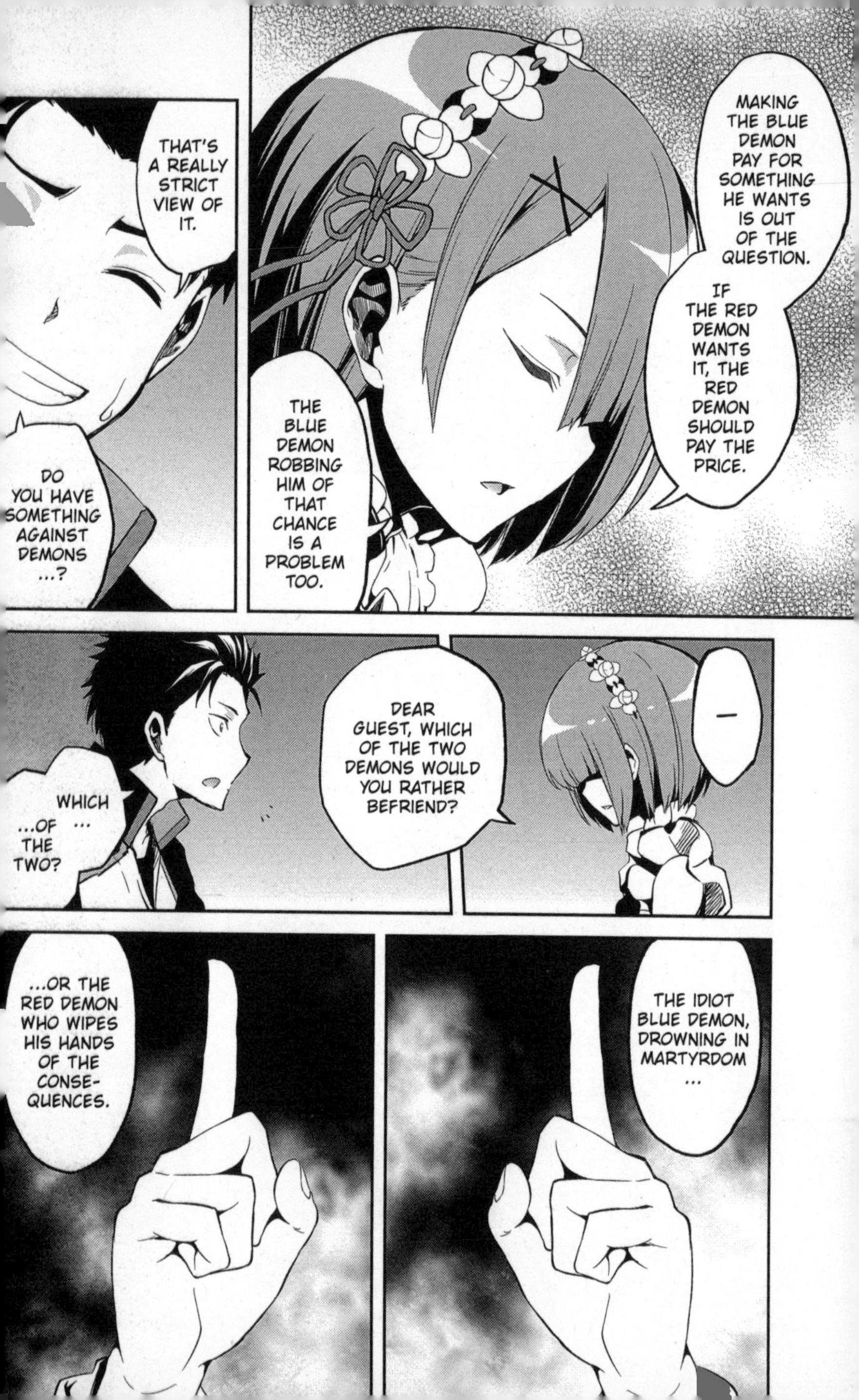
MAKING THE BLUE DEMON PAY FOR SOMETHING HE WANTS IS OUT OF THE QUESTION.
IF THE RED DEMON WANTS IT, THE RED DEMON SHOULD PAY THE PRICE.
THE BLUE DEMON ROBBING HIM OF THAT CHANCE IS A PROBLEM TOO.
THAT'S A REALLY STRICT VIEW OF IT.
DO YOU HAVE SOMETHING AGAINST DEMONS ...?
—
DEAR GUEST, WHICH OF THE TWO DEMONS WOULD YOU RATHER BEFRIEND?
WHICH ... ...OF THE TWO?
THE IDIOT BLUE DEMON, DROWNING IN MARTYRDOM ...
...OR THE RED DEMON WHO WIPES HIS HANDS OF THE CONSE-QUENCES.

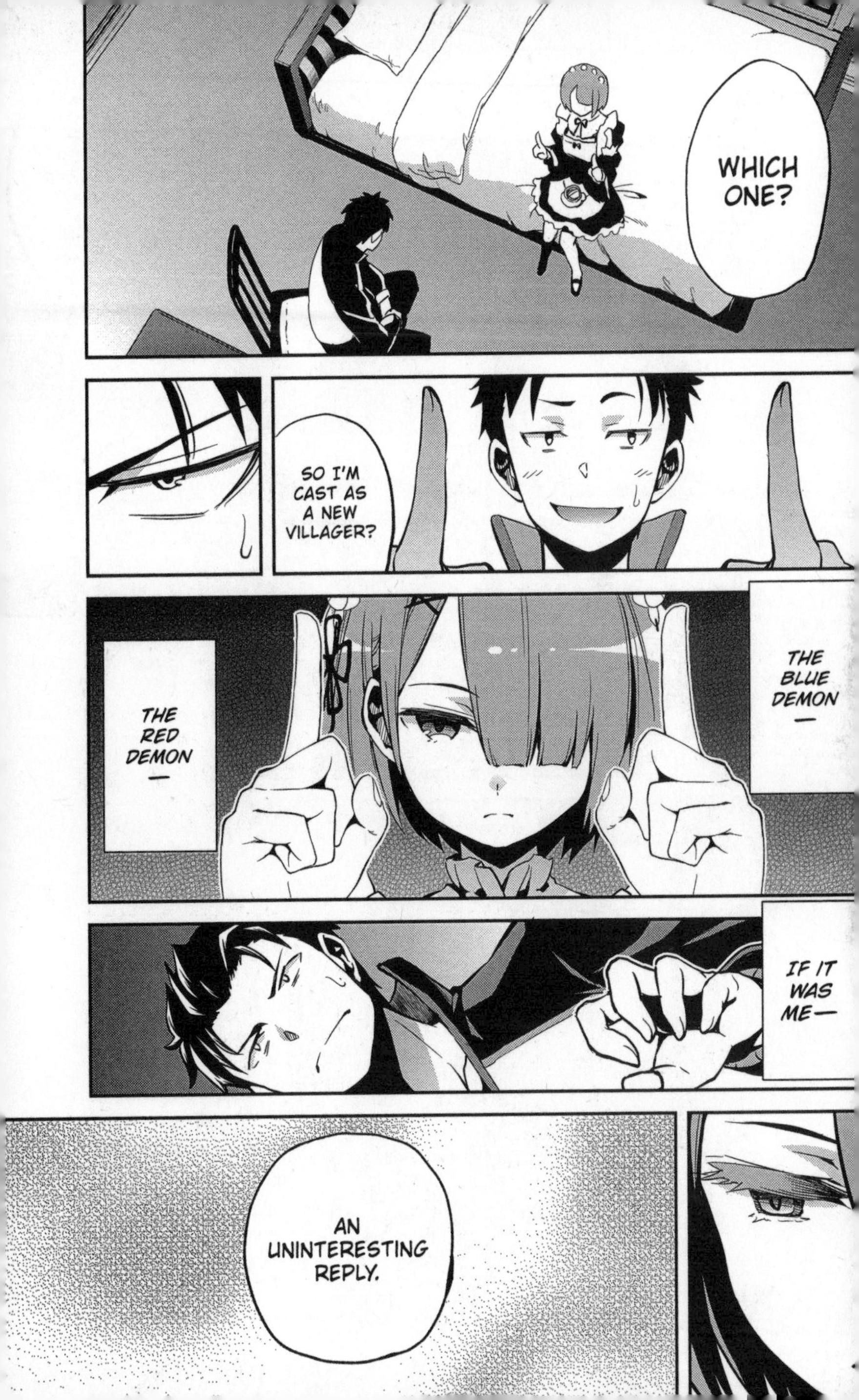
WHICH ONE?
SO I'M CAST AS A NEW VILLAGER?
THE BLUE DEMON—
THE RED DEMON—
IF IT WAS ME—
AN UNINTERESTING REPLY.

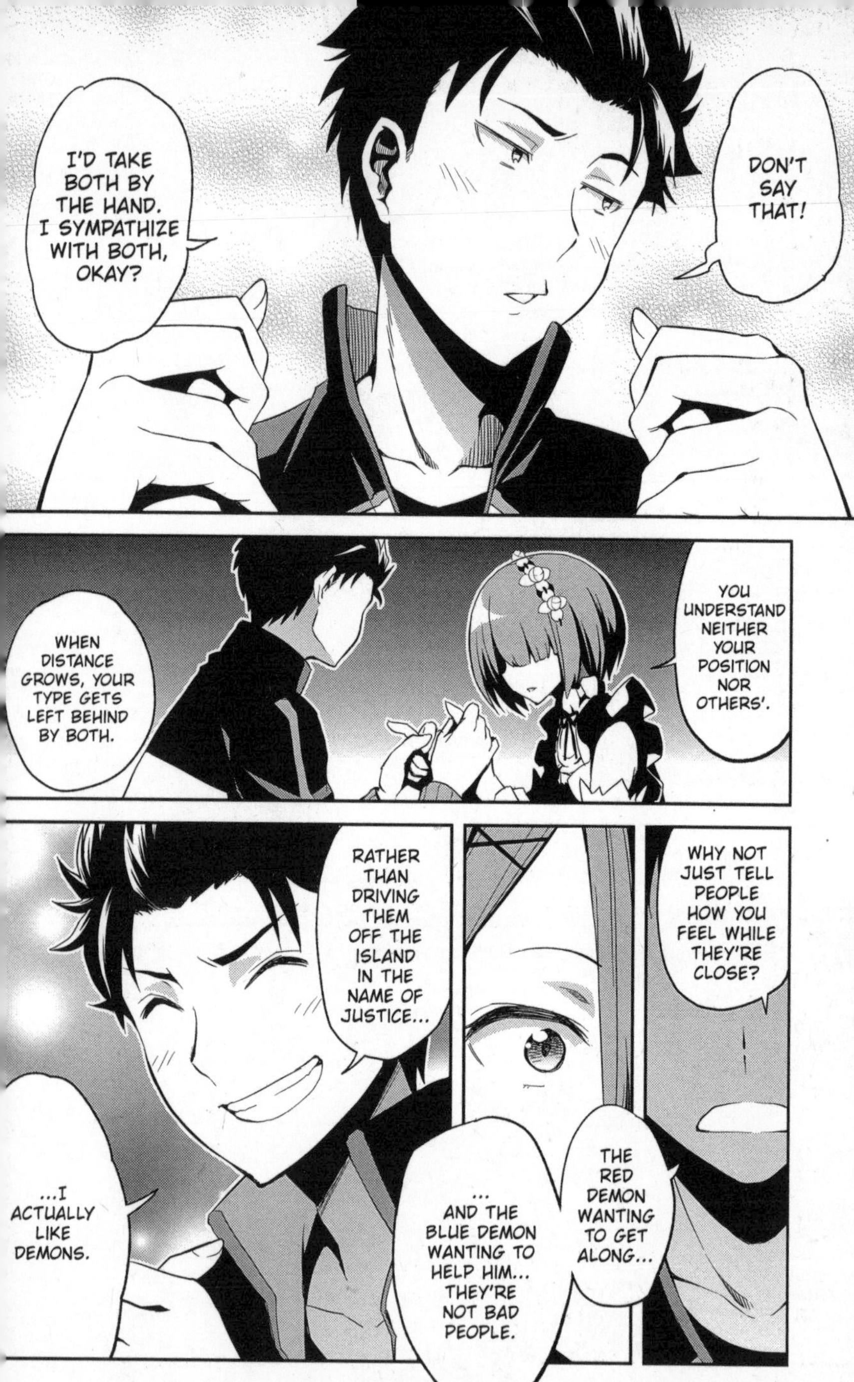
DON'T SAY THAT!
I'D TAKE BOTH BY THE HAND. I SYMPATHIZE WITH BOTH, OKAY?
YOU UNDERSTAND NEITHER YOUR POSITION NOR OTHERS'.
WHEN DISTANCE GROWS, YOUR TYPE GETS LEFT BEHIND BY BOTH.
WHY NOT JUST TELL PEOPLE HOW YOU FEEL WHILE THEY'RE CLOSE?
RATHER THAN DRIVING THEM OFF THE ISLAND IN THE NAME OF JUSTICE...
THE RED DEMON WANTING TO GET ALONG...
...AND THE BLUE DEMON WANTING TO HELP HIM... THEY'RE NOT BAD PEOPLE.
...I ACTUALLY LIKE DEMONS.

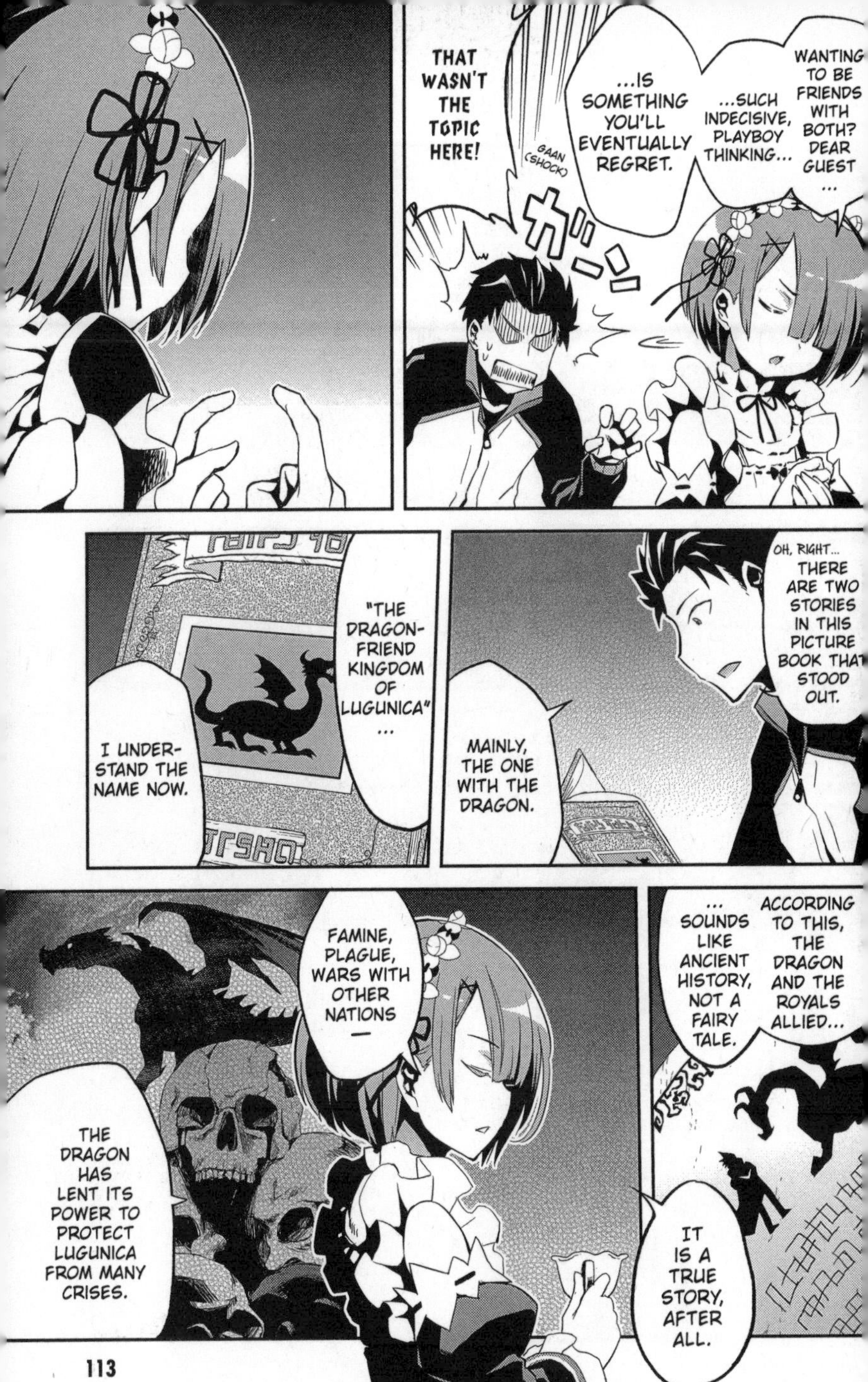
WANTING TO BE FRIENDS WITH BOTH? DEAR GUEST ...
...SUCH INDECISIVE, PLAYBOY THINKING...
...IS SOMETHING YOU'LL EVENTUALLY REGRET.
THAT WASN'T THE TOPIC HERE!
GAAN (SHOCK)
ガーン
OH, RIGHT... THERE ARE TWO STORIES IN THIS PICTURE BOOK THAT STOOD OUT.
MAINLY, THE ONE WITH THE DRAGON.
"THE DRAGON-FRIEND KINGDOM OF LUGUNICA" ...
I UNDERSTAND THE NAME NOW.
ACCORDING TO THIS, THE DRAGON AND THE ROYALS ALLIED...
... SOUNDS LIKE ANCIENT HISTORY, NOT A FAIRY TALE.
IT IS A TRUE STORY, AFTER ALL.
FAMINE, PLAGUE, WARS WITH OTHER NATIONS —
THE DRAGON HAS LENT ITS POWER TO PROTECT LUGUNICA FROM MANY CRISES.

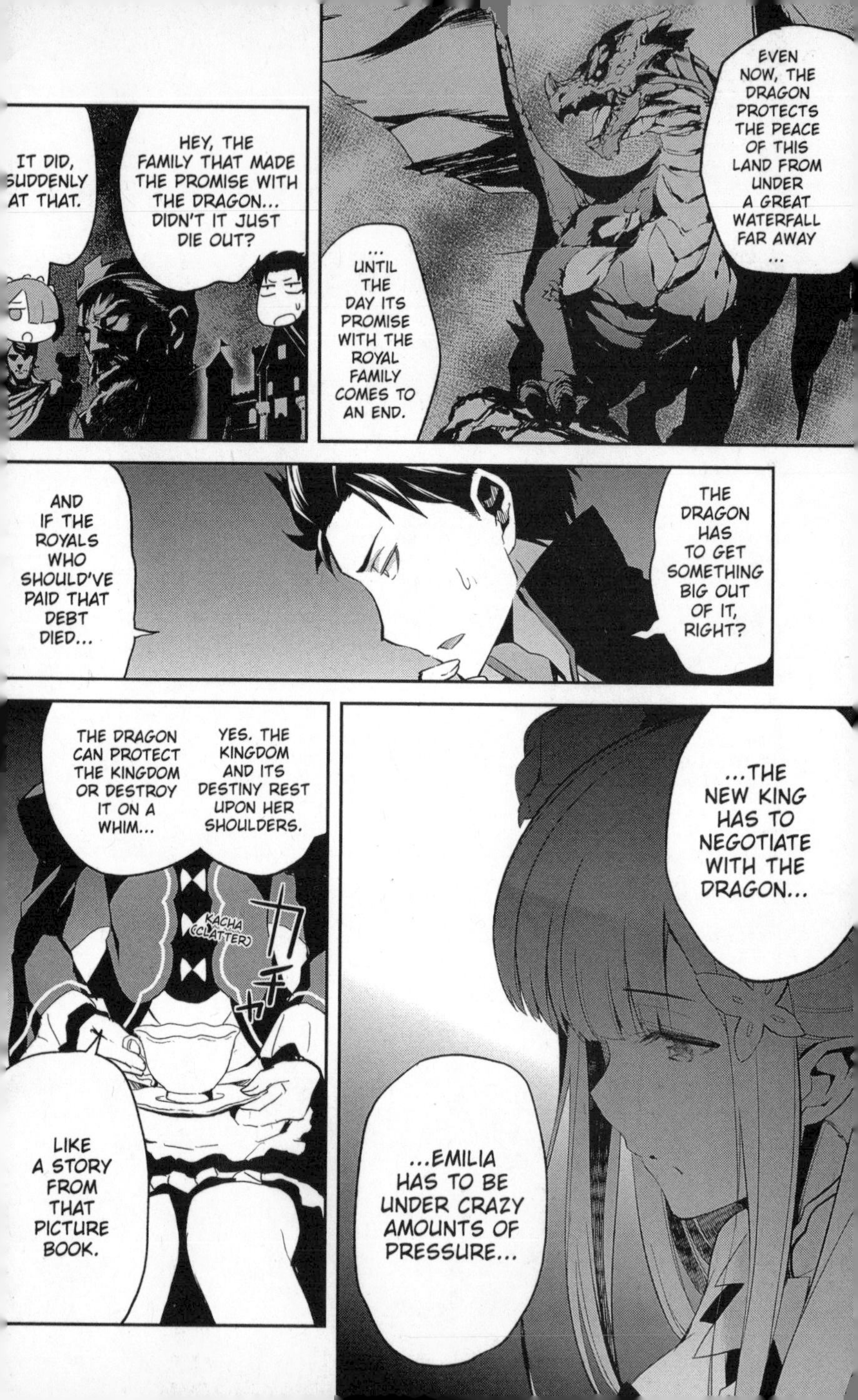
EVEN NOW, THE DRAGON PROTECTS THE PEACE OF THIS LAND FROM UNDER A GREAT WATERFALL FAR AWAY...
...UNTIL THE DAY ITS PROMISE WITH THE ROYAL FAMILY COMES TO AN END.
HEY, THE FAMILY THAT MADE THE PROMISE WITH THE DRAGON... DIDN'T IT JUST DIE OUT?
IT DID, SUDDENLY AT THAT.
THE DRAGON HAS TO GET SOMETHING BIG OUT OF IT, RIGHT?
AND IF THE ROYALS WHO SHOULD'VE PAID THAT DEBT DIED...
...THE NEW KING HAS TO NEGOTIATE WITH THE DRAGON...
...EMILIA HAS TO BE UNDER CRAZY AMOUNTS OF PRESSURE...
YES. THE KINGDOM AND ITS DESTINY REST UPON HER SHOULDERS.
THE DRAGON CAN PROTECT THE KINGDOM OR DESTROY IT ON A WHIM...
カチャ
KACHA (CLATTER)
LIKE A STORY FROM THAT PICTURE BOOK.

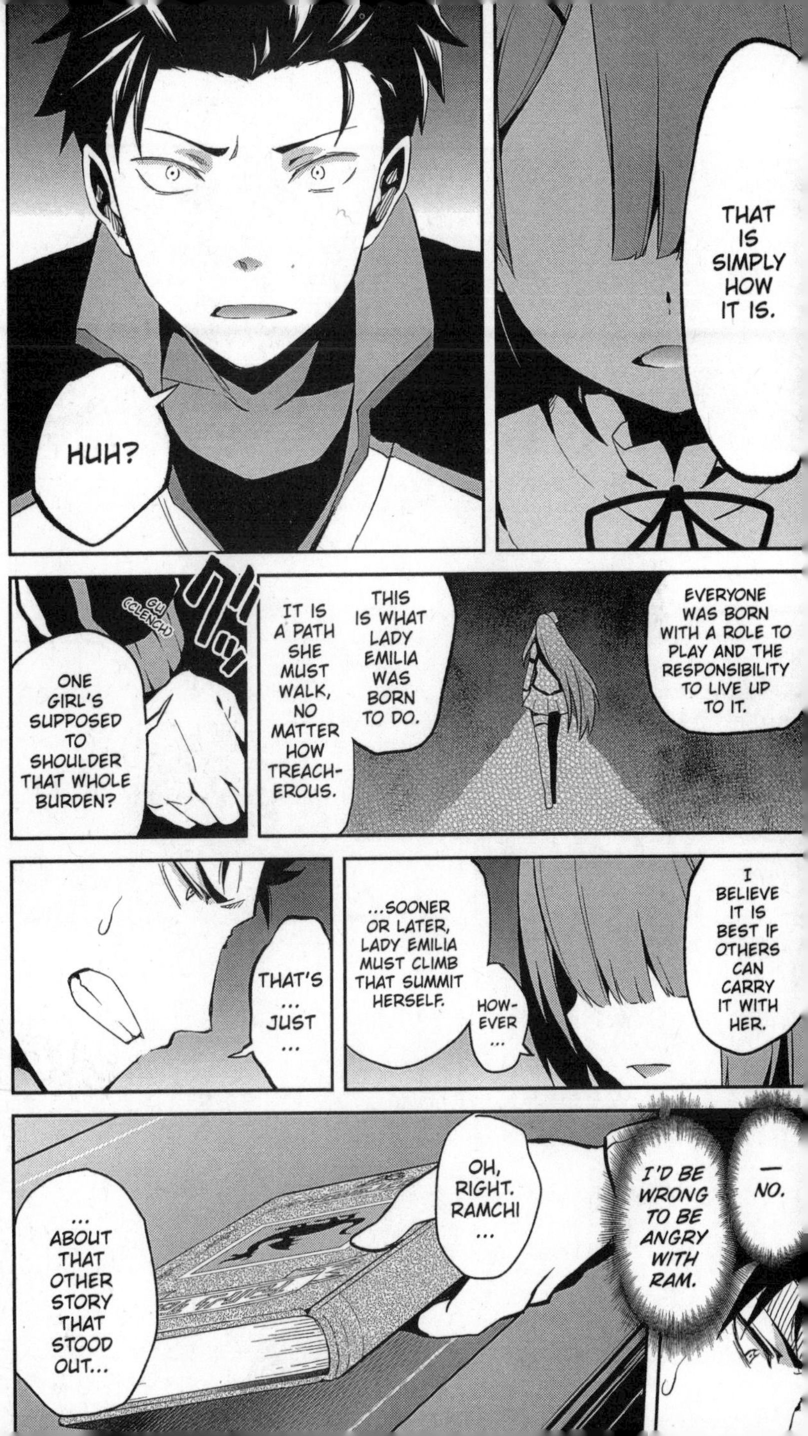
THAT IS SIMPLY HOW IT IS.
HUH?
EVERYONE WAS BORN WITH A ROLE TO PLAY AND THE RESPONSIBILITY TO LIVE UP TO IT.
THIS IS WHAT LADY EMILIA WAS BORN TO DO.
IT IS A PATH SHE MUST WALK, NO MATTER HOW TREACH-EROUS.
GU (CLENCH)
ONE GIRL'S SUPPOSED TO SHOULDER THAT WHOLE BURDEN?
I BELIEVE IT IS BEST IF OTHERS CAN CARRY IT WITH HER.
HOW-EVER...
...SOONER OR LATER, LADY EMILIA MUST CLIMB THAT SUMMIT HERSELF.
THAT'S... JUST...
—NO.
I'D BE WRONG TO BE ANGRY WITH RAM.
OH, RIGHT. RAMCHI...
...ABOUT THAT OTHER STORY THAT STOOD OUT...

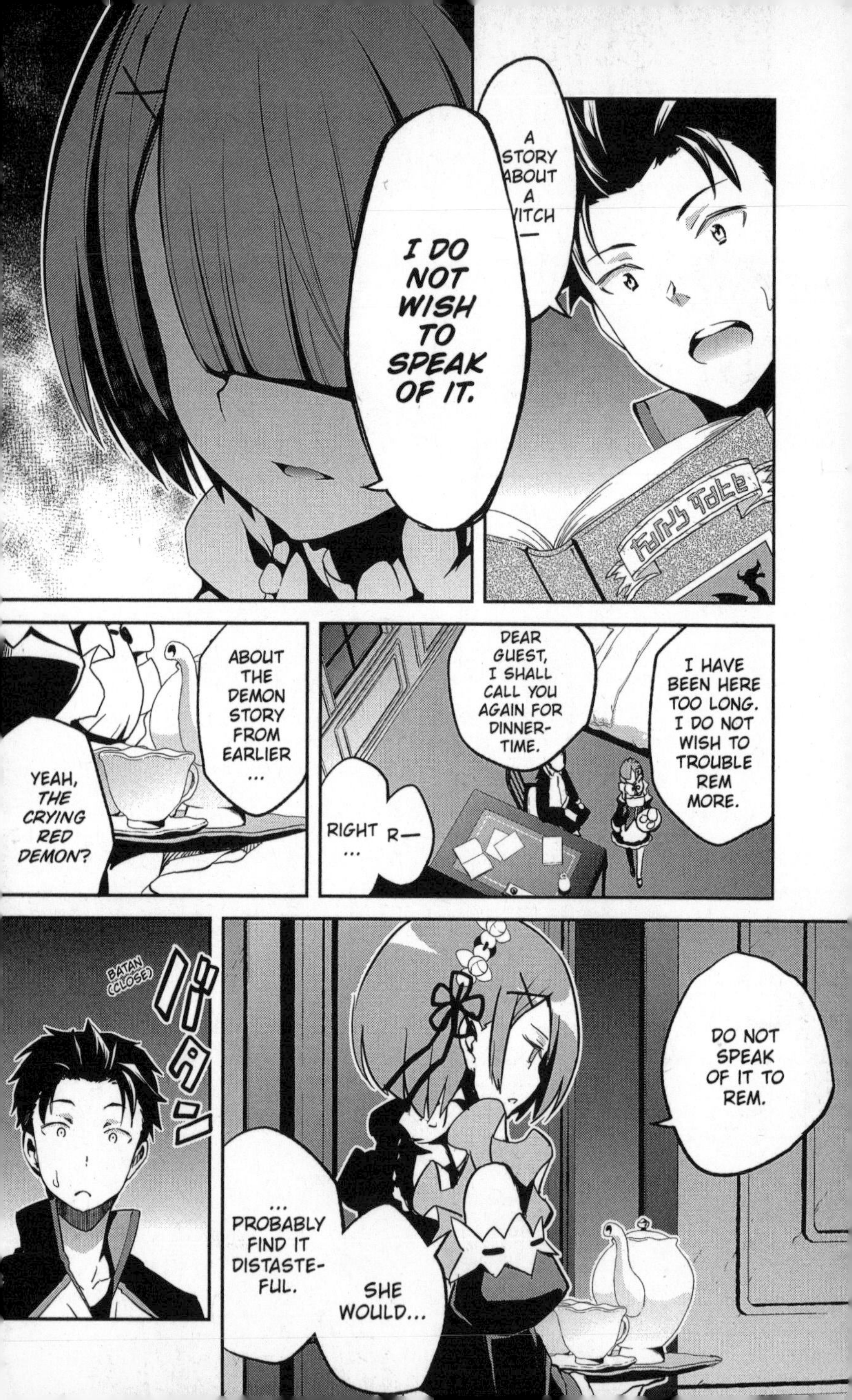
A STORY ABOUT A WITCH—
I DO NOT WISH TO SPEAK OF IT.
I HAVE BEEN HERE TOO LONG. I DO NOT WISH TO TROUBLE REM MORE.
DEAR GUEST, I SHALL CALL YOU AGAIN FOR DINNER-TIME.
R—
RIGHT ...
ABOUT THE DEMON STORY FROM EARLIER ...
YEAH, THE CRYING RED DEMON?
DO NOT SPEAK OF IT TO REM.
SHE WOULD...
... PROBABLY FIND IT DISTASTE-FUL.
BATAN (CLOSE)

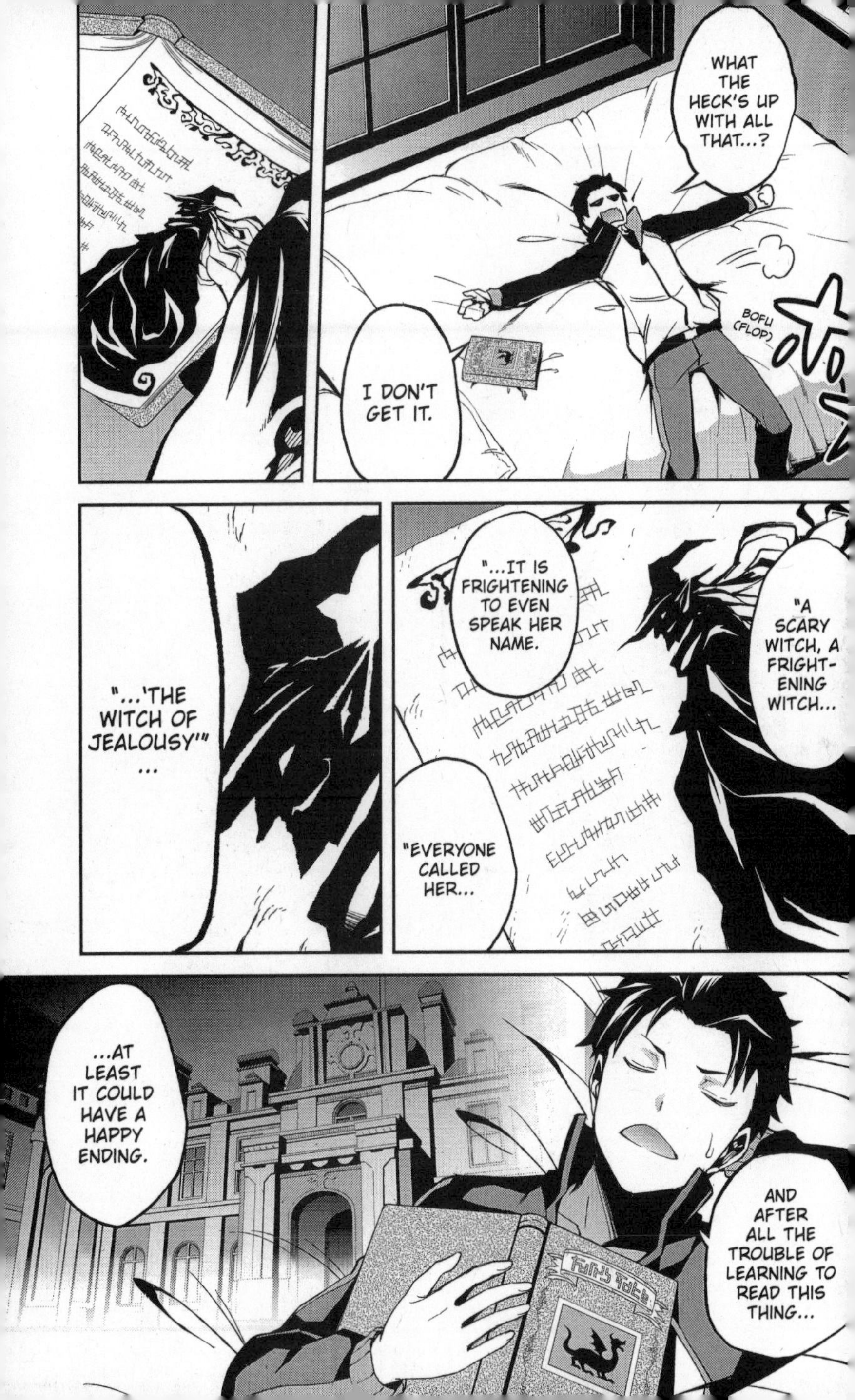
WHAT THE HECK'S UP WITH ALL THAT...?
BOFU (FLOP)
I DON'T GET IT.
"A SCARY WITCH, A FRIGHT-ENING WITCH...
"...IT IS FRIGHTENING TO EVEN SPEAK HER NAME.
"EVERYONE CALLED HER...
"...'THE WITCH OF JEALOUSY'"...
AND AFTER ALL THE TROUBLE OF LEARNING TO READ THIS THING...
...AT LEAST IT COULD HAVE A HAPPY ENDING.

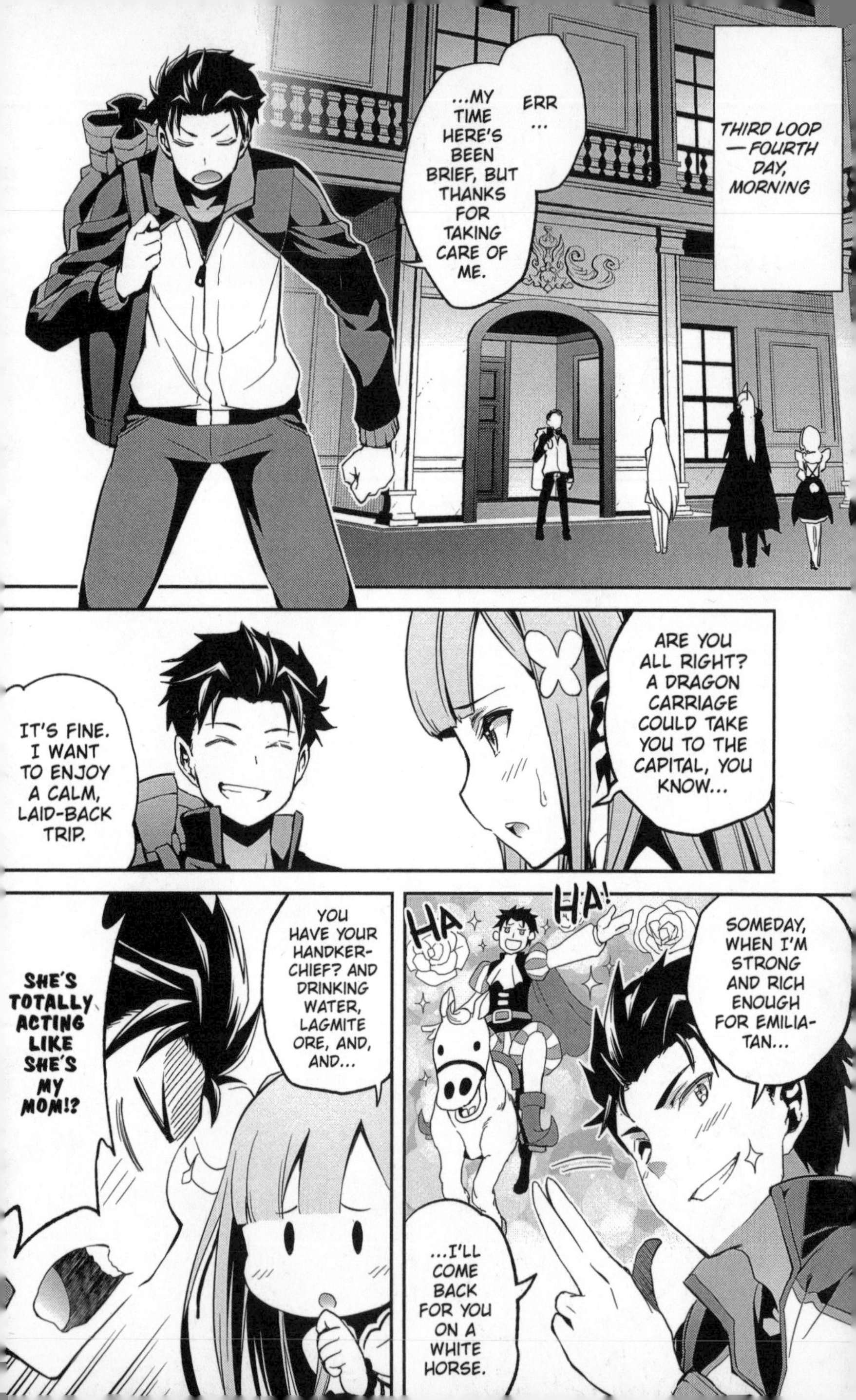
THIRD LOOP —FOURTH DAY, MORNING
ERR...
...MY TIME HERE'S BEEN BRIEF, BUT THANKS FOR TAKING CARE OF ME.
ARE YOU ALL RIGHT? A DRAGON CARRIAGE COULD TAKE YOU TO THE CAPITAL, YOU KNOW...
IT'S FINE. I WANT TO ENJOY A CALM, LAID-BACK TRIP.
SOMEDAY, WHEN I'M STRONG AND RICH ENOUGH FOR EMILIA-TAN...
HA HA!
...I'LL COME BACK FOR YOU ON A WHITE HORSE.
YOU HAVE YOUR HANDKER-CHIEF? AND DRINKING WATER, LAGMITE ORE, AND, AND...
SHE'S TOTALLY ACTING LIKE SHE'S MY MOM!?

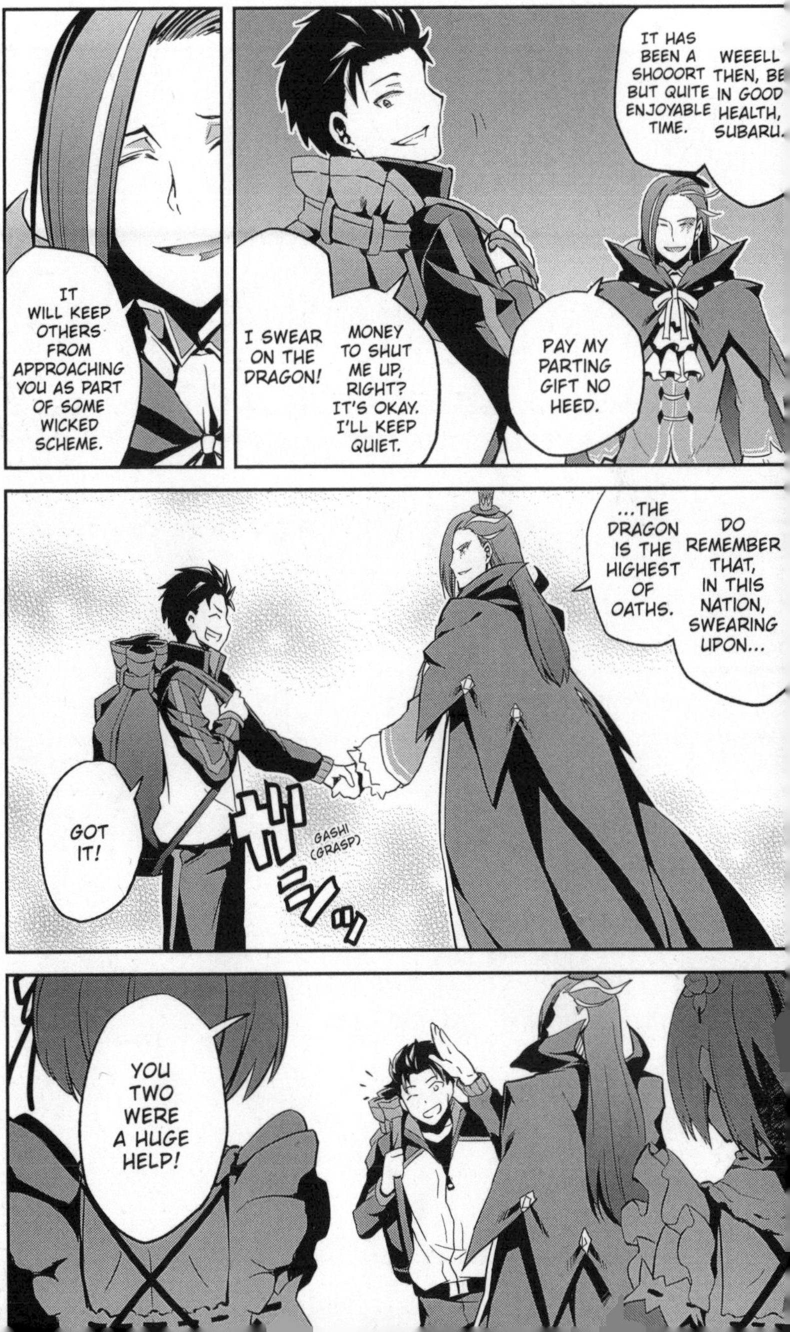
WEEELL THEN, BE IN GOOD HEALTH, SUBARU.
IT HAS BEEN A SHOOORT BUT QUITE ENJOYABLE TIME.
PAY MY PARTING GIFT NO HEED.
MONEY TO SHUT ME UP, RIGHT? IT'S OKAY. I'LL KEEP QUIET.
I SWEAR ON THE DRAGON!
IT WILL KEEP OTHERS FROM APPROACHING YOU AS PART OF SOME WICKED SCHEME.
DO REMEMBER THAT, IN THIS NATION, SWEARING UPON...
...THE DRAGON IS THE HIGHEST OF OATHS.
GASHI (GRASP)
GOT IT!
YOU TWO WERE A HUGE HELP!

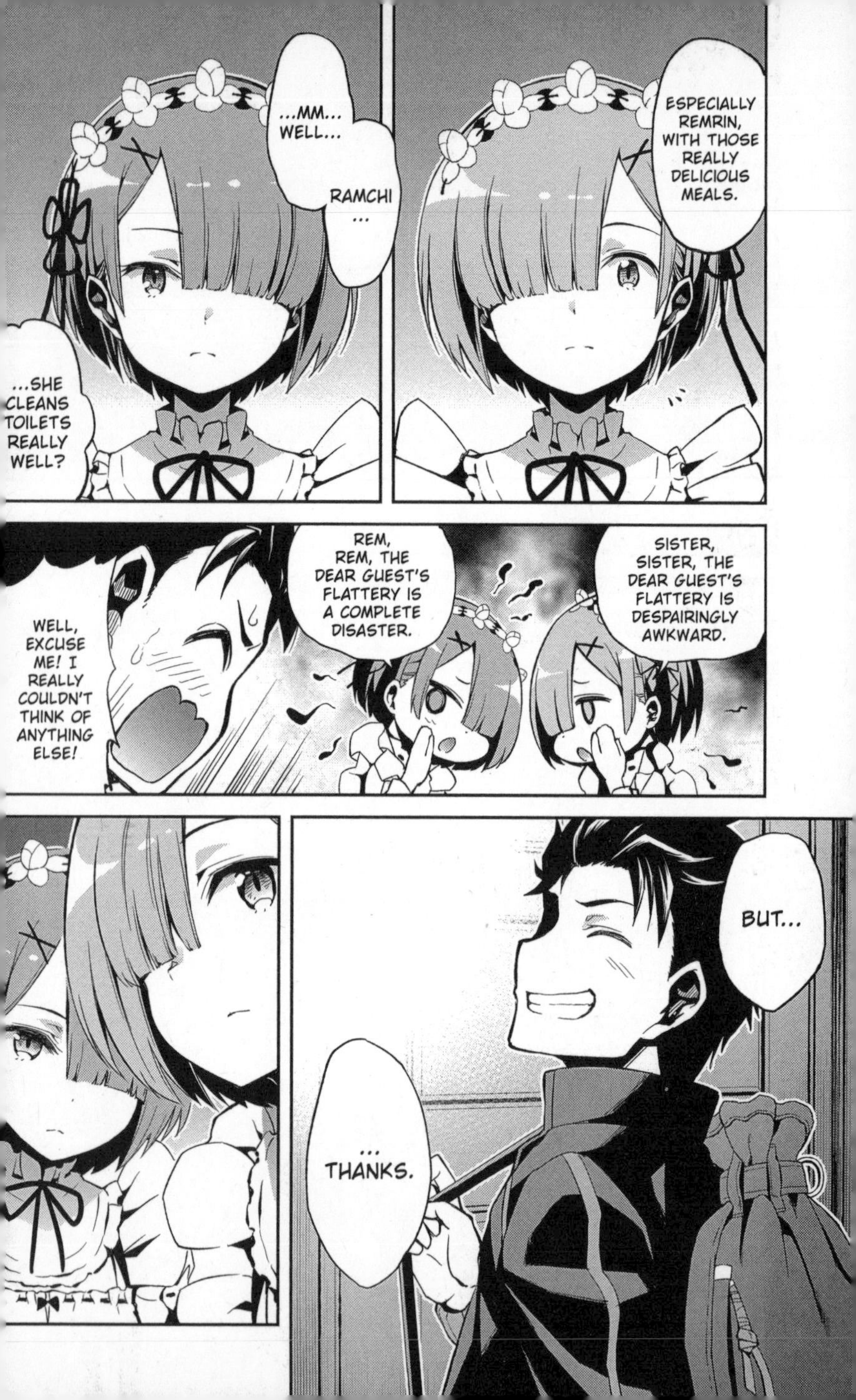
ESPECIALLY REMRIN, WITH THOSE REALLY DELICIOUS MEALS.
...MM... WELL...
RAMCHI ...
...SHE CLEANS TOILETS REALLY WELL?
SISTER, SISTER, THE DEAR GUEST'S FLATTERY IS DESPAIRINGLY AWKWARD.
REM, REM, THE DEAR GUEST'S FLATTERY IS A COMPLETE DISASTER.
WELL, EXCUSE ME! I REALLY COULDN'T THINK OF ANYTHING ELSE!
BUT...
... THANKS.

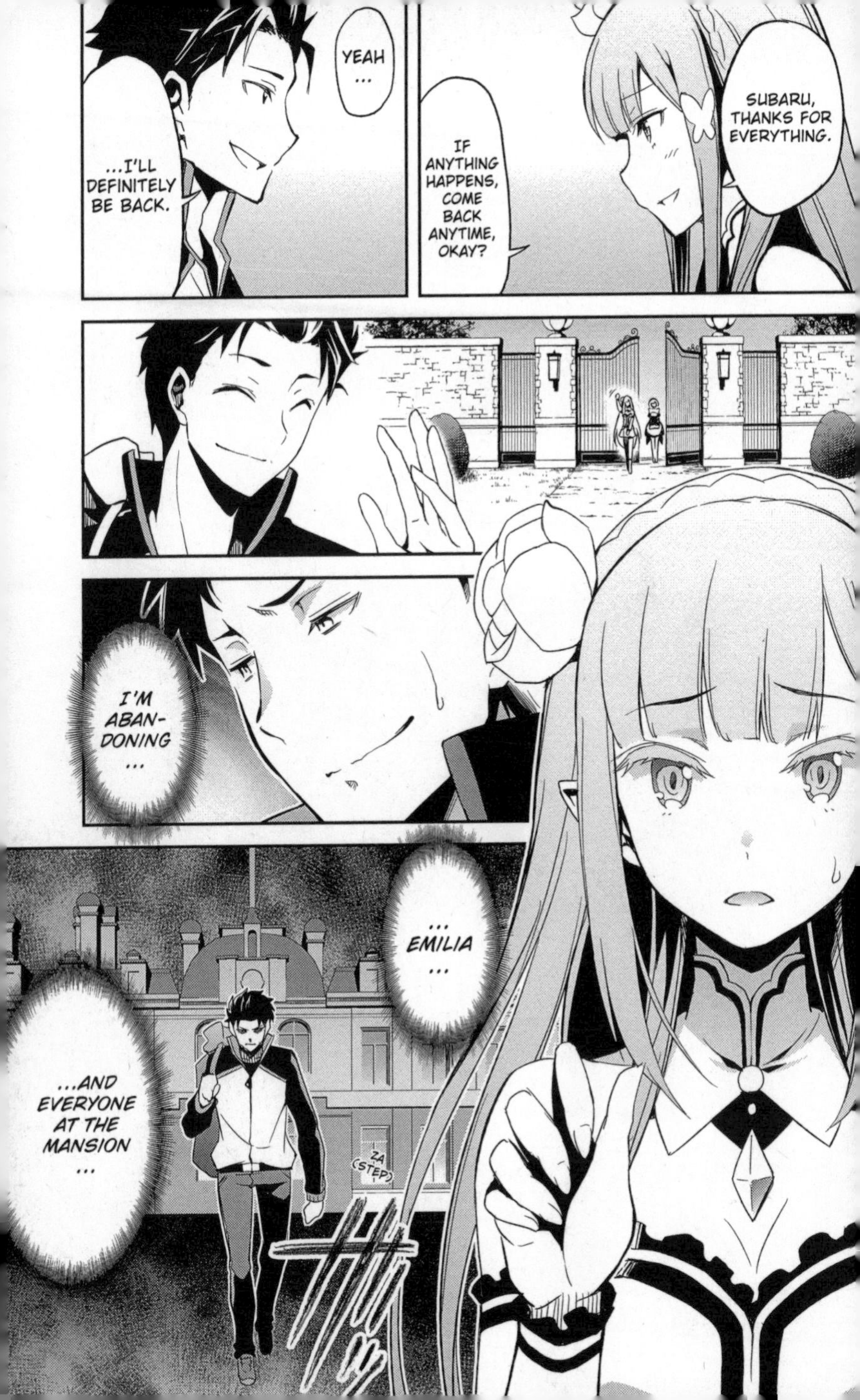
SUBARU, THANKS FOR EVERYTHING.
IF ANYTHING HAPPENS, COME BACK ANYTIME, OKAY?
YEAH ...
...I'LL DEFINITELY BE BACK.
I'M ABAN-DONING ...
... EMILIA ...
...AND EVERYONE AT THE MANSION ...
ZA (STEP)

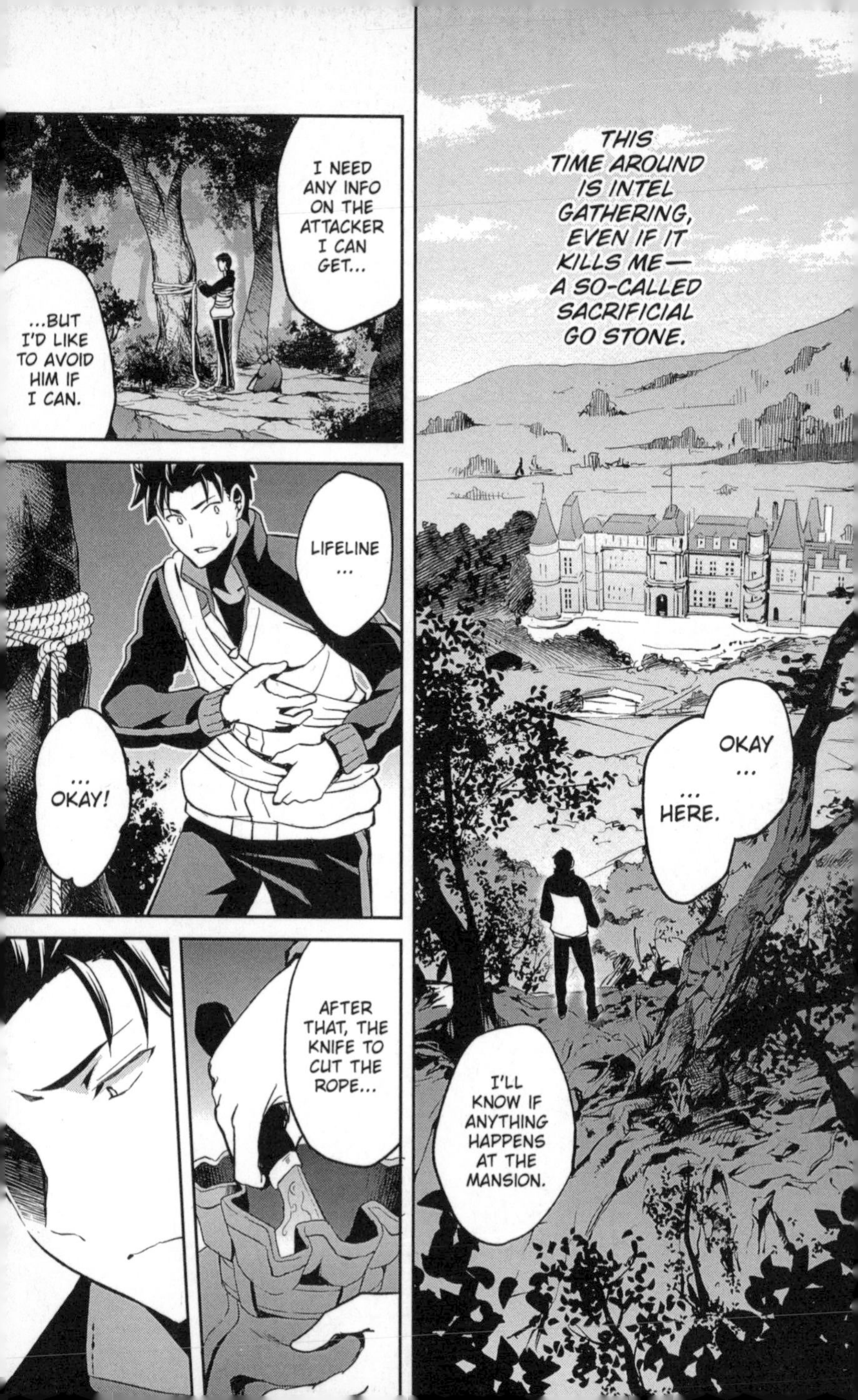
THIS TIME AROUND IS INTEL GATHERING, EVEN IF IT KILLS ME— A SO-CALLED SACRIFICIAL GO STONE.
OKAY... ...HERE.
I'LL KNOW IF ANYTHING HAPPENS AT THE MANSION.
I NEED ANY INFO ON THE ATTACKER I CAN GET...
...BUT I'D LIKE TO AVOID HIM IF I CAN.
LIFELINE...
...OKAY!
AFTER THAT, THE KNIFE TO CUT THE ROPE...

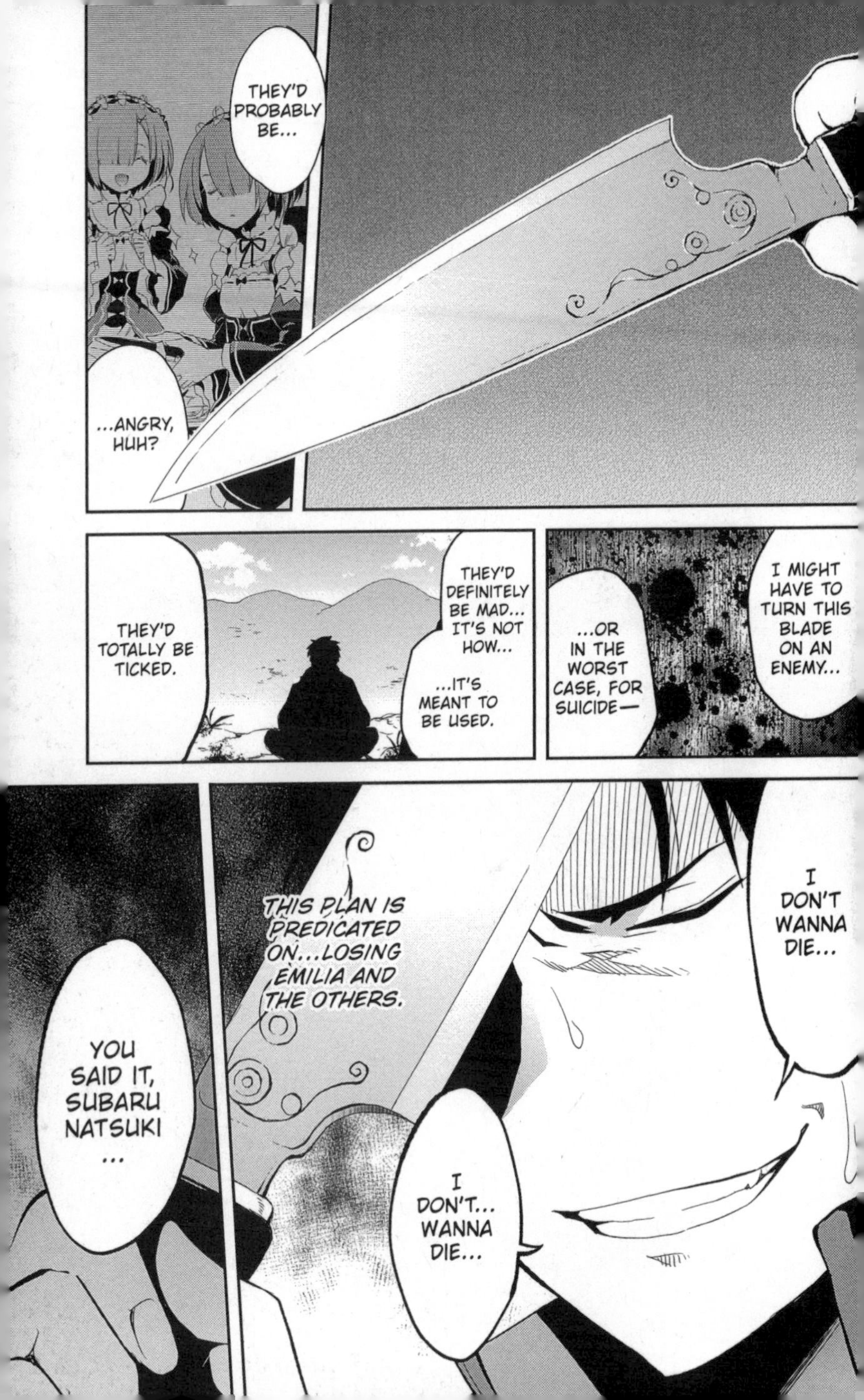
THEY'D PROBABLY BE...
...ANGRY, HUH?
I MIGHT HAVE TO TURN THIS BLADE ON AN ENEMY...
...OR IN THE WORST CASE, FOR SUICIDE—
THEY'D DEFINITELY BE MAD... IT'S NOT HOW...
...IT'S MEANT TO BE USED.
THEY'D TOTALLY BE TICKED.
I DON'T WANNA DIE...
I DON'T... WANNA DIE...
THIS PLAN IS PREDICATED ON...LOSING EMILIA AND THE OTHERS.
YOU SAID IT, SUBARU NATSUKI...

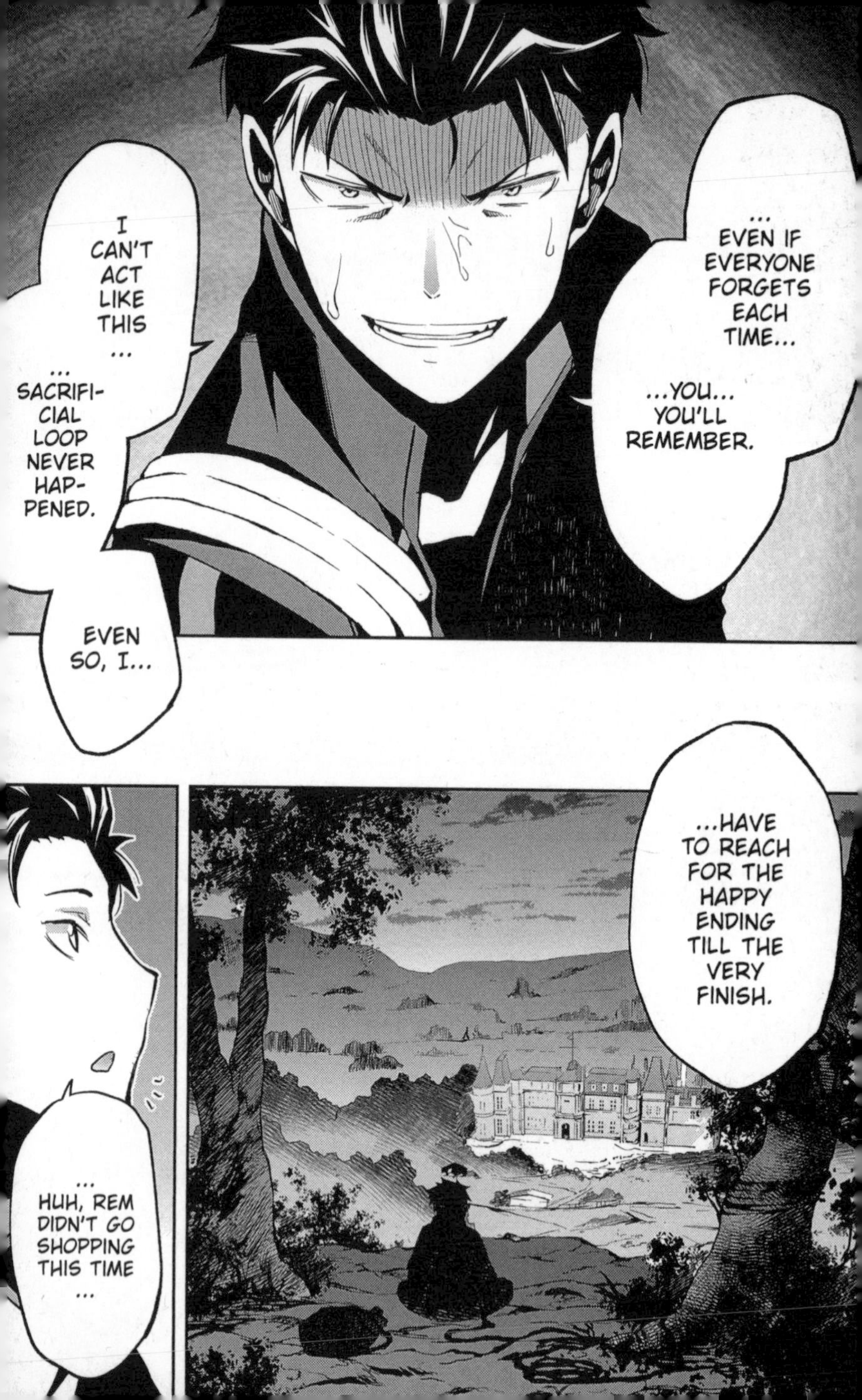
... EVEN IF EVERYONE FORGETS EACH TIME...
...YOU... YOU'LL REMEMBER.
I CAN'T ACT LIKE THIS ... ... SACRIFICIAL LOOP NEVER HAPPENED.
EVEN SO, I...
...HAVE TO REACH FOR THE HAPPY ENDING TILL THE VERY FINISH.
... HUH, REM DIDN'T GO SHOPPING THIS TIME ...

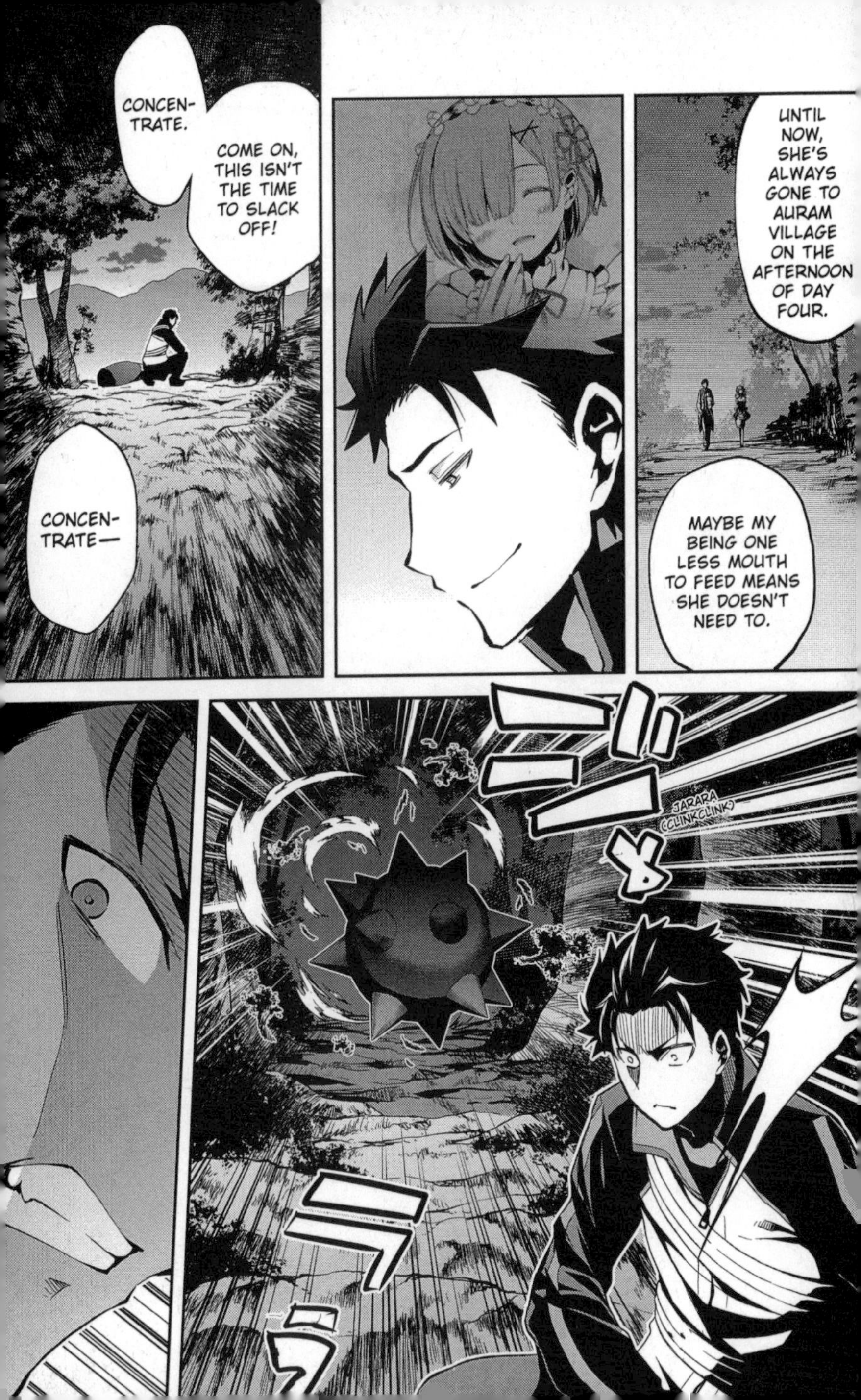
UNTIL NOW, SHE'S ALWAYS GONE TO AURAM VILLAGE ON THE AFTERNOON OF DAY FOUR.
MAYBE MY BEING ONE LESS MOUTH TO FEED MEANS SHE DOESN'T NEED TO.
CONCEN-TRATE.
COME ON, THIS ISN'T THE TIME TO SLACK OFF!
CONCEN-TRATE—
JARARA (CLINKCLINK)

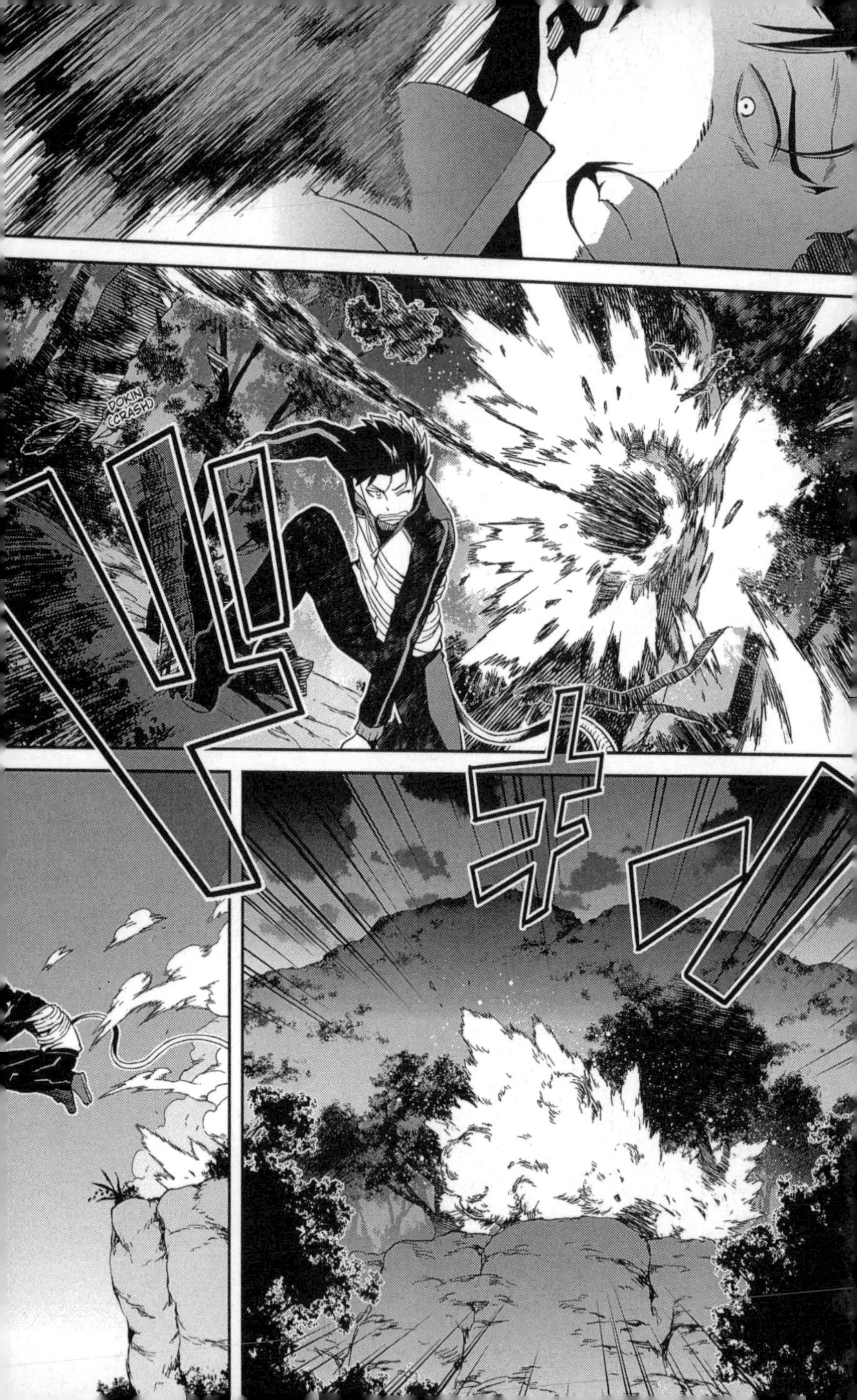
DOKIN
(CRASH)

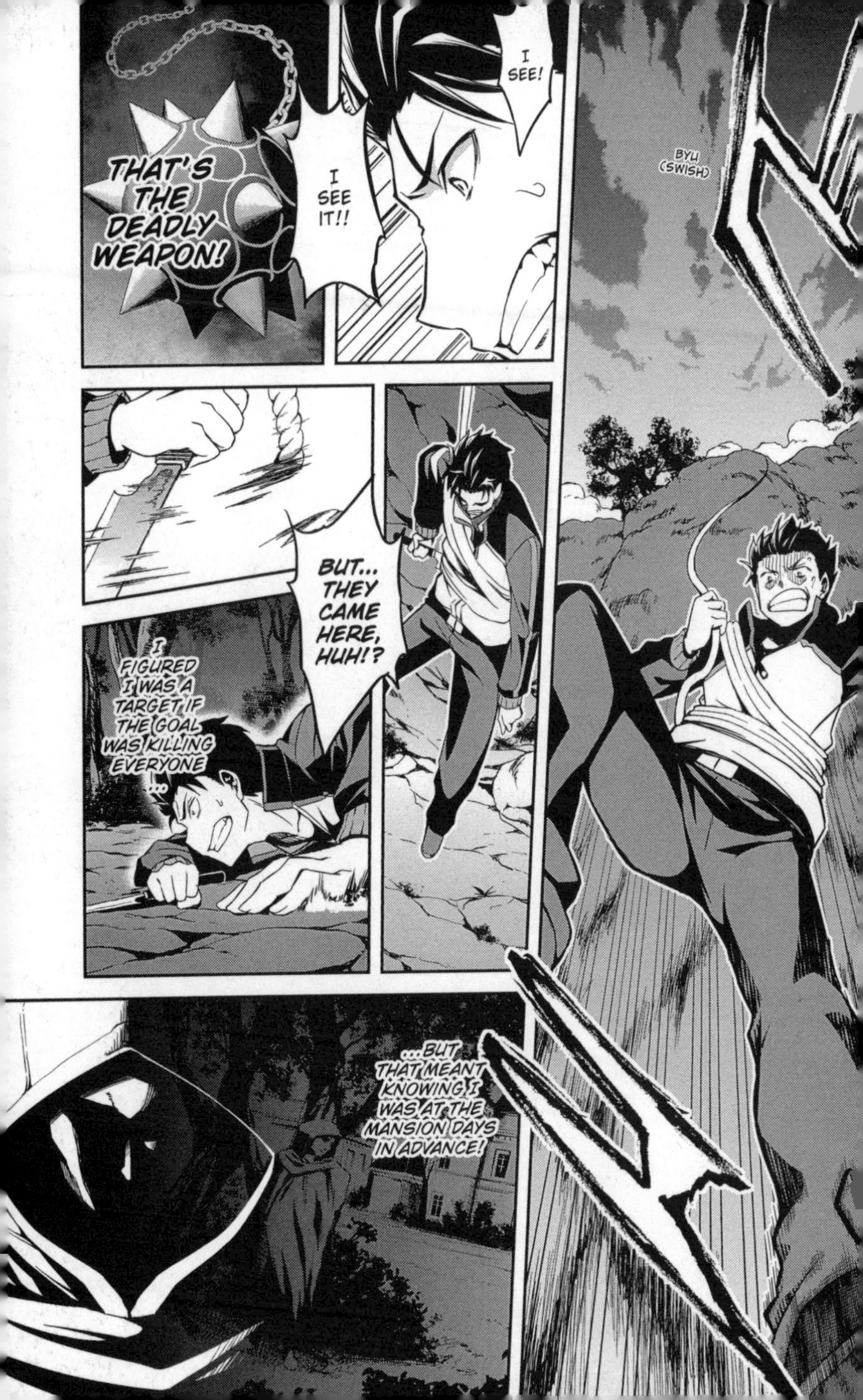
BYU (SWISH)
I SEE!
I SEE IT!!
THAT'S THE DEADLY WEAPON!
BUT... THEY CAME HERE, HUH!?
I FIGURED I WAS A TARGET IF THE GOAL WAS KILLING EVERYONE...
...BUT THAT MEANT KNOWING I WAS AT THE MANSION DAYS IN ADVANCE!

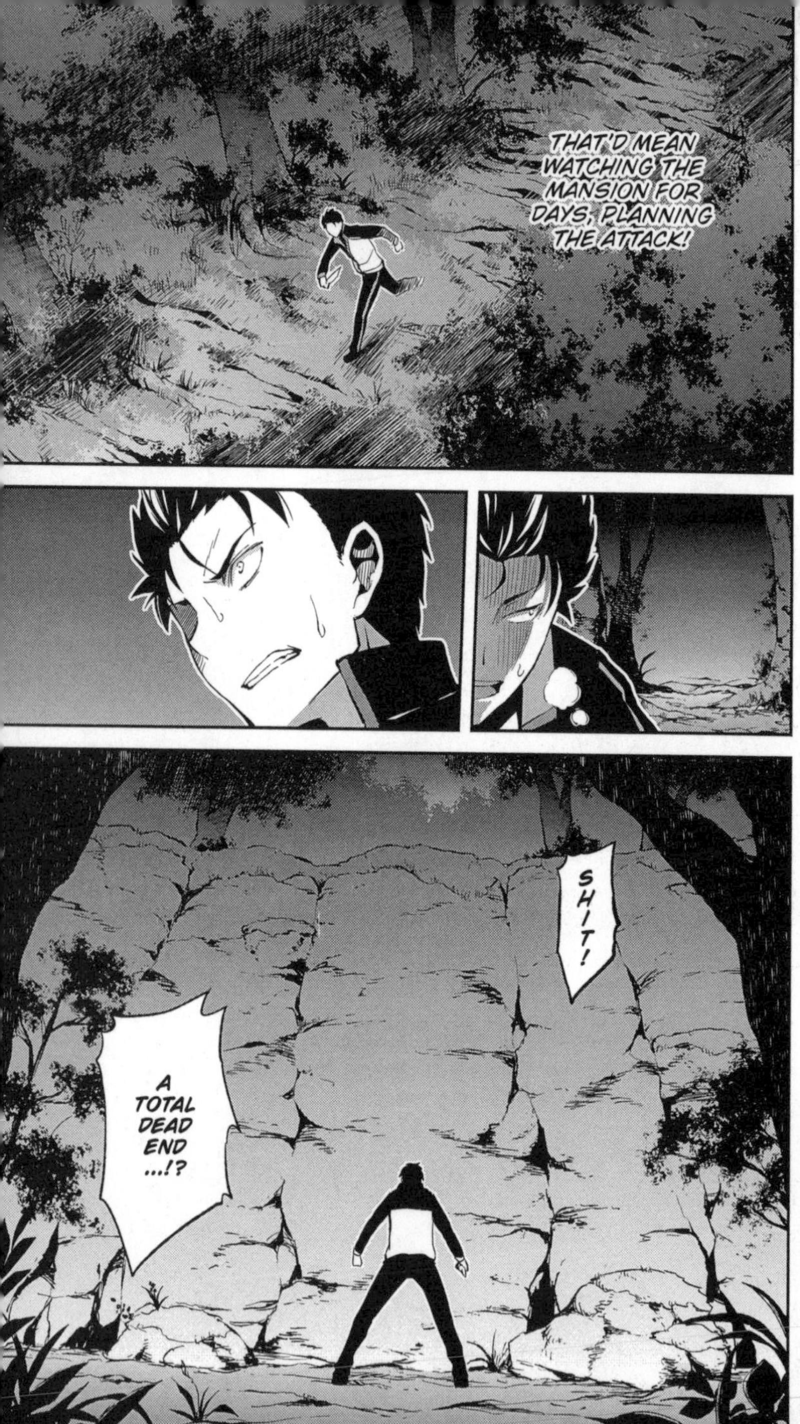
THAT'D MEAN WATCHING THE MANSION FOR DAYS, PLANNING THE ATTACK!
SHIT!
A TOTAL DEAD END ...!?

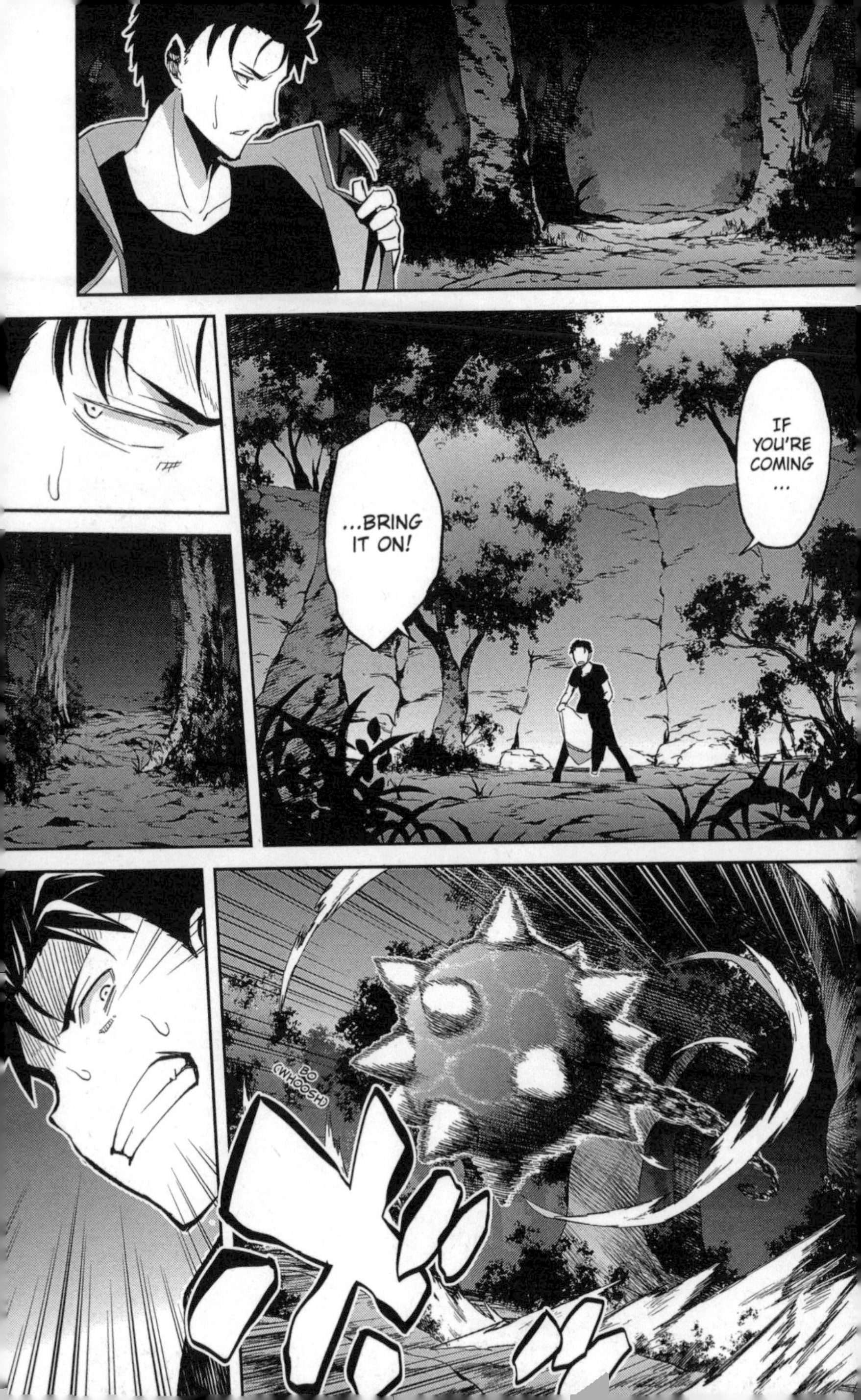
IF YOU'RE COMING...
...BRING IT ON!
BO (WHOOSH)

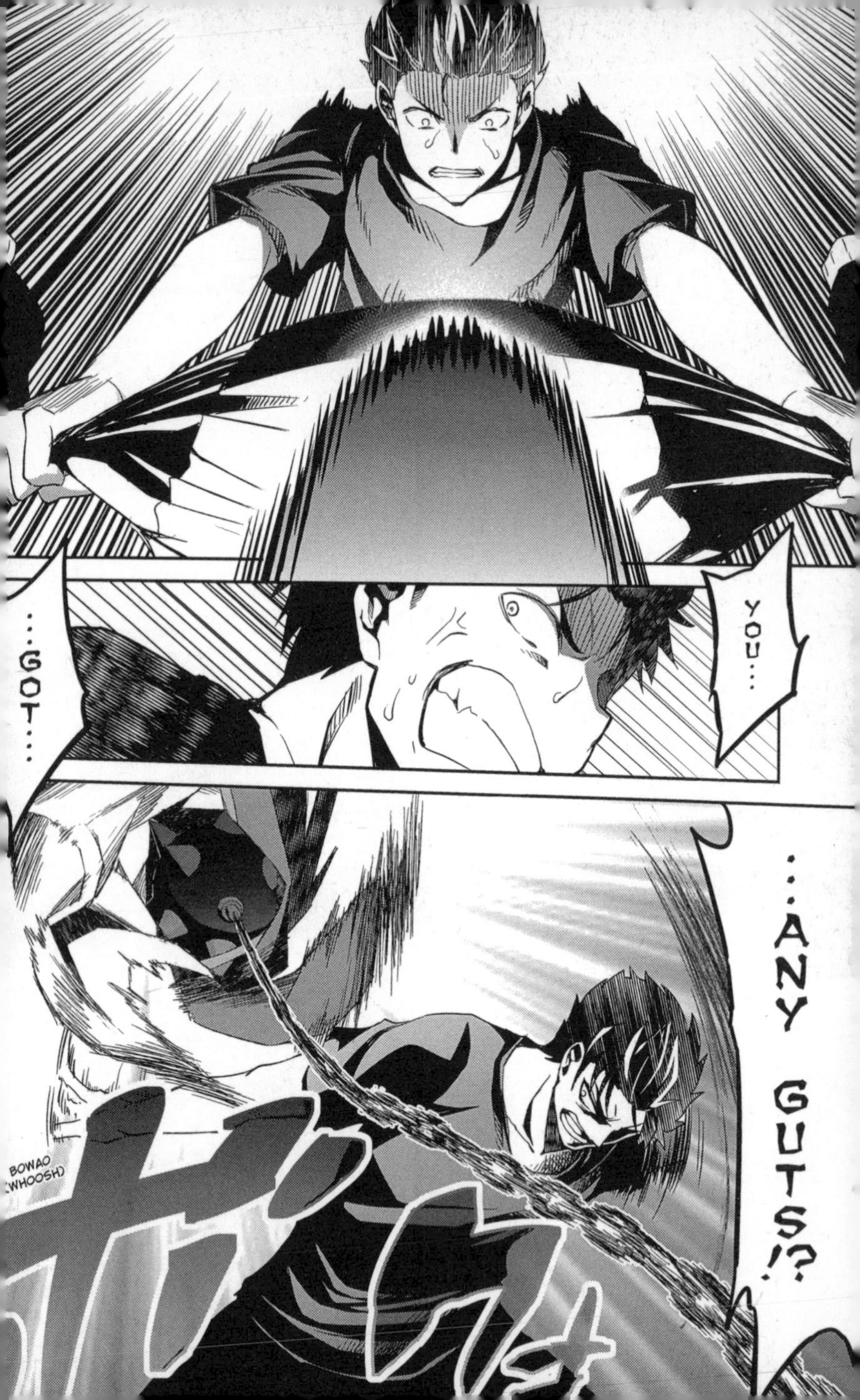
YOU...
...GOT...
...ANY GUTS!?
BOWAO (WHOOSH)

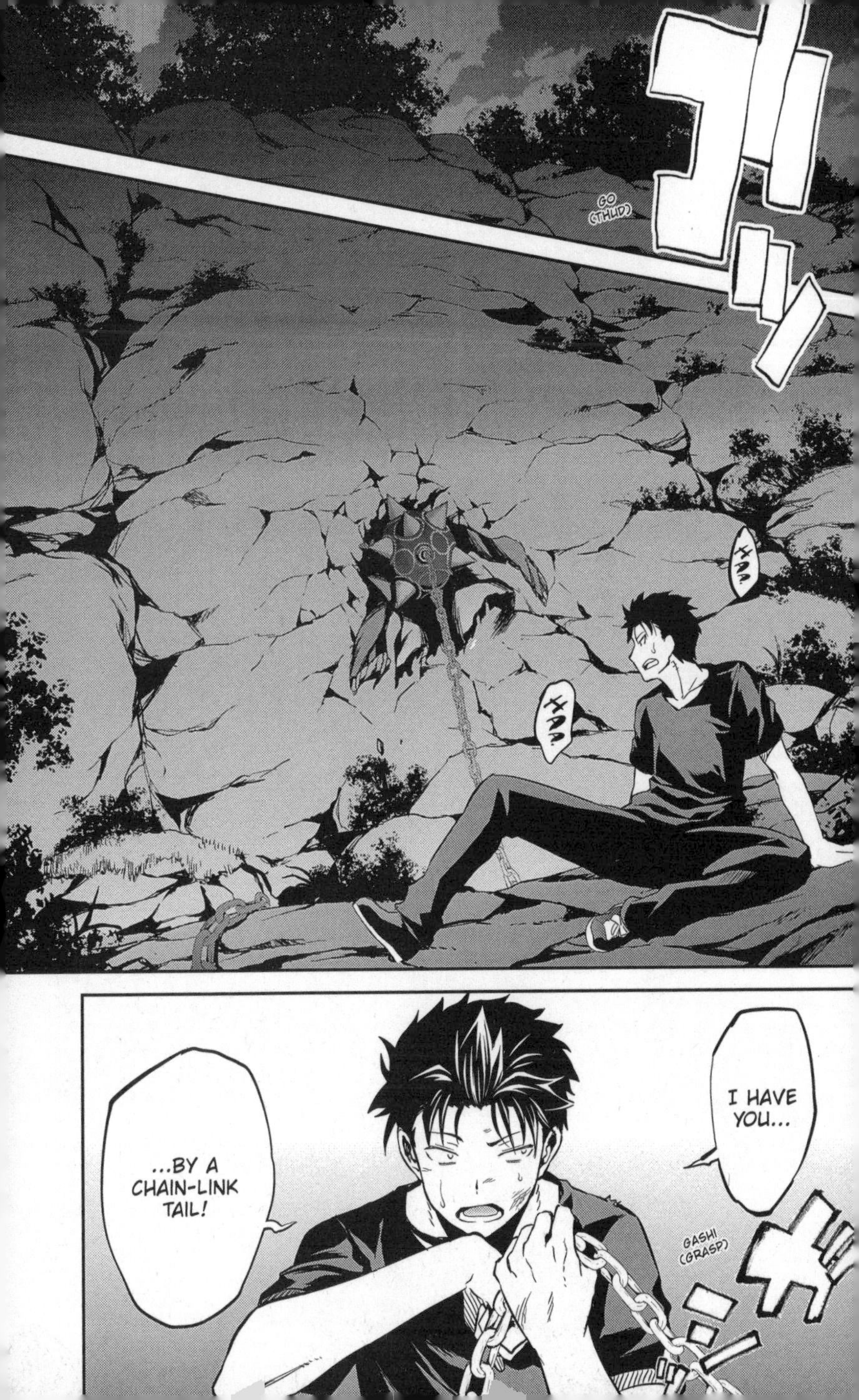
GO
(THUD)
HAA.
HAA.
I HAVE YOU...
GASHI
(GRASP)
...BY A CHAIN-LINK TAIL!

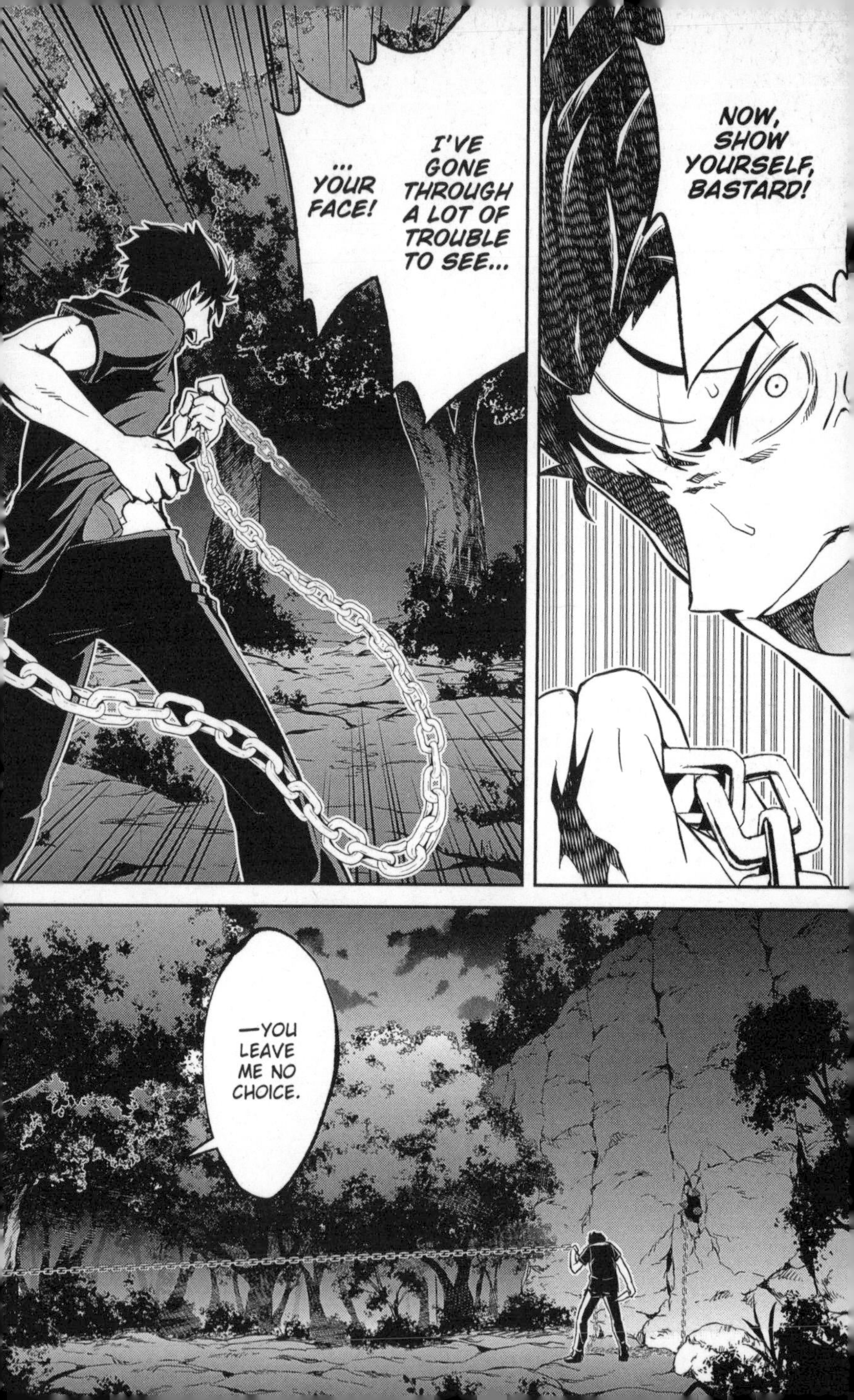
NOW, SHOW YOURSELF, BASTARD!
I'VE GONE THROUGH A LOT OF TROUBLE TO SEE...
... YOUR FACE!
—YOU LEAVE ME NO CHOICE.

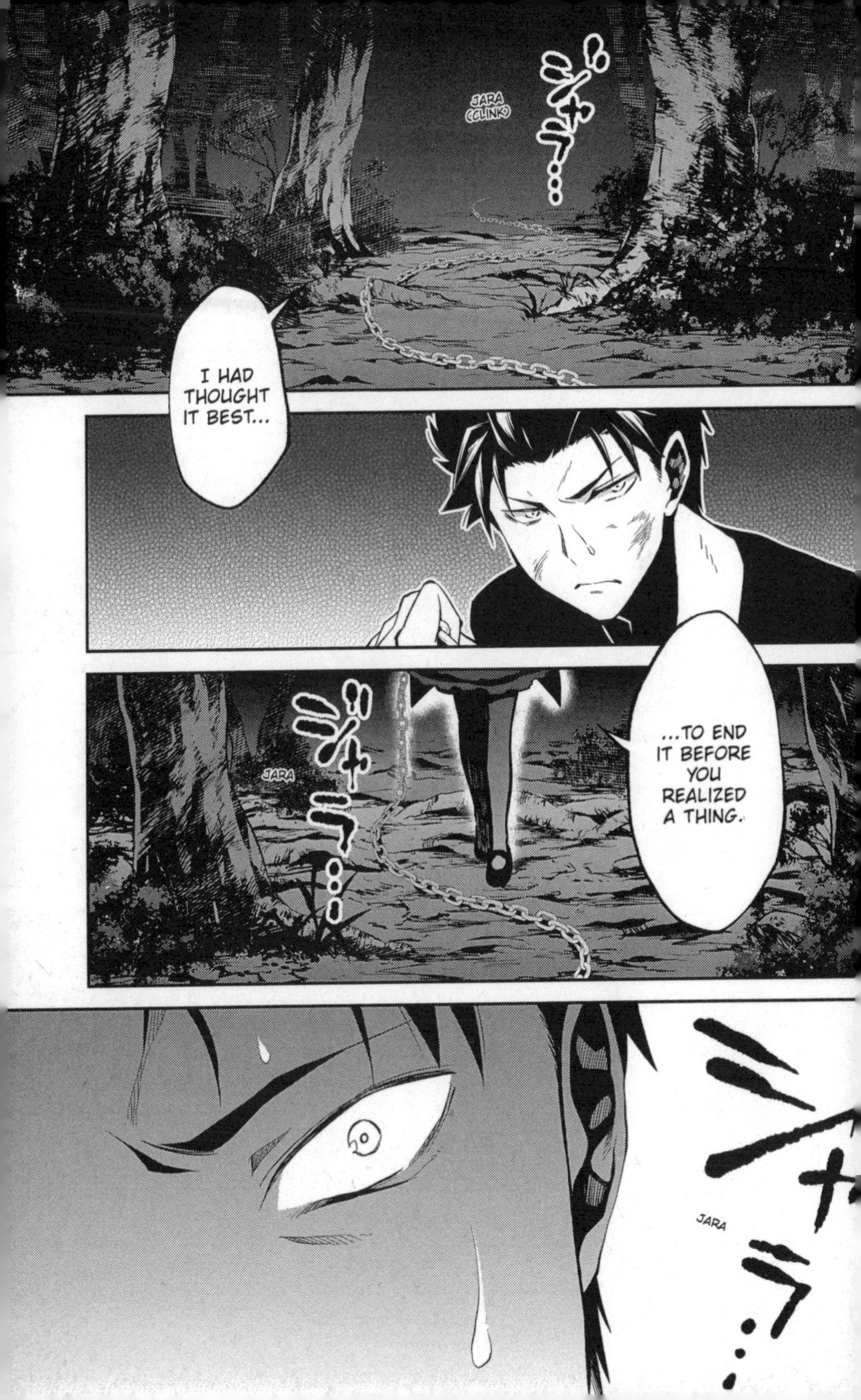

ジャラ…
JARA (CLINK)
I HAD THOUGHT IT BEST...
...TO END IT BEFORE YOU REALIZED A THING.
ジャラ…
JARA
ジャラ…
JARA

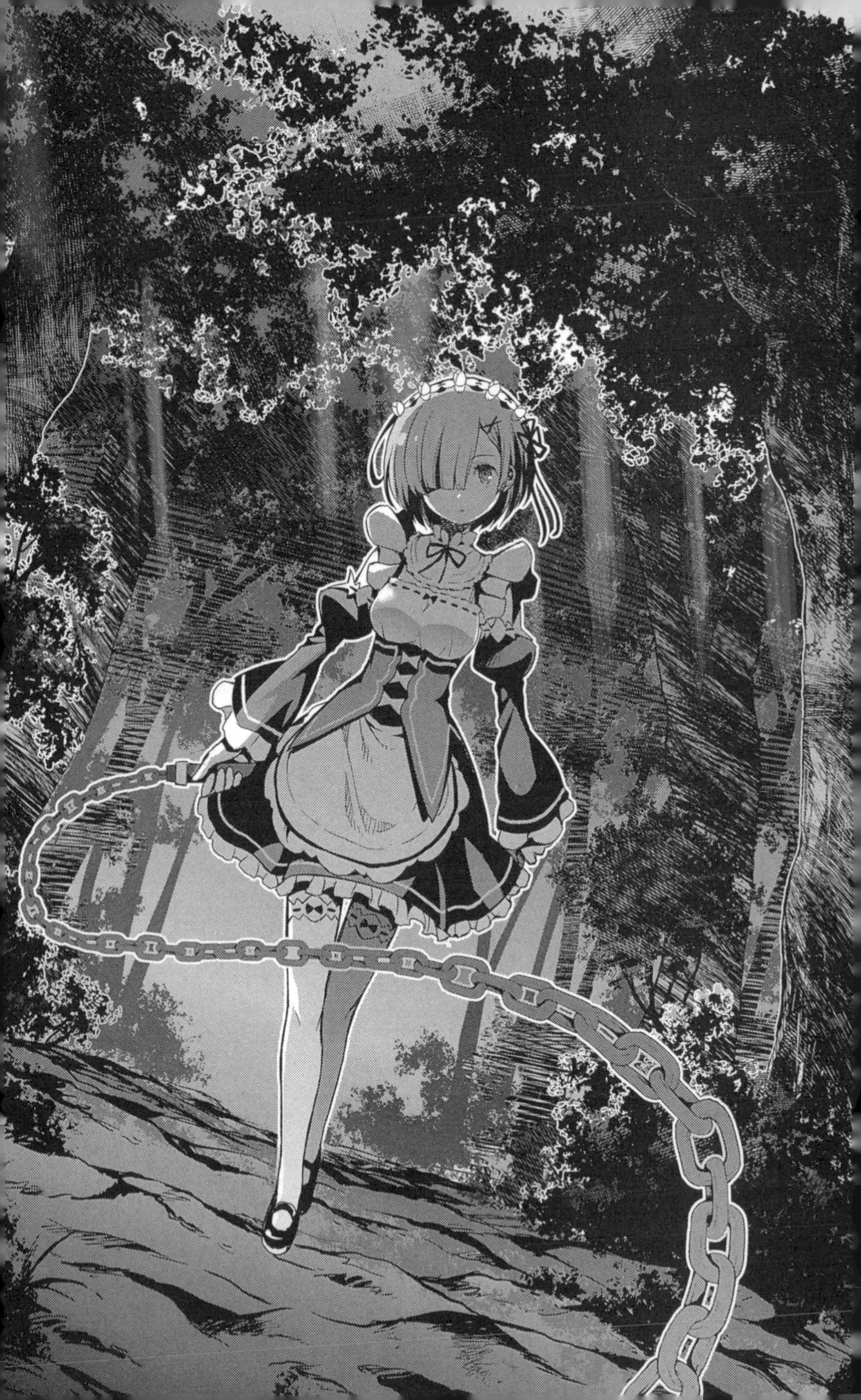

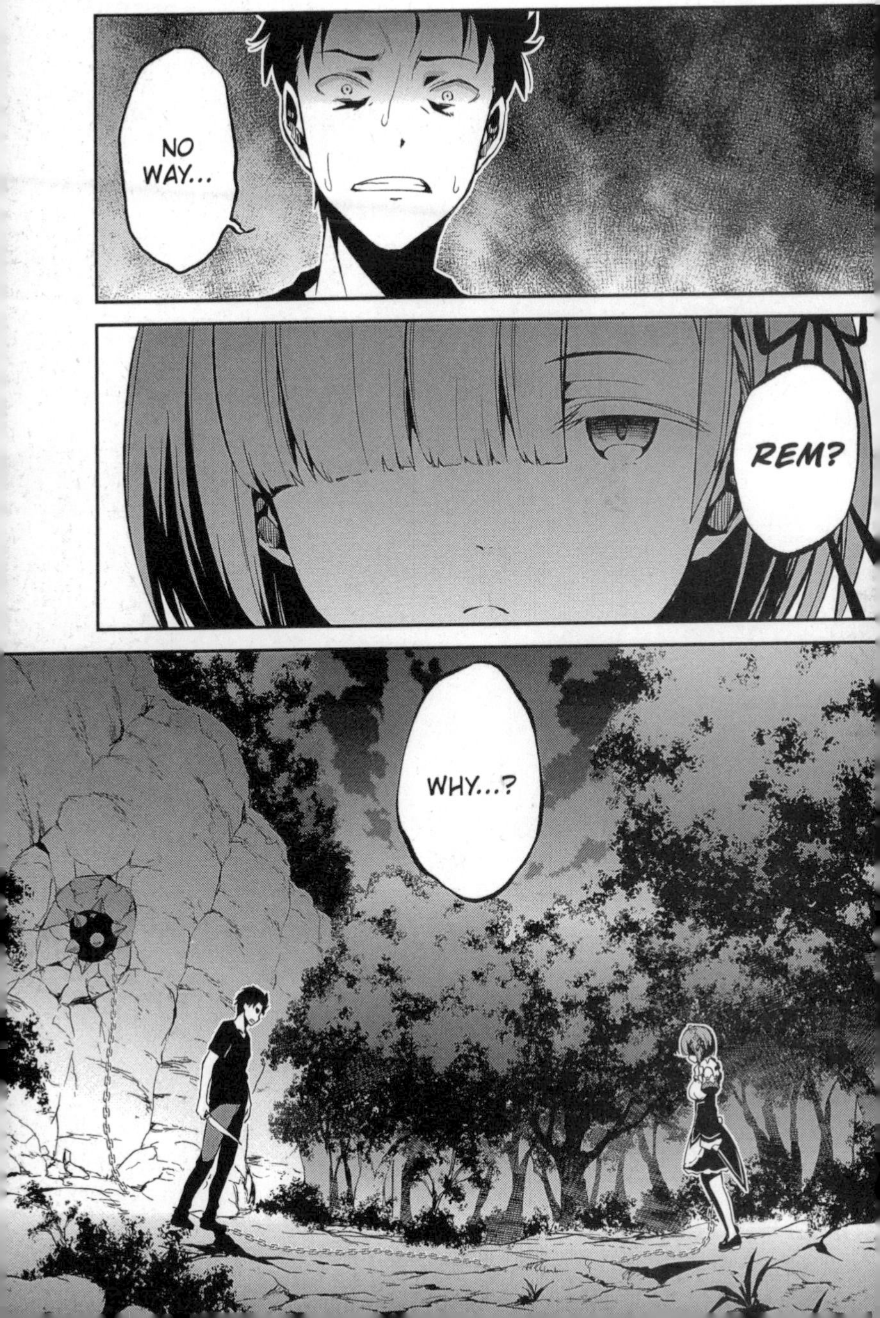
NO WAY...
REM?
WHY...?

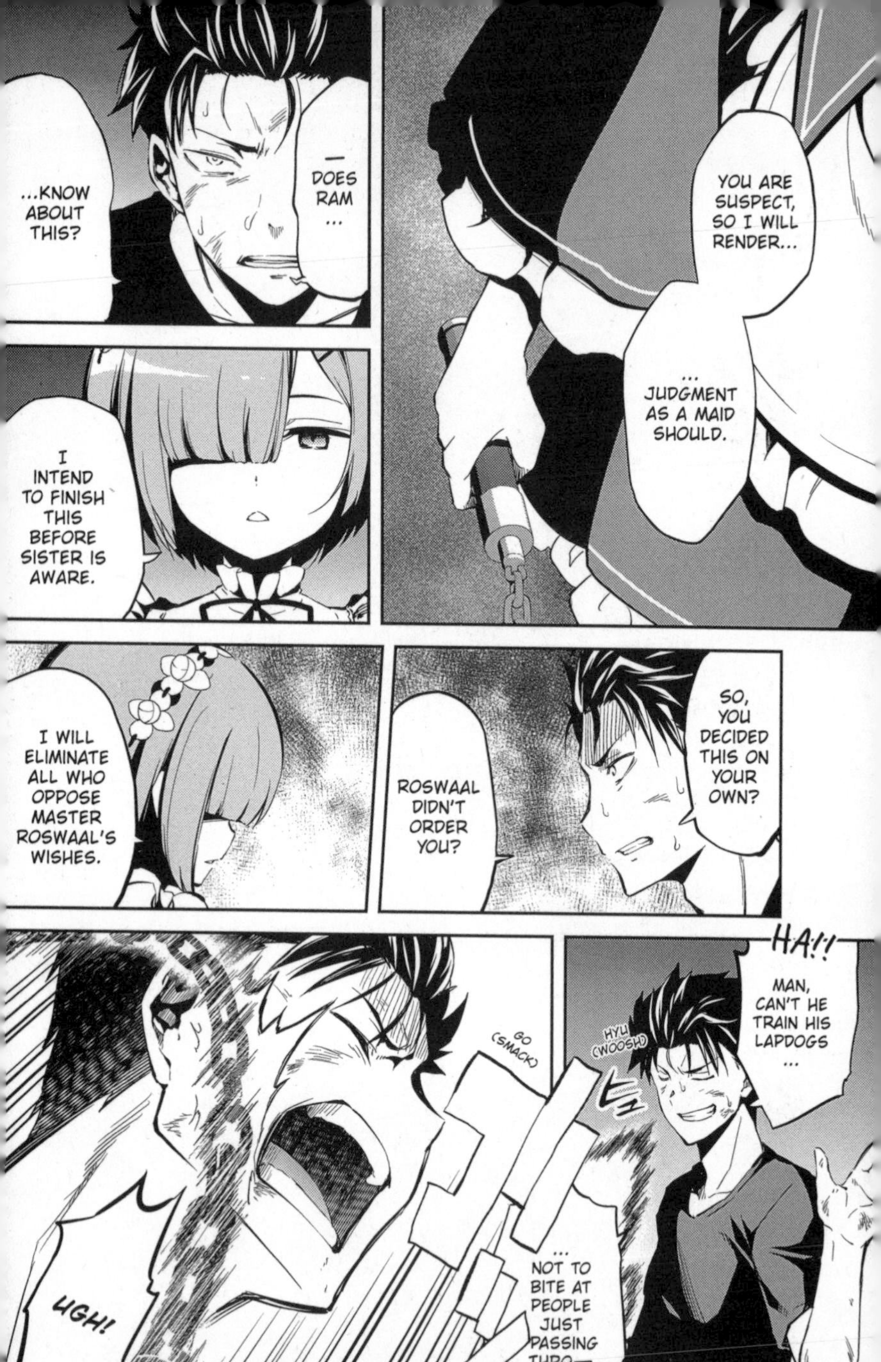
YOU ARE SUSPECT, SO I WILL RENDER...
...JUDGMENT AS A MAID SHOULD.
—DOES RAM...
...KNOW ABOUT THIS?
I INTEND TO FINISH THIS BEFORE SISTER IS AWARE.
SO, YOU DECIDED THIS ON YOUR OWN?
ROSWAAL DIDN'T ORDER YOU?
I WILL ELIMINATE ALL WHO OPPOSE MASTER ROSWAAL'S WISHES.
HA!!
MAN, CAN'T HE TRAIN HIS LAPDOGS...
HYU (WOOSH)
...NOT TO BITE AT PEOPLE JUST PASSING THRO—
GO (SMACK)
UGH!

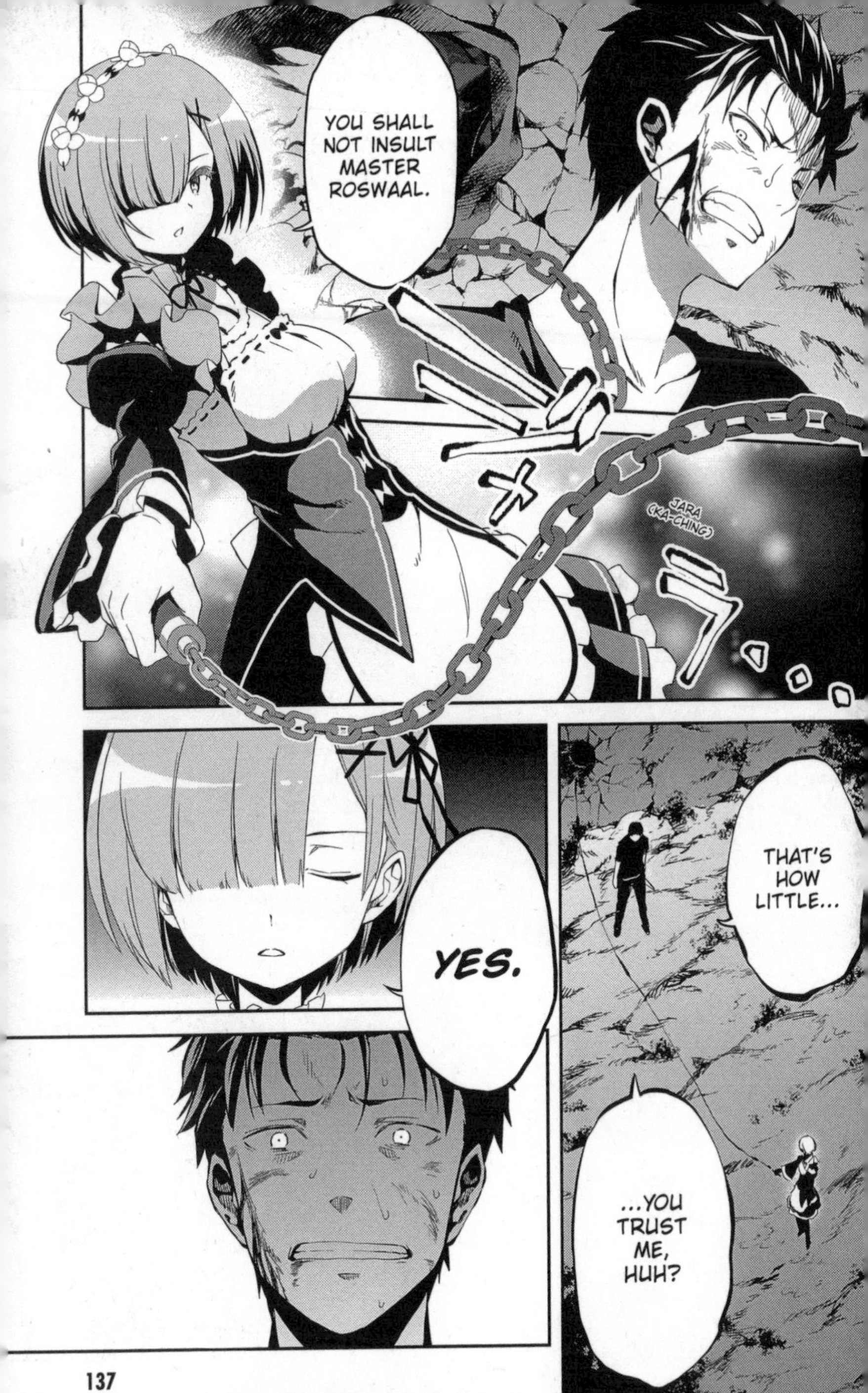
YOU SHALL NOT INSULT MASTER ROSWAAL.
JARA (KA-CHING)
THAT'S HOW LITTLE...
...YOU TRUST ME, HUH?
YES.

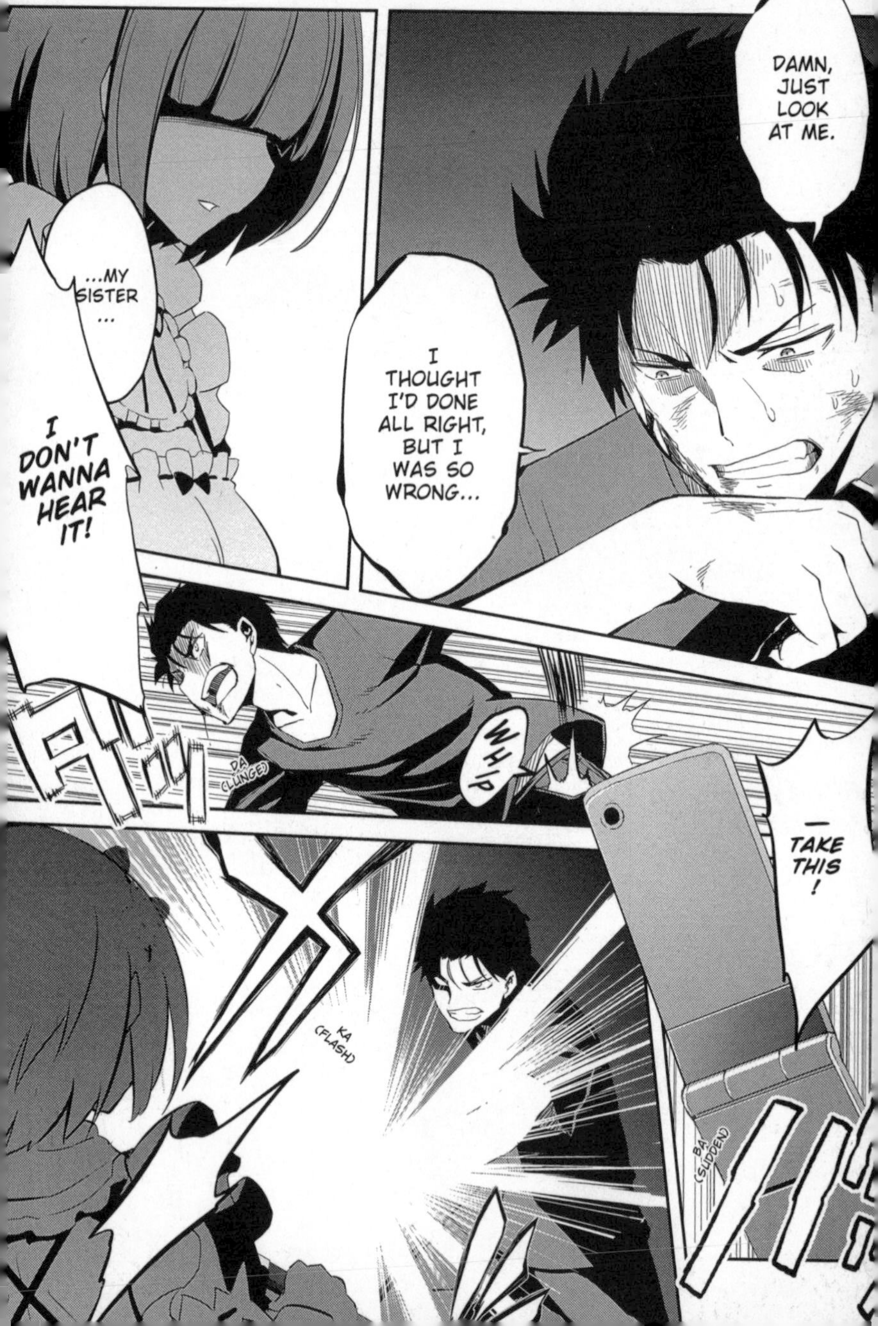
DAMN, JUST LOOK AT ME.
I THOUGHT I'D DONE ALL RIGHT, BUT I WAS SO WRONG...
...MY SISTER ...
I DON'T WANNA HEAR IT!
WHIP
DA (LUNGE)
—TAKE THIS!
BA (SUDDEN)
KA (FLASH)

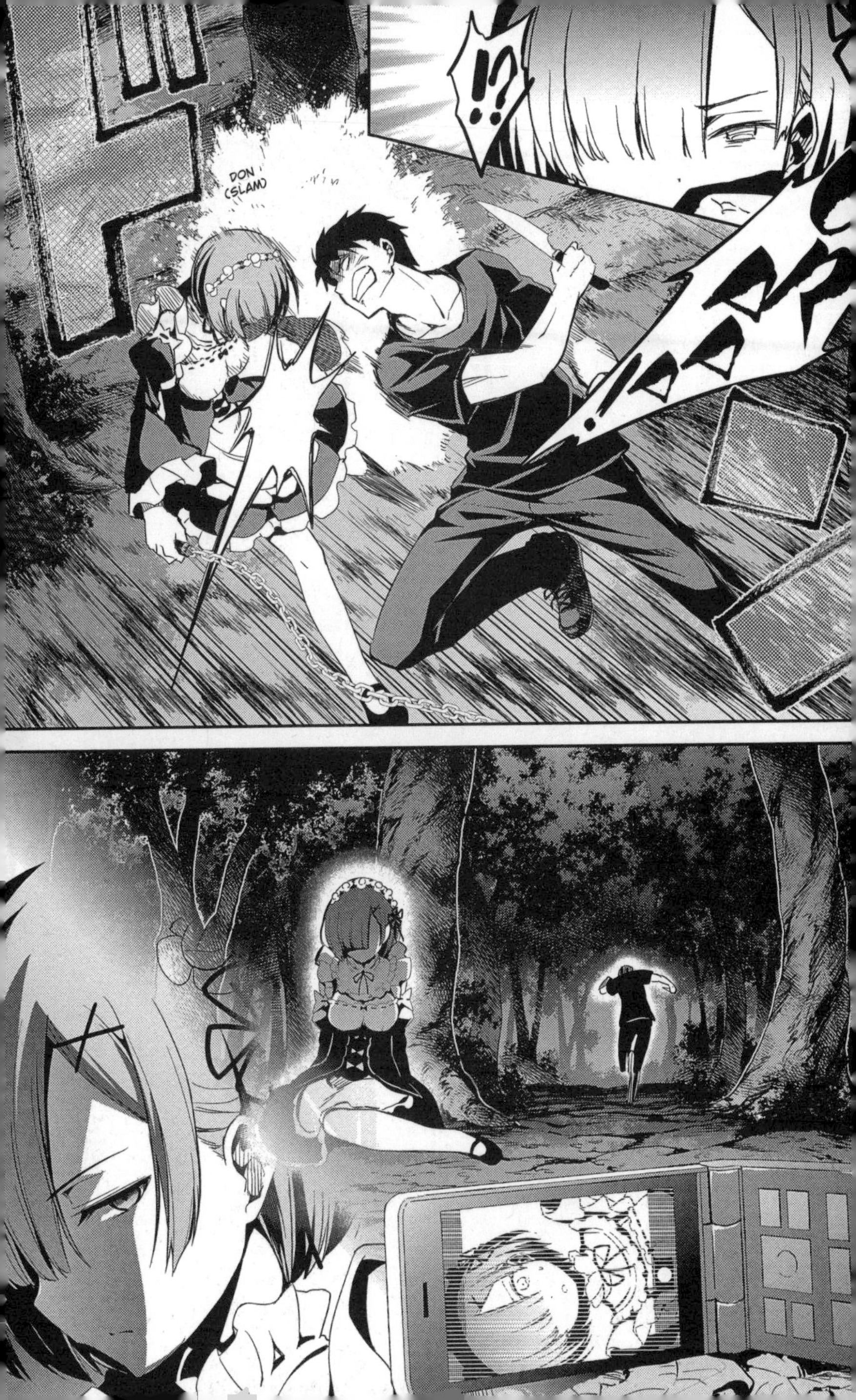
!?
CRAAA!
DON (SLAM)

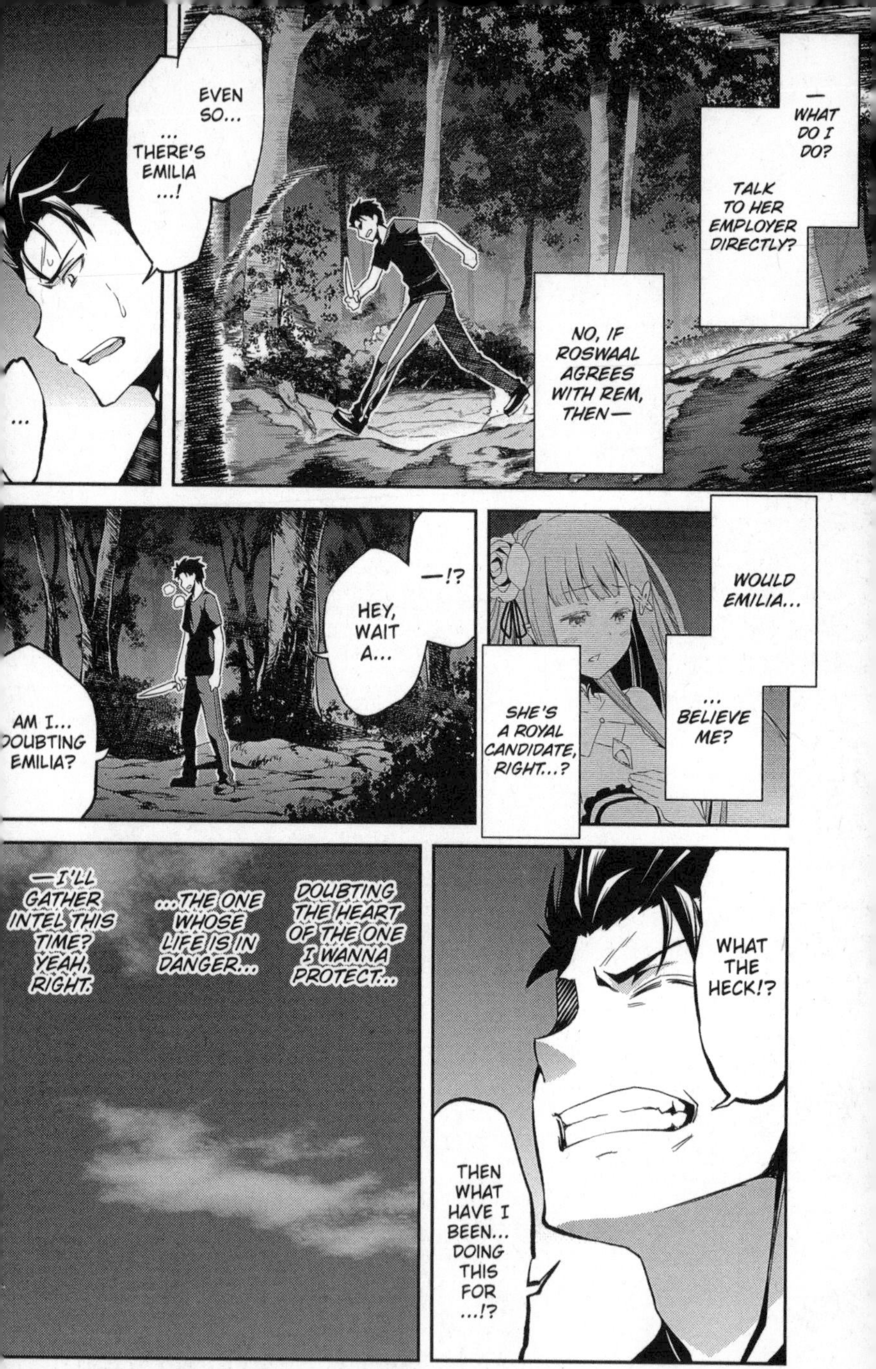
—WHAT DO I DO?
TALK TO HER EMPLOYER DIRECTLY?
NO, IF ROSWAAL AGREES WITH REM, THEN—
EVEN SO... ...THERE'S EMILIA ...!
...
WOULD EMILIA...
...BELIEVE ME?
SHE'S A ROYAL CANDIDATE, RIGHT...?
—!? HEY, WAIT A...
AM I... DOUBTING EMILIA?
WHAT THE HECK!?
THEN WHAT HAVE I BEEN... DOING THIS FOR ...!?
DOUBTING THE HEART OF THE ONE I WANNA PROTECT...
...THE ONE WHOSE LIFE IS IN DANGER...
—I'LL GATHER INTEL THIS TIME? YEAH, RIGHT.

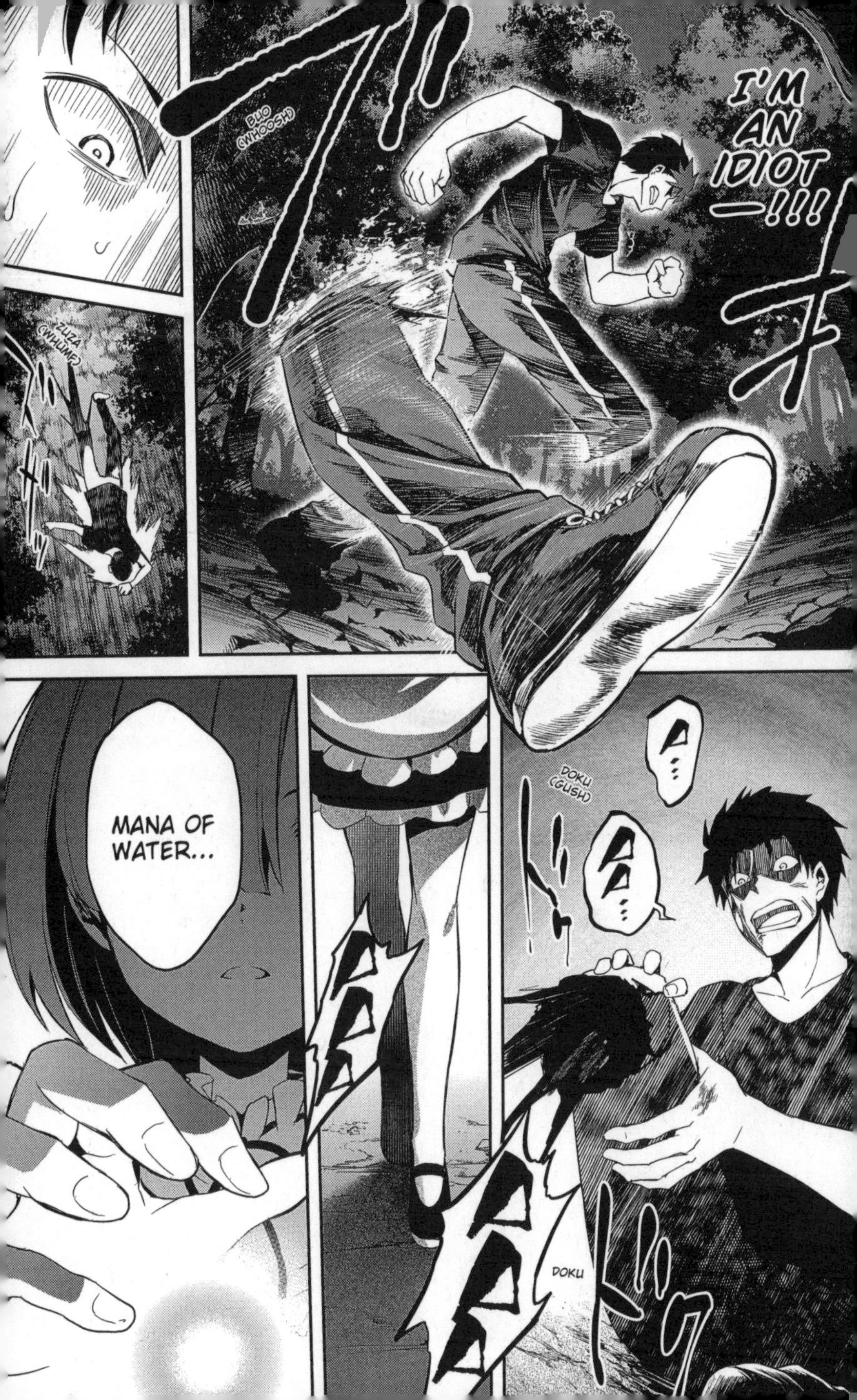
I'M AN IDIOT—!!!
BUO (WHOOSH)
ZUZA (WHUMP)
A...
AA...
DOKU (GUSH)
DOKU
MANA OF WATER...

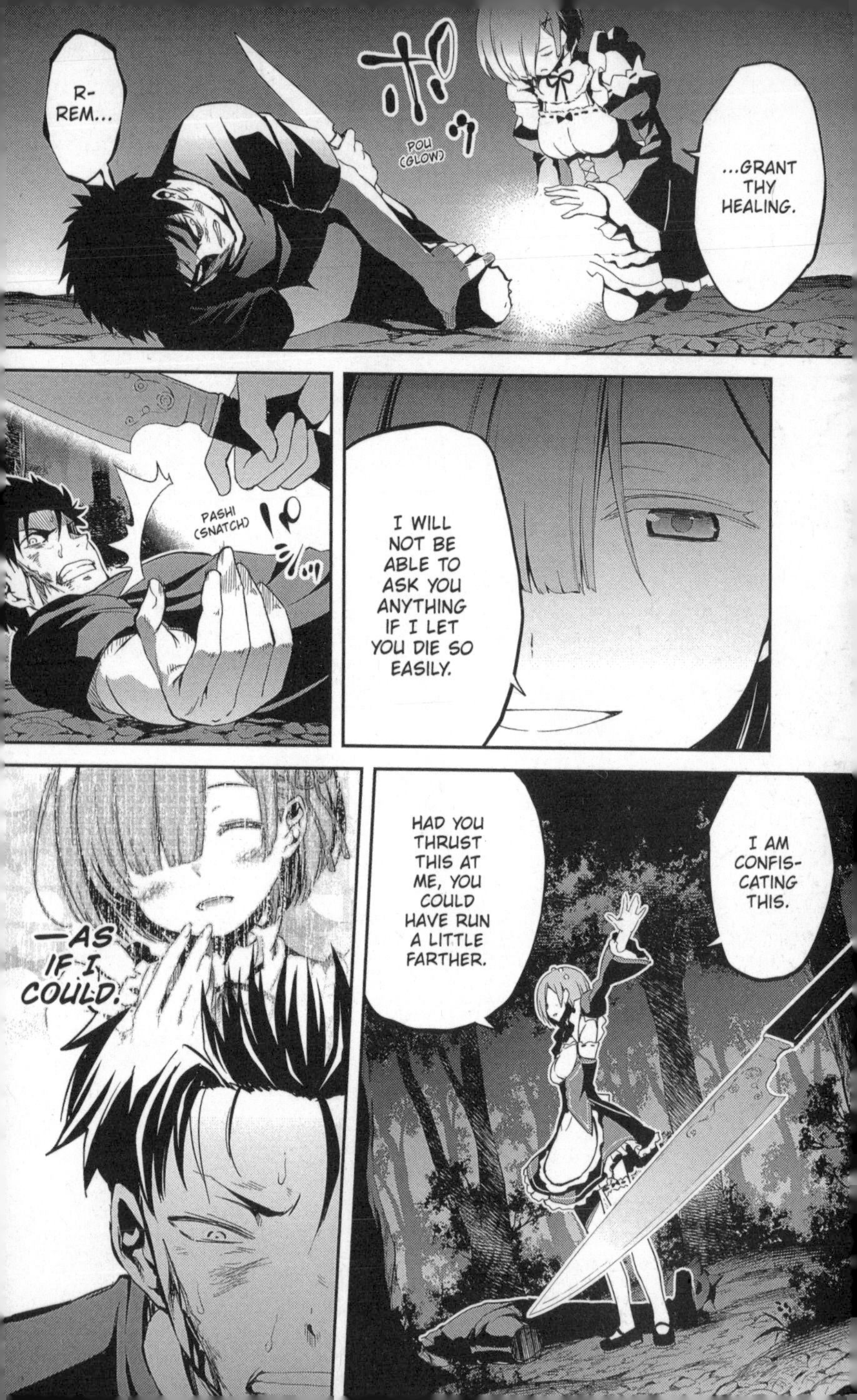
...GRANT THY HEALING.
POU (GLOW)
R- REM...
I WILL NOT BE ABLE TO ASK YOU ANYTHING IF I LET YOU DIE SO EASILY.
PASHI (SNATCH)
I AM CONFIS- CATING THIS.
HAD YOU THRUST THIS AT ME, YOU COULD HAVE RUN A LITTLE FARTHER.
—AS IF I COULD!

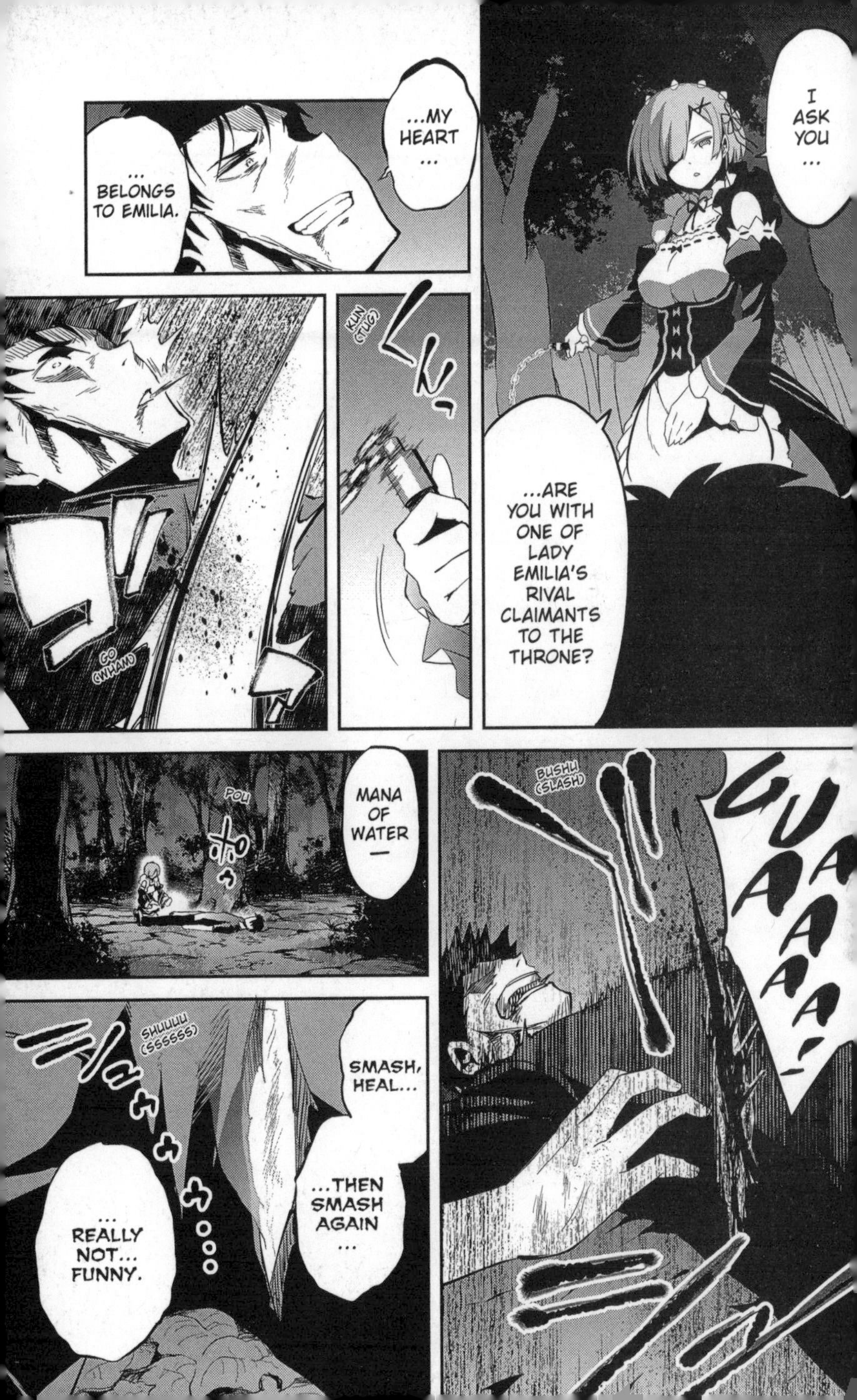
I ASK YOU ...
...ARE YOU WITH ONE OF LADY EMILIA'S RIVAL CLAIMANTS TO THE THRONE?
...MY HEART ...
... BELONGS TO EMILIA.
KUN (TUG)
GO (WHAN)
BUSHU (SLASH)
GUAAAAAAA!
MANA OF WATER —
POU
SHUUUU (SSSSSS)
SMASH, HEAL...
...THEN SMASH AGAIN ...
... REALLY NOT... FUNNY.

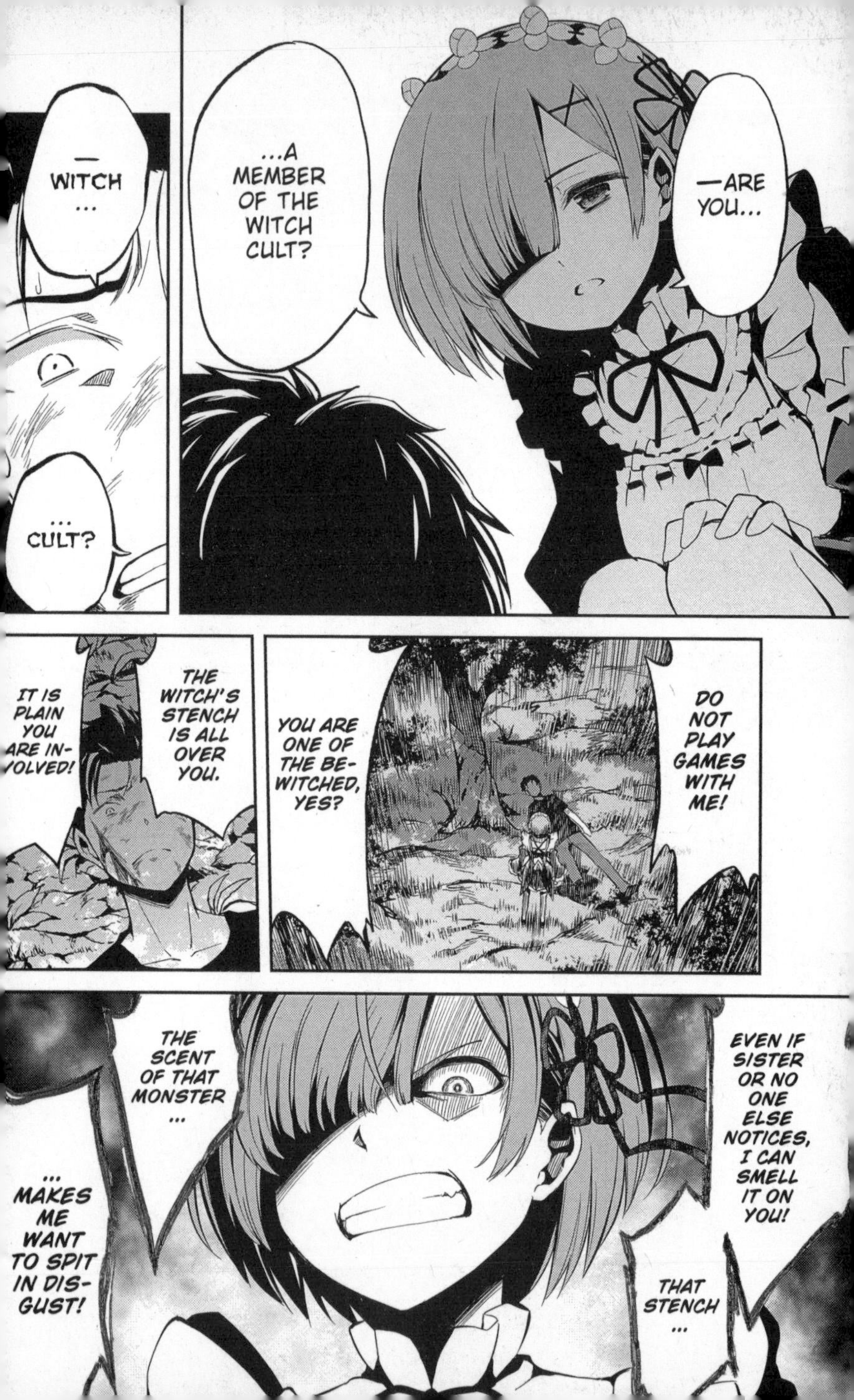
—ARE YOU...
...A MEMBER OF THE WITCH CULT?
—WITCH ...
... CULT?
DO NOT PLAY GAMES WITH ME!
YOU ARE ONE OF THE BE-WITCHED, YES?
THE WITCH'S STENCH IS ALL OVER YOU.
IT IS PLAIN YOU ARE IN-VOLVED!
EVEN IF SISTER OR NO ONE ELSE NOTICES, I CAN SMELL IT ON YOU!
THAT STENCH ...
THE SCENT OF THAT MONSTER ...
... MAKES ME WANT TO SPIT IN DIS-GUST!

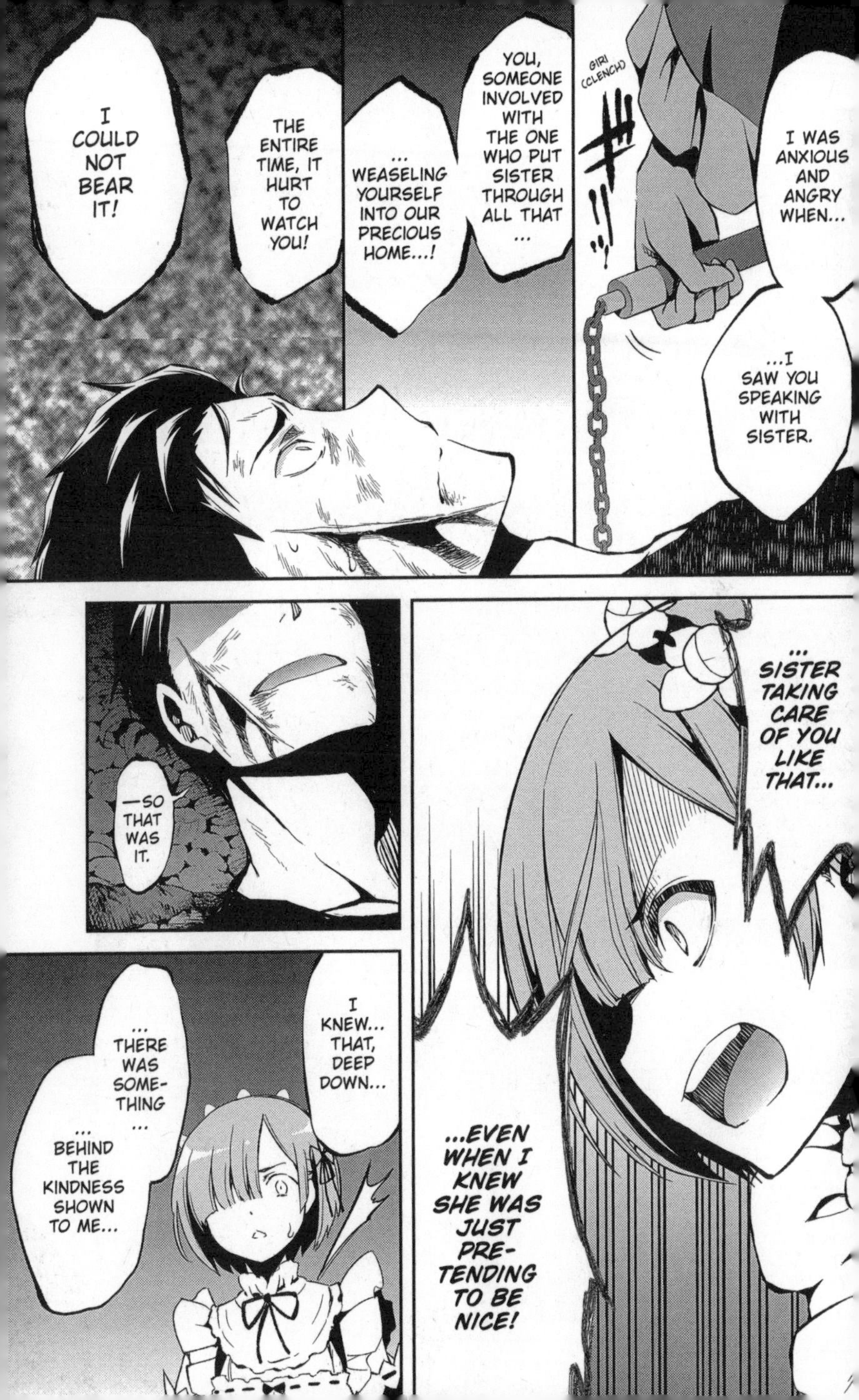
I WAS ANXIOUS AND ANGRY WHEN...
GIRI (CLENCH)
...I SAW YOU SPEAKING WITH SISTER.
YOU, SOMEONE INVOLVED WITH THE ONE WHO PUT SISTER THROUGH ALL THAT ...
... WEASELING YOURSELF INTO OUR PRECIOUS HOME...!
THE ENTIRE TIME, IT HURT TO WATCH YOU!
I COULD NOT BEAR IT!
... SISTER TAKING CARE OF YOU LIKE THAT...
...EVEN WHEN I KNEW SHE WAS JUST PRE-TENDING TO BE NICE!
—SO THAT WAS IT.
I KNEW... THAT, DEEP DOWN...
... THERE WAS SOME-THING ... BEHIND THE KINDNESS SHOWN TO ME...

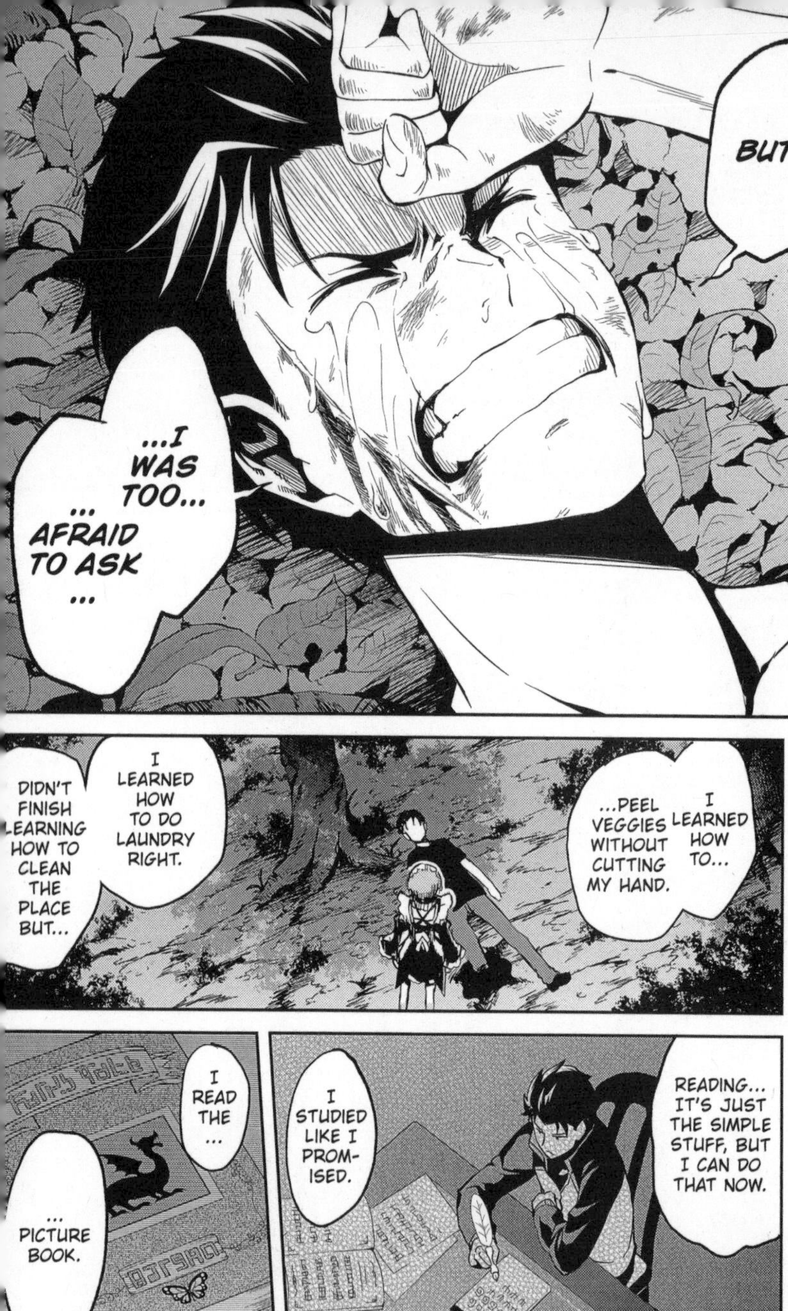
BUT...
...I WAS TOO... ...AFRAID TO ASK...
I LEARNED HOW TO...
...PEEL VEGGIES WITHOUT CUTTING MY HAND.
I LEARNED HOW TO DO LAUNDRY RIGHT.
DIDN'T FINISH LEARNING HOW TO CLEAN THE PLACE BUT...
READING... IT'S JUST THE SIMPLE STUFF, BUT I CAN DO THAT NOW.
I STUDIED LIKE I PROMISED.
I READ THE...
...PICTURE BOOK.

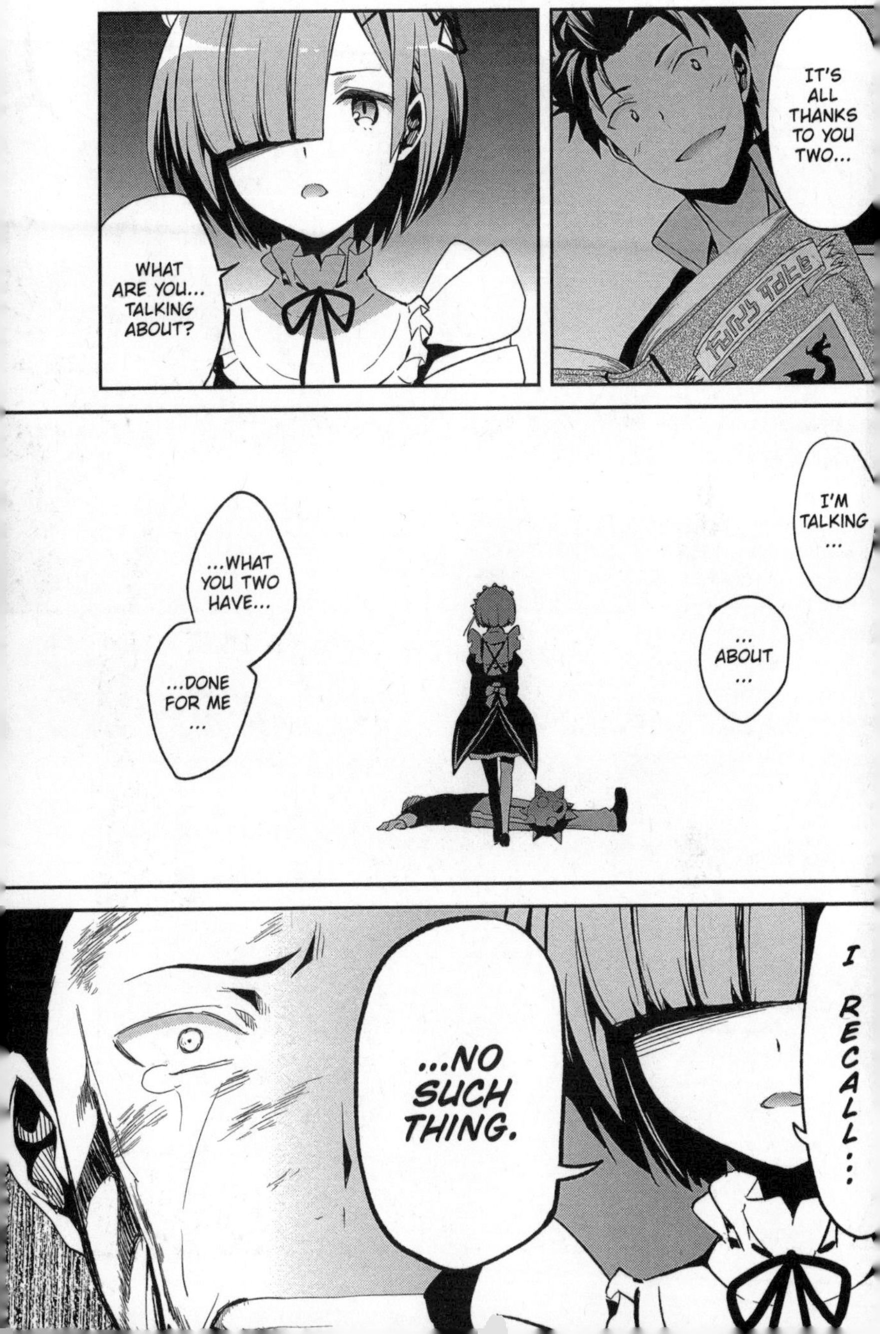
IT'S ALL THANKS TO YOU TWO...
WHAT ARE YOU... TALKING ABOUT?
I'M TALKING ...
... ABOUT ...
...WHAT YOU TWO HAVE...
...DONE FOR ME ...
I RECALL...
...NO SUCH THING.

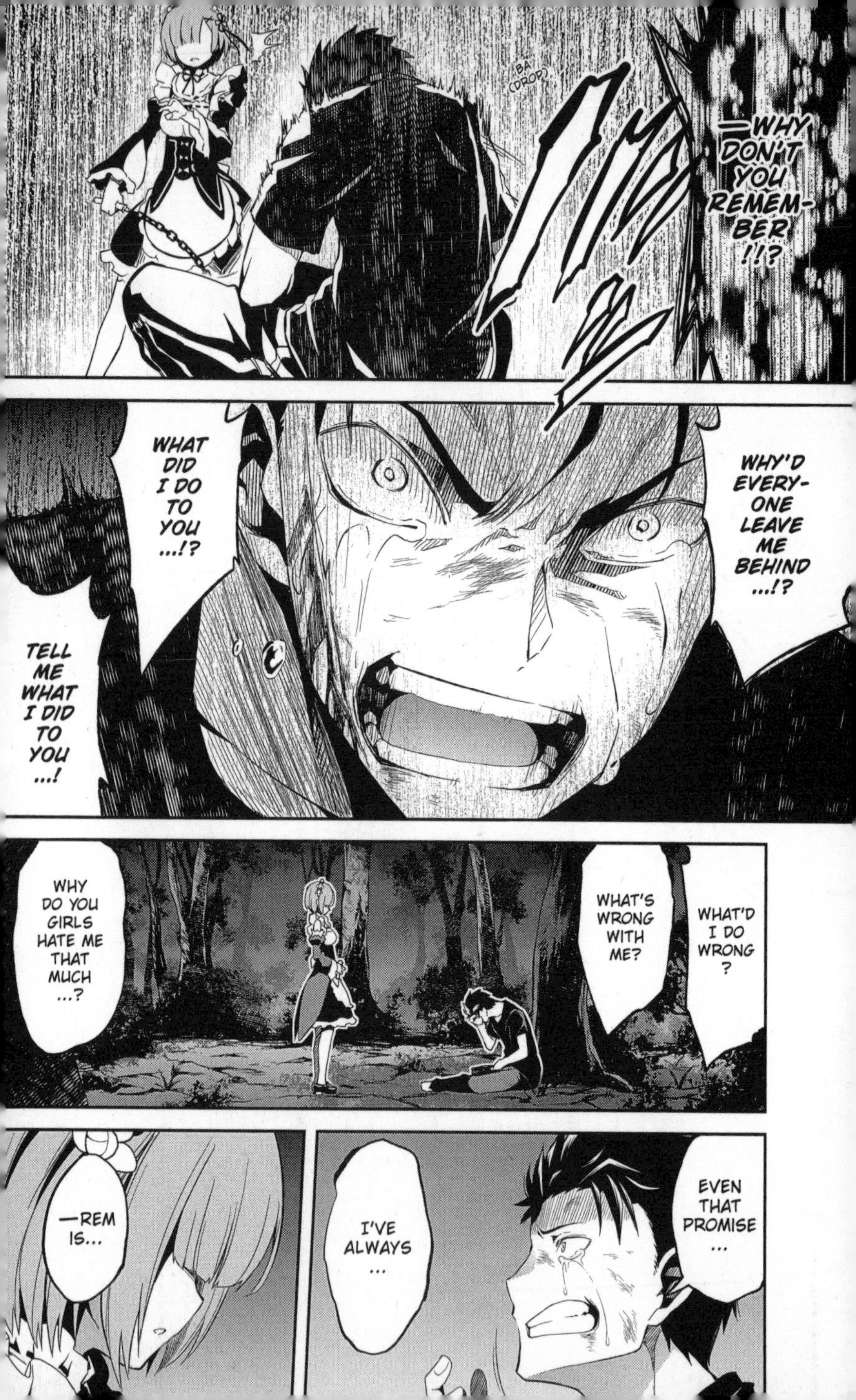
—WHY DON'T YOU REMEMBER!!?
BA (DROP)
WHY'D EVERYONE LEAVE ME BEHIND...!?
WHAT DID I DO TO YOU...!?
TELL ME WHAT I DID TO YOU...!
WHAT'D I DO WRONG?
WHAT'S WRONG WITH ME?
WHY DO YOU GIRLS HATE ME THAT MUCH...?
EVEN THAT PROMISE...
I'VE ALWAYS...
—REM IS...

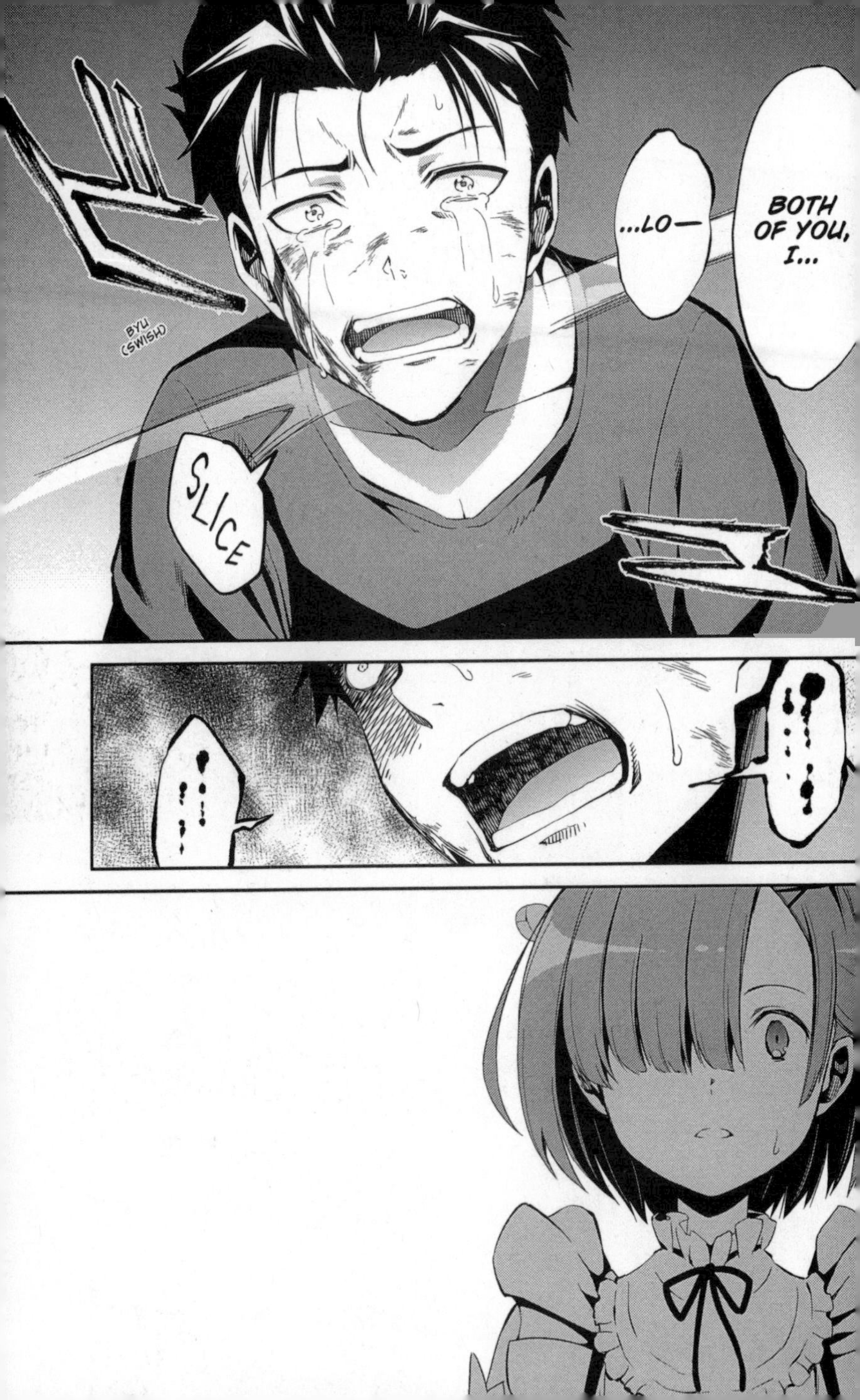
BOTH OF YOU, I...
...LO—
BYU (SWISH)
SLICE

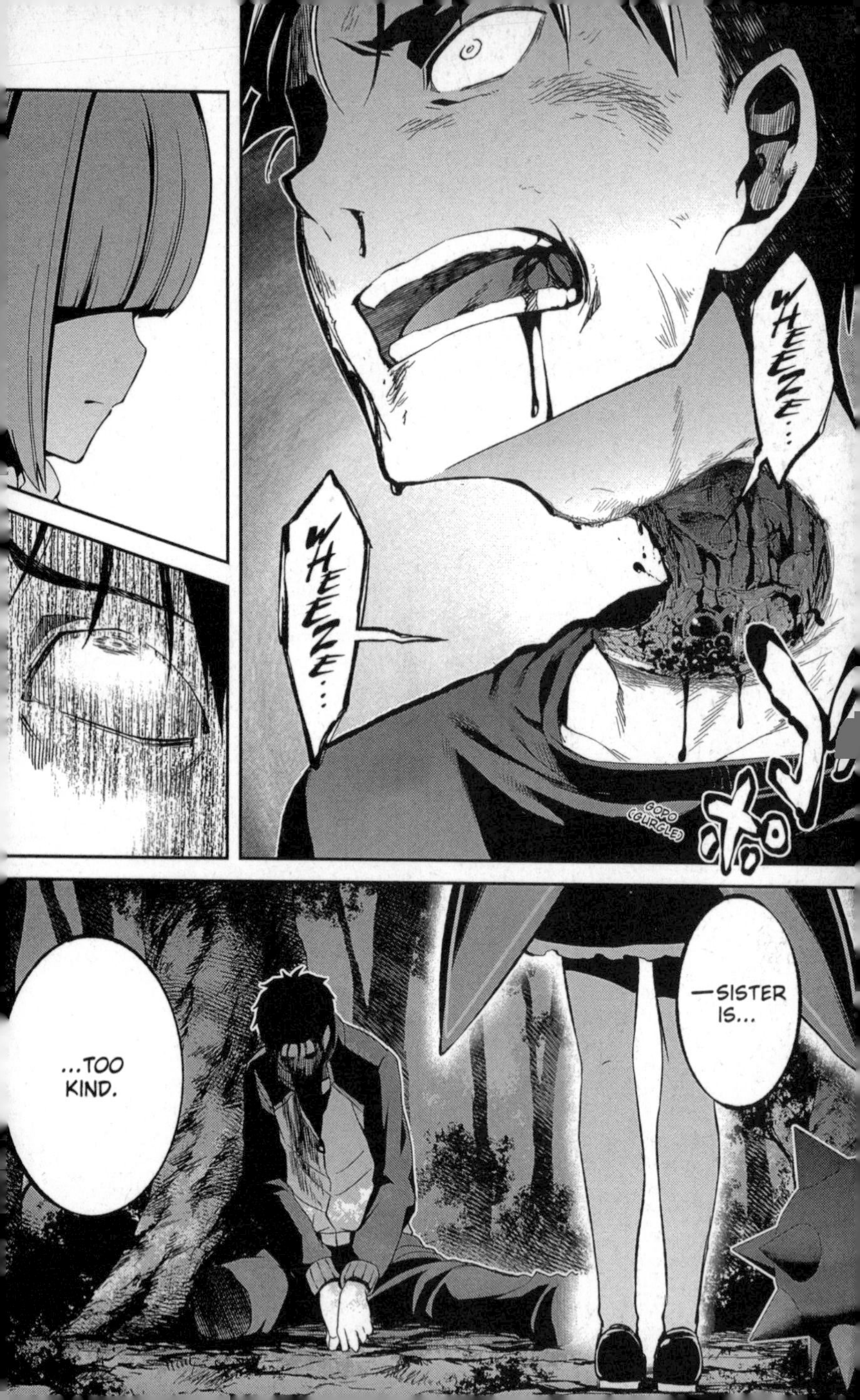
WHEEZE...
WHEEZE...
GOPO (GURGLE)
—SISTER IS...
...TOO KIND.

The shocking scene of the second chapter...

I hope I was able to convey with the manga the same impact this scene had for me when I experienced it as just another reader. The second chapter of *Re:ZERO* will accelerate faster from this point on.

Let's meet again in Volume 3.

# Re:Zero

## -Starting Life in Another World-

### A Week at the Mansion

The only ability Subaru Natsuki gets when he's summoned to another world is time travel via his own death. But to save her, he'll die as many times as it takes.

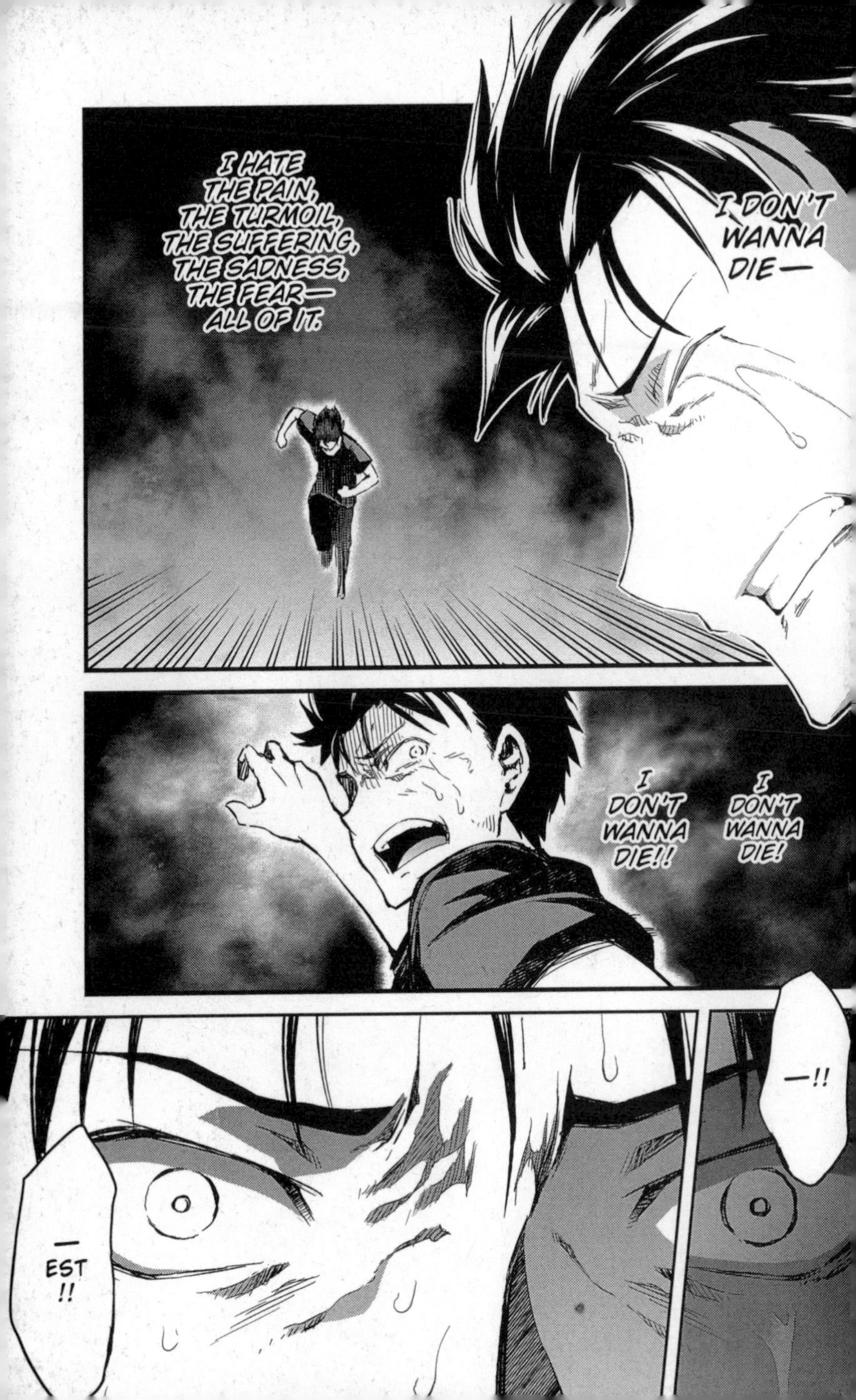
I DON'T WANNA DIE—
I HATE THE PAIN, THE TURMOIL, THE SUFFERING, THE SADNESS, THE FEAR—ALL OF IT.
I DON'T WANNA DIE!
I DON'T WANNA DIE!!
—!!
—EST!!

## Episode 9 "Hands"

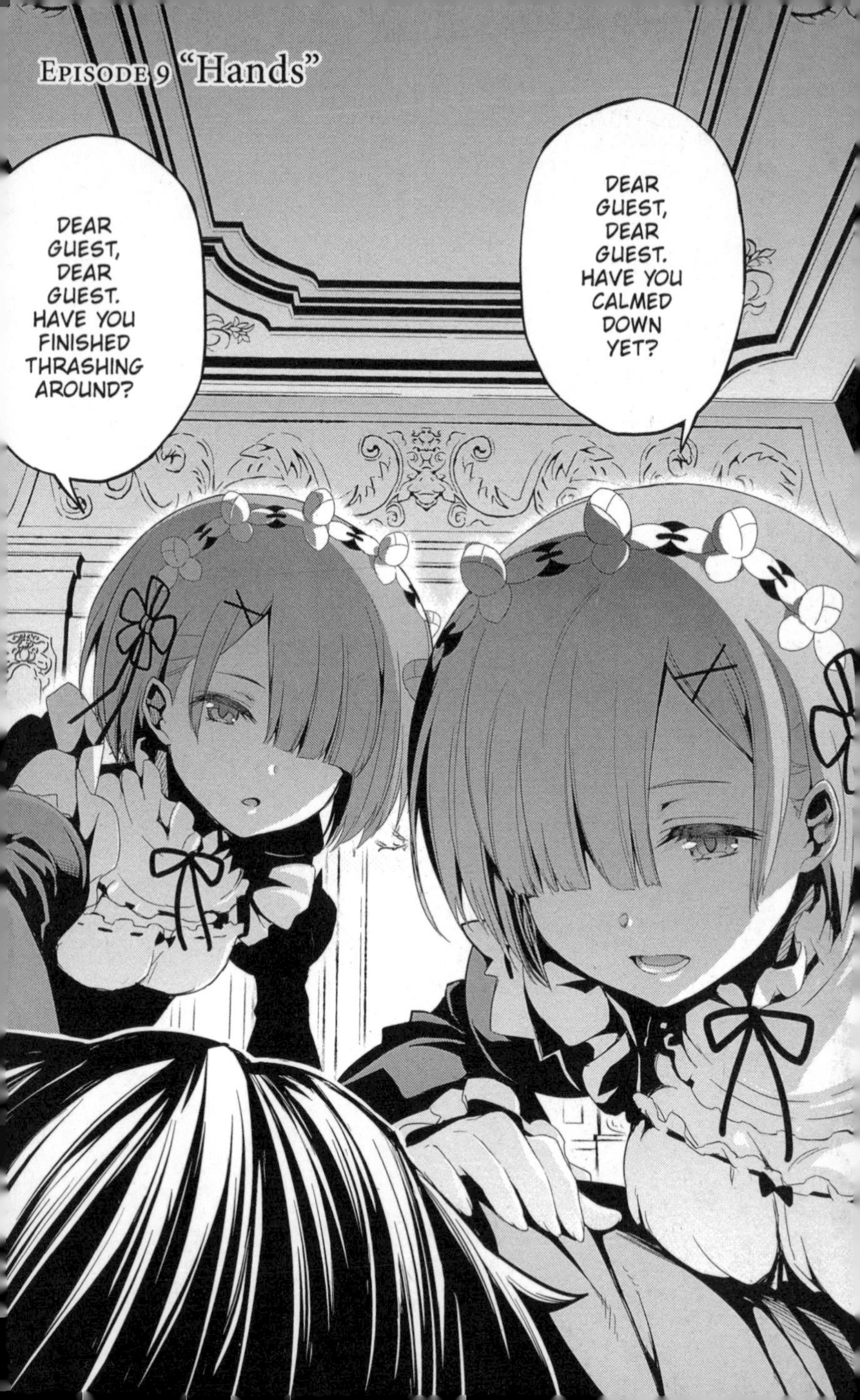
DEAR GUEST, DEAR GUEST. HAVE YOU CALMED DOWN YET?
DEAR GUEST, DEAR GUEST. HAVE YOU FINISHED THRASHING AROUND?

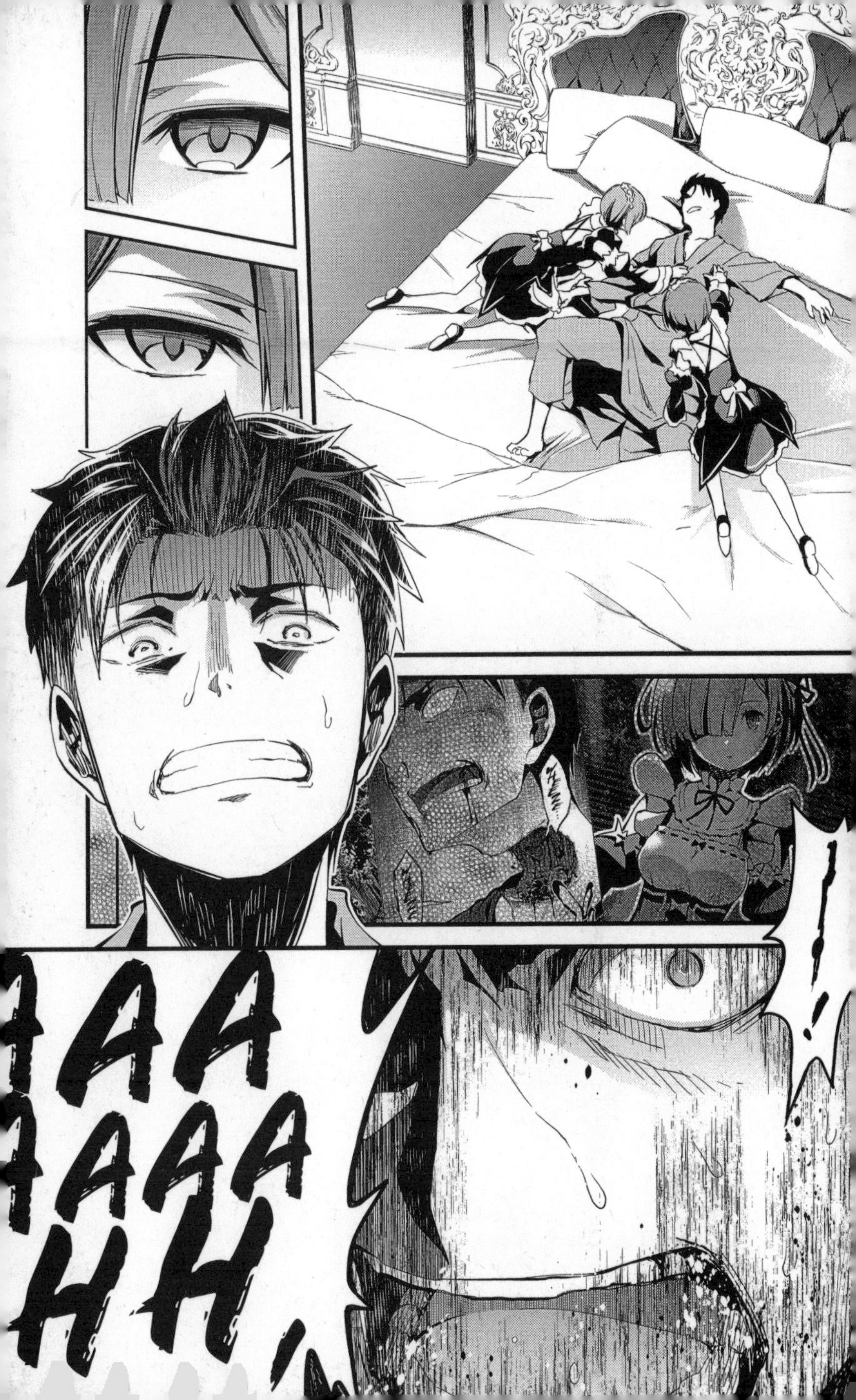
AA
AAA
HH...

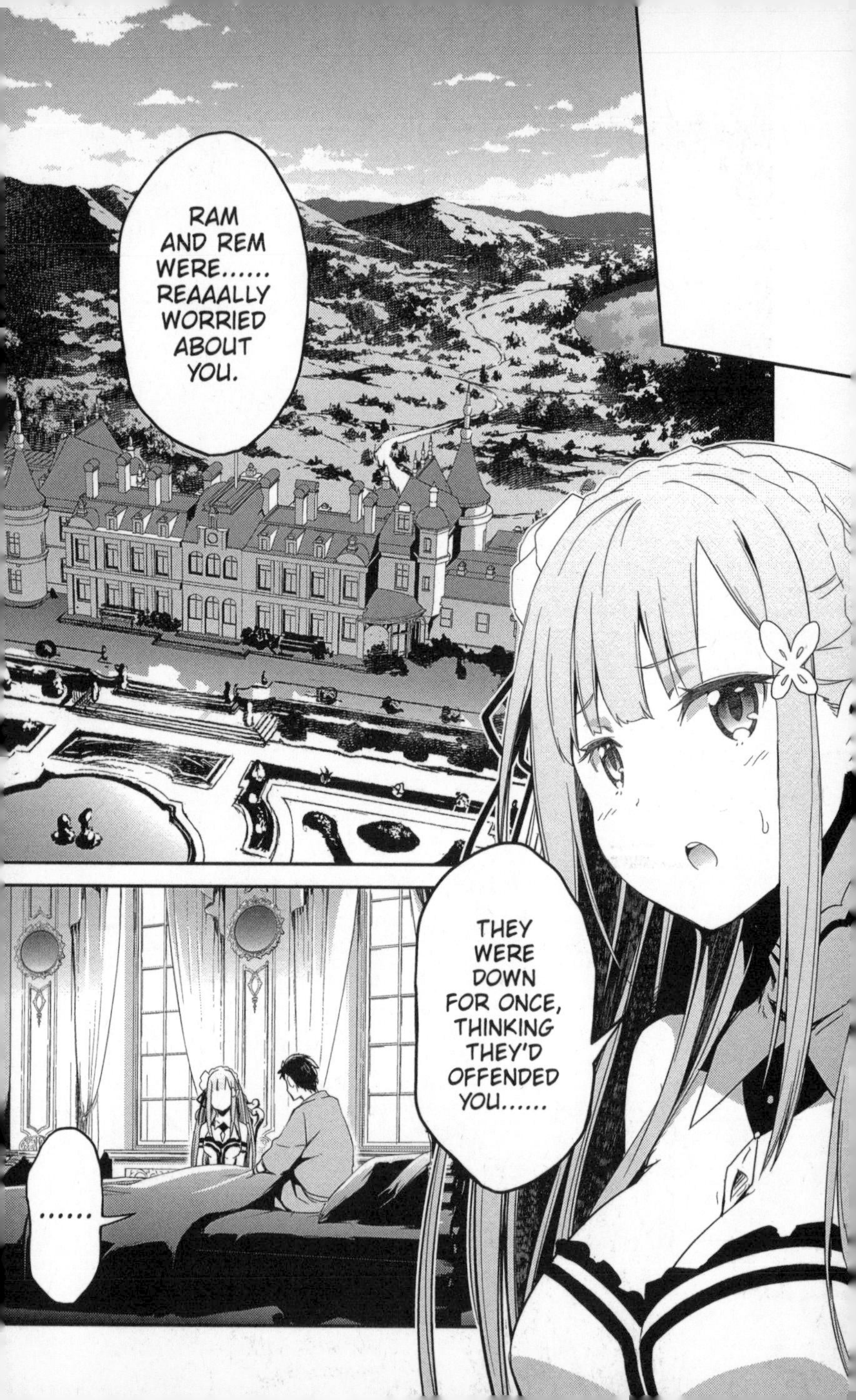
RAM AND REM WERE...... REAAALLY WORRIED ABOUT YOU.
THEY WERE DOWN FOR ONCE, THINKING THEY'D OFFENDED YOU......
......

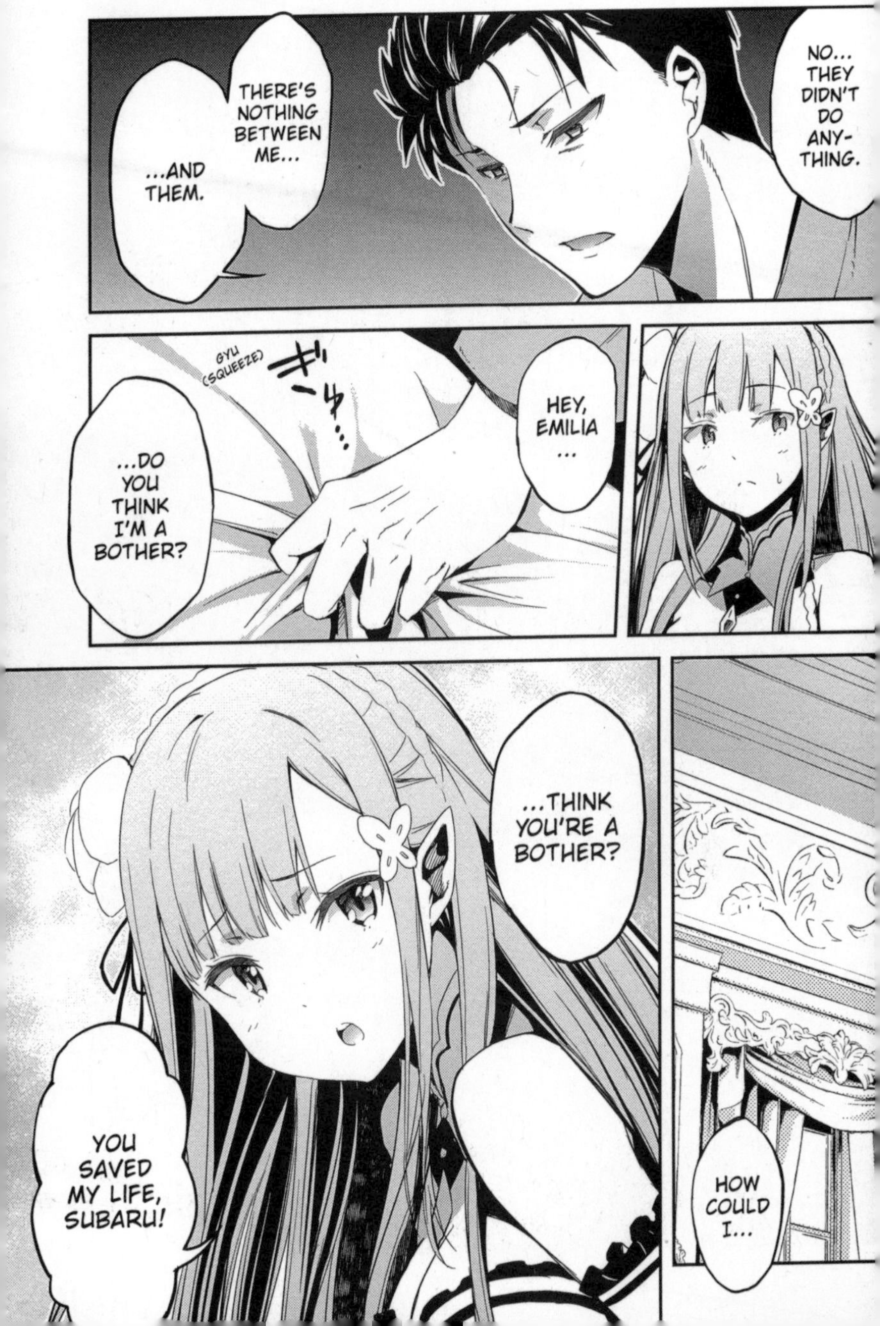
NO... THEY DIDN'T DO ANY-THING.
THERE'S NOTHING BETWEEN ME...
...AND THEM.
HEY, EMILIA...
GYU (SQUEEZE)
...DO YOU THINK I'M A BOTHER?
HOW COULD I...
...THINK YOU'RE A BOTHER?
YOU SAVED MY LIFE, SUBARU!

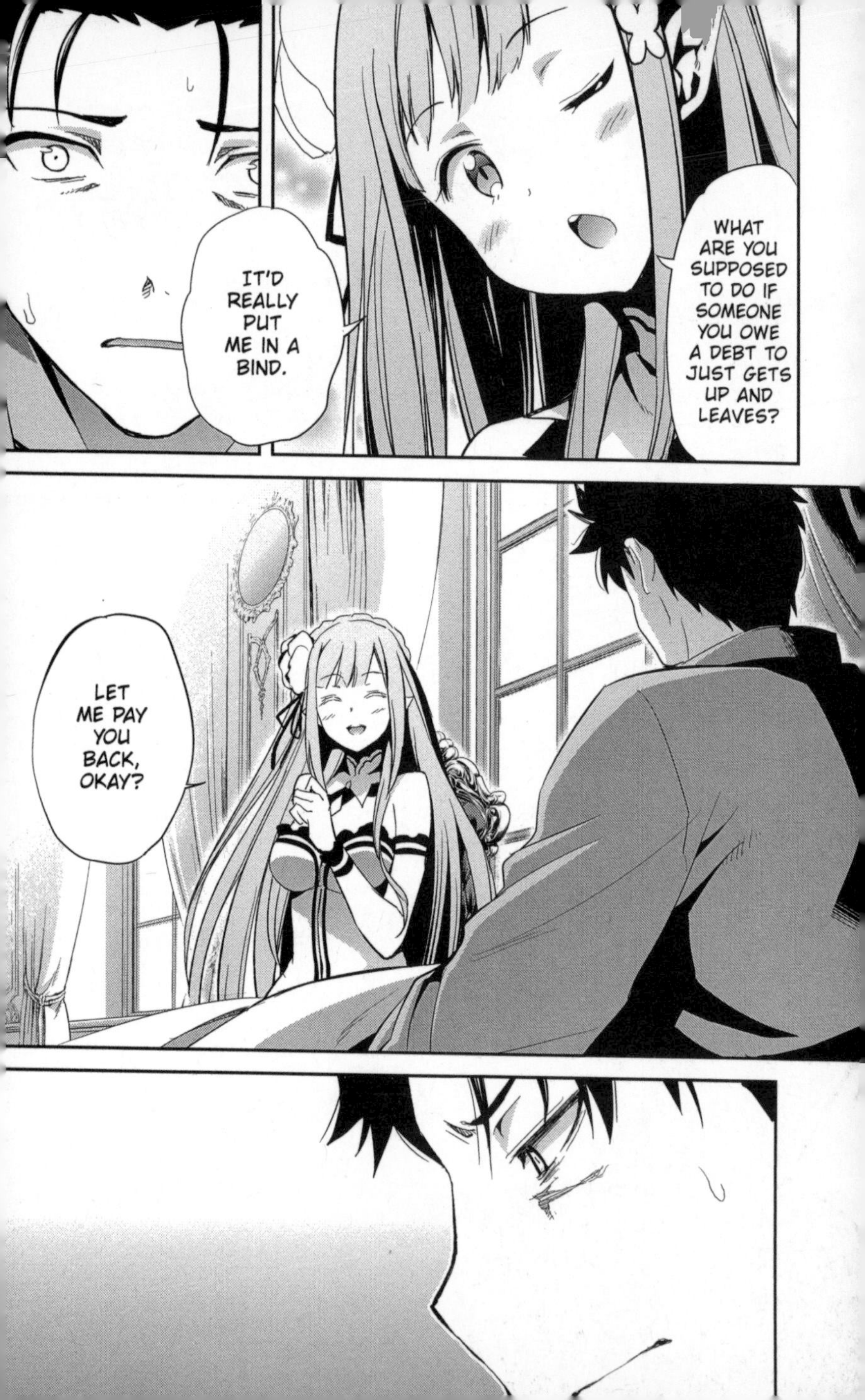
WHAT ARE YOU SUPPOSED TO DO IF SOMEONE YOU OWE A DEBT TO JUST GETS UP AND LEAVES?
IT'D REALLY PUT ME IN A BIND.
LET ME PAY YOU BACK, OKAY?

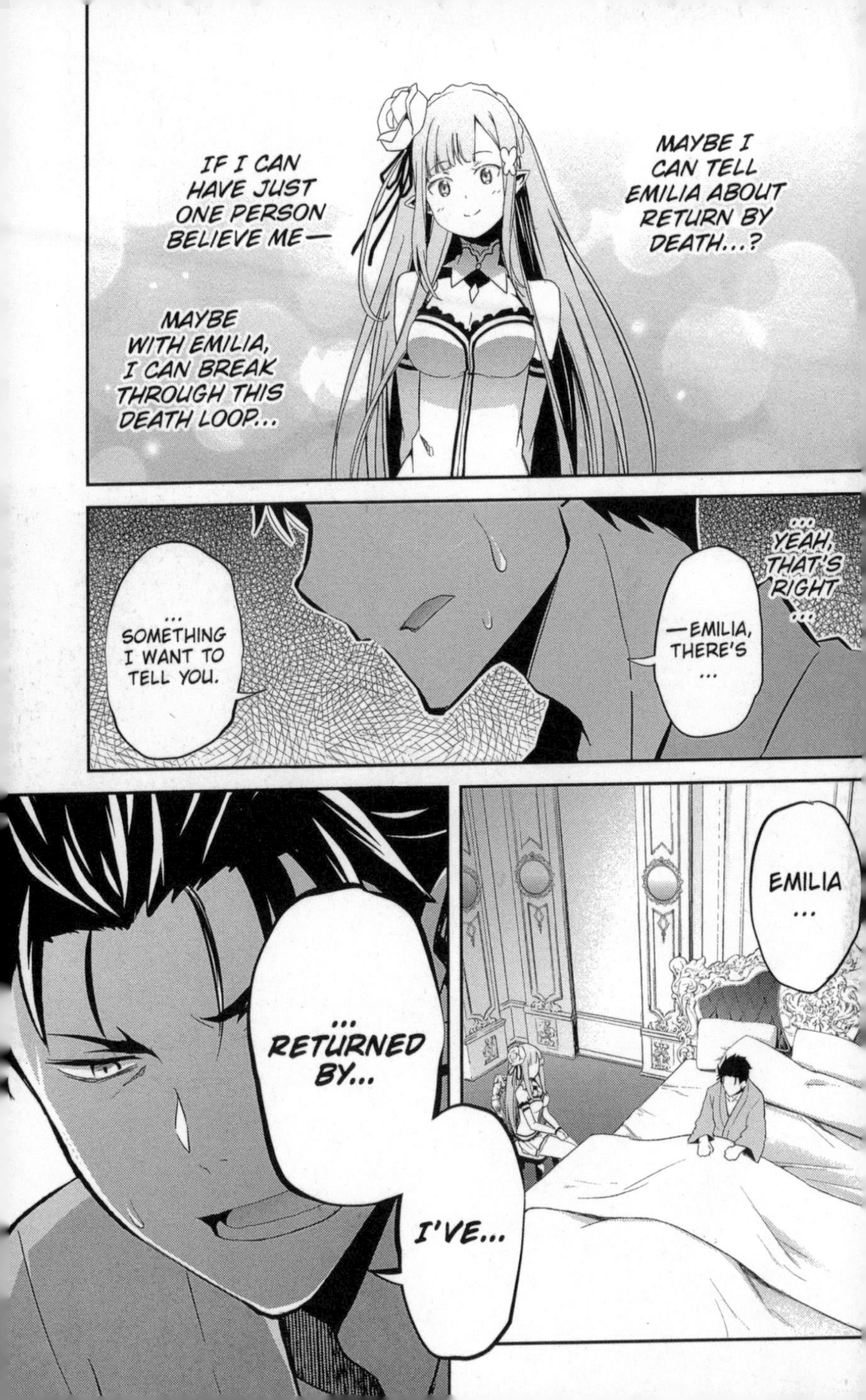
MAYBE I CAN TELL EMILIA ABOUT RETURN BY DEATH...?
IF I CAN HAVE JUST ONE PERSON BELIEVE ME—
MAYBE WITH EMILIA, I CAN BREAK THROUGH THIS DEATH LOOP...
...YEAH, THAT'S RIGHT...
—EMILIA, THERE'S ...
... SOMETHING I WANT TO TELL YOU.
EMILIA ...
... RETURNED BY...
I'VE...

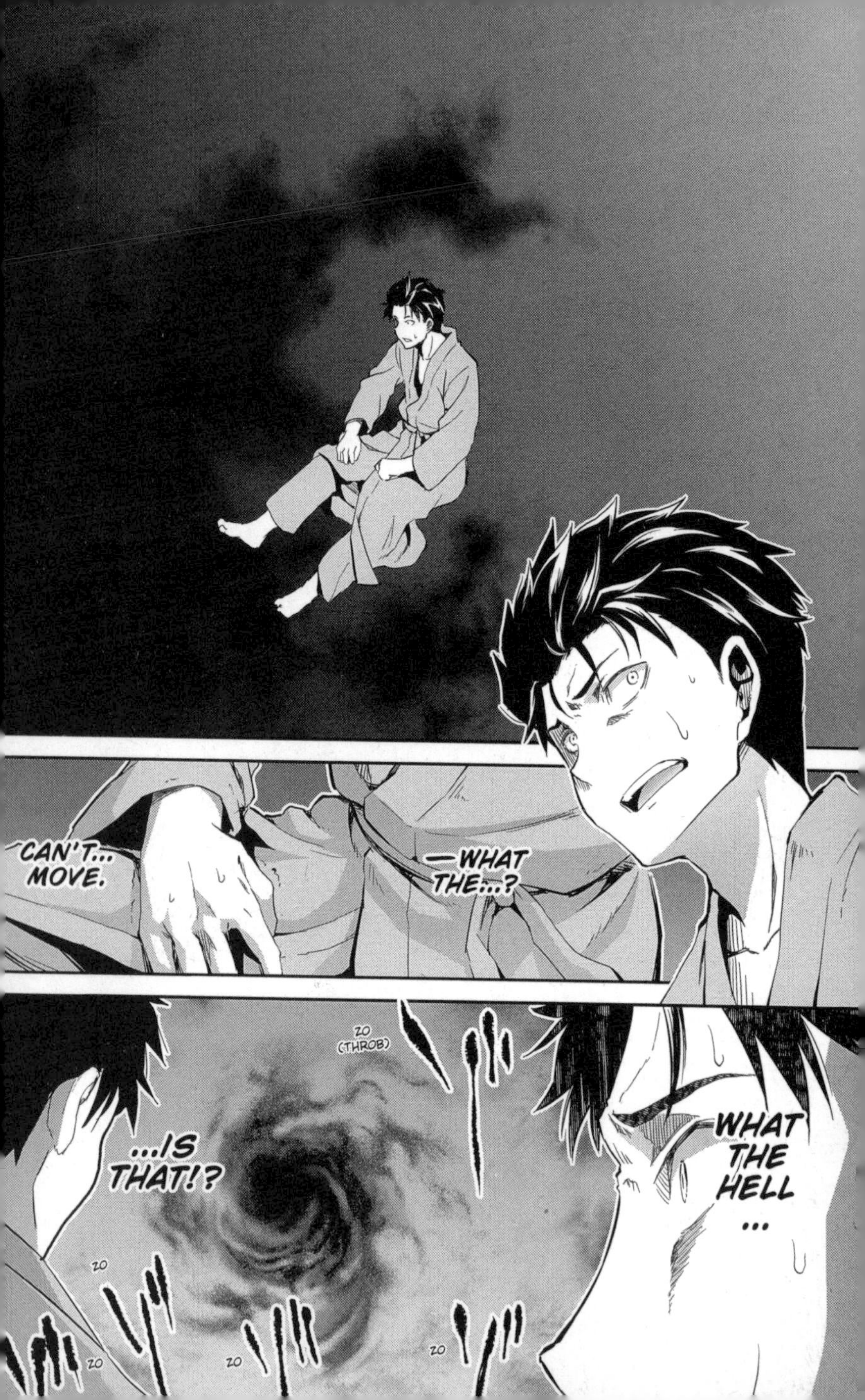
—WHAT THE...?
CAN'T... MOVE.
ZO (THROB)
WHAT THE HELL ...
...IS THAT!?
ZO
ZO
ZO
ZO

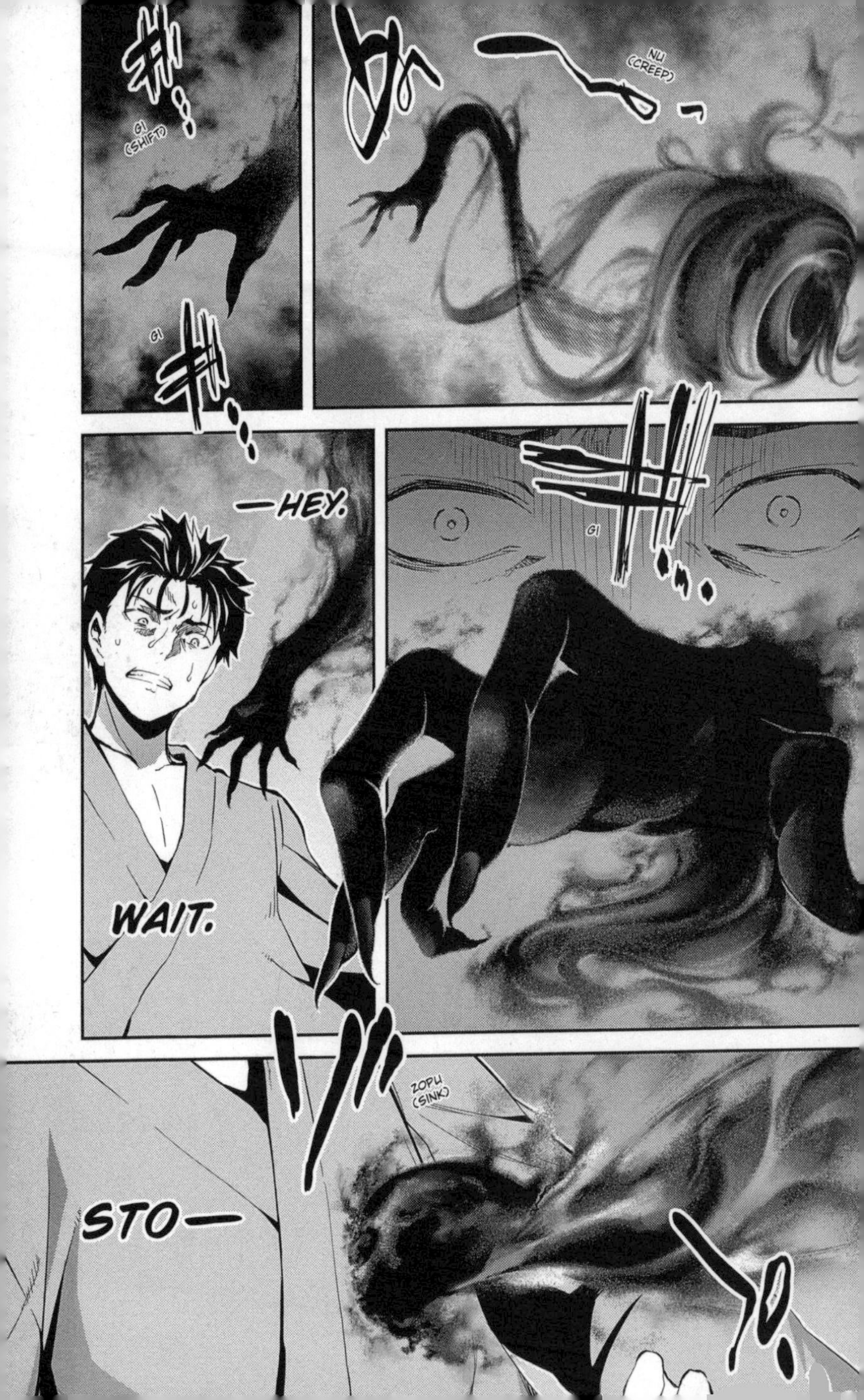
NU
(CREEP)
GI
(SHIFT)
GI
GI
—HEY.
WAIT.
ZOPU
(SINK)
STO—

GUAAAAH!!

GIRI
(GRIP)

—BARU?

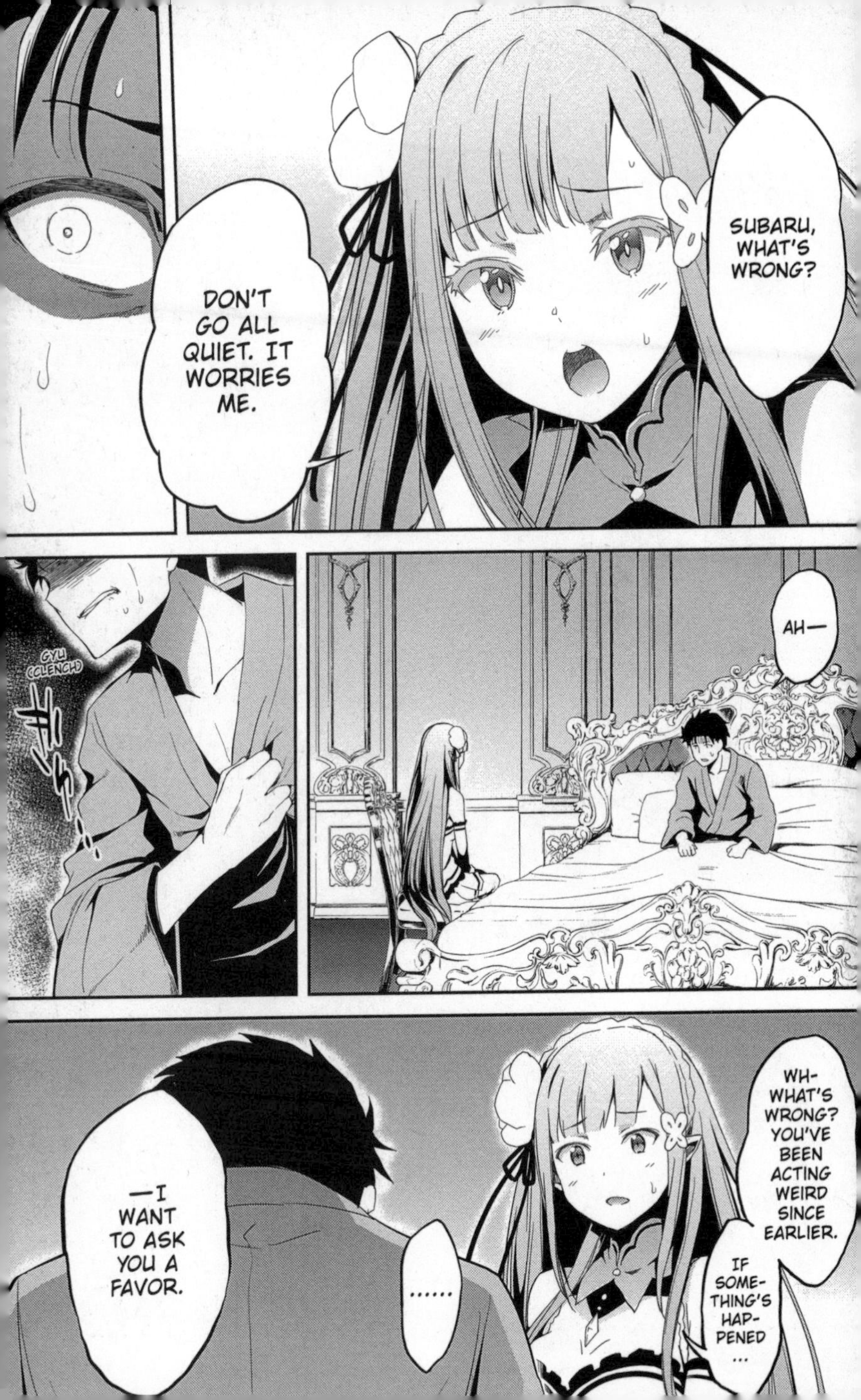
SUBARU, WHAT'S WRONG?
DON'T GO ALL QUIET. IT WORRIES ME.
AH—
GYU (CLENCH)
WH-WHAT'S WRONG? YOU'VE BEEN ACTING WEIRD SINCE EARLIER.
IF SOMETHING'S HAPPENED...
......
—I WANT TO ASK YOU A FAVOR.

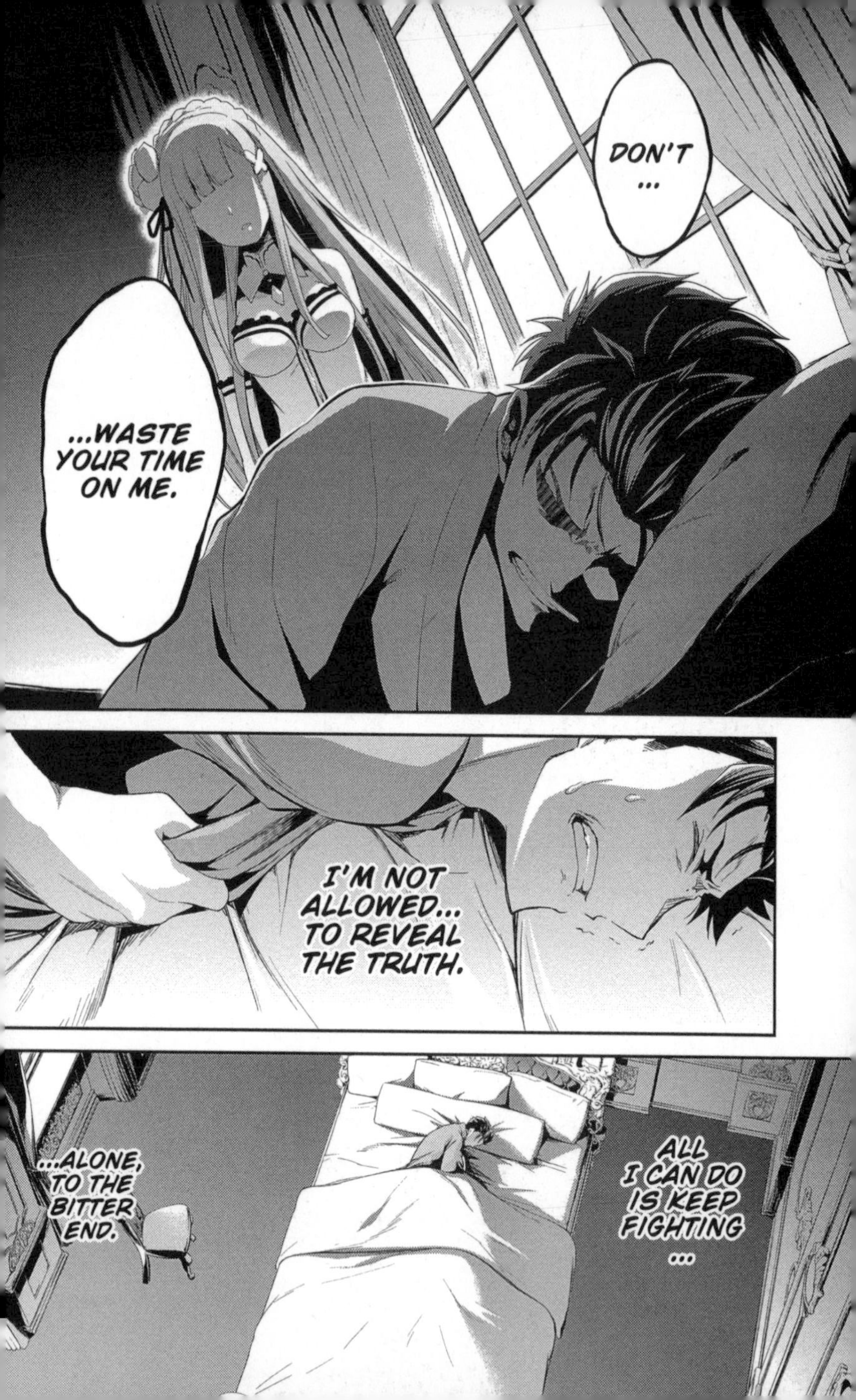
DON'T ...
...WASTE YOUR TIME ON ME.
I'M NOT ALLOWED... TO REVEAL THE TRUTH.
ALL I CAN DO IS KEEP FIGHTING ...
...ALONE, TO THE BITTER END.

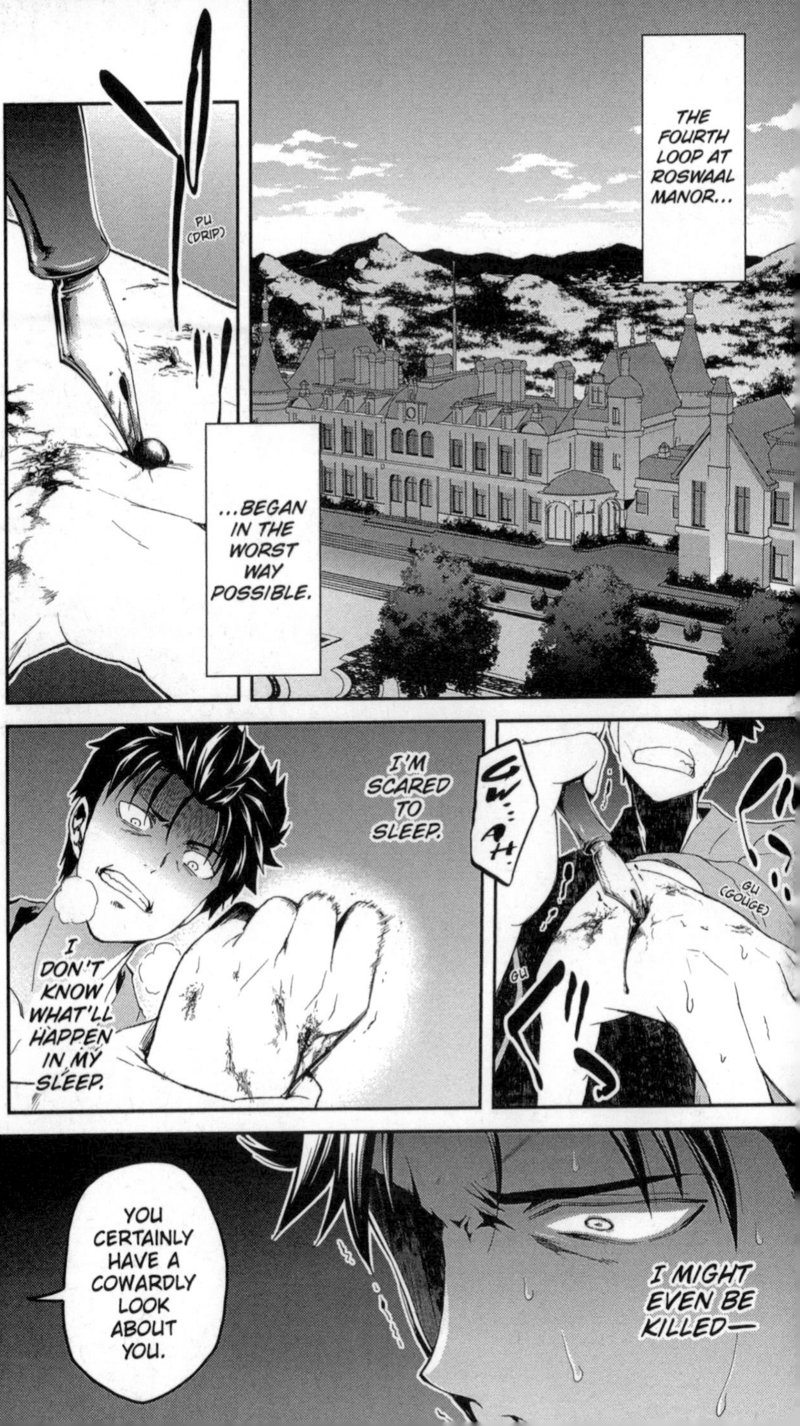
THE FOURTH LOOP AT ROSWAAL MANOR...
...BEGAN IN THE WORST WAY POSSIBLE.
PU (DRIP)
GU (GOUGE)
GU
I'M SCARED TO SLEEP.
I DON'T KNOW WHAT'LL HAPPEN IN MY SLEEP.
I MIGHT EVEN BE KILLED—
YOU CERTAINLY HAVE A COWARDLY LOOK ABOUT YOU.

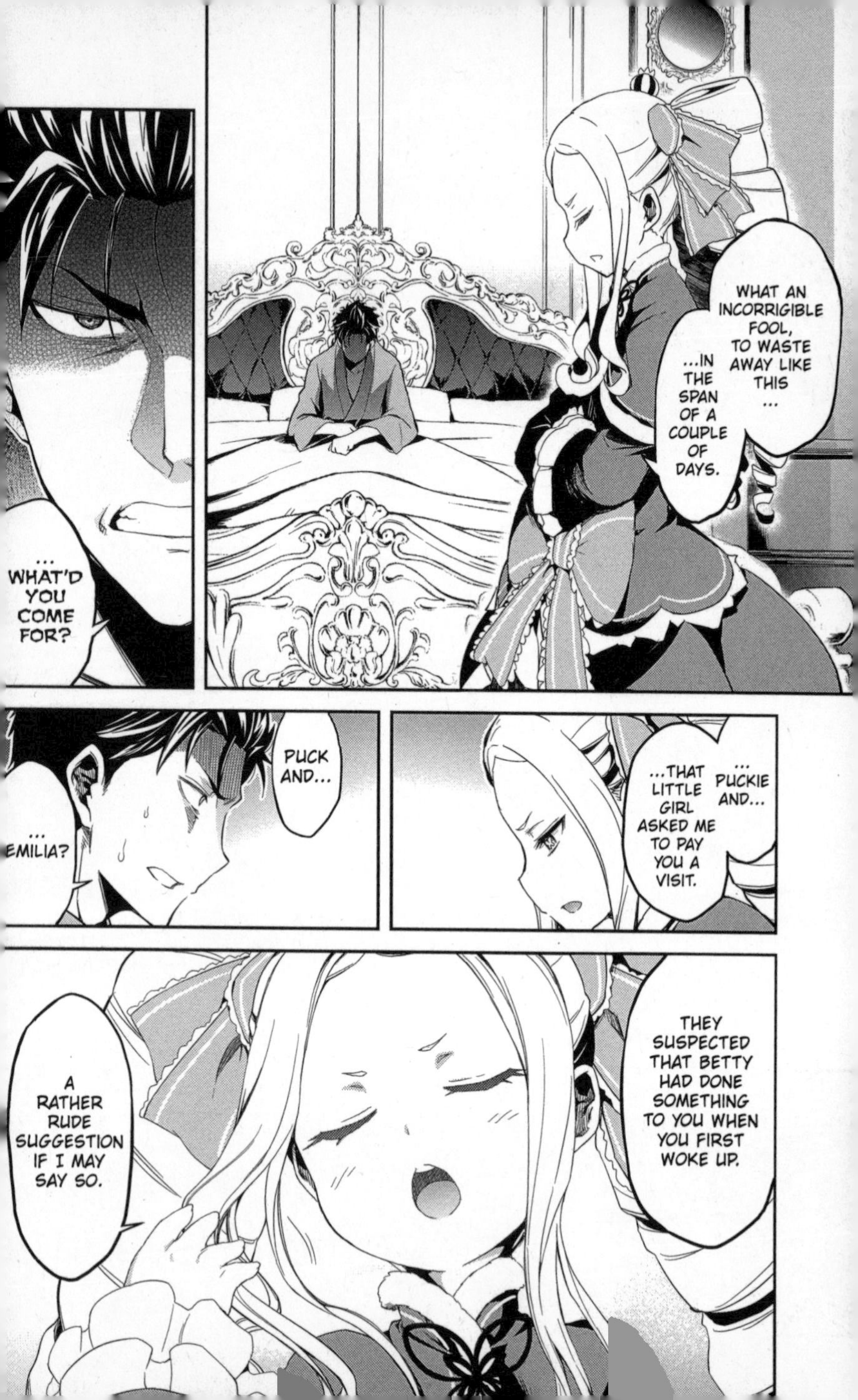
WHAT AN INCORRIGIBLE FOOL, TO WASTE AWAY LIKE THIS...
...IN THE SPAN OF A COUPLE OF DAYS.
...WHAT'D YOU COME FOR?
...PUCKIE AND...
...THAT LITTLE GIRL ASKED ME TO PAY YOU A VISIT.
PUCK AND...
...EMILIA?
THEY SUSPECTED THAT BETTY HAD DONE SOMETHING TO YOU WHEN YOU FIRST WOKE UP.
A RATHER RUDE SUGGESTION IF I MAY SAY SO.

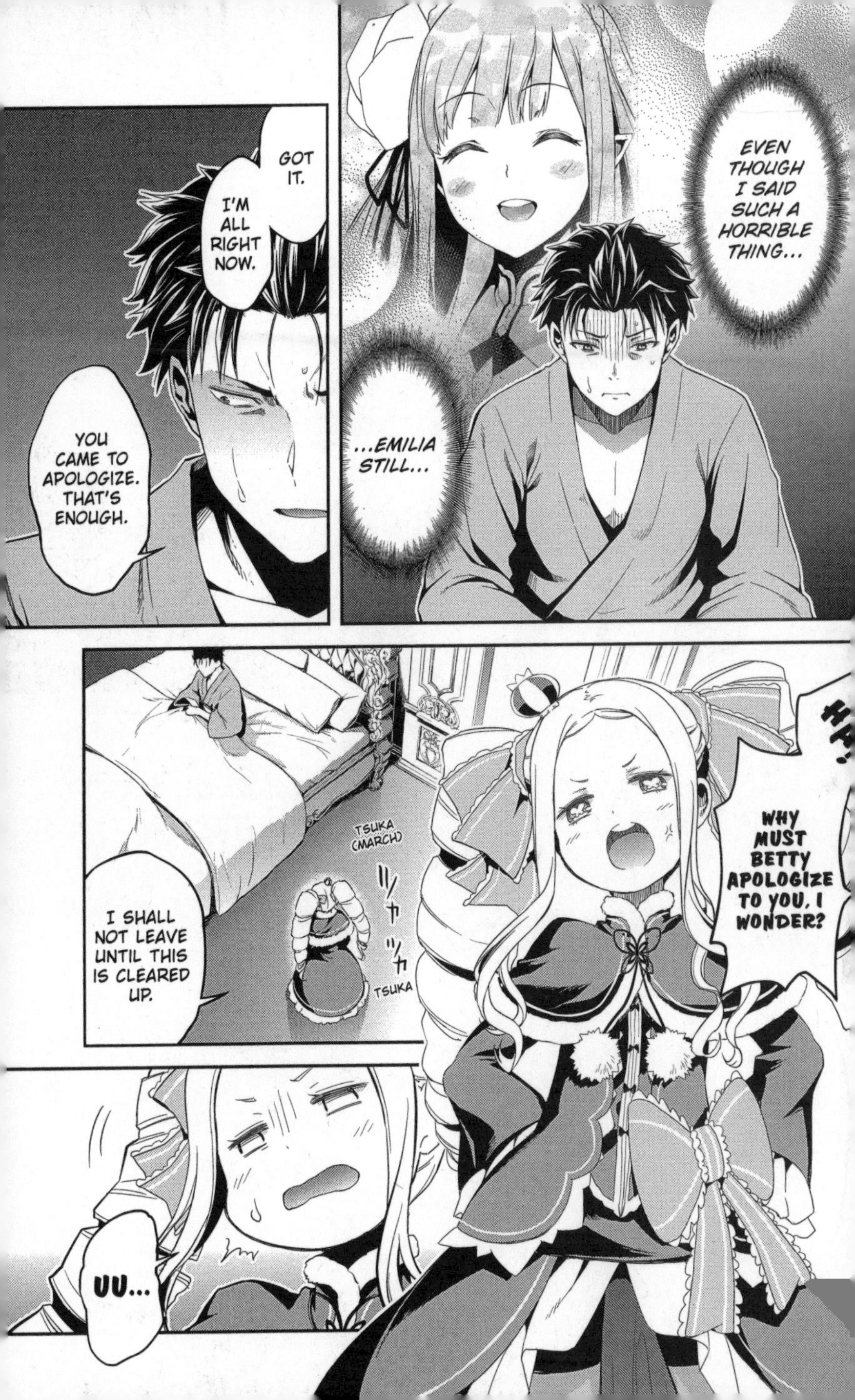
EVEN THOUGH I SAID SUCH A HORRIBLE THING...
...EMILIA STILL...
GOT IT.
I'M ALL RIGHT NOW.
YOU CAME TO APOLOGIZE. THAT'S ENOUGH.
WHY MUST BETTY APOLOGIZE TO YOU, I WONDER?
TSUKA (MARCH)
ツカ
ツカ
TSUKA
I SHALL NOT LEAVE UNTIL THIS IS CLEARED UP.
UU...

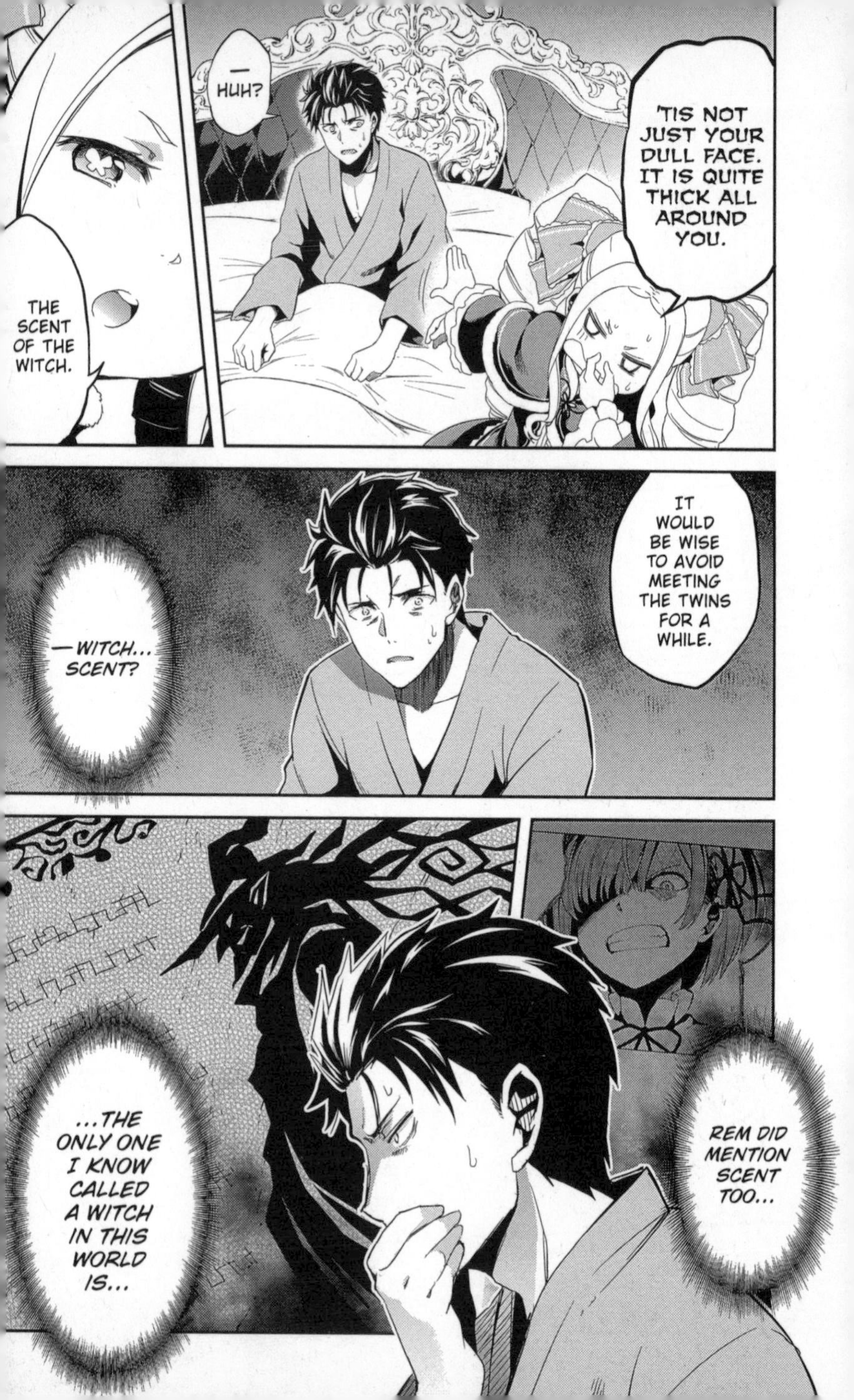
'TIS NOT JUST YOUR DULL FACE. IT IS QUITE THICK ALL AROUND YOU.
—HUH?
THE SCENT OF THE WITCH.
IT WOULD BE WISE TO AVOID MEETING THE TWINS FOR A WHILE.
—WITCH... SCENT?
REM DID MENTION SCENT TOO...
...THE ONLY ONE I KNOW CALLED A WITCH IN THIS WORLD IS...

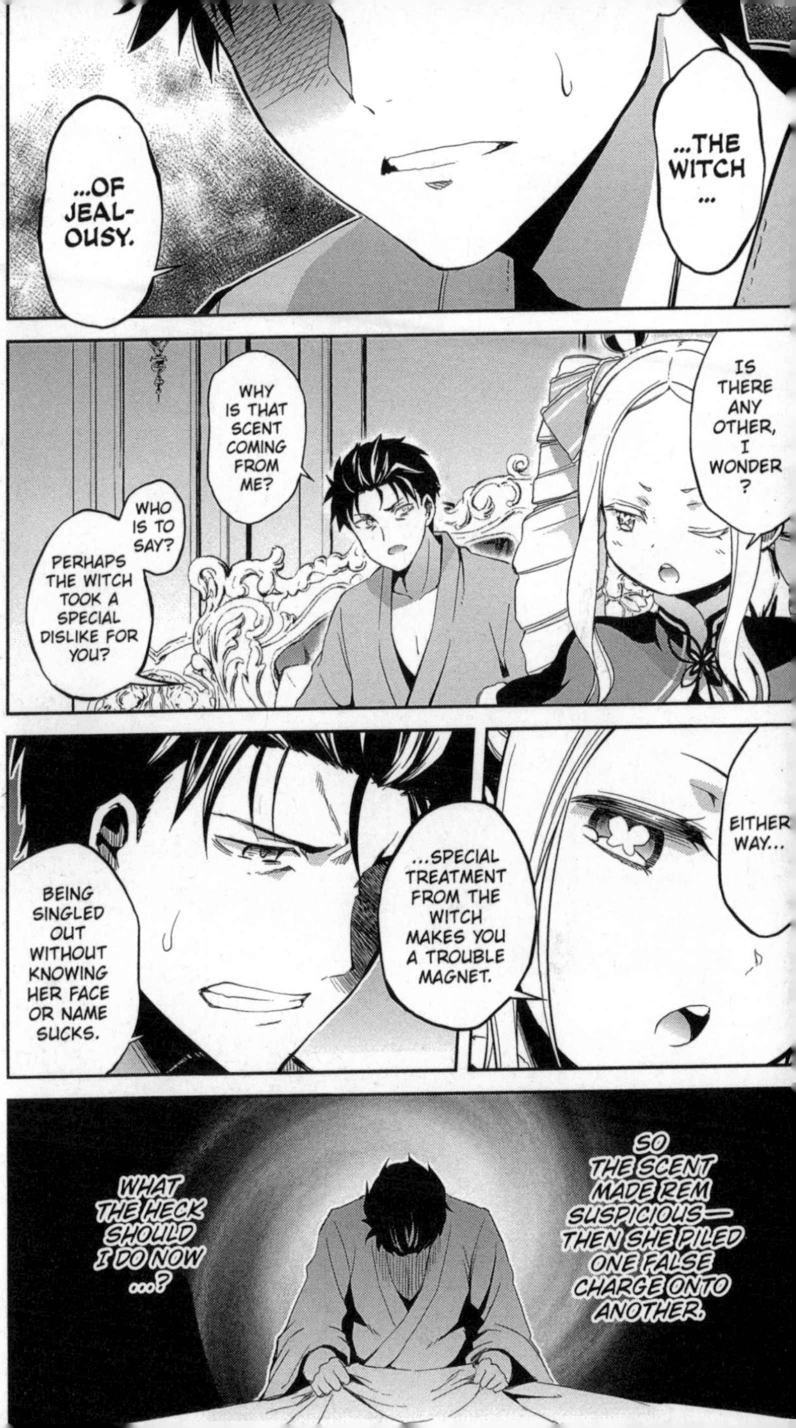

...THE WITCH...
...OF JEALOUSY.
IS THERE ANY OTHER, I WONDER?
WHY IS THAT SCENT COMING FROM ME?
WHO IS TO SAY?
PERHAPS THE WITCH TOOK A SPECIAL DISLIKE FOR YOU?
EITHER WAY...
...SPECIAL TREATMENT FROM THE WITCH MAKES YOU A TROUBLE MAGNET.
BEING SINGLED OUT WITHOUT KNOWING HER FACE OR NAME SUCKS.
SO THE SCENT MADE REM SUSPICIOUS—THEN SHE PILED ONE FALSE CHARGE ONTO ANOTHER.
WHAT THE HECK SHOULD I DO NOW...?

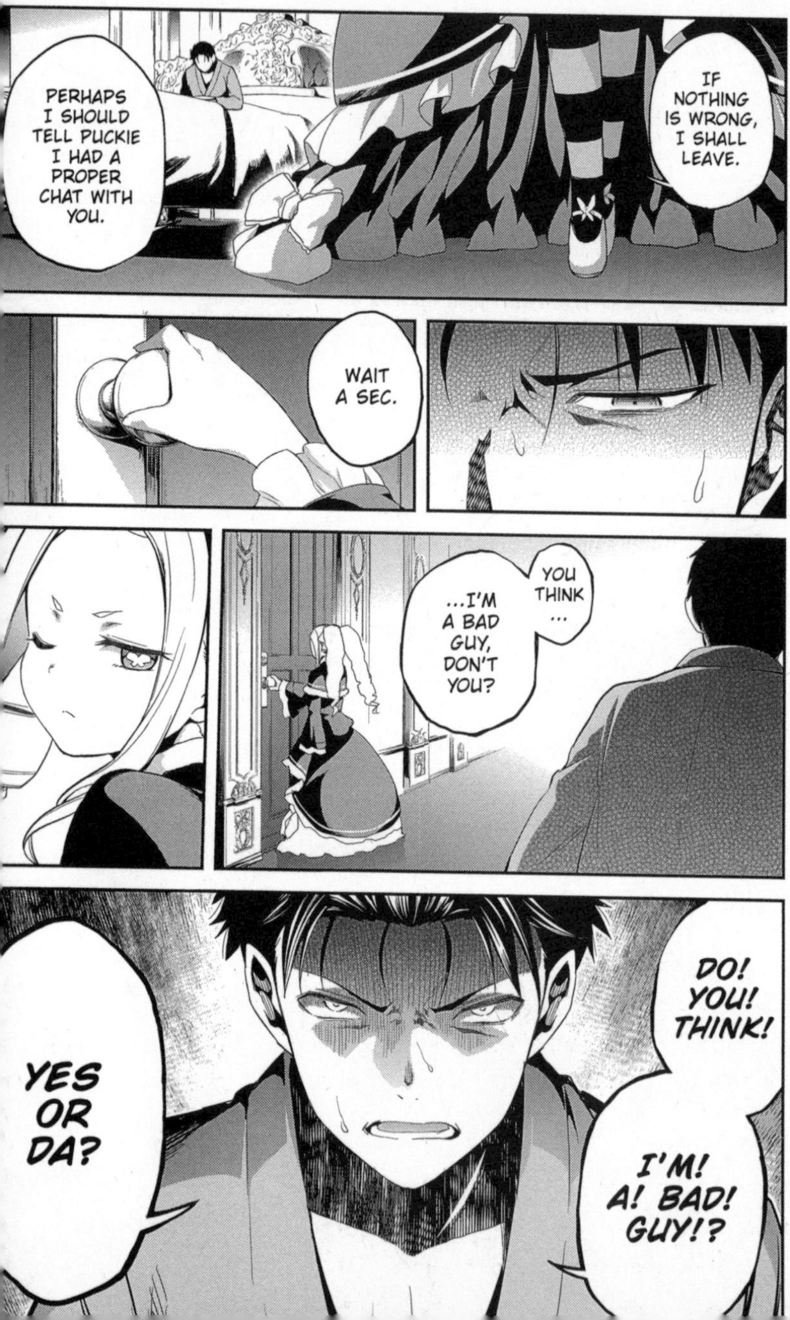
IF NOTHING IS WRONG, I SHALL LEAVE.
PERHAPS I SHOULD TELL PUCKIE I HAD A PROPER CHAT WITH YOU.
WAIT A SEC.
YOU THINK ...
...I'M A BAD GUY, DON'T YOU?
DO! YOU! THINK!
I'M! A! BAD! GUY!?
YES OR DA?

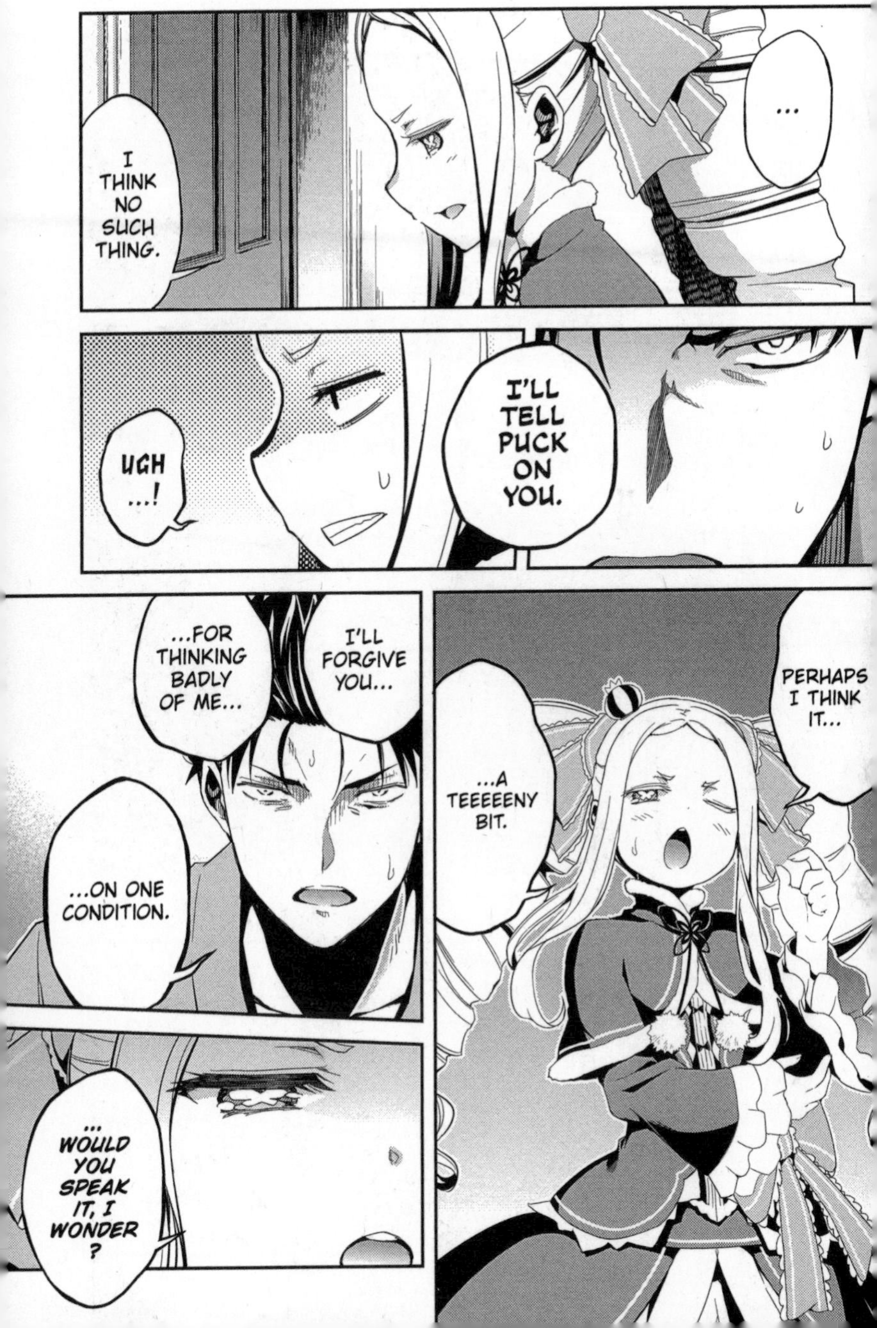
...
I THINK NO SUCH THING.
I'LL TELL PUCK ON YOU.
UGH ...!
PERHAPS I THINK IT...
...A TEEEEENY BIT.
I'LL FORGIVE YOU...
...FOR THINKING BADLY OF ME...
...ON ONE CONDITION.
... WOULD YOU SPEAK IT, I WONDER?

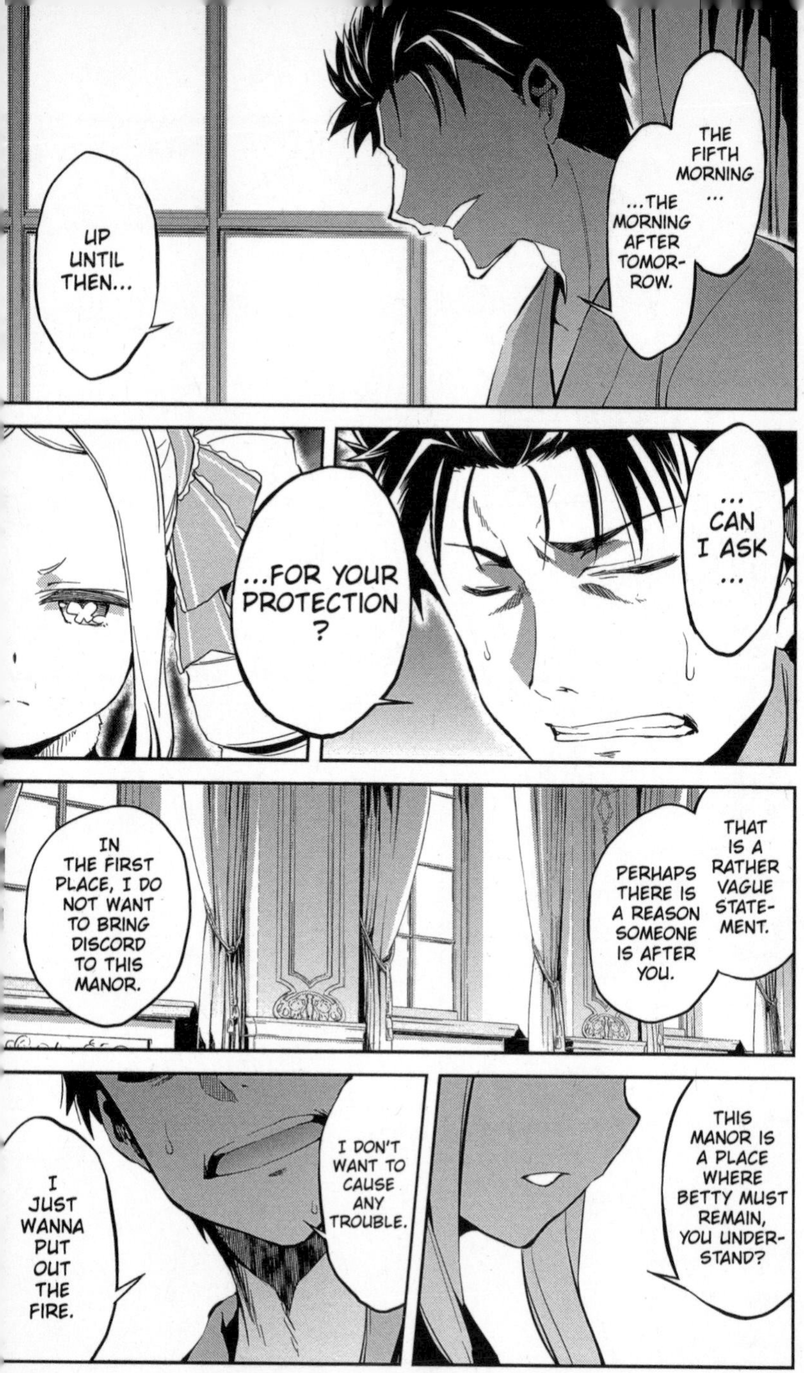
THE FIFTH MORNING...
...THE MORNING AFTER TOMOR-ROW.
UP UNTIL THEN...
...CAN I ASK...
...FOR YOUR PROTECTION?
THAT IS A RATHER VAGUE STATE-MENT.
PERHAPS THERE IS A REASON SOMEONE IS AFTER YOU.
IN THE FIRST PLACE, I DO NOT WANT TO BRING DISCORD TO THIS MANOR.
THIS MANOR IS A PLACE WHERE BETTY MUST REMAIN, YOU UNDER-STAND?
I DON'T WANT TO CAUSE ANY TROUBLE.
I JUST WANNA PUT OUT THE FIRE.

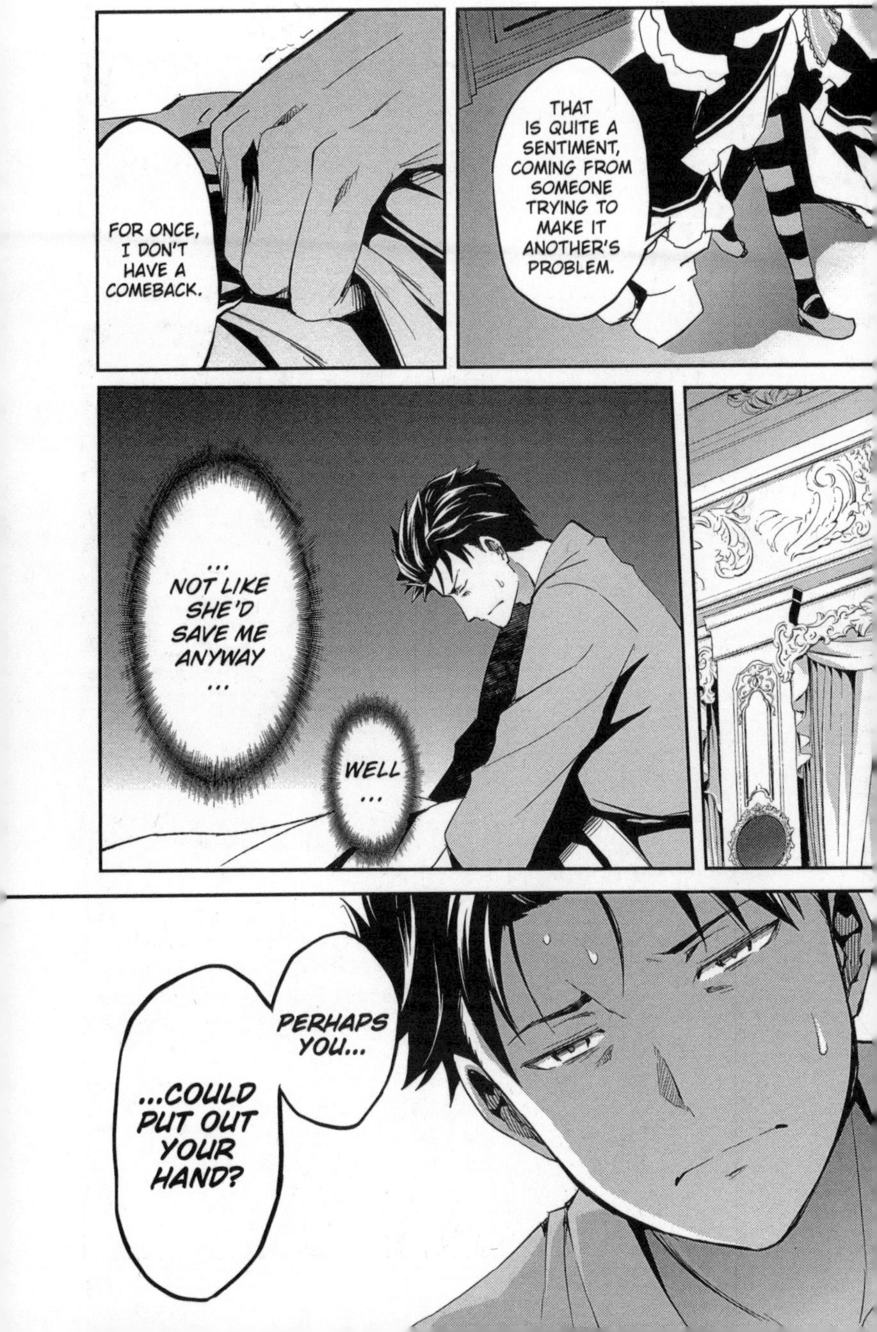
THAT IS QUITE A SENTIMENT, COMING FROM SOMEONE TRYING TO MAKE IT ANOTHER'S PROBLEM.
FOR ONCE, I DON'T HAVE A COMEBACK.
... NOT LIKE SHE'D SAVE ME ANYWAY ...
WELL ...
PERHAPS YOU...
...COULD PUT OUT YOUR HAND?

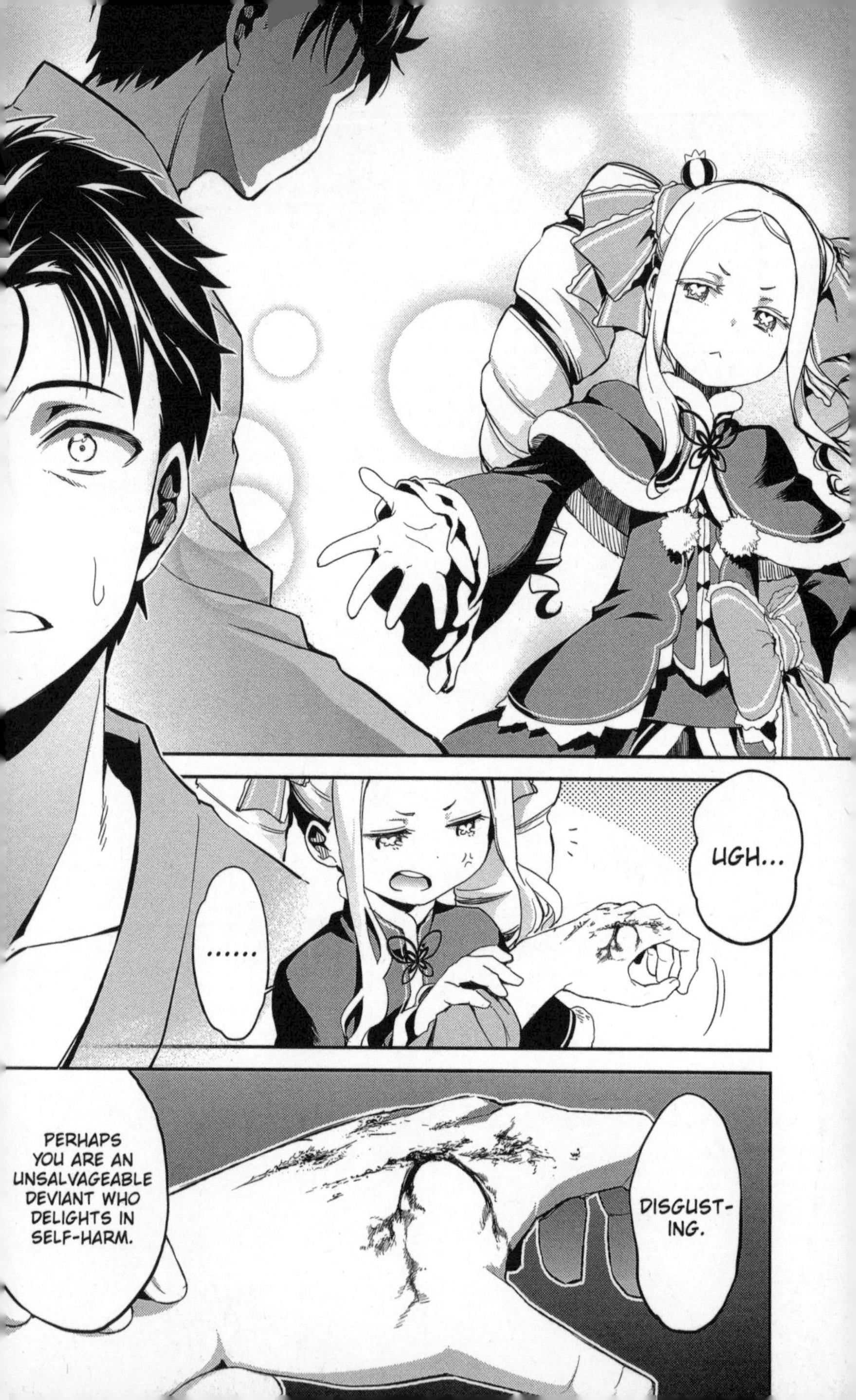
UGH...
......
DISGUST-ING.
PERHAPS YOU ARE AN UNSALVAGEABLE DEVIANT WHO DELIGHTS IN SELF-HARM.

I WAS JUST ...

...TRYING TO GIVE MYSELF A TATTOO AND BOTCHED IT.

YOUR ARTISTIC SENSE, SKILL...

...AND TALENT FOR LIES ARE SORELY LACKING ...

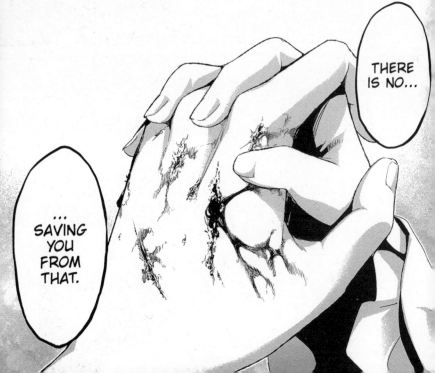

THERE IS NO...

... SAVING YOU FROM THAT.

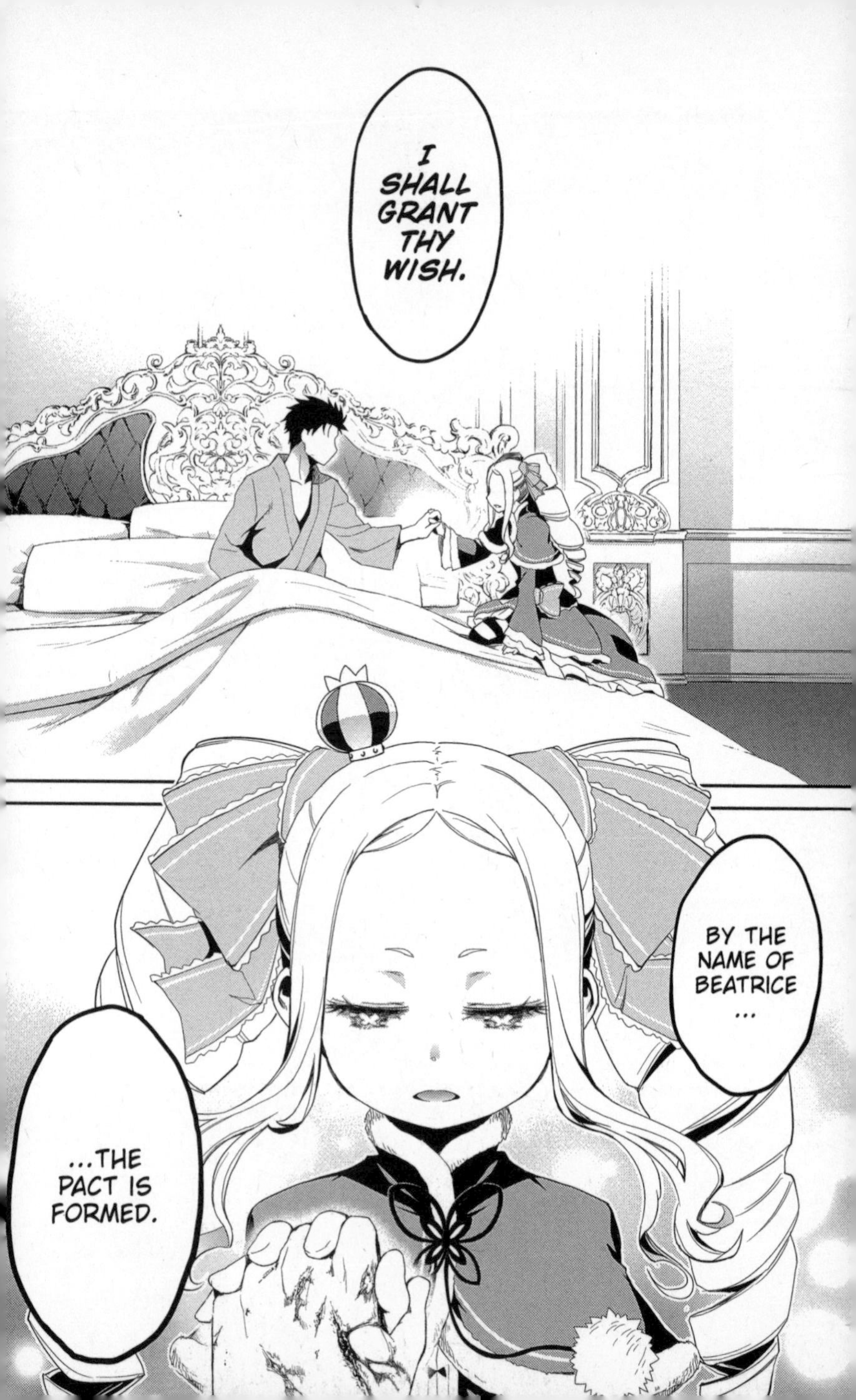
I SHALL GRANT THY WISH.
BY THE NAME OF BEATRICE ...
...THE PACT IS FORMED.

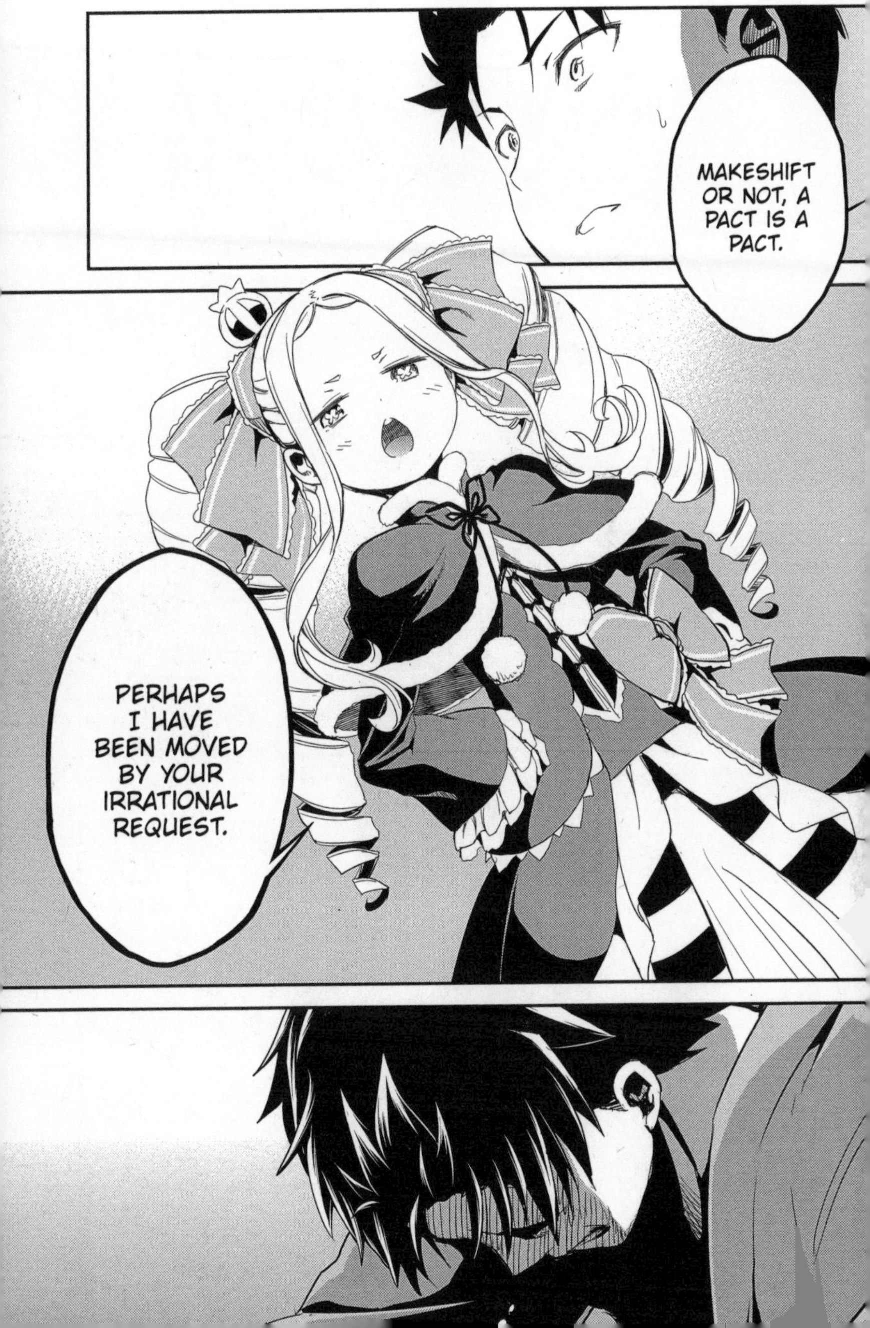
MAKESHIFT OR NOT, A PACT IS A PACT.
PERHAPS I HAVE BEEN MOVED BY YOUR IRRATIONAL REQUEST.

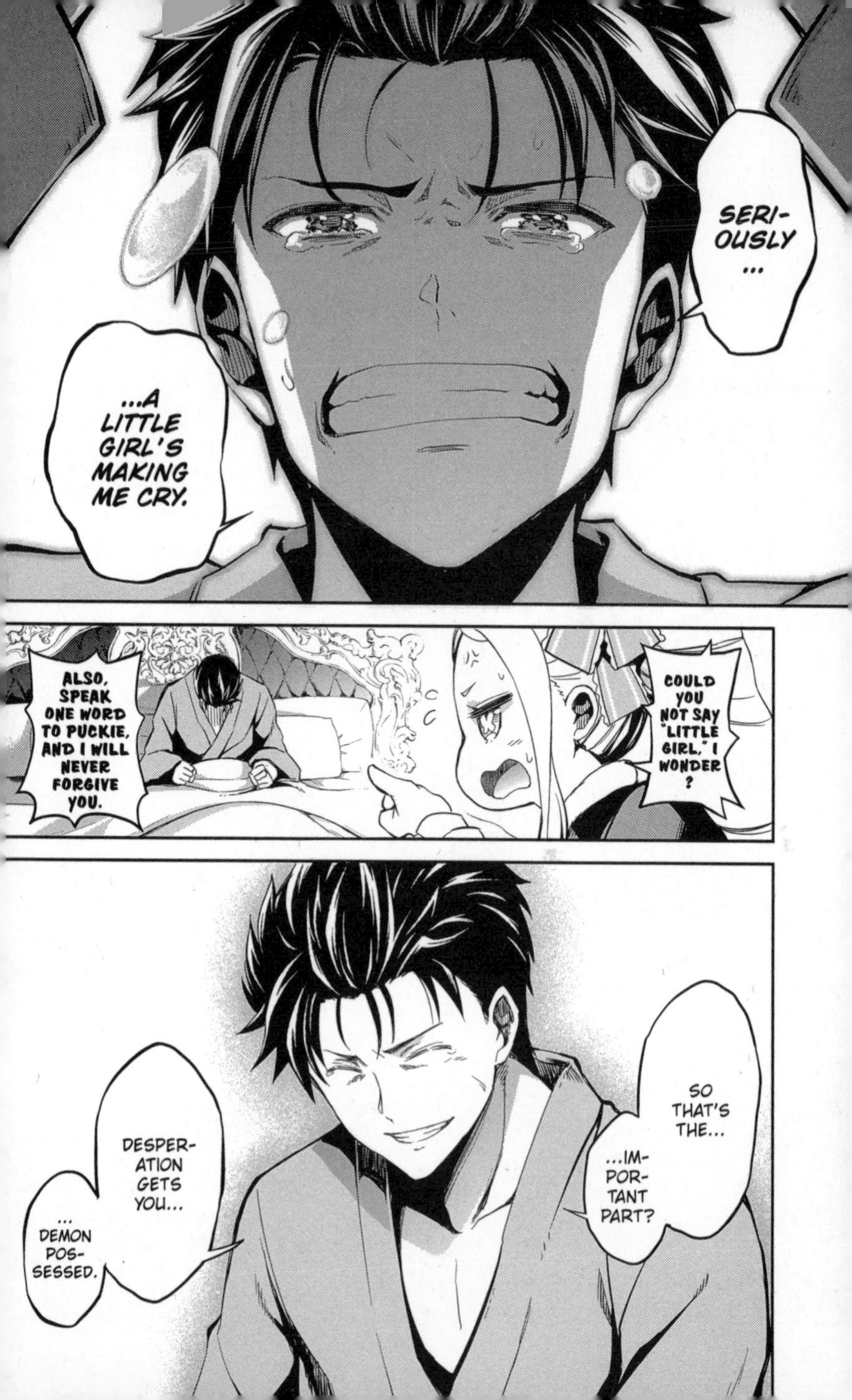
SERI-OUSLY...
...A LITTLE GIRL'S MAKING ME CRY.
COULD YOU NOT SAY "LITTLE GIRL," I WONDER?
ALSO, SPEAK ONE WORD TO PUCKIE, AND I WILL NEVER FORGIVE YOU.
SO THAT'S THE...
...IM-POR-TANT PART?
DESPER-ATION GETS YOU...
...DEMON POS-SESSED.

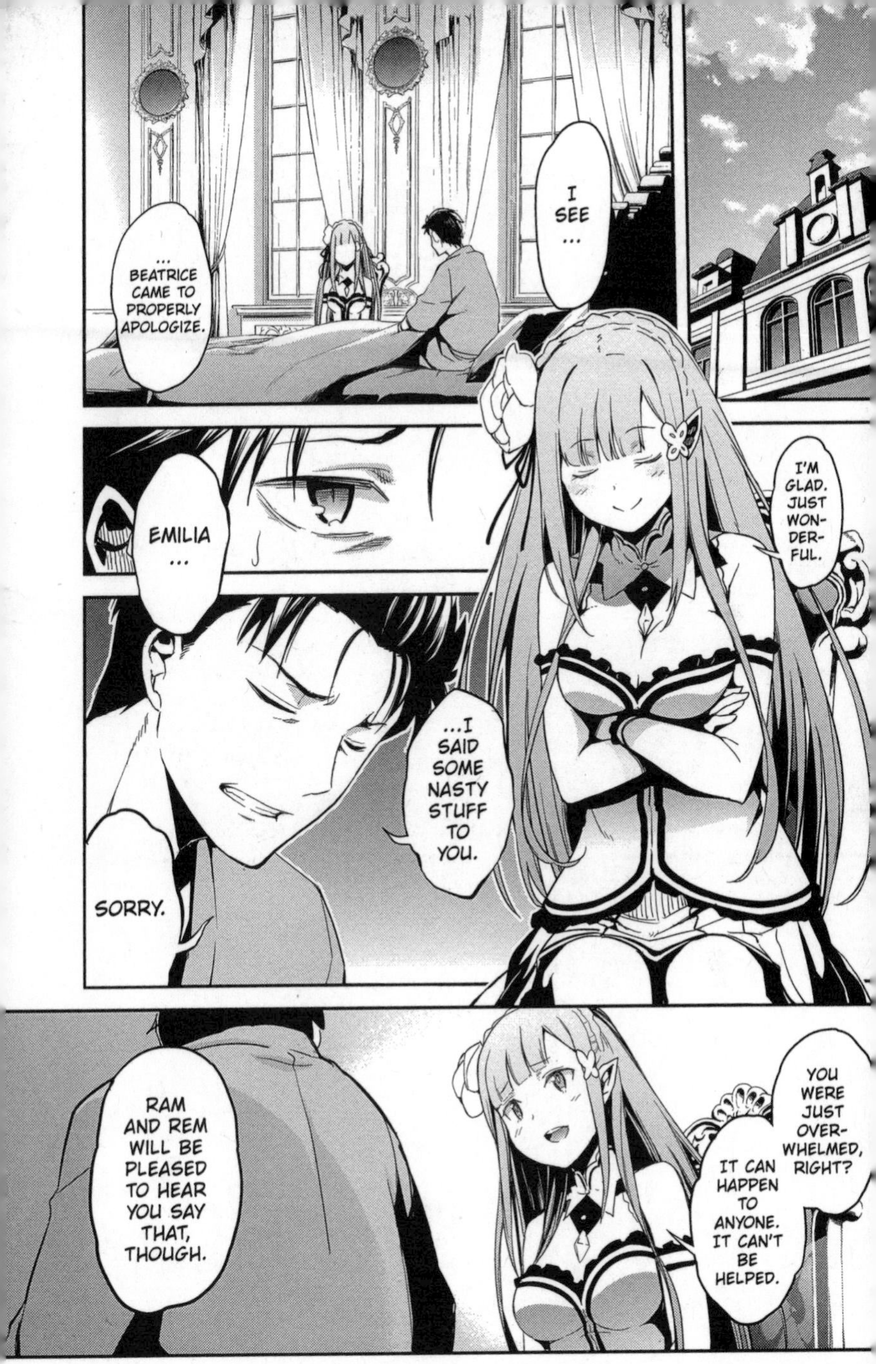
I SEE ...
... BEATRICE CAME TO PROPERLY APOLOGIZE.
I'M GLAD. JUST WONDERFUL.
EMILIA ...
...I SAID SOME NASTY STUFF TO YOU.
SORRY.
YOU WERE JUST OVERWHELMED, RIGHT?
IT CAN HAPPEN TO ANYONE. IT CAN'T BE HELPED.
RAM AND REM WILL BE PLEASED TO HEAR YOU SAY THAT, THOUGH.

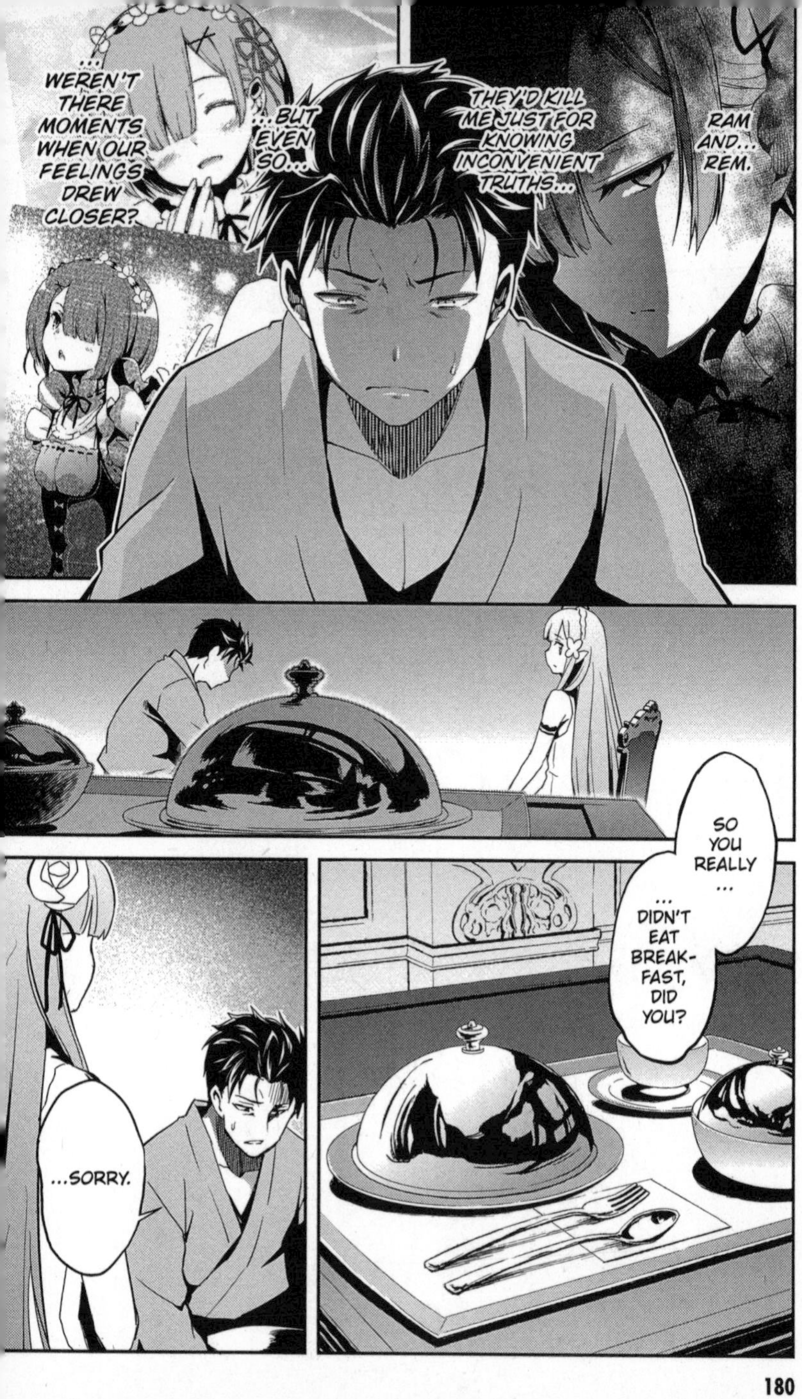
RAM AND... REM.
THEY'D KILL ME JUST FOR KNOWING INCONVENIENT TRUTHS...
...BUT EVEN SO...
...WEREN'T THERE MOMENTS WHEN OUR FEELINGS DREW CLOSER?
SO YOU REALLY ...
...DIDN'T EAT BREAK-FAST, DID YOU?
...SORRY.

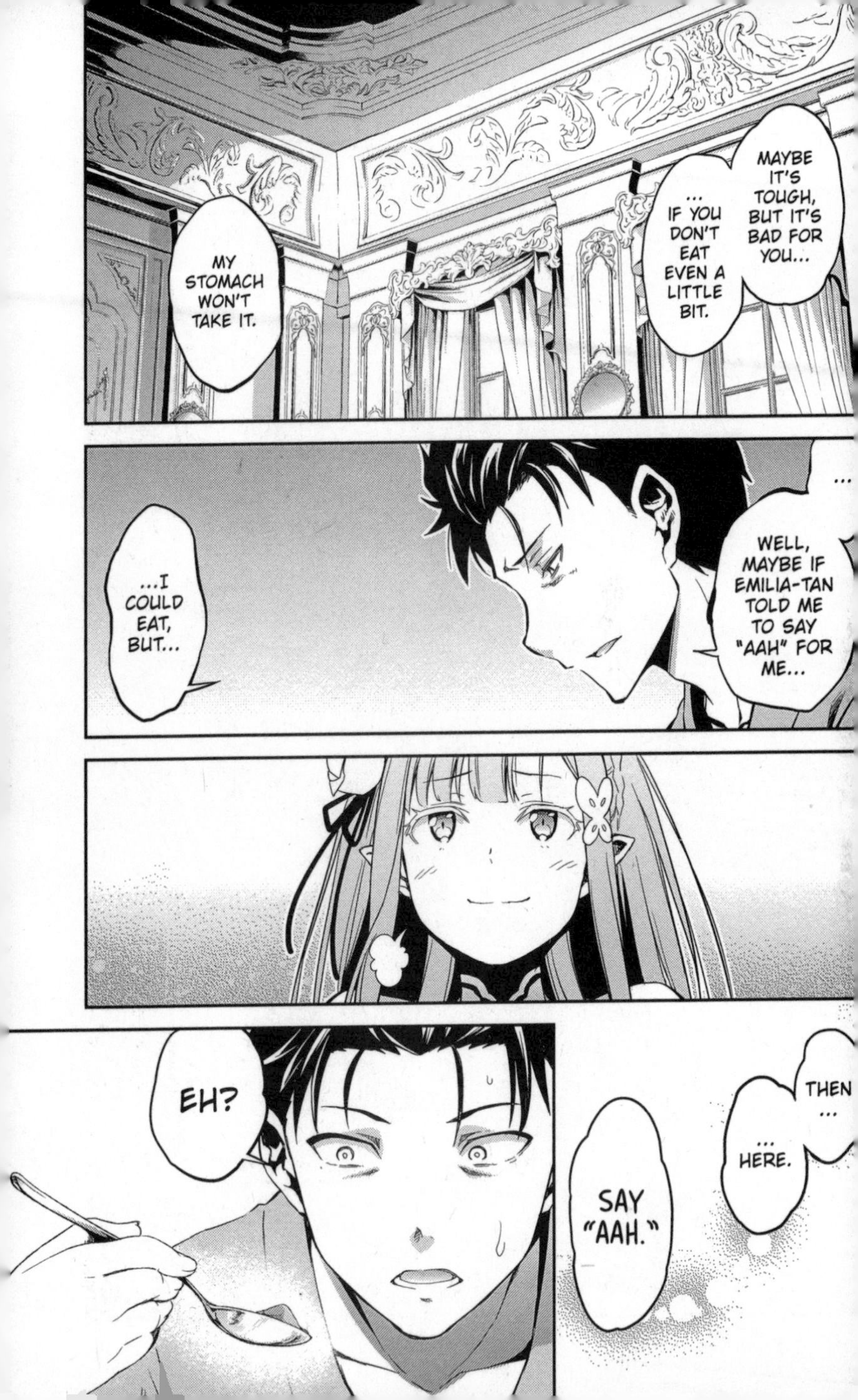
MAYBE IT'S TOUGH, BUT IT'S BAD FOR YOU...
...IF YOU DON'T EAT EVEN A LITTLE BIT.
MY STOMACH WON'T TAKE IT.
...
WELL, MAYBE IF EMILIA-TAN TOLD ME TO SAY "AAH" FOR ME...
...I COULD EAT, BUT...
THEN...
...HERE.
SAY "AAH."
EH?

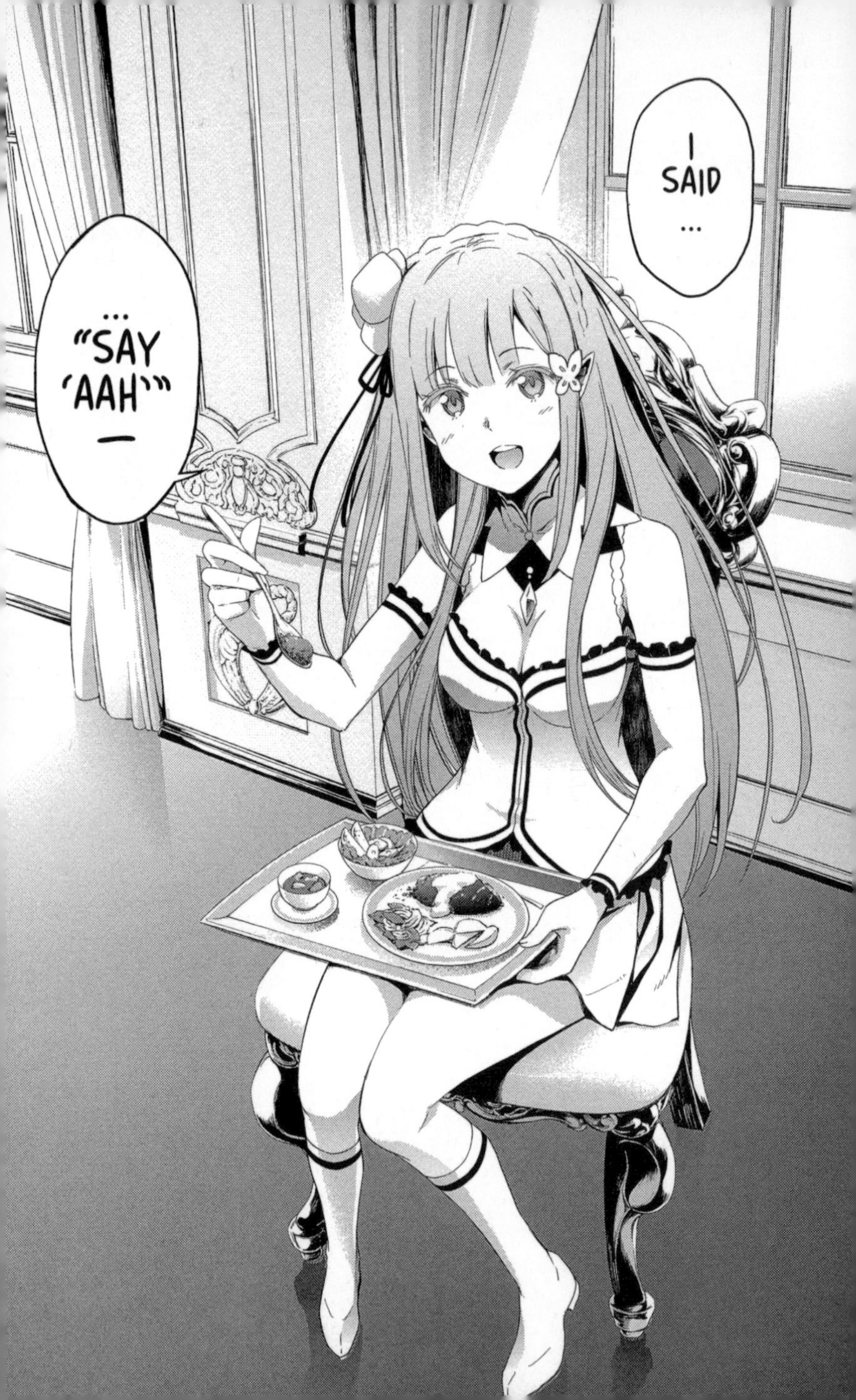
I SAID ...
... "SAY 'AAH'" —

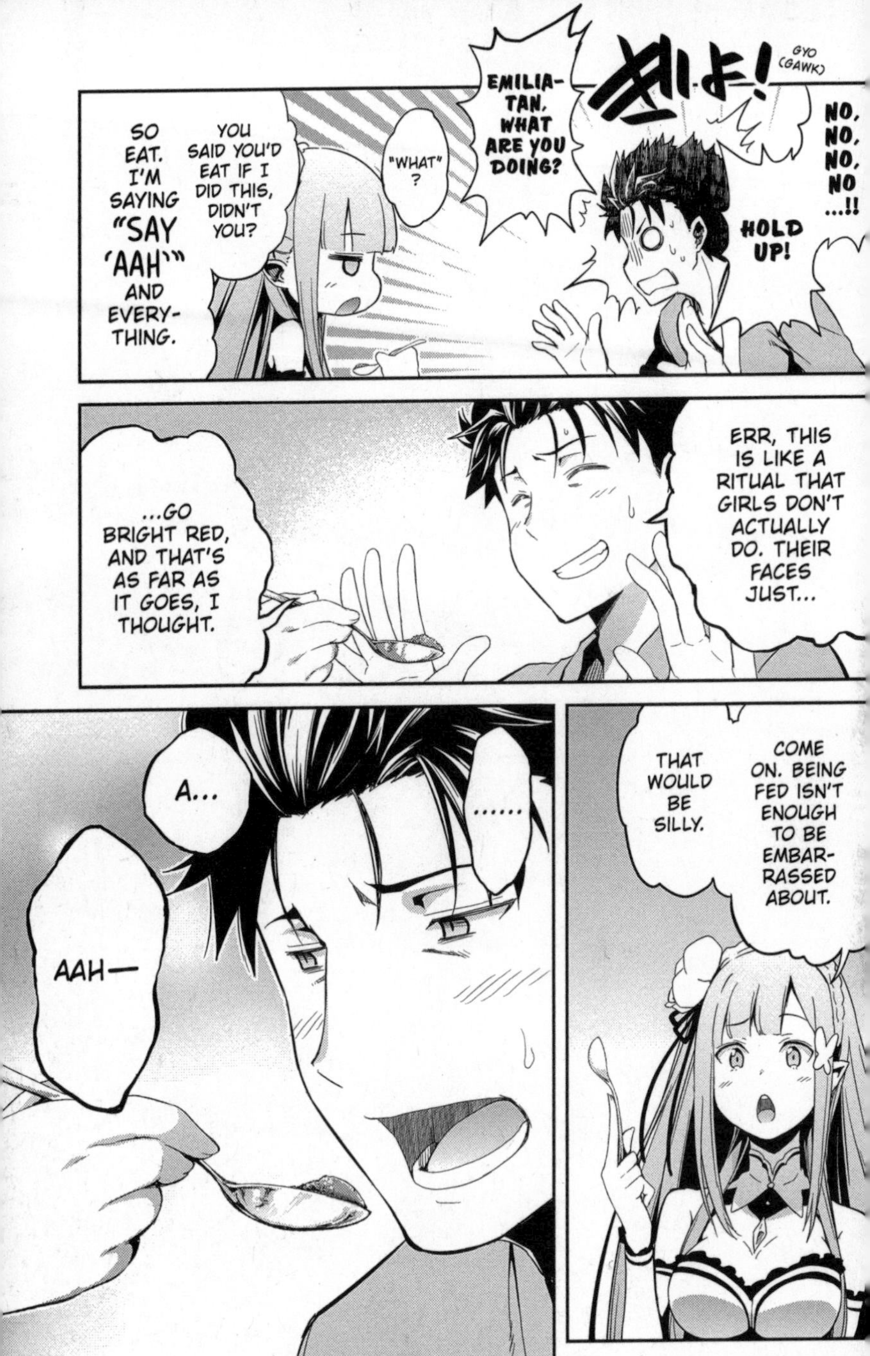
GYO (GAWK)
EMILIA-TAN, WHAT ARE YOU DOING?
NO, NO, NO, NO ...!!
HOLD UP!
"WHAT"?
YOU SAID YOU'D EAT IF I DID THIS, DIDN'T YOU?
SO EAT. I'M SAYING "SAY 'AAH'" AND EVERYTHING.
ERR, THIS IS LIKE A RITUAL THAT GIRLS DON'T ACTUALLY DO. THEIR FACES JUST...
...GO BRIGHT RED, AND THAT'S AS FAR AS IT GOES, I THOUGHT.
COME ON. BEING FED ISN'T ENOUGH TO BE EMBARRASSED ABOUT.
THAT WOULD BE SILLY.
......
A...
AAH—

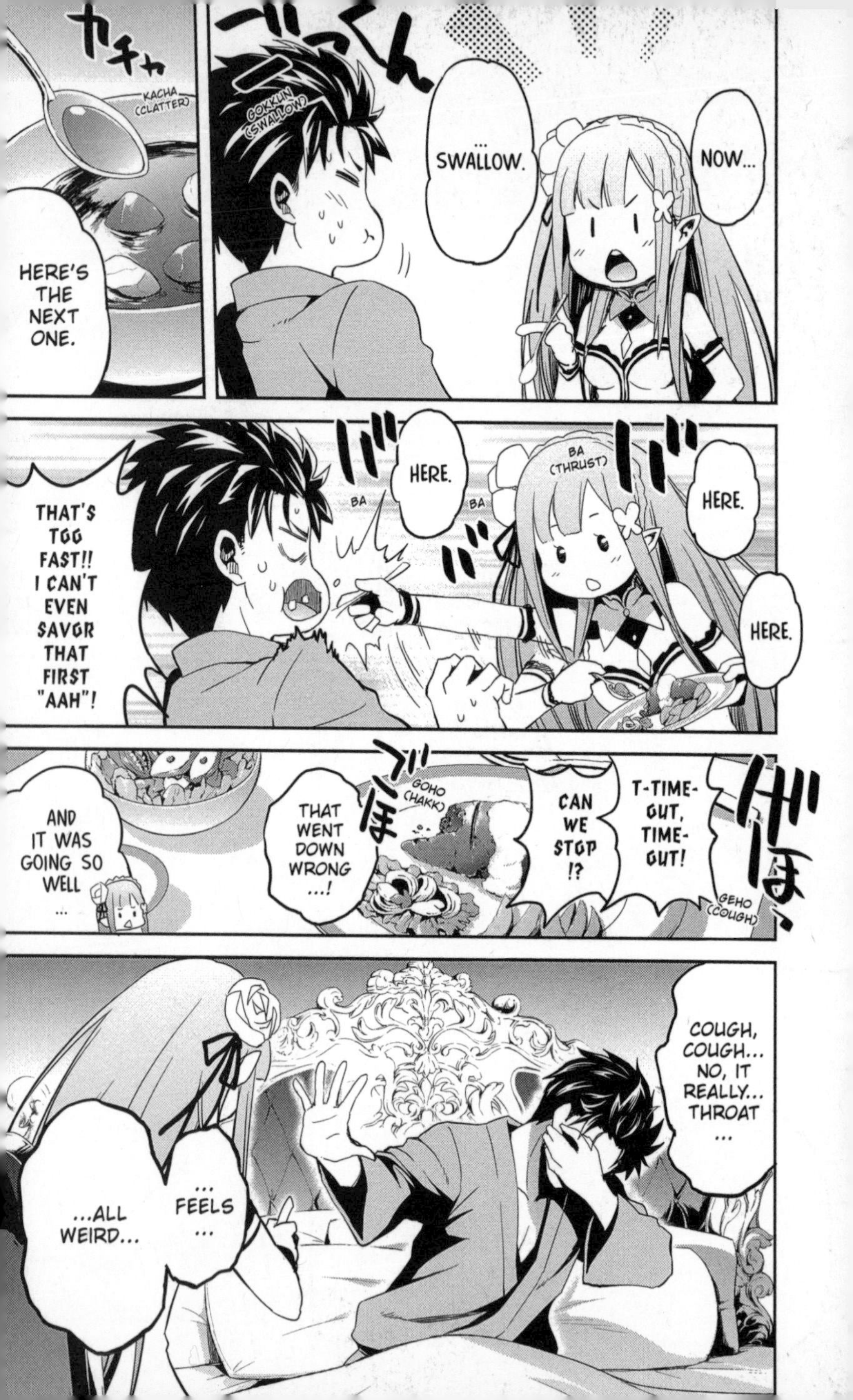
NOW...
... SWALLOW.
GOKKUN (SWALLOW)
KACHA (CLATTER)
HERE'S THE NEXT ONE.
HERE.
BA (THRUST)
HERE.
HERE.
BA
BA
THAT'S TOO FAST!! I CAN'T EVEN SAVOR THAT FIRST "AAH"!
GEHO (COUGH)
T-TIME-OUT, TIME-OUT!
CAN WE STOP!?
GOHO (HAKK)
THAT WENT DOWN WRONG ...!
AND IT WAS GOING SO WELL ...
COUGH, COUGH... NO, IT REALLY... THROAT ...
... FEELS ...
...ALL WEIRD...

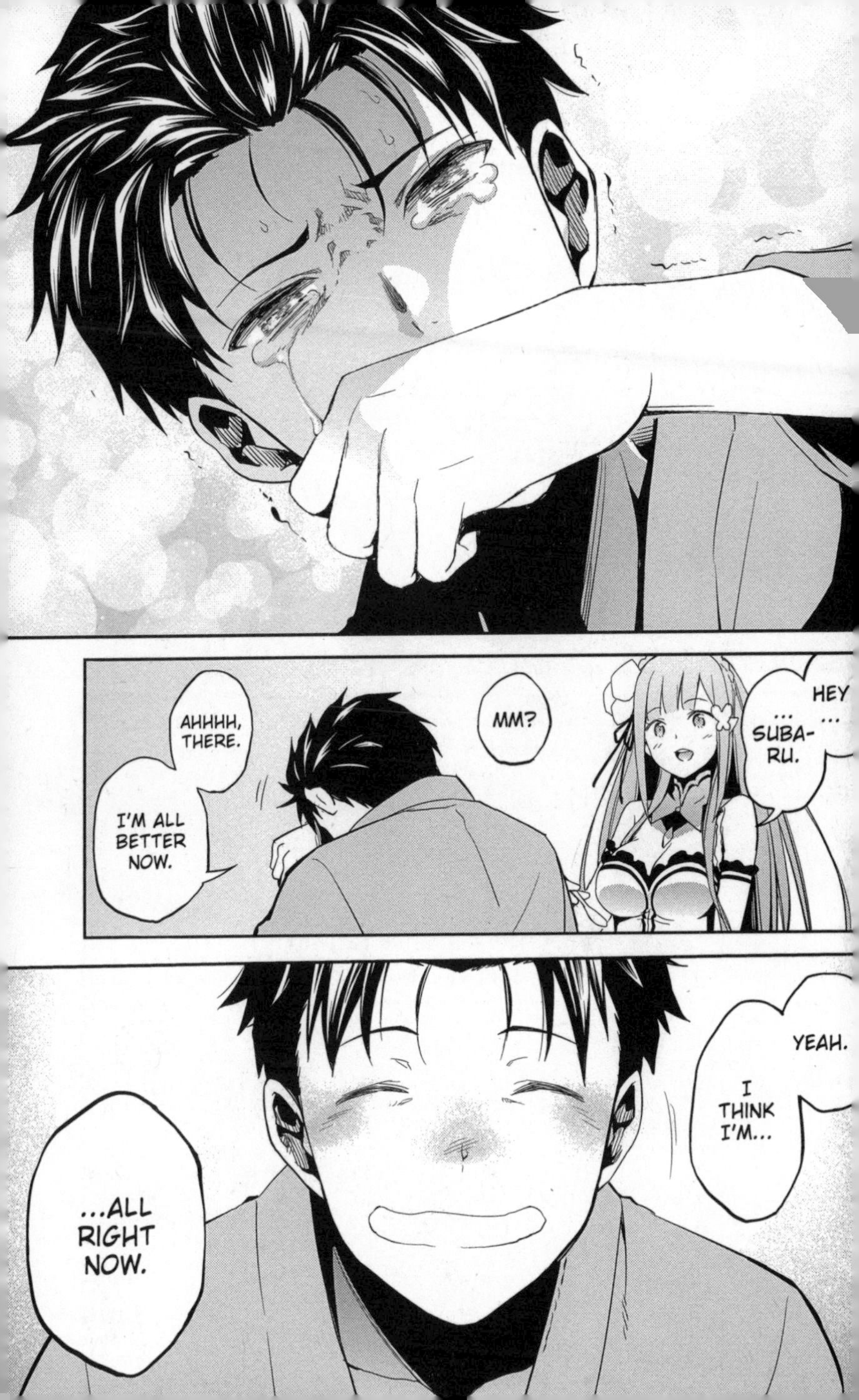
HEY ... SUBA-RU.
MM?
AHHHH, THERE.
I'M ALL BETTER NOW.
YEAH. I THINK I'M...
...ALL RIGHT NOW.

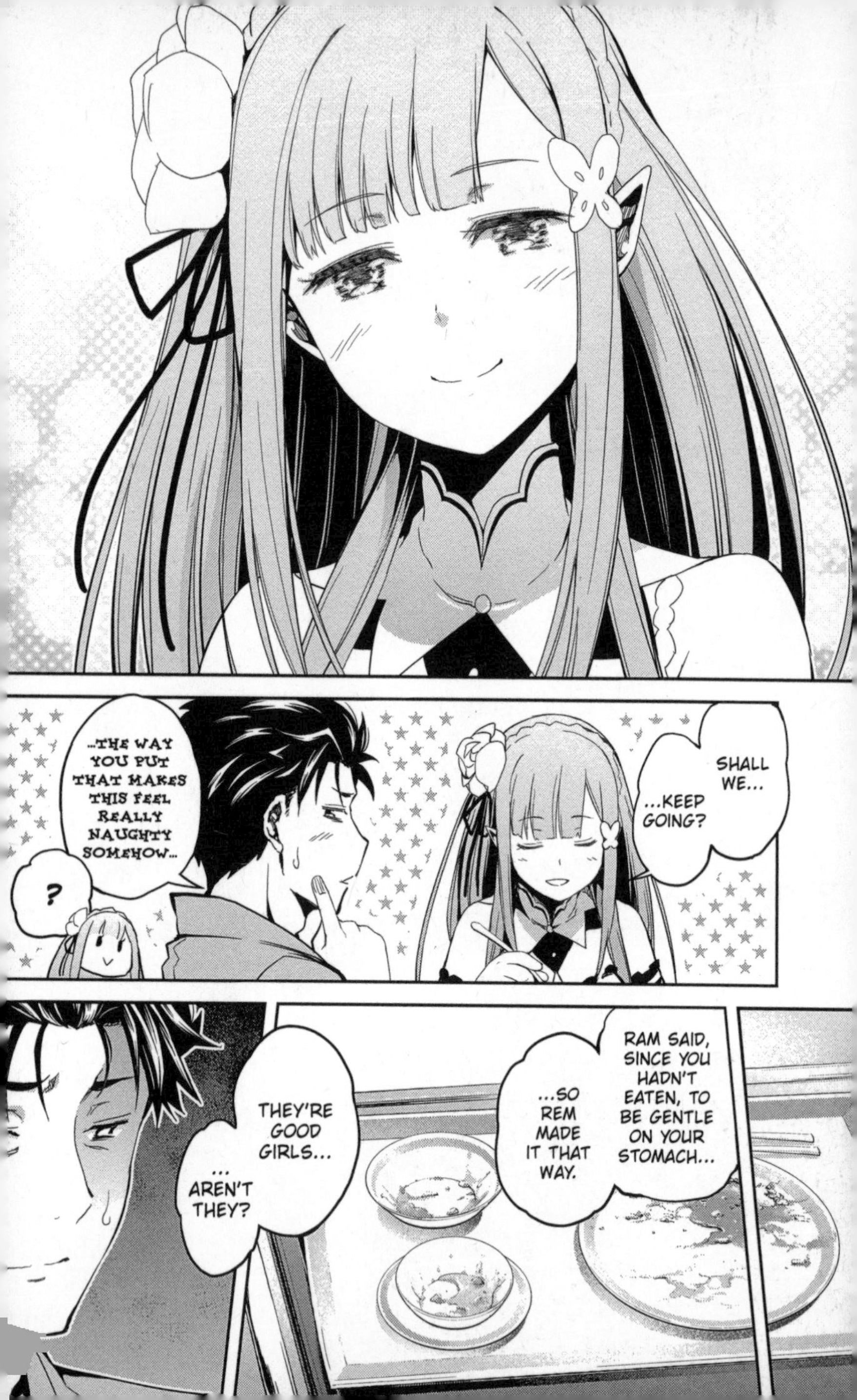
SHALL WE...
...KEEP GOING?
...THE WAY YOU PUT THAT MAKES THIS FEEL REALLY NAUGHTY SOMEHOW...
?
RAM SAID, SINCE YOU HADN'T EATEN, TO BE GENTLE ON YOUR STOMACH...
...SO REM MADE IT THAT WAY.
THEY'RE GOOD GIRLS...
...AREN'T THEY?

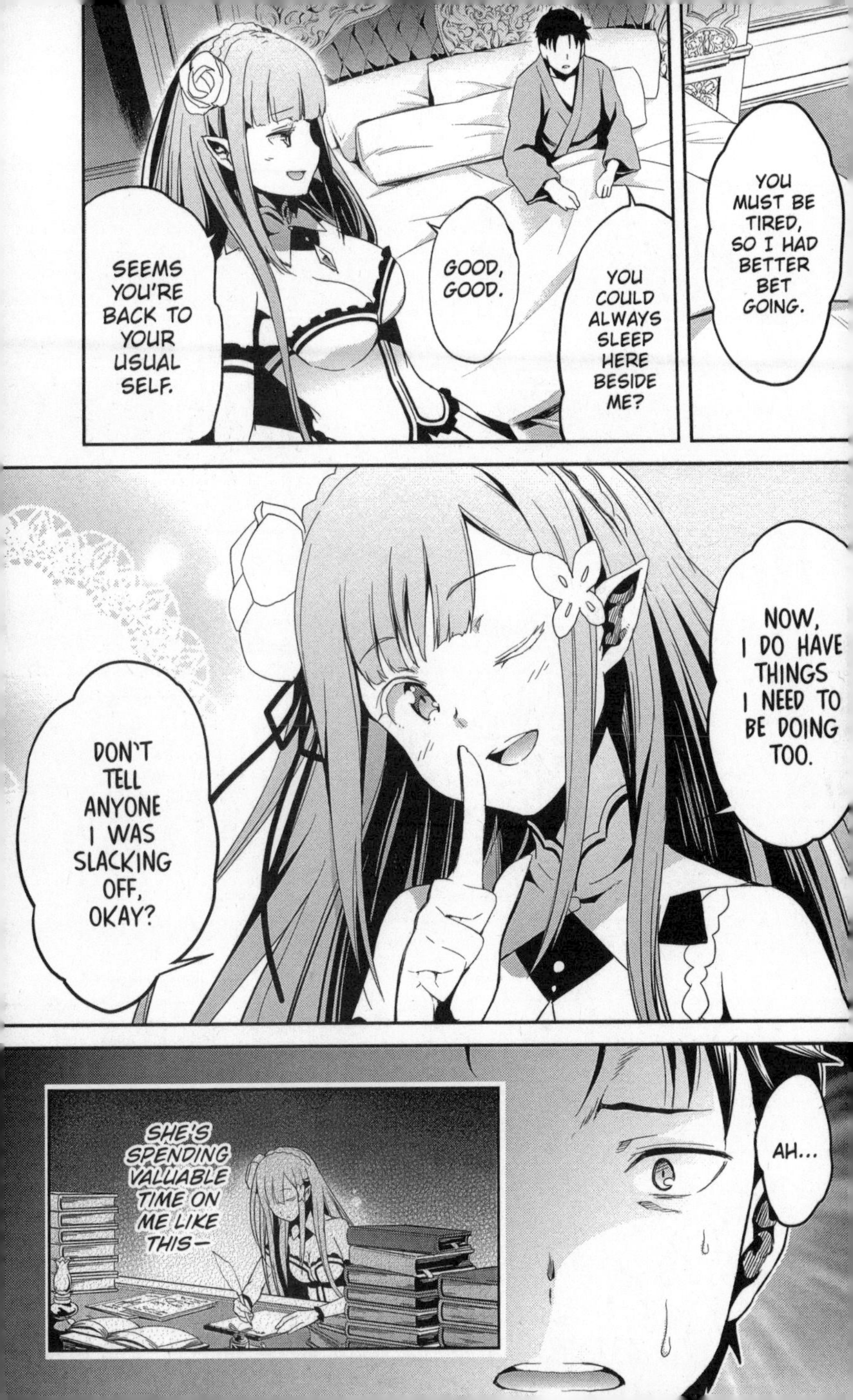
YOU MUST BE TIRED, SO I HAD BETTER BET GOING.
YOU COULD ALWAYS SLEEP HERE BESIDE ME?
GOOD, GOOD.
SEEMS YOU'RE BACK TO YOUR USUAL SELF.
NOW, I DO HAVE THINGS I NEED TO BE DOING TOO.
DON'T TELL ANYONE I WAS SLACKING OFF, OKAY?
AH...
SHE'S SPENDING VALUABLE TIME ON ME LIKE THIS—

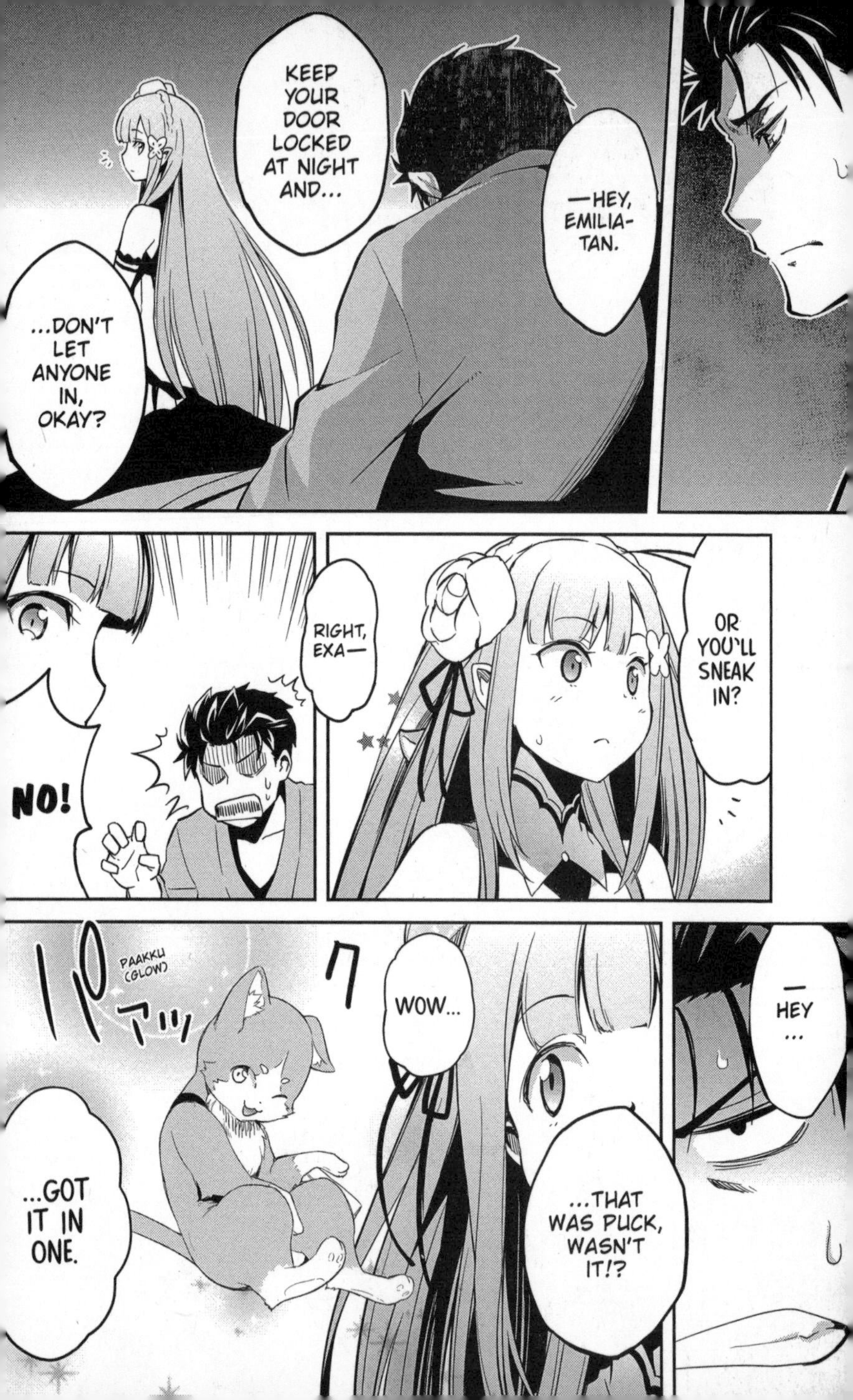
—HEY, EMILIA-TAN.
KEEP YOUR DOOR LOCKED AT NIGHT AND...
...DON'T LET ANYONE IN, OKAY?
OR YOU'LL SNEAK IN?
RIGHT, EXA—
NO!
—HEY...
...THAT WAS PUCK, WASN'T IT!?
WOW...
PAAKKU (GLOW)
...GOT IT IN ONE.

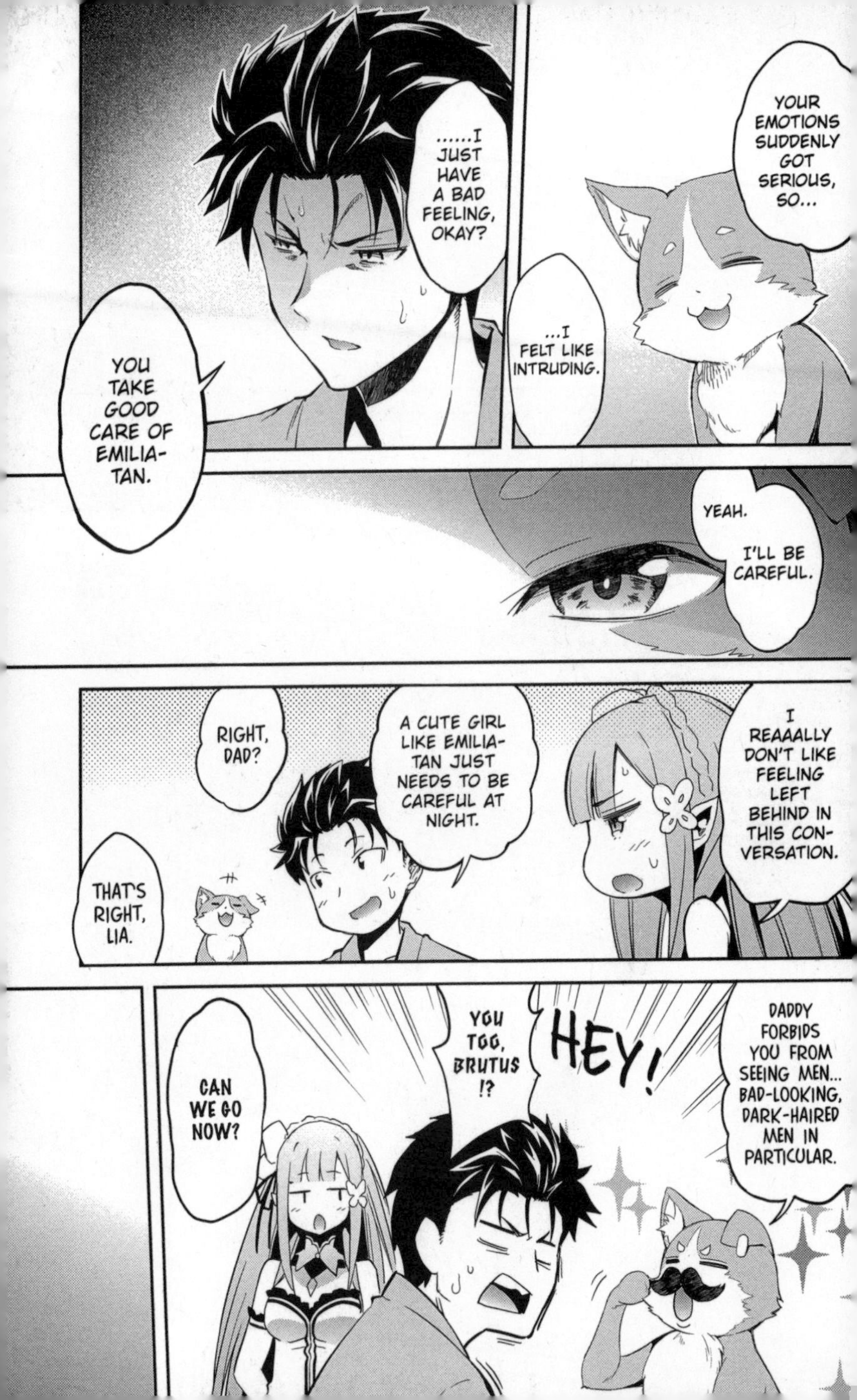
YOUR EMOTIONS SUDDENLY GOT SERIOUS, SO...
...I FELT LIKE INTRUDING.
......I JUST HAVE A BAD FEELING, OKAY?
YOU TAKE GOOD CARE OF EMILIA-TAN.
YEAH.
I'LL BE CAREFUL.
I REAAALLY DON'T LIKE FEELING LEFT BEHIND IN THIS CON-VERSATION.
A CUTE GIRL LIKE EMILIA-TAN JUST NEEDS TO BE CAREFUL AT NIGHT.
RIGHT, DAD?
THAT'S RIGHT, LIA.
DADDY FORBIDS YOU FROM SEEING MEN... BAD-LOOKING, DARK-HAIRED MEN IN PARTICULAR.
HEY!
YOU TOO, BRUTUS!?
CAN WE GO NOW?

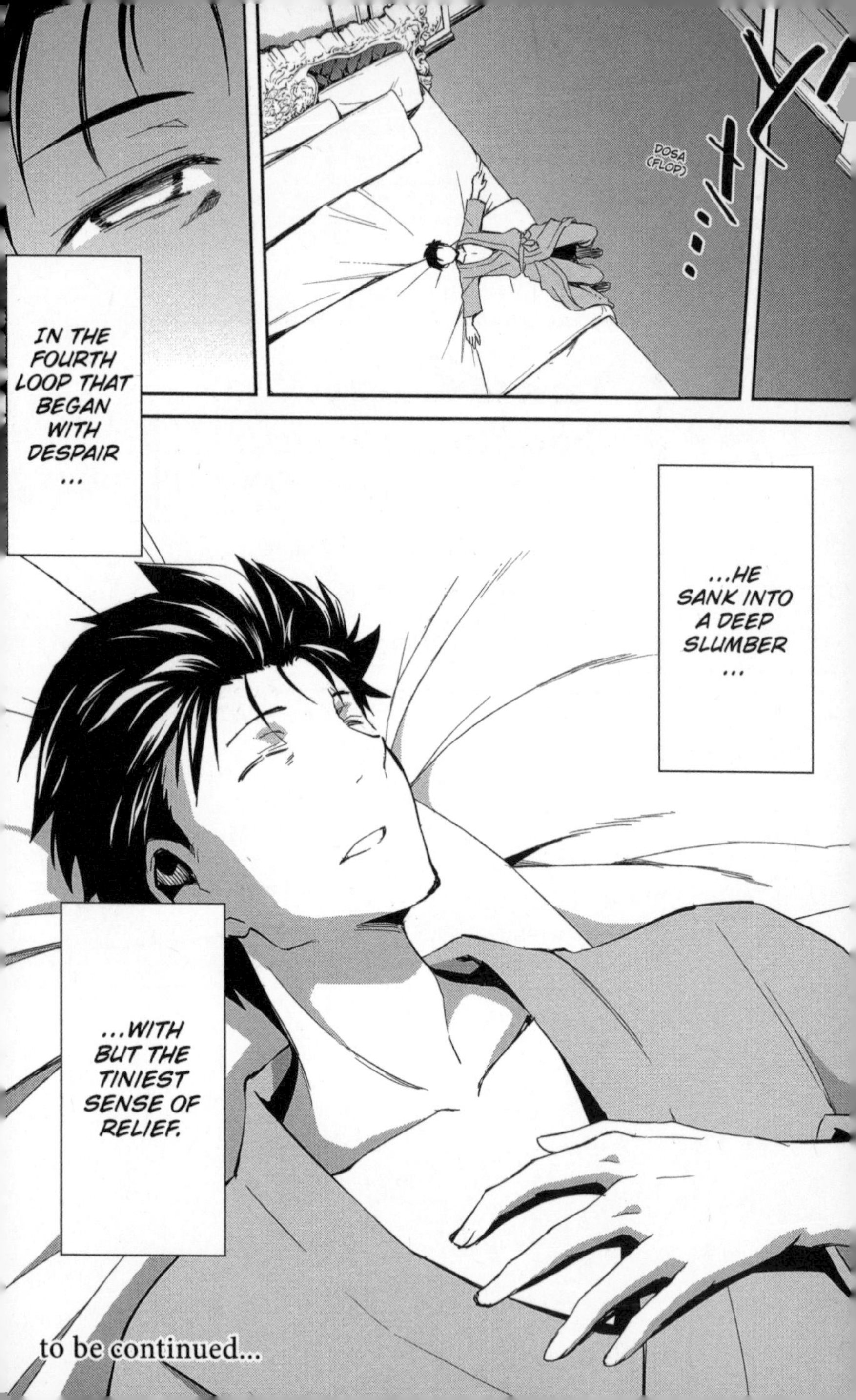
DOSA (FLOP)
IN THE FOURTH LOOP THAT BEGAN WITH DESPAIR ...
...HE SANK INTO A DEEP SLUMBER ...
...WITH BUT THE TINIEST SENSE OF RELIEF.
to be continued...

Turn to the end of the book for an original *Re:ZERO* short story from the light novel author, Tappei Nagatsuki!

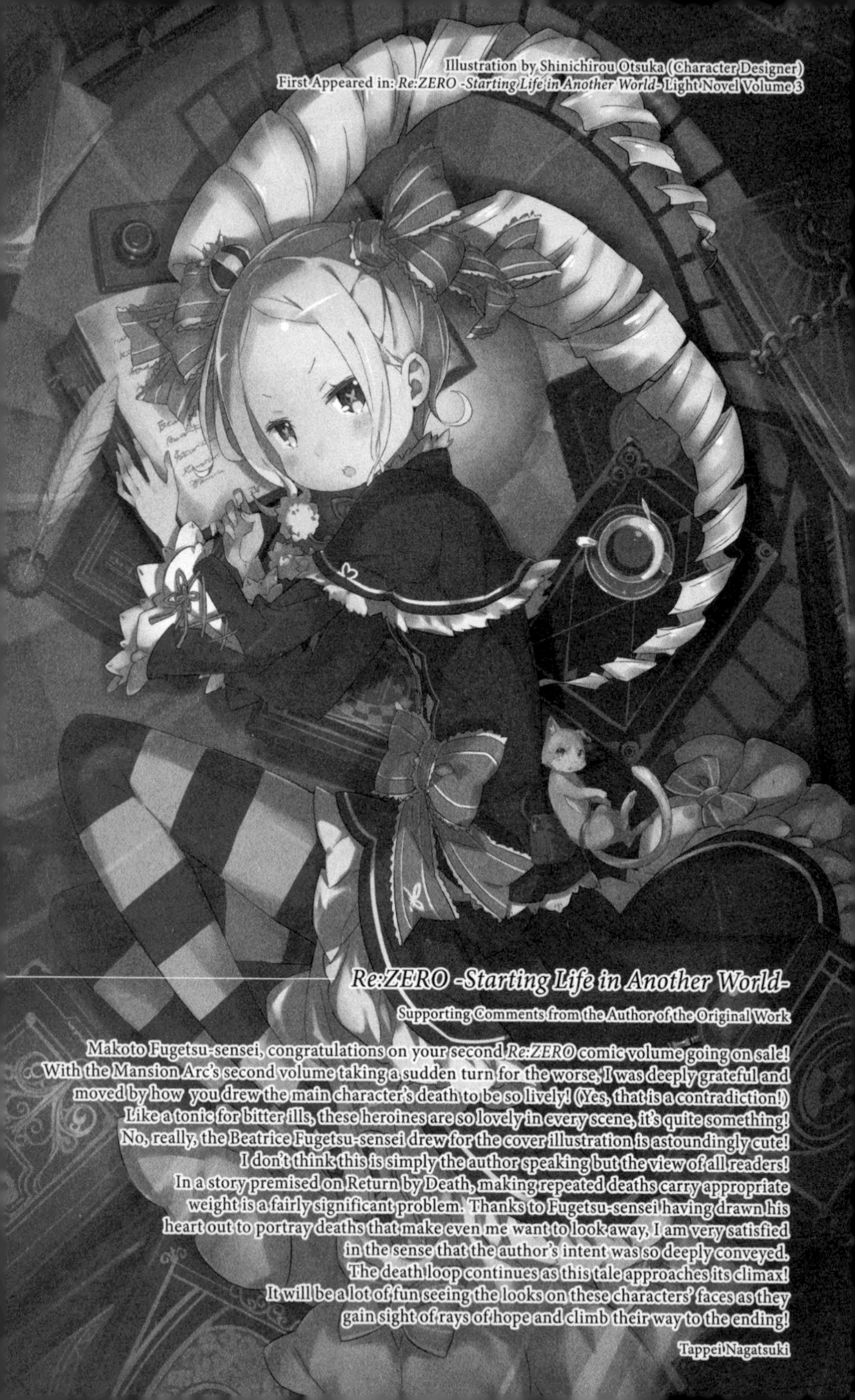

Illustration by Shinichirou Otsuka (Character Designer)
First Appeared in: *Re:ZERO -Starting Life in Another World-* Light Novel Volume 3

## *Re:ZERO -Starting Life in Another World-*

Supporting Comments from the Author of the Original Work

Makoto Fugetsu-sensei, congratulations on your second *Re:ZERO* comic volume going on sale!
With the Mansion Arc's second volume taking a sudden turn for the worse, I was deeply grateful and moved by how you drew the main character's death to be so lively! (Yes, that is a contradiction!)
Like a tonic for bitter ills, these heroines are so lovely in every scene, it's quite something!
No, really, the Beatrice Fugetsu-sensei drew for the cover illustration is astoundingly cute!
I don't think this is simply the author speaking but the view of all readers!
In a story premised on Return by Death, making repeated deaths carry appropriate weight is a fairly significant problem. Thanks to Fugetsu-sensei having drawn his heart out to portray deaths that make even me want to look away, I am very satisfied in the sense that the author's intent was so deeply conveyed.
The death loop continues as this tale approaches its climax!
It will be a lot of fun seeing the looks on these characters' faces as they gain sight of rays of hope and climb their way to the ending!

Tappei Nagatsuki

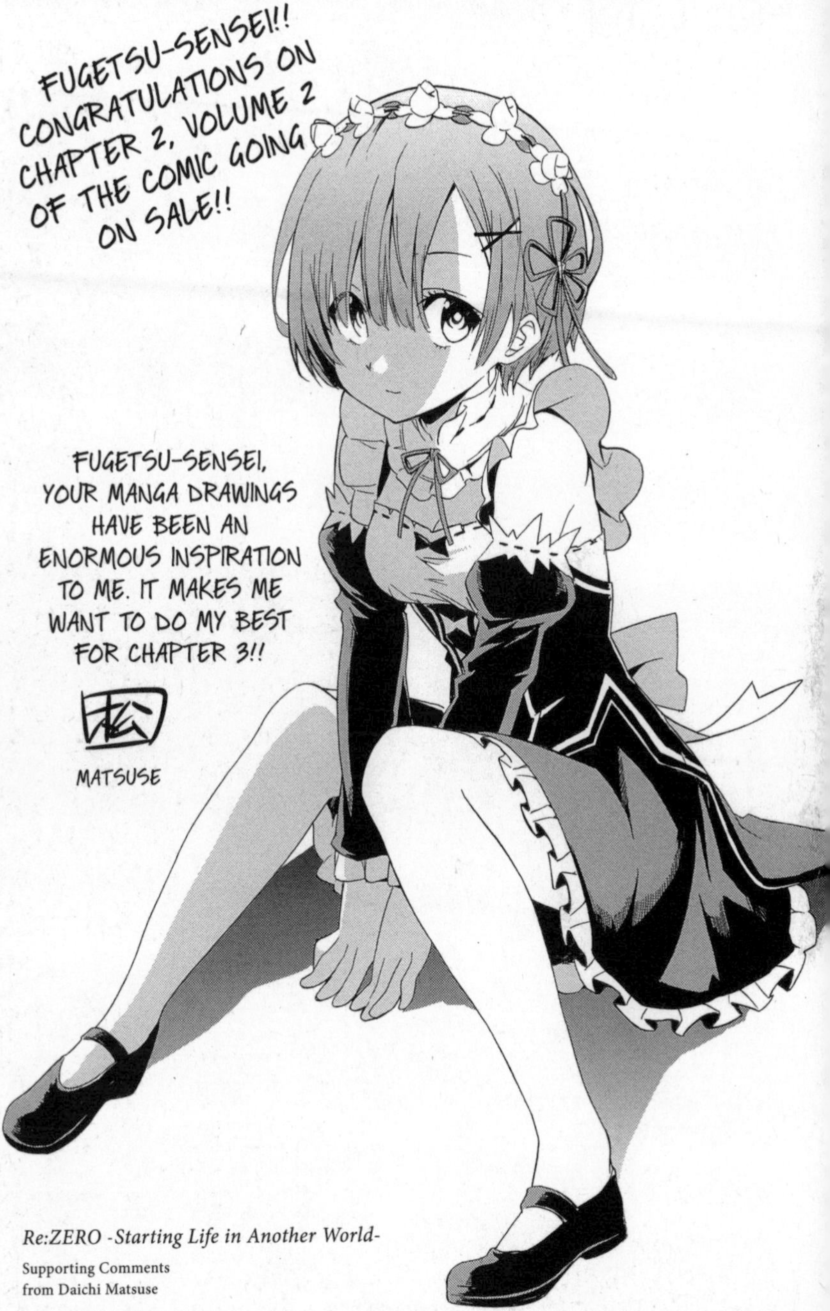
FUGETSU-SENSEI!! CONGRATULATIONS ON CHAPTER 2, VOLUME 2 OF THE COMIC GOING ON SALE!!
FUGETSU-SENSEI, YOUR MANGA DRAWINGS HAVE BEEN AN ENORMOUS INSPIRATION TO ME. IT MAKES ME WANT TO DO MY BEST FOR CHAPTER 3!!
MATSUSE

*Re:ZERO -Starting Life in Another World-*

Supporting Comments
from Daichi Matsuse

# NEXT

Re:ZERO *-Starting Life in Another World-*

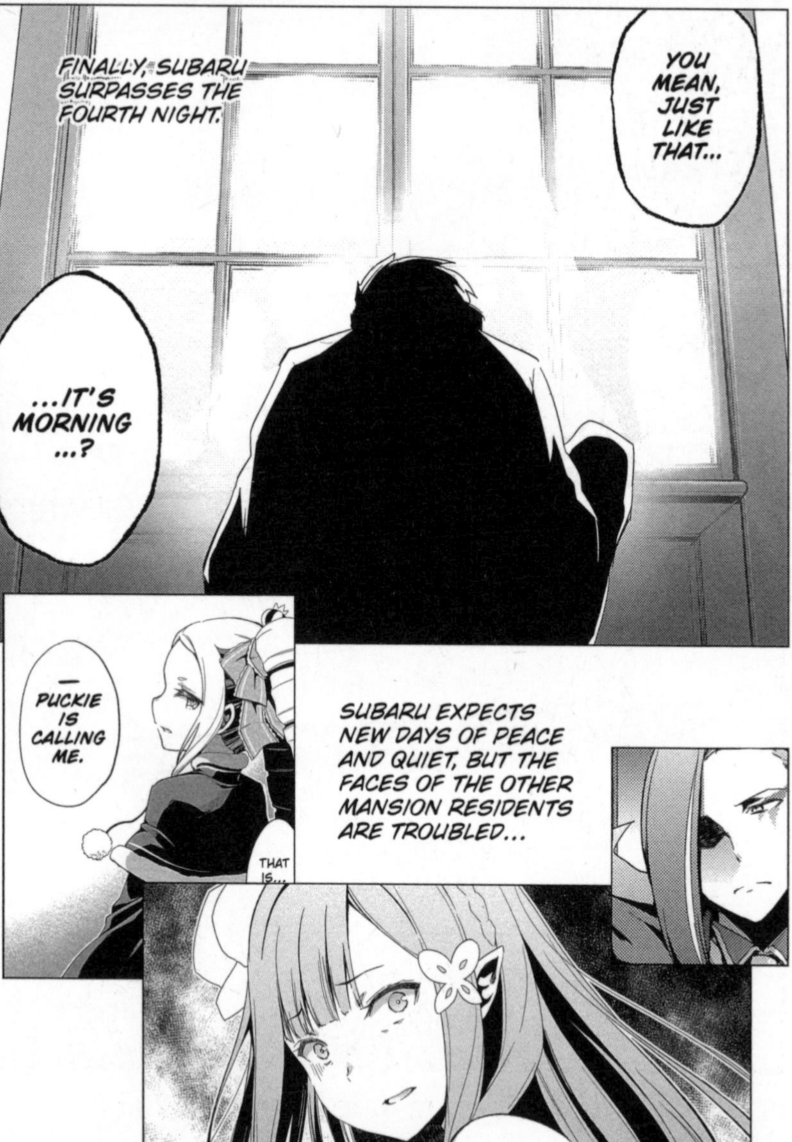
YOU MEAN, JUST LIKE THAT...
FINALLY, SUBARU SURPASSES THE FOURTH NIGHT.
...IT'S MORNING...?
SUBARU EXPECTS NEW DAYS OF PEACE AND QUIET, BUT THE FACES OF THE OTHER MANSION RESIDENTS ARE TROUBLED...
—PUCKIE IS CALLING ME.
THAT IS...

I'LL FIND A WAY TO END THIS WITHOUT YOU HAVING TO CRY—

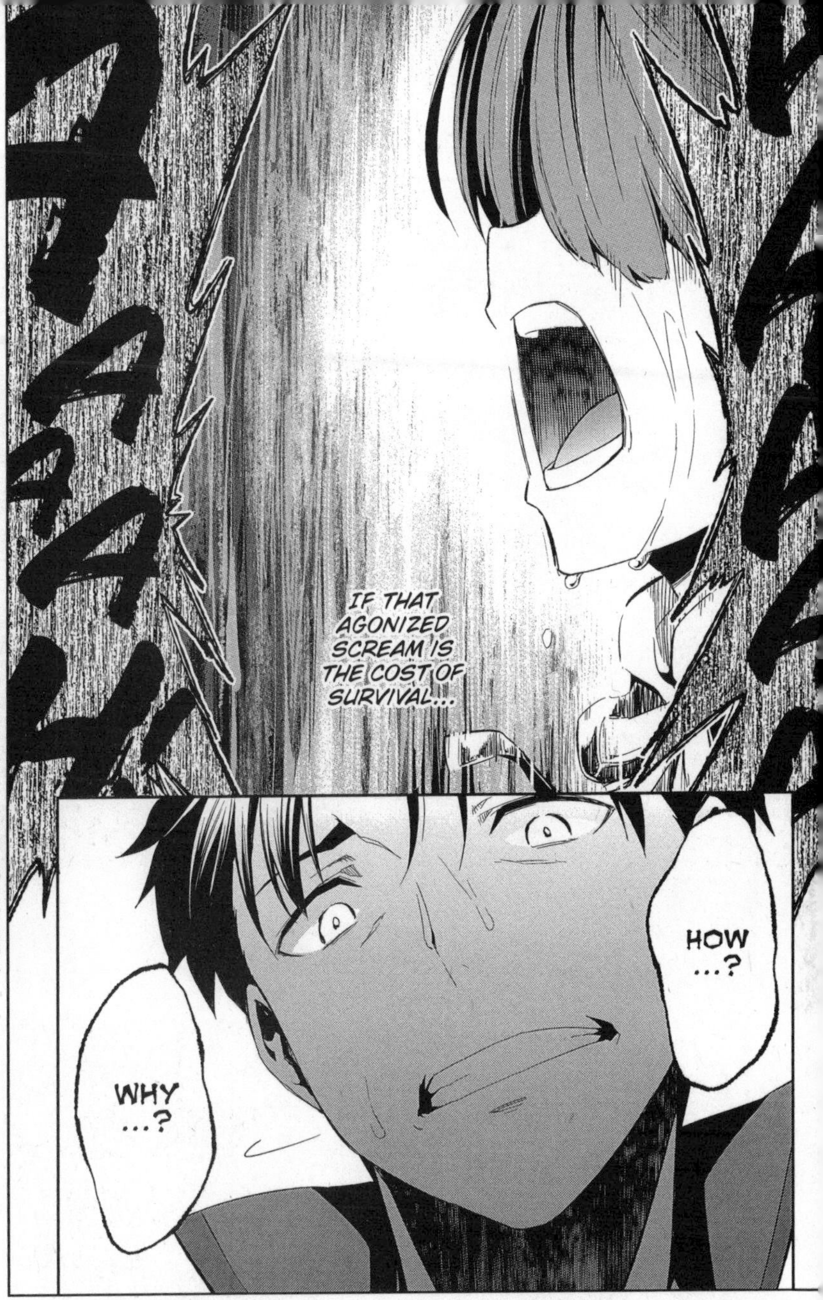
IF THAT AGONIZED SCREAM IS THE COST OF SURVIVAL...
HOW ...?
WHY ...?

## VOLUME ③ on sale October 2017

The only ability Subaru Natsuki gets when he's summoned to another world is time travel via his own death. But to save her, he'll die as many times as it takes.

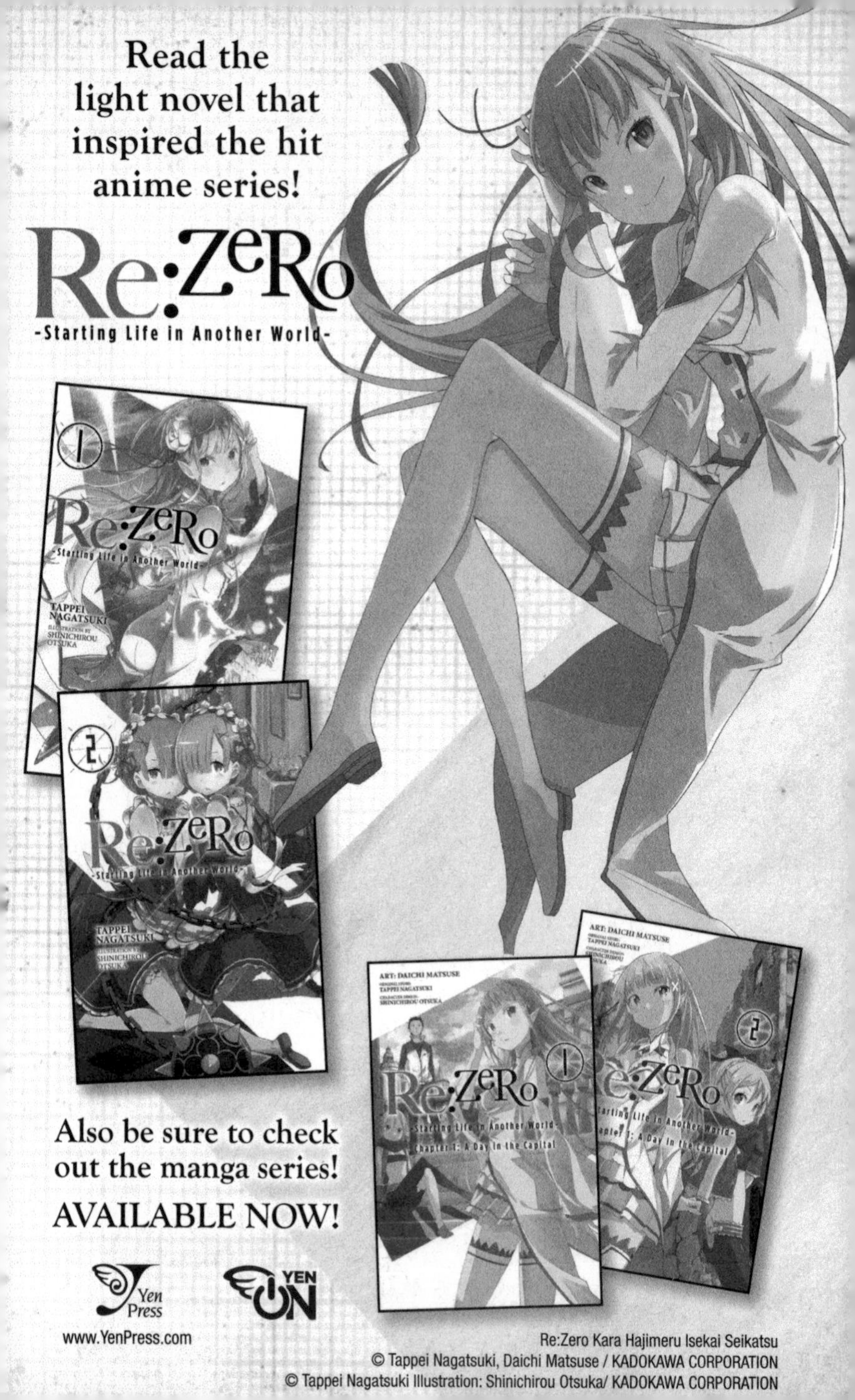
Read the light novel that inspired the hit anime series!
Re:ZeRo
-Starting Life in Another World-
Also be sure to check out the manga series!
AVAILABLE NOW!
Yen Press
YEN ON
www.YenPress.com
Re:Zero Kara Hajimeru Isekai Seikatsu
© Tappei Nagatsuki, Daichi Matsuse / KADOKAWA CORPORATION
© Tappei Nagatsuki Illustration: Shinichirou Otsuka/ KADOKAWA CORPORATION

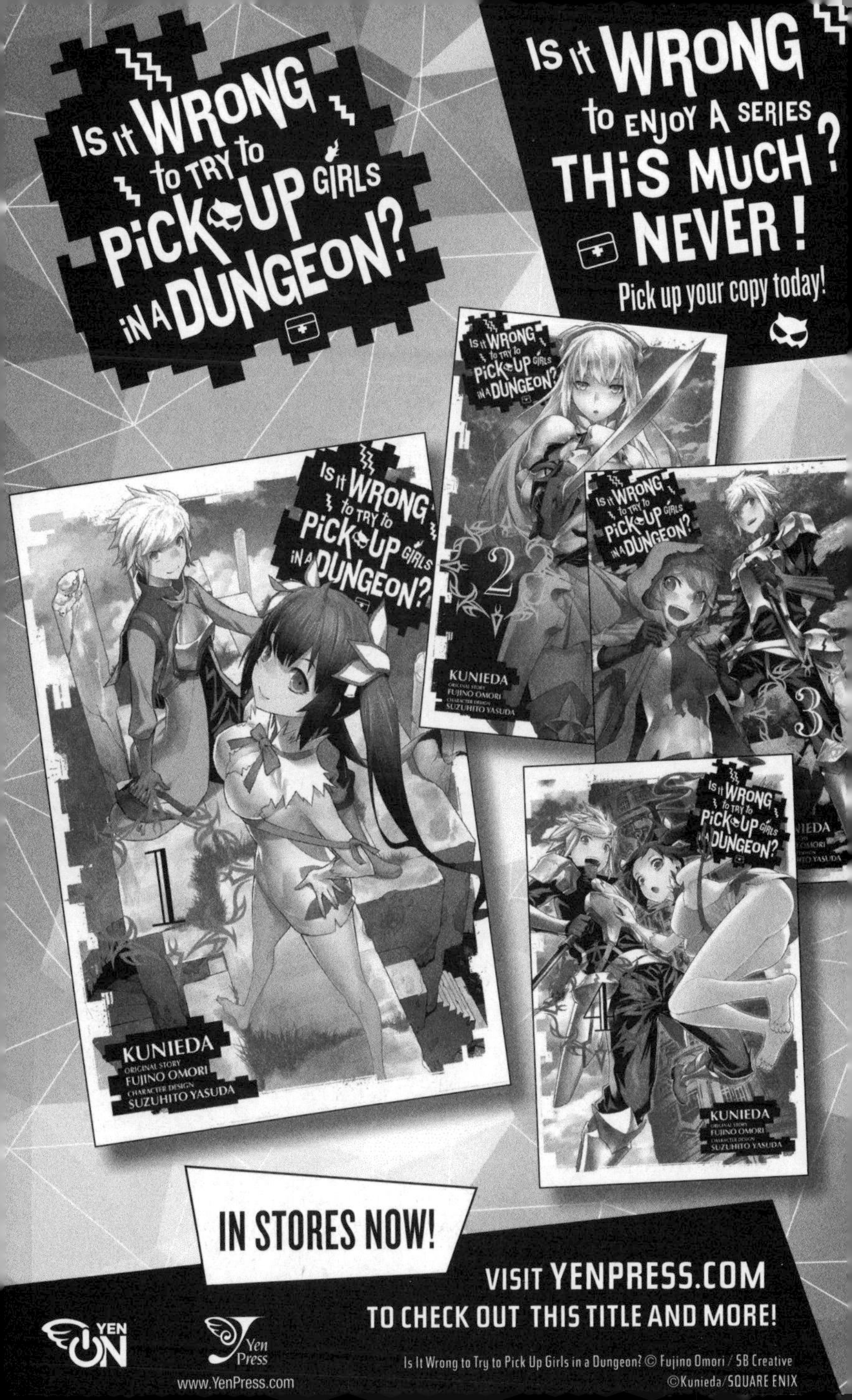
IS IT WRONG TO TRY TO PICK UP GIRLS IN A DUNGEON?
IS IT WRONG TO ENJOY A SERIES THIS MUCH?
NEVER!
Pick up your copy today!
KUNIEDA
ORIGINAL STORY FUJINO OMORI
CHARACTER DESIGN SUZUHITO YASUDA
IN STORES NOW!
VISIT YENPRESS.COM
TO CHECK OUT THIS TITLE AND MORE!
YEN ON
Yen Press
www.YenPress.com
Is It Wrong to Try to Pick Up Girls in a Dungeon? © Fujino Omori / SB Creative
©Kunieda/SQUARE ENIX

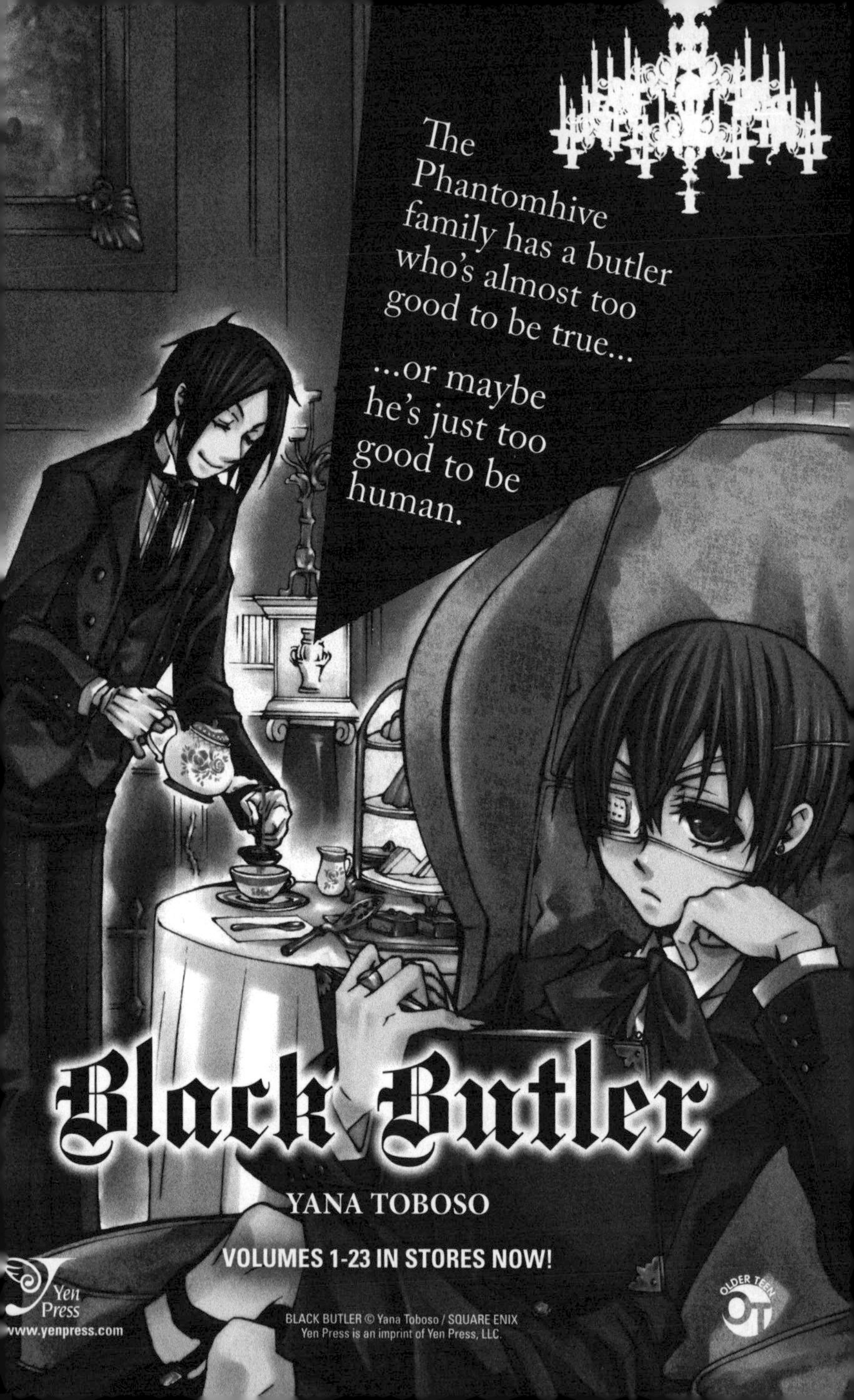

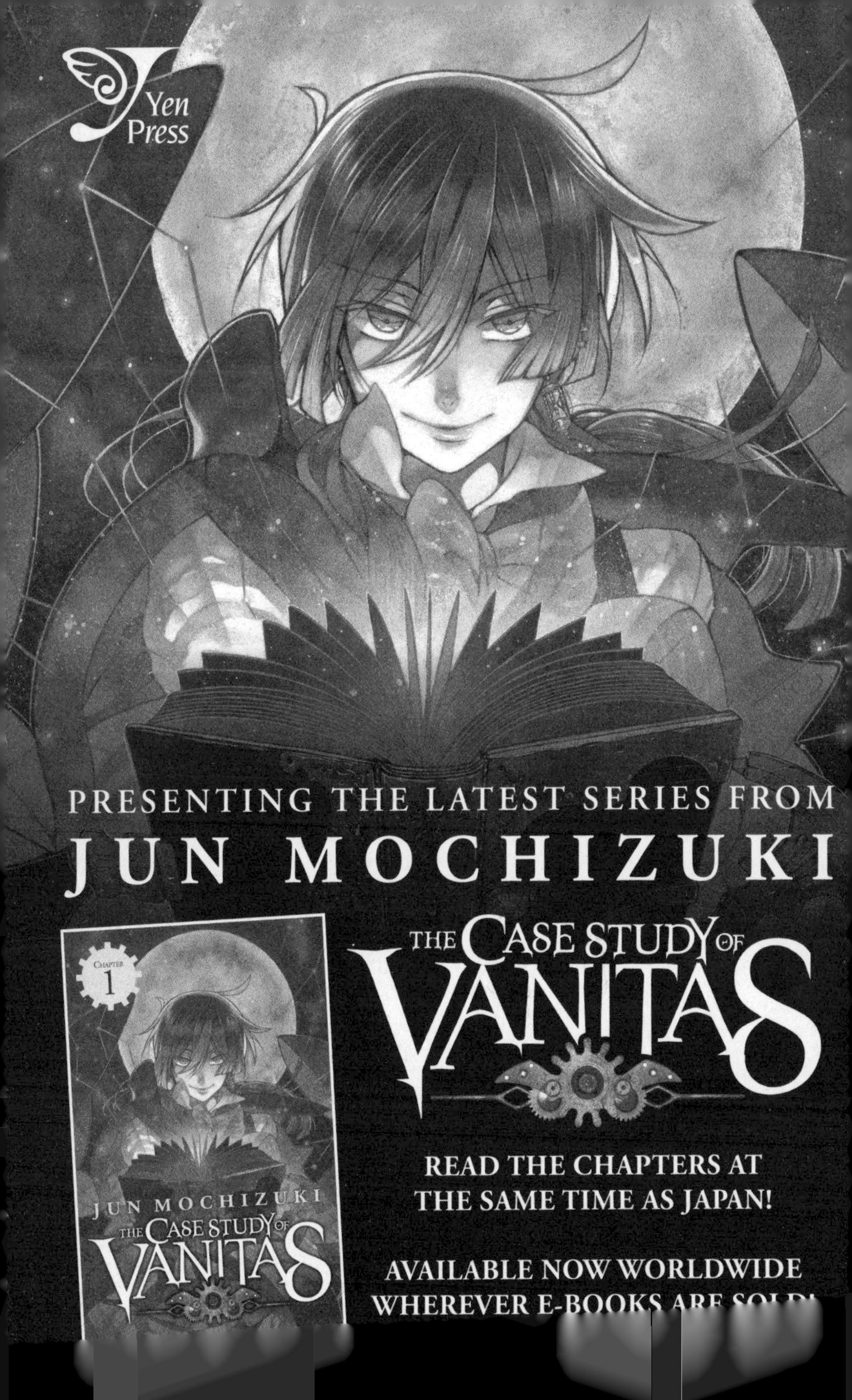
Yen Press
PRESENTING THE LATEST SERIES FROM
JUN MOCHIZUKI
CHAPTER 1
JUN MOCHIZUKI
THE CASE STUDY OF VANITAS
THE CASE STUDY OF VANITAS
READ THE CHAPTERS AT
THE SAME TIME AS JAPAN!
AVAILABLE NOW WORLDWIDE
WHEREVER E-BOOKS ARE SOLD!

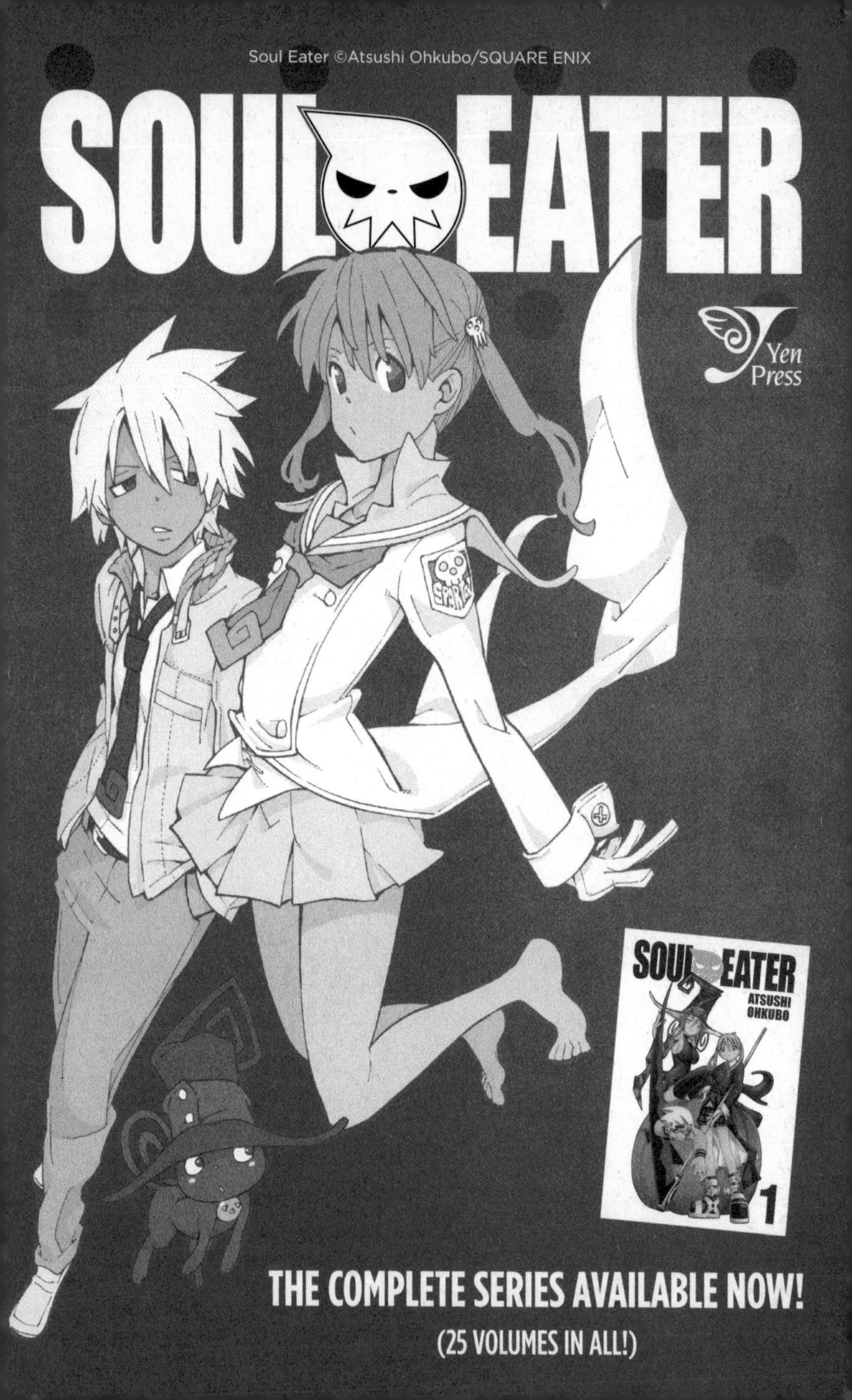

Soul Eater ©Atsushi Ohkubo/SQUARE ENIX
SOUL EATER
Yen Press
SOUL EATER
ATSUSHI OHKUBO
1
THE COMPLETE SERIES AVAILABLE NOW!
(25 VOLUMES IN ALL!)

# Re:ZERO

−Starting Life in Another World−

# RE:ZERO -STARTING LIFE IN ANOTHER WORLD- ❷
## Chapter 2: A Week at the Mansion

Art: **Makoto Fugetsu**
Original Story: **Tappei Nagatsuki**
Character Design: **Shinichirou Otsuka**

Translation: ZephyrRZ
Lettering: Bianca Pistillo

RE:ZERO KARA HAJIMERU ISEKAI SEIKATSU DAINISHO YASHIKI NO ISSHUKAN-HEN Vol. 2
© Tappei Nagatsuki 2014
Licensed by KADOKAWA CORPORATION
© 2015 Makoto Fugetsu / SQUARE ENIX CO., LTD.
First published in Japan in 2015 by SQUARE ENIX CO., LTD. English translation rights arranged with SQUARE ENIX CO., LTD. and Yen Press, LLC through TUTTLE-MORI AGENCY, Inc.

English translation © 2017 by SQUARE ENIX CO., LTD.

Yen Press
1290 Avenue of the Americas
New York, NY 10104

Visit us at yenpress.com
facebook.com/yenpress
twitter.com/yenpress
yenpress.tumblr.com
instagram.com/yenpress

First Yen Press Edition: August 2017

Yen Press is an imprint of Yen Press, LLC.
The Yen Press name and logo are trademarks of Yen Press, LLC.

Library of Congress Control Number: 2016936537

ISBNs: 978-0-316-47238-8 (paperback)
       978-0-316-41474-6 (ebook)

10 9 8 7 6 5 4 3 2 1

BVG

Printed in the United States of America

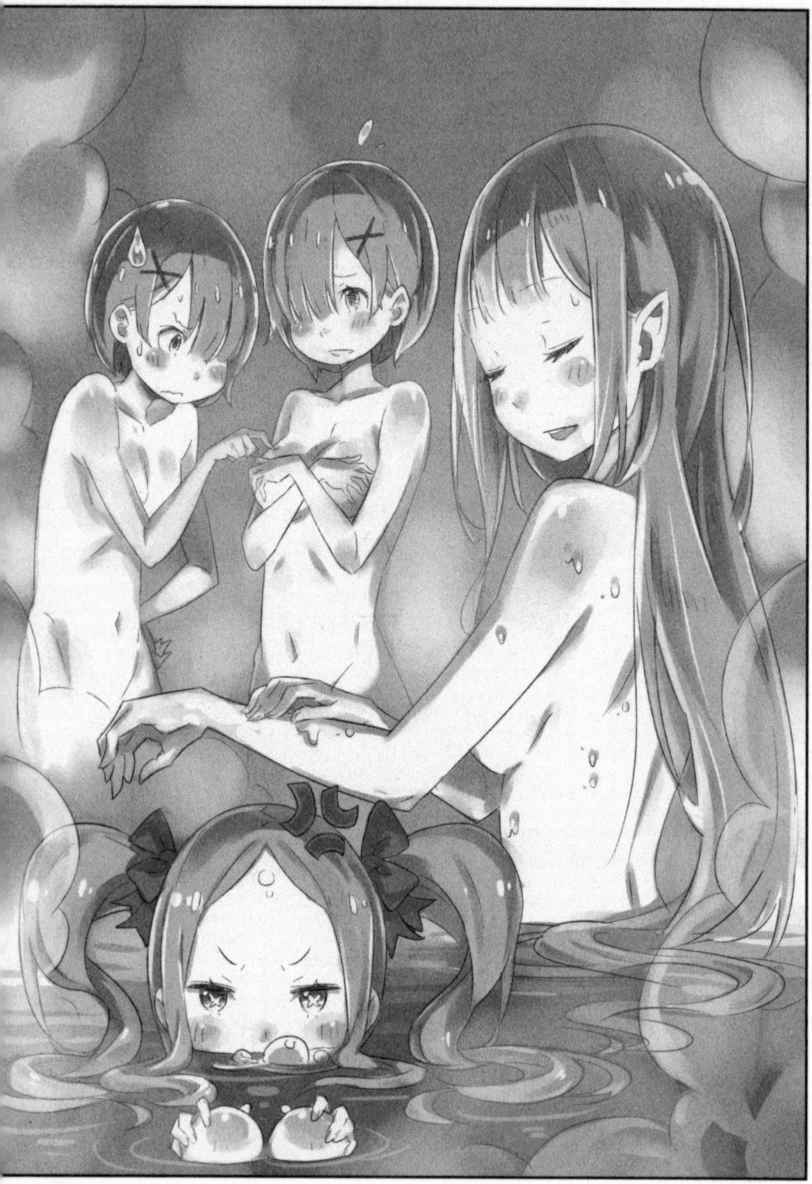

Beatrice raised a cry as she flew toward the tub. As she arced through the air, though, she suddenly stopped.

"What do you think you are...?! But this is not enough against me!"

She'd used magic to hover mid-hurl and proceeded to gently float down to the edge of the bath—

Just as Beatrice seemed set to flee, Ram and Rem caught her by the sleeves of her dress. Ram said, "My, Miss Beatrice, do not say that."

Ram added, "Let us be together tonight. I have long wanted to wash Miss Beatrice's hair."

Beatrice shouted, "B-both of you, too—?!"

Unable to resist their combined strength, Beatrice plunged headfirst into the tub.

Rising with a sheet of spray, Beatrice was dripping wet as she spat out the bathwater she'd swallowed, glaring at the three of them.

With that, her voice resounded like a lament—

"You have all been completely corrupted by that strange boy—!"

Emilia laughed. *That really might be true*, she mused but kept laughing.

—That day, the girls' lovely voices would continue echoing through the great bath of Roswaal Manor for a while longer.

*<END>*

strung, happy-go-lucky boy in a situation like that.

Ram commented, "I did wonder if you were anxious about that, Lady Emilia."

"Ram?"

"Whatever Barusu may decide, if he is of no use as a servant, we shall hurl him far away. That decision has been entrusted to Rem and myself. There is no need for you to be concerned."

After a slight pause, Emilia expressed her gratitude to Ram.

"...Thank you."

The maid's deliberately harsh phrasing was a means of erecting a fence around Emilia's heart. The message was that, if necessary, she would do the dirty work.

Emilia reflected, "I feel like Naked Ram and Naked Rem really are nice people..."

Ram replied, "Could you please not affix 'Naked' to my name?"

Rem added, "That's right, Lady Emilia. Sister is a nice person even when she is not naked."

Ram sighed deeply as Rem's response to Emilia went wide. As she did, the changing room opened, and she caught the rare sight of a fourth joining the three already in the bath. The girl revealing herself wore a most elegant dress. She had cream-colored hair in long rolls and was as adorable as a finely crafted doll.

"—Ahh, good grief. You step on him and kick him, and it isn't enough!"

Her cheeks were red and puffed up like a ripened fruit. She grandly raised her round eyes and glared at the three in the tub.

Ram asked, "What is the matter, Miss Beatrice? Is it Barusu?"

"You are quite correct, but it is perhaps annoying you guessed so easily. He is truly a vexing person! The Passage does not work on him, so perhaps this is the only place I can escape him?"

"Indeed, it is unlikely even Barusu would barge into the bath."

"That is precisely what it is. Perhaps I may kill some time here?"

Beatrice crossed her little arms, standing in the corner of the bathroom with an arrogant look that clashed with her appearance. Emilia emerged from the tub and walked to Beatrice's side.

Beatrice looked up peevishly at the naked Emilia.

"...What do you want, I wonder? Perhaps all I wish is to spend a little time here?"

"Oh, don't say that. You've come all this way, and for once, Ram and Rem are here, too. Wouldn't it be good if you joined us, Beatrice?"

"It most certainly would not! What are you saying all of a sudden, I wonder? Goodness, it is not funny at all."

*Shoo, shoo,* Beatrice motioned with her hand, as if to brush Emilia away like an insect.

Perhaps that obstinate attitude would normally have made Emilia retreat. However, the Emilia present that night was a different flavor than the norm. She glanced over her shoulder. She saw a pair of nods in return.

Beatrice said, "...Could you wait, I wonder? What is the purpose of those signals just now?"

Emilia replied, "Nothing at all. —Aa! Beatrice, Puck's bathing!"

"Eh?! Where, I wonder?!"

Beatrice looked in the direction Emilia was pointing, falling for a very old trick. The next instant, Emilia lifted Beatrice's tiny frame and proceeded to toss her in the direction of the bath.

"Nyaa?!"

"I think Sister is splendid when she is firm all the time, but I think Sister is adorable when she soaks in the bath and lets her guard down a little."

"Ah, you mean she's always like this?" Emilia wondered aloud.

"Yes, it is a small secret of Sister's."

Rem's cheeks reddened slightly as she made an uncharacteristic attempt at dry humor.

In one sense, Rem had built higher walls between herself and others than Ram. It was Emilia's impression of Rem that made her current demeanor unexpectedly charming.

"...Rem, do not say anything overly embarrassing," Ram chided.

"I am sorry, Sister. I cannot resist expressing how wonderful Sister is."

"I see, then it cannot be helped. It is natural I would inspire boasting from my little sister."

Ram was always gentle with Rem, but Emilia felt it particularly pronounced that day. Compounded with Rem's demeanor, Emilia regarded it as a splendid change. She wondered aloud:

"Wait, maybe being naked in the bath lets you talk while forgetting all your worries...?!"

Ram replied, "Lady Emilia, is something wrong?"

"Wh-what got into me just now...? It's like...I just realized an essential truth of the world..."

"Sister, Sister, oh no. It seems Lady Emilia has become dizzy."

"Rem, Rem, oh no. It seems Lady Emilia has fallen half-asleep."

"Even though I'm in the bath?!" Emilia asked.

Emilia, being treated as if she were addled or half-conscious, had a dumbfounded look as she submerged herself in the tub. She blew some bubbles for a while before popping back up.

"Pwah! Ohhh, you two are so mean..."

Rem pointed out, "Lady Emilia, I feel as if your expressions have been poisoned by Subaru."

Emilia looked conflicted.

"I-is that so? I, ahh, don't believe that is the case, but..."

Subaru was the boy who had been living at the manor as a servant since the upheaval in the capital a few days before. Emilia often found herself taken aback during her encounters with him, for his words and behavior frequently thwarted her expectations.

Certainly, the eccentric boy might have influenced her just a little—

"But in that regard, haven't the two of you spent more time with him than I have? Maybe Subaru has impacted your behavior on matters beyond merely lounging naked in the bath?"

"That is..."

"...absolutely not the case."

The twins blew off Emilia's comeback in perfect sync. The statement was harsh, but Emilia didn't feel they were denying it all that hard. From Emilia's point of view, the sisters didn't have what she'd characterize as a bad relationship with Subaru, prompting her to remark:

"I was thinking, do I really wanna involve him in this for too long...?"

"—"

Ram and Rem simply narrowed their eyes at Emilia's sullen murmur, saying nothing.

What awaited Emilia was the royal selection—a dispute over the future monarch of the kingdom. Whoever instigated the theft of her badge at the royal capital did so with the intent of damaging her royal candidacy. No doubt similar incidents would arise around Emilia, which could place their very lives in danger. She was hesitant to involve a high-

She sullenly counted on her fingers the things she'd promised Puck she'd do after her soak.

"After getting out of the bath, stretching, doing my hair, doing my nails, err..."

She might have felt the wear of going through the same routine day after day. Perhaps she was exhausted both physically and mentally in the days following events in the capital—the theft of her badge and the day-long uproar involved in getting it back.

"Goodness, this isn't the time for me to be saying something so weak."

Emilia slapped both cheeks as if to put such ruminations behind her.

She could use her fatigue as an excuse, but the path she had chosen was not an easy one. She was starting out well behind the pack. It would be a hard fight just to pull even.

Just as Emilia was motivating herself anew—

The door of the changing room opened, and she heard someone stepping toward the bath. When she heard a voice, she turned to see a pink-haired girl with a towel covering her otherwise naked body.

"Ah, Lady Emilia?"

She was shorter than Emilia, but her flesh was no less delicate nor her face any less lovely than Emilia's own. The towel over her absorbed moisture from the air, greatly accentuating the lines of her elegant body. She gazed at Emilia in the bath and tilted her head slightly.

"It is rare for you to bathe at this hour. Should I come back another time?"

Emilia, still soaking in the bath, replied, "No, it's all right. I wouldn't say anything so unkind."

The girl—Ram—lowered her head without altering her expression.

"Is that so? Thank you very much."

Then, she called out in the direction of the changing room to her little sister.

"—Come on in, Rem."

A second girl, with blue hair and an identical face, followed Ram into the chamber. "Sister, it is good that it was Emilia in the bath ahead of us, but what would you have done if it had been Subaru? That would not do at all."

Compared to Ram, Rem gave a slightly softer impression, but beyond that, she resembled her older sister in most respects. Her face and elegant body were identical—Emilia supposed that the only other difference was that Rem's breasts were larger.

Ram mulled over the towel-clad Rem's words. "I suppose not," she remarked. Had the previous occupant been their male guest rather than Emilia—

"I could not endure it if Subaru gazed indecently at Sister."

"Then I would simply gouge out his eyes. I would be the last thing he ever saw."

Emilia responded, "Don't say such scary things. Subaru's a good boy, isn't he?"

Ram wiped away a bit of sweat and gently dipped a foot into the water as her younger sister bluntly answered Emilia.

"Perhaps your assessments differ somewhat because of different tastes?"

The usually expressionless Ram took a position off to the side of Emilia as her cheeks softened somewhat. Emilia noted this and smiled wryly.

Ram asked, "...What is it, Lady Emilia? You are grinning oddly."

"Mm, just a little. I'm a bit relieved to know that you take baths, too, Ram."

Ram's cheek tightened as she asserted firmly:

"I am not a doll, after all. I do not, however, deny that I am as lovely as one."

Emilia found Ram's embarrassed reaction at being seen somewhat relaxed unfortunate, but Rem chimed in, soaking herself opposite Ram.

## The Roswaal Manor Girls' Meet (Hot Bath Edition)

"...Nn."

Beginning with the tips of her toes, she slowly slid her long pale legs into the slightly clouded water.

The heat of the bathwater made her thighs shudder momentarily. The girl's throat made a faint sound from the shock as she sank her legs into the water. With a flick of her hand, she put her silver hair in order, exhaling as she immersed her entire body.

"A...hh..."

She was a beautiful girl. The silver of her hair seemed reminiscent of the rays of the moon at night. Her violet eyes were like embedded jewels. Her light skin, which seemed as pale as the snow, held slightly more color than usual. A charming atmosphere hovered around her that would have made anyone who saw her fall for her, male or female alike.

Her name was Emilia, a maiden through whom coursed the blood of the elves, known for their comeliness.

Emilia leaned back against the edge of the bath, her face red as she let out a groan of ecstasy.

"It really does feel good soaking your whole body in a bath like this..."

The tub was so enormous that Emilia could stretch out her long legs and not come close to touching the other side. She supposed one should expect a bath of this size in Marquis Roswaal's personal residence. His grandeur didn't really register with Emilia very much, but from time to time, she became painfully aware of just how important an individual was taking care of her needs while she lived at the mansion day in and day out.

Roswaal was her guardian and protector—and she could not fail to meet his expectations.

Because she recognized this, she strove every day to study a variety of things, even amidst a lifestyle to which she was unaccustomed.

All that said, even someone as hard-driven as Emilia became just another girl—no, a most lovely girl—when she stripped off her clothes and got into the bath where no one else could see.

Lifting her arms and pinching her pale upper arm between two fingers, her voice trembled.

"Ahh... I may have put on a little weight."

Mansion life had meant regular meals, so recent overeating might have been the cause. Compared to her previous lifestyle, life at the mansion gave her fewer opportunities to exert herself. It was natural that she'd get fatter.

"Puck's going to chew me out again..."

Truth be told, Emilia didn't obsess over her figure very much. The little cat spirit, Puck, with whom she had a pact, though, was more vocal about Emilia than she herself.

To Puck, her self-appointed surrogate father who had spent as much time with her as any real family, Emilia was almost too precious, which led him to criticize many of her habits. Of course, she was grateful for this, but having little comments piled up still annoyed her.

# Re:ZERO -Starting Life in Another World-

## THE ROSWAAL MANOR GIRLS' MEET (HOT BATH EDITION)

Tappei Nagatsuki
Illustration: Shinichirou Otsuka

Re:ZERO -Starting Life in Another World- Chapter 2: A Week at the Mansion ②
**Short Story Extra**